A STUDY OF
HISTORY

The Royal Institute of International Affairs is an unofficial and non-political body, founded in 1920 to encourage and facilitate the scientific study of international questions.

The Institute, as such, is precluded by its rules from expressing an opinion on any aspect of international affairs; opinions expressed in this book are, therefore, purely individual.

A STUDY OF HISTORY

BY

ARNOLD J. TOYNBEE

Doloris
Sopitam recreant volnera viva animam.
Anon.

ABRIDGEMENT
OF VOLUMES VII–X

BY

D. C. SOMERVELL

OXFORD UNIVERSITY PRESS
New York   Oxford

Oxford University Press

Oxford   New York   Toronto
Delhi   Bombay   Calcutta   Madras   Karachi
Petaling Jaya   Singapore   Hong Kong   Tokyo
Nairobi   Dar es Salaam   Cape Town
Melbourne   Auckland

and associated companies in
Beirut   Berlin   Ibadan   Nicosia

© 1957 by Oxford University Press, Inc.;
renewed 1985 by Robert Somervell, Mary Brautaset, and Lawrence Toynbee

First published in 1957 in Great Britain by Oxford University Press,
Walton Street, Oxford OX2 6DP, and in the United States by
Oxford University Press, Inc., 200 Madison Avenue, New York, New York 10016

First issued as an Oxford University Press paperback, 1987

Oxford is a registered trademark of Oxford University Press

Library of Congress Cataloging-in-Publication Data

Toynbee, Arnold Joseph, 1889–1975.
A study of history.

Includes indexes.
1. Civilization.   2. History—Philosophy.   I. Somervell,
D. C. (David Churchill), 1885–1965.   II. Title.
CB63.T6433   1987   909   87-12291
ISBN 0-19-500198-2 (v. 1)
ISBN 0-19-505080-0 (pbk. : v. 1)
ISBN 0-19-500199-0 (v. 2)
ISBN 0-19-505081-9 (pbk. : v. 2)

2 4 6 8 10 9 7 5 3 1

Printed in the United States of America

PREFACE

I AM fortunate in having twice had Mr. Somervell for my partner.
After having first abridged volumes i–vi of *A Study of History*,
he has now done the same skilful work on volumes vii–x. So
the reader now has at his command a uniform Abridgement of the
whole book, made by a clear mind that has not only mastered the
contents but has entered into the writer's outlook and purpose.

In the production of this second instalment of the Abridgement,
Mr. Somervell and I have worked together in the same way as
before. In going through Mr. Somervell's script before publication, I have rarely suggested putting in again anything that he has
left out. A writer is usually not a good judge of what it is best to
cut out of his own work, and Mr. Somervell has a wonderfully
good eye for this—as will have been found by anyone who has
compared the first instalment of his Abridgement with the original.
This time, as before, I have practically confined myself to working
over the passages that he has retained, and so making them my
own as well as his. This has not been difficult, as he has managed,
as before, to keep to my words to a large extent in reproducing the
gist of my meaning. Where he has added points and illustrations
of his own, as he has done here and there, I have been glad to see
something that is his coalesce with what is mine.

For a long book like mine, in a busy age like this, it is a boon to
be abbreviated in a first-rate Abridgement, such as Mr. Somervell's
is. This makes the book accessible to readers who might not have
had the patience, or at any rate not the time, to read the original.
To my mind, the original and the Abridgement are complementary.
Some readers of the second instalment of the Abridgement may,
I hope, be led on, as I know some readers of the first have been,
to dip into the original, if not to read the whole of it; and some
intrepid readers of the original may find the Abridgement, too,
useful for recalling the general argument and structure of the book.
In some ways, the deftest piece of Mr. Somervell's work seems
to me to be the concluding summary of his Abridgement of all
ten volumes of the original.

Our co-operation over both instalments of the Abridgement has
been a very happy experience for me.

1 December 1955   ARNOLD TOYNBEE

NOTE

BY THE MAKER OF THIS ABRIDGEMENT

THE fact that this volume starts with Part VI, chapter XXIII, is a reminder that this is not a complete work but the latter part of one, and a reader who entered upon it without any knowledge of what had gone before would find himself involved in much the same difficulties as would beset him if he began reading the third volume of one of the Victorian 'three-volume' novels. At the end of this volume will be found an 'Argument', summarizing the course of the whole work. It may be useful to those who have read the earlier part of Mr. Toynbee's *Study*, either in its original or its abridged form, and partly forgotten it.

I am very grateful to Miss O. P. Self for compiling the Index to this book:

1955   D. C. S.

CONTENTS

VIII. HEROIC AGES

IX. CONTACTS BETWEEN CIVILIZATIONS IN SPACE

XII. THE PROSPECTS OF THE WESTERN CIVILIZATION

XIII. CONCLUSION

A STUDY OF
HISTORY

VI

UNIVERSAL STATES

XXIII. ENDS OR MEANS?

THE starting-point of this book was a search for fields of historical study which would be intelligible in themselves within their own limits of space and time, without reference to extraneous historical events. The search for these self-contained units led us to find them in Societies of the species we called Civilizations, and so far we have been working on the assumption that a comparative study of the geneses, growths, breakdowns, and disintegrations of the twenty-one Civilizations that we have succeeded in identifying would comprehend everything of any significance in the history of Mankind since the time when the first Civilizations emerged from the Primitive Societies. Yet from time to time we have stumbled upon indications that this, our first, master-key might not serve to unlock all the doors through which we have to pass to reach our mental journey's end.

Near the outset, in the act of identifying as many Civilizations as were known to have existed, we found that certain of them were related to one another in a manner which we called 'apparentation-and-affiliation', and we found also that the evidences of this relationship were certain characteristic social products of a Dominant Minority, an Internal Proletariat, and an External Proletariat, into which the 'apparented' Society split up in the course of its disintegration. It appeared that dominant minorities produced philosophies which sometimes gave inspirations to universal states, that internal proletariats produced higher religions which sought to embody themselves in universal churches, and that external proletariats produced heroic ages which were the tragedies of barbarian war-bands. In the aggregate these experiences and institutions manifestly constitute a link between an 'apparented' and an 'affiliated' Civilization.

Moreover, this link in the time-dimension between two non-contemporary Civilizations is not the only kind of relation between Civilizations that a comparative study of universal states, universal churches, and heroic ages brings to light. These fractions, into which Civilizations, after breakdown, disintegrate, acquire a liberty to enter into social and cultural combinations with alien elements derived from other contemporary Civilizations. Some universal states have been the handiwork of alien empire-builders; some higher religions have been animated by alien inspirations, and some barbarian war-bands have imbibed a tincture of alien culture.

Universal states, universal churches, and heroic ages thus link together contemporary, as well as non-contemporary, Civilizations, and this raises the question whether we have been justified in treating them as mere by-products of the disintegration of some single Civilization. Ought we not now to try to study them on their own merits? Until we have examined the claims of institutions of each of these three kinds to be intelligible fields of study in themselves, and have also considered the alternative possibility that they might be parts of some larger whole embracing them and the Civilizations alike, we cannot be sure that we have brought within our purview the whole of human history above the primitive level. Thus further inquiry was the task that we set ourselves at the end of Part V of this Study, and we shall now try to acquit ourselves of it in Parts VI, VII, and VIII.

For the present, then, we are concerned with the universal states, and we may begin by asking whether they are ends in themselves or means towards something beyond them. Our best approach to this question may be to remind ourselves of certain salient features of universal states that we have already ascertained. In the first place, they arise after, and not before, the breakdowns of the civilizations to whose bodies social they bring political unity. They are not summers but 'Indian summers', masking autumn and presaging winter. In the second place, they are the products of dominant minorities; that is, of once creative minorities that have lost their creative power. This negativeness is the hallmark of their authorship and also the essential condition of their establishment and maintenance. This, however, is not the whole picture; for besides being accompaniments of social breakdown and products of dominant minorities, universal states display a third salient feature: they are the expressions of a rally—and a particularly notable one—in a process of disintegration that works itself out in successive pulsations of lapse-and-rally followed by relapse; and it is this last feature that strikes the imagination and evokes the gratitude of the generation that lives to see the successful establishment of a universal state set a term at last to a Time of Troubles that had previously been gathering momentum from successive failures of the repeated attempts to stem it.

Taken together, these features present a picture of universal states that, at first sight, looks ambiguous. They are symptoms of social disintegration, yet at the same time they are attempts to check this disintegration and defy it. The tenacity with which universal states, when once established, cling to life is one of their most conspicuous features, but it should not be mistaken for true vitality. It is rather the obstinate longevity of the old who refuse to die. In fact, universal states show a strong tendency to behave as if they were ends in themselves, whereas in truth they represent a phase in a process of social disintegration and, if they have any significance beyond that, can only have it in virtue of being a means to some end that is outside and beyond them.

XXIV. THE MIRAGE OF IMMORTALITY

IF we look at these universal states, not as alien observers but through the eyes of their own citizens, we shall find that these not only desire that these earthly commonwealths of theirs should live for ever but actually believe that the immortality of these human institutions is assured, and this sometimes in the teeth of contemporary events which, to an observer posted at a different standpoint in time or space, declare beyond question that this particular universal state is at that very moment in its last agonies. Why is it, such an observer might well ask, that, in defiance of apparently plain facts, the citizens of a universal state are prone to regard it, not as a night's shelter in the wilderness, but as the Promised Land, the goal of human endeavours? It should be said, however, that this sentiment is confined to the citizens of universal states established by indigenous empire-builders. No Indian, for example, either desired or foretold the immortality of the British Rāj.

In the history of the Roman Empire, which was the universal state of the Hellenic civilization, we find the generation that had witnessed the establishment of the *Pax Augusta* asserting, in evidently sincere good faith, that the Empire and the City that had built it have been endowed with a common immortality. Tibullus (*circa* 54–18 B.C.) sings of 'the walls of the eternal city' while Virgil (70–19 B.C.) makes his Iuppiter, speaking of the future Roman scions of Aeneas' race, say: 'I give them empire without end.' Livy writes with the same assurance of 'the city founded for eternity'. Horace, sceptic though he was, in claiming immortality for his Odes, takes as his concrete measure of eternity the repetition of the annual round of the religious ritual of the Roman city state. The Odes are still alive on the lips of men. How much longer their 'immortality' will continue is uncertain, for the number of those who can quote them has been sadly diminished in recent times by changes in educational fashions; but at least they have lived four or five times as long as the Roman pagan ritual. More than four hundred years after the age of Horace and Virgil, after the sack of Rome by Alaric has already announced the end, we find the Gallic poet Rutilius Namatianus still defiantly asserting Rome's immortality and Saint Jerome, in scholarly retreat at Jerusalem, interrupting his theological labours to express his grief and stupefaction in language almost identical with that of Rutilius. The pagan official and the Christian Father are united in their emotional reactions to an event which, as we now see it, had been inevitable for generations.

The shock administered by the fall of Rome in A.D. 410 to the citizens of a transient universal state which they had mistaken for an everlasting habitation has its counterpart in the shock suffered by the subjects of the Arab Caliphate when Baghdad fell to the Mongols in A.D. 1258. In the Roman world the shock was felt from Palestine to Gaul; in the Arab world from Farghānah to Andalusia. The intensity of the psychological effect is even more remarkable in this than in the Roman case; for, by the time when Hūlāgū gave the 'Abbasid Caliphate its *coup de grâce*, its sovereignty had been ineffective for three or four centuries over the greater part of the vast domain nominally subject to it. This halo of an illusory immortality, worn by moribund universal states, often persuades the more prudent barbarian leaders, in the very act of parcelling out their dominions among themselves, to acknowledge an equally illusory subjection. The Amalung leaders of the Arian Ostrogoths and the Buwayhid leaders of the Shī'ī Daylamīs sought title for their conquests by ruling them, in official theory, as vicegerents of the Emperor at Constantinople and the Caliph at Baghdad respectively; and, though this tactful handling of a senile universal state did not avail, in their case, to avert the doom to which both these war-bands condemned themselves by clinging to their distinctive religious heresies, the same political manoeuvre was brilliantly successful when executed by fellow barbarians who had the sagacity or good fortune to be at the same time impeccable in their professions of religious faith. Clovis the Frank, for example, the most successful of all the founders of barbarian successor-states of the Roman Empire, followed up his conversion to Catholicism by obtaining from the Emperor Anastasius in distant Constantinople the title of proconsul with the consular insignia. His success is attested by the fact that in later ages no less than eighteen royal Louis, reigning in the land that he conquered, bore a modified variant of his name.

The Ottoman Empire, which became, as we have seen in an earlier part of this Study, the universal state of a Byzantine civilization, exhibited the same characteristics of illusory immortality at a time when it had already become 'the Sick Man of Europe'. The ambitious war-lords who were carving out for themselves successor-states—a Mehmed 'Alī in Egypt and Syria, an 'Alī of Yannina in Albania and Greece, and a Pasvānoghlu of Viddin in the north-western corner of Rumelia—were sedulous in doing in the Pādishāh's name all that they were doing to his detriment in their own private interests. When the Western

Powers followed in their footsteps, they adopted the same fictions. Great Britain, for example, administered Cyprus from 1878 and Egypt from 1882 in the name of the Sultan at Constantinople until she found herself at war with Turkey in 1914. The Mughal universal state of the Hindu civilization displays the same features. Within half a century of the Emperor Awrangzīb's death in A.D. 1707, an empire which had once exercised effective sovereignty over the greater part of the Indian subcontinent had been whittled down to a torso some 250 miles long and 100 miles broad. After another half-century it had been reduced to the circuit of the walls of the Red Fort at Delhi. Yet, 150 years after A.D. 1707, a descendant of Akbar and Awrangzīb was still squatting on their throne, and might have been left there much longer if the Mutineers of 1857 had not forced this poor puppet, against his wishes, to give his blessing to their revolt against a rāj from overseas which had, after a period of anarchy, replaced the long-extinct Mughal Rāj which he still symbolized.

A still more remarkable testimony to the tenacity of the belief in the immortality of universal states is the practice of evoking their ghosts after they have proved themselves mortal by expiring. The 'Abbasid Caliphate of Baghdad was thus resuscitated in the shape of the 'Abbasid Caliphate of Cairo, and the Roman Empire in the shape of the Holy Roman Empire of the West and the East Roman Empire of Orthodox Christendom; and the empire of the Ts'in and Han dynasties in the shape of the Sui and T'ang Empire of the Far Eastern civilization. The surname of the founder of the Roman Empire was revived in the titles Kaiser and Czar, and the title of Caliph, which originally meant successor of Muhammad, after haunting Cairo, passed on to Istanbul, where it survived until its abolition at the hands of Westernizing revolutionists in the twentieth century.

These are only a selection from the wealth of historical examples illustrating the fact that the belief in the immortality of universal states survives for centuries after it has been confuted by plain hard facts. What are the causes of this strange phenomenon?

One manifest cause is the potency of the impression made by the founders and the great rulers of universal states, an impression handed on to a receptive posterity with an emphasis which exaggerates an imposing truth into an overwhelming legend. Another cause is the impressiveness of the institution itself, apart from the genius displayed by its greatest rulers. A universal state captivates hearts and minds because it is the embodiment of a rally from the long-unhalted rout of a Time of Troubles, and it was this aspect of the Roman Empire that eventually won the admiration of originally hostile Greek men of letters, writing in the Age of the Antonines, which Gibbon long afterwards was to adjudge the period when the human race attained its highest point of felicity.

'There is no salvation in the exercise of a dominion divorced from power. To find oneself under the dominion of one's superiors is a "second best" alternative; but this "second best" proved to be the best of all in our present experience of the Roman Empire. This happy experience has moved the whole World to cleave to Rome with might and main. The World would no more think of seceding from Rome than a ship's crew would think of parting company with the pilot. You must have seen bats in a cave clinging tight to one another and to the rocks; and this is an apt image of the whole World's dependence on Rome. In every heart today the focus of anxiety is the fear of becoming detached from the cluster. The thought of being abandoned by Rome is so appalling that it precludes any thought of wantonly abandoning her.

'There is an end of those disputes over sovereignty and prestige which were the causes of the outbreak of all the wars of the past; and, while some of the nations, like noiselessly flowing water, are delightfully quiet—rejoicing in their release from toil and trouble, and aware at last that all their old struggles were to no purpose—there are other nations which do not even know or remember whether they once sat in the seat of power. In fact we are witnessing a new version of the Pamphylian's myth (or is it Plato's own?). At a moment when the states of the World were already laid out on the funeral pyre as the victims of their own fratricidal strife and turmoil, they were all at once presented with the [Roman] dominion and straightway came to life again. How they arrived at this condition they are unable to say. They know nothing about it, and can only marvel at their present well-being. They are like sleepers awakened who have come to themselves and now dismiss from their thoughts the dreams that obsessed them only a moment ago. They no longer find it credible that there were ever such things as wars. . . . The entire Inhabited World now keeps perpetual holiday. . . . So that the only people who still need pity for the good things that they are missing are those outside your empire—if there are any such people left. . . .'[1]

This quaint scepticism on the question whether there were in fact any people worth mentioning outside the Roman Empire is characteristic, and is our justification for calling such institutions universal states. They were universal not geographically but psychologically. Horace, for example, in one of his Odes, tells us that he does not bother about 'the threats of Tiridates'. The King of Parthia no doubt existed, but he simply did not matter. In a similar vein the Manchu Emperors of the Far Eastern universal state assumed in their diplomatic dealings that all governments,

[1] Aristeides, P. Aelius (A.D. 117–89): *In Romam.*

including those of the Western world, had at some unspecified period in the past received permission to exist from the Chinese authorities.

And yet the reality of these universal states was something very different from the brilliant surface that they presented to Aelius Aristeides and their other panegyrists in varicus ages and various climes.

An obscure divinity of the Nubian marches of the Egyptiac universal state was transfigured by the genius of Hellenic mythology into a mortal king of the Ethiopians who had the misfortune to be loved by Eôs, the immortal Goddess of the Dawn. The goddess besought her fellow Olympians to confer on her human lover the immortality which she and her peers enjoyed; and, jealous though they were of their divine privileges, she teased them into yielding at last to her feminine importunity. Yet even this grudging gift was marred by a fatal flaw; for the eager goddess had forgotten that the Olympians' immortality was mated with an everlasting youth, and the other immortals had spitefully taken care to grant her no more than her bare request. The consequence was both ironic and tragic. After a honeymoon that flashed past in the twinkling of an Olympian eye, Eôs and her now immortal but still inexorably ageing mate found themselves condemned for eternity to grieve together over Tithonus's hapless plight. A senility to which the merciful hand of death could never set a term was an affliction that no mortal man could ever be made to suffer, and an eternal grief was an obsession that left no room for any other thought or feeling.

For any human soul or human institution an immortality in This World would prove a martyrdom, even if it were unaccompanied by either physical decrepitude or mental senility. 'In this sense', wrote the philosophic Emperor Marcus Aurelius (A.D. 161–80), 'it would be true to say that any man of forty who is endowed with moderate intelligence has seen—in the light of the uniformity of Nature—the entire Past and Future'; and, if this estimate of the capacity of human souls for experience strikes the reader as an inordinately low one, he may find the reason in the age in which Marcus lived; for an 'Indian Summer' is an age of boredom. The price of the Roman Peace was the forfeiture of Hellenic liberty; and, though that liberty might always have been the privilege of a minority, and this privileged minority might have turned irresponsible and oppressive, it was manifest in retrospect that the turbulent wickedness of the Ciceronian climax of an Hellenic 'Time of Troubles' had provided a wealth of exciting and inspiring themes for Roman public speakers which their epigoni in a smugly ordered Trajanic epoch might conventionally condemn as horrors, not *nostri saeculi*, but must secretly envy as they found themselves perpetually failing in their laborious efforts to substitute far-fetched artifice for the stimulus of importunate life.

On the morrow of the breakdown of the Hellenic society Plato, anxiously seeking to safeguard it against a further fall by pegging it in a securely rigid posture, had idealized the comparative stability of the Egyptiac culture; and a thousand years later, when this Egyptiac culture was still in being while the Hellenic civilization had arrived at its last agonies, the last of the Neoplatonists pushed their reputed master's sentiment to an almost frenzied pitch of uncritical admiration.

Thanks to the obstinacy of the Egyptiac universal state in again and again insisting on returning to life after its body had been duly laid on the salutary funeral pyre, the Egyptiac civilization lived to see its contemporaries—the Minoan, the Sumeric, and the Indus culture—all pass away and give place to successors of a younger generation, some of which had passed away in their turn while the Egyptiac society still kept alive. Egyptiac students of history could have observed the birth and death of the First Syriac, Hittite, and Babylonic offspring of the Sumeric civilization and the rise and decline of the Syriac and Hellenic offspring of the Minoan. Yet the fabulously long-drawn-out epilogue to the broken-down Egyptiac society's natural term of life was but an alternation of long stretches of boredom with hectic bouts of demonic energy, into which this somnolent society was galvanized by the impact of alien bodies social.

The same rhythm of trance-like somnolence alternating with outbursts of fanatical xenophobia can be discerned in the epilogue to the history of the Far Eastern civilization in China. The tincture of Far Eastern Christian culture in the Mongols who had forced upon China an alien universal state evoked a reaction in which the Mongols were evicted and their dominion replaced by the indigenous universal state of the Ming. Even the Manchu barbarians, who stepped into the political vacuum created by the Ming's collapse, and whose taint of Far Eastern Christian culture was less noticeable than their receptivity in adopting the Chinese way of life, aroused a popular opposition which, in Southern China at any rate, never ceased to maintain itself underground and broke out into the open again in the T'aip'ing insurrection of A.D. 1852–64. The infiltration of the Early Modern Western civilization, in its Catholic Christian form, in the sixteenth and seventeenth centuries provoked the proscription of Catholicism in the first quarter of the eighteenth century. The blasting open of the sea-gates of China for Western trade between A.D. 1839 and A.D. 1861 provoked the retort of the anti-Western 'Boxer' rising of A.D. 1900; and the Manchu Dynasty was overthrown in A.D. 1911 in retribution for the double crime of being ineradicably alien itself and at the same time showing itself incompetent to keep the now far more formidable alien force of Western penetration at bay.

Happily life is kinder than legend, and the sentence of immortality which mythology passed on Tithonus is commuted, for the benefit of the universal states of history, to a not interminable longevity. Marcus's disillusioned man of forty must die at last though he may outlive his zest for life by fifty or sixty years, and a universal state that kicks again and again against the pricks of death will weather away in the course of ages, like the pillar of salt that was fabled to be the petrified substance of a once living woman.

XXV. *SIC VOS NON VOBIS*

'Sᴵᴄ vos non vobis mellificatis, apes.' Thus you bees make honey, but not only for yourselves.[1] The hackneyed quotation expresses through a homely simile the paradoxical position of universal states in the scheme of history. These imposing polities are the last works of dominant minorities in the disintegrating bodies social of moribund civilizations. Their conscious purpose is to preserve themselves by conserving the wasting energies of the society with whose fortunes their own are bound up. This purpose is never in the long run fulfilled. None the less, these by-products of social disintegration have a part to play in fresh acts of creation. They serve others when they fail to save themselves.

If a universal state finds its significance as a means for the performance of services, who are its beneficiaries? They must be one or other of three possible candidates for the part—the internal proletariat or external proletariat of the moribund society itself, or some alien civilization which is its contemporary; and in serving the internal proletariat a universal state will be ministering to one of the higher religions that make their epiphany in the internal proletariat's bosom. In the words of Bossuet, 'All the great empires which we have seen on the Earth have contributed by divers means to the good of religion and the glory of God, as God himself has declared by His prophets'.

(I) THE CONDUCTIVITY OF UNIVERSAL STATES

Our next task is to make an empirical survey of the services involuntarily offered by universal states and of the uses made of these facilities by internal proletariats, external proletariats, and alien civilizations; but we have first to find the answer to a preliminary question: how can any services be rendered to anyone by an institution which is passive, conservative, archaistic, and in fact negative in every respect? How—in the terms of the expressive Sinic notation for the rhythm of the universe—can so unpromising a Yin-state give rise to a new burst of Yang-activity? It is easy, of course, to see that, if once a spark of creative energy has been kindled in the shelter of a universal state, it will have a chance of swelling into a steady flame which it might never have had if it had been exposed to the buffeting blast of a 'Time of Troubles'. But

---

[1] The 'only' is not in the Latin, but it might well be, for the poet must have known that if the bees do not get any honey for themselves they go on strike.

this service, though valuable, is negative. What feature in the social situation arising under a universal state is the positive source of that new capacity to create which is the supreme benefit that a universal state confers on its beneficiaries, though apparently it cannot profit by it in the long run for its own account? Perhaps one clue is to be found in the tendency shown by Archaism to defeat itself by being inveigled into construction in its efforts to 'make things work'.

For example, the inclusion of the surviving fabric of the shattered society within the universal state's political framework does not avail either to restore what has already perished or to prevent the progressive collapse of the remainder; and the menace of this immense and constantly extending social vacuum compels the Government to act against its own inclinations and construct stop-gap institutions to fill the void. A classic example of this necessity of stepping ever farther into an ever-widening breach is afforded by the administrative history of the Roman Empire during the two centuries following its establishment. The Roman secret of government was the principle of indirect rule. The Hellenic universal state was conceived of by its Roman founders as an association of self-governing cities with a fringe of autonomous principalities in regions where the Hellenic culture had not yet struck political root. The burden of administration was to be left to these local authorities. This policy was never deliberately revised; yet, if we resurvey the Empire at the end of two centuries of the Roman Peace, we shall find that the administrative structure has been in fact transformed. The client principalities have been turned into provinces, and the provinces themselves have become organs of direct and centralized administration. The human resources for the conduct of local government gradually ran dry, and the central government, faced with this increasing dearth of local administrative talent, found itself constrained not only to replace client princes by imperial governors but to put the administration of the city-states into the hands of appointed 'managers'. By the end of the story the whole administration of the Empire had passed into the hands of a hierarchically organized bureaucracy.

The central authorities had been no more eager to impose these changes than the local authorities to suffer them; both alike had been victims of *force majeure*. None the less, the consequences were revolutionary, because these new institutions were highly 'conductive'. In a previous context (pp. 455–505) we have seen that two leading features of an age of social disintegration are a sense of promiscuity and a sense of unity; and, though these two psychological tendencies may be antithetical from a subjective standpoint, they conspire to produce an identical objective result. This dominant spirit of the age endows these new stop-gap institutions thrown up by a universal state with a 'conductivity' comparable to that which the Ocean and the Steppe derive, not from their human psychological atmosphere, but from their own physical nature.

'As the surface of the Earth bears all mankind, so Rome receives all the peoples of the Earth into her bosom, as the rivers are received by the sea.' Thus wrote Aelius Aristeides, whom we have quoted already, and the same simile was employed by the writer of this Study in a passage written before he had become acquainted with the work of Aristeides.

'The writer can best express his personal feeling about the Empire in a parable. It was like the sea round whose shores its network of city-states was strung. The Mediterranean seems at first sight a poor substitute for the rivers that have given their waters to make it. Those were living waters, whether they ran muddy or clear; the sea seems just salt and still and dead. But, as soon as we study the sea, we find movement and life there also. There are silent currents circulating perpetually from one part of the sea to another, and the surface water that seems to be lost by evaporation is not really lost, but will descend in distant places and seasons, with its bitterness all distilled away, as life-giving rain. And, as those surface-waters are drawn off into the clouds, their place is taken by lower layers continually rising from the depths. The sea itself is in constant and creative motion, but the influence of this great body of waters extends far beyond its shores. One finds it softening the extremes of temperature, quickening the vegetation, and prospering the life of animals and men, in the distant heart of continents and among peoples that have never heard its name.'[1]

The social movements that make their way through the conductive medium of a universal state are in fact both horizontal and vertical. Examples of horizontal motion are the circulation of medicinal herbs in the Roman Empire, according to the testimony of the Elder Pliny in his *Historia Naturalis*, and the spread of the use of paper from the eastern to the western extremity of the Arab Caliphate. Reaching Samarqand from China in A.D. 751, its use had spread to Baghdad by A.D. 793, to Cairo by A.D. 900, to Fez (Fas), almost within sight of the Atlantic, by about A.D. 1100, and to Jativa in the Iberian Peninsula by A.D. 1150.

The vertical movements are sometimes more elusive but often more important in their social effects—as is illustrated by the history of the Tokugawa Shogunate, which was the universal state of the Far Eastern society in Japan. The Tokugawa régime set itself

---

[1] Toynbee, A. J., in *The Legacy of Greece* (Oxford 1922, Clarendon Press), p. 320.

to insulate Japan from the rest of the World, and was successful for nearly two centuries in maintaining this political *tour de force*; but it found itself powerless to arrest the course of social change within an insulated Japanese Empire, in spite of an effort to petrify a feudal system, inherited from the preceding Time of Troubles, into a permanent dispensation.

'The penetration of money economy into Japan . . . caused a slow but irresistible revolution, culminating in the breakdown of feudal government and the resumption of intercourse with foreign countries after more than two hundred years of seclusion. What opened the doors was not a summons from without but an explosion from within. . . . One of [the] first effects [of the new economic forces] was an increase in the wealth of the townspeople, gained at the expense of the samurai and also of the peasants. . . . The daimyō and their retainers spent their money on luxuries produced by the artisans and sold by the tradesmen, so that by about the year [A.D.] 1700, it is said, nearly all their gold and silver had passed into the hands of the townspeople. They then began to buy goods on credit. Before long they were deeply in debt to the merchant class, and were obliged to pledge, or to make forced sales of, their tax-rice. . . . Abuses and disaster followed thick and fast. The merchants took to rice-broking, and then to speculating. . . . It was the members of one class only, and not all of them, who profited by these conditions. These were the merchants, in particular the brokers and money lenders, despised chōnin or townsmen, who in theory might be killed with impunity by any samurai for mere disrespectful language. Their social status still remained low, but they held the purse and they were in the ascendant. By the year 1700 they were already one of the strongest and most enterprising elements in the state, and the military caste was slowly losing its influence.'[1]

If we regard the year A.D. 1590, in which Hideyoshi overcame the last resistance to his dictatorship, as the date of the foundation of the Japanese universal state, we perceive that it took little more than a century for the rising of the lower layers of water from the depths to the surface to produce a bloodless social revolution in a society which Hideyoshi's successors had sought to freeze into an almost Platonically Utopian immobility. The result is the more impressive by reason of the fact that the universal state of the Tokugawa Shogunate was culturally homogeneous to an unusually high degree.

Illustrations of the 'conductivity' of universal states can be drawn from every other instance of which we have sufficient historical knowledge.

[1] Sansom, G. B.: *Japan: a Short Cultural History* (London 1932, Cresset Press), pp. 460–2.

(2) THE PSYCHOLOGY OF PEACE

A universal state is imposed by its founders, and accepted by its subjects, as a panacea for the ills of a Time of Troubles. In psychological terms it is an institution for establishing and maintaining concord; and this is the true remedy for a rightly diagnosed disease. The disease is that of a house being divided against itself, and this schism cuts both ways. There is the horizontal schism between contending social classes and the vertical schism between warring states. The paramount aim of the empire-builders, in making a universal state out of the Power that emerges as the sole survivor of the wars between the parochial states of the preceding age, is to establish concord with their fellow members of the dominant minorities in the parochial states which they have conquered. Nonviolence, however, is a state of mind and a principle of behaviour that cannot be confined to one compartment of social life. Therefore the concord which a dominant minority is moved to seek in its own domestic relations has to be extended to the dominant minority's relations with the internal and external proletariats and with any alien civilizations with which the disintegrating civilization is in contact.

This universal concord profits its divers beneficiaries in different degrees. While it enables the dominant minority to recuperate to some extent, it brings a greater relative access of strength to the proletariat. For the life has already gone out of the dominant minority, and 'all the spices' of concord can 'but prolong decay'—to adapt Byron's irreverent comment on the corpse of King George III; whereas these same spices serve as fertilizers to the proletariat. Accordingly, during the armistice established by a universal state, the proletariat must increase and the dominant minority must decrease. The toleration practised by the founders of a universal state, for the negative purpose of eliminating strife among themselves, gives the internal proletariat a chance to found a universal church, while the atrophy of the martial spirit among the subjects of the universal state gives the external proletariat of barbarians, or a neighbouring alien Civilization, a chance of breaking in and seizing for itself the dominion over an internal proletariat that has been conditioned to be passive on the political plane, however active on the religious.

The relative incapacity of the dominant minority to profit by the conditions that this minority itself has called into existence is illustrated by its almost invariable failure to propagate a philosophy or a 'fancy religion' of its own from above downwards. On the other hand, it is remarkable to observe how effective a use the internal proletariat are apt to make of the pacific atmosphere of a universal state for propagating, from below upwards, a higher religion, and eventually establishing a universal church.

'The Middle Empire' of Egypt, for instance, which was the original Egyptiac universal state, was used to this effect by the Osirian church. The Neo-Babylonian Empire, which was the Babylonic universal state, and its successive alien successor-states, the Achaemenian (Persian) Empire and the Seleucid Monarchy, were similarly used by Judaism and its sister-religion Zoroastrianism. The opportunities offered by the Roman Peace were seized by a number of competing proletarian religions—by the worships of Cybele and Isis and by Mithraism and Christianity. The corresponding opportunities offered by the *Pax Hanica* in the Sinic world were competed for by an Indic proletarian religion, the Mahāyāna, and by the indigenous Sinic proletarian religion of Taoism. The Arab Caliphate provided a comparable opportunity for Islam, and the Gupta Rāj in the Indic world for Hinduism. The Mongol Empire, which for a moment extended an effective *Pax Nomadica* from the west coast of the Pacific to the east coast of the Baltic and from the southern fringes of the Siberian tundra to the northern fringes of the Arabian Desert and the Burmese jungle, struck the imaginations of the missionaries of a host of rival religions with the opportunities that it offered; and, considering how brief this passing moment was, it is remarkable to observe how successfully it was turned to account by the Nestorian and the Western Catholic Christian churches and by Islam, as well as by the Lamaist Tantric sect of Mahāyānian Buddhism.

The exponents of the higher religions that had thus so frequently profited by the favourable social and psychological climate of a universal state had in some cases been conscious of the boon and had ascribed its bestowal to the One True God in whose name they had been preaching. In the eyes of the authors of the Books of Deutero-Isaiah, Ezra, and Nehemiah the Achaemenian Empire was the chosen instrument of Yahweh for the propagation of Judaism, and Pope Leo the Great (A.D. 440–61) similarly regarded the Roman Empire as providentially ordained by God to facilitate the spread of Christianity. In his eighty-second sermon he wrote: 'In order that the effects of this ineffable act of grace (i.e. the Incarnation) might be spread throughout the World, God's providence previously brought into existence the Roman Empire.'

The idea became a commonplace of Christian thought, and reappears, for example, in Milton's *Ode on the Morning of Christ's Nativity*.

No war or battle's sound
Was heard the world around:
The idle spear and shield were high uphung;
The hookèd chariot stood
Unstain'd by hostile blood;
The trumpet spake not to the armèd throng;
And kings sat still with awful eye,
As if they surely knew their sovran Lord was by.

An opportunity so marvellous might well seem heaven-sent; yet, in the relation between a successful missionary church and the universal state within which it works, the climate of toleration, which gives it a favourable start, does not always persist till the end of the story, and is sometimes transformed into its opposite. There have, no doubt, been cases in which there was no such sinister outcome. The Osirian church never suffered persecution and was ultimately amalgamated with the religion of the Egyptiac dominant minority. Peace likewise seems to have been preserved in the Sinic world between the Mahāyāna and the Taoist church on the one side and the Han Empire on the other until the Sinic universal state went into dissolution towards the end of the second century of the Christian Era.

When we come to Judaism and Zoroastrianism, we cannot tell what their ultimate relations would have been with either the Neo-Babylonian or the Achaemenian Empire, since each of these universal states had its life cut short at an early stage of its history. We only know that, when the Achaemenian régime was abruptly replaced by the Seleucid and eventually, west of the Euphrates, by the Roman, the impact of an alien Hellenic culture, of which the Seleucid and the Roman Powers were the successive political instruments, deflected both Judaism and Zoroastrianism from their original mission of preaching a gospel of salvation to all Mankind, and transformed them into weapons of cultural warfare in the Syriac society's retort to the Hellenic society's aggression. If the Achaemenian Empire, like its post-Hellenic avatar, the Arab Caliphate, had run out its full course, we may conjecture that, under the auspices of a tolerant Achaemenian imperial government, either Zoroastrianism or Judaism would have anticipated the achievement of Islam, which—profiting by the indifference of the Umayyads and the conscientious observance, by the 'Abbasids, of the tolerance prescribed towards non-Muslims who were 'Peoples of the Book'—made gradual headway, uncompromised by any frustrating assistance from the civil arm, until the collapse of the 'Abbasid régime brought a landslide of voluntary mass conversions seeking shelter, in the courtyard of the Mosque, from the storm of an approaching political interregnum.

Similarly, under a Guptan Empire which was a reintegration of the original Mauryan Indic universal state, the ousting of the philosophy of Buddhism by the post-Buddhaic higher religion of Hinduism was not only unopposed by the dynasty but was also unimpeded by any acts of official persecution, which would have been alien to the tolerant and syncretistic religious ethos of the Indic civilization.

In contrast to these cases in which a higher religion, profiting by the peace of a universal state, has been tolerated by its government from first to last, there are others in which its peaceful progress have been interrupted by official persecutions that had either nipped it in the bud or have denatured it by goading it into going into politics or taking up arms. Western Catholic Christianity, for example, was almost completely extirpated in Japan in the seventeenth century and in China in the eighteenth. Islam in China under the Mongols gained a footing only in two provinces, and never became more than an alien minority, goaded by the precariousness of its position into recurrent outbursts of militancy.

The untoward after-effects on Christianity of the trial of strength that was the prelude to its triumph over the Roman Imperial régime were comparatively slight. During the three centuries ending with the conversion of Constantine the Church was never out of danger of falling foul of Roman policy; for, besides the suspicion of private associations of all kinds that haunted the Roman state in the Imperial Age, there was an older and more deeply graven Roman tradition of special hostility to private societies for the practice and propagation of foreign religions; and, though the Roman Government had relaxed this hardset policy in two notable instances—in its official reception of the worship of Cybele at the crisis of the Hannibalic War and in its persistent toleration of Judaism as a religion, even when the Jewish Zealots provoked Rome into obliterating the Jewish state—the suppression of the Bacchanals in the second century B.C. was an augury of what the Christians were to suffer in the third century of their era. But the Christian Church resisted the temptation to retort to official persecution by perverting itself into a politico-military association, and was rewarded by becoming a universal church and an heir of the future.

Yet the Christian Church did not come through this ordeal unscathed. Instead of taking to heart the lesson of the triumph of Christian gentleness over Roman force, she presented her discomfited persecutors with a gratuitous vindication and a posthumous moral revenge by taking to her bosom the sin which had consummated their failure. She quickly became and long remained a persecutor herself.

While the internal proletariat, as the creator of higher religions, is thus the principal beneficiary on the spiritual plane of the dominant minority's achievement in creating and maintaining universal states, the benefits on the political plane are harvested by other hands. The psychology of peace under the auspices of a universal state unfits its rulers for the task of maintaining their political heritage. Accordingly the beneficiaries of this process of psychological disarmament are neither the rulers nor the ruled, neither the dominant minority nor the internal proletariat; they are the intruders from beyond the imperial frontiers, who may be either members of the disintegrating Society's external proletariat or representatives of some alien civilization.

At an earlier point in this Study we have observed that the event which registers the extinction of a civilization—as distinct from its antecedent breakdown and disintegration—is usually the occupation of the domain of the defunct Society's universal state either by barbarian war-lords from beyond the pale or by conquerors coming from another society with a different culture, or in some cases by both kinds, one following at the heels of the other. The benefits secured by barbarian or alien aggressors who have succeeded in taking advantage, for their own predatory purposes, of the psychological climate induced by a universal state are obvious and, on a short view, imposing. Yet we have observed already that the barbarian invaders of the derelict domain of a crumbling universal state are heroes without a future; and Posterity would surely have recognized them as being the disreputable adventurers that they are but for the retrospective glamour cast over their sordid escapades by their gift for writing their own epitaphs in the language of epic poetry. Even an Achilles can be transformed into a 'hero' by an *Iliad*. As for the achievements of the militant missionaries of an alien civilization, these too are delusive and disappointing compared with the historic achievement of the churches.

In two instances in which we know the whole story we have seen that a civilization whose universal state has been prematurely cut short by alien conquerors is capable of going to earth, hibernating for centuries, biding its time, and eventually finding its opportunity to expel the intrusive civilization and resume the universal state phase of its history at the point where this had been interrupted. The Indic civilization achieved this *tour de force* after nearly six hundred years, and the Syriac after nearly a thousand years, of submergence beneath a Hellenic flood. The monuments of their achievement were the Guptan Empire and the Arab Caliphate, in which they respectively resumed the universal states originally embodied in the Mauryan Empire and the Achaemenian Empire. On the other hand the Babylonic and Egyptiac societies were eventually absorbed into the body social of the Syriac, though the Babylonic succeeded in preserving its cultural identity for about six hundred years after the overthrow of the Neo-Babylonian Empire of Nebuchadnezzar by Cyrus, while the Egyptiac society maintained itself for no less than two thousand years after the termination of its natural expectation of life with the collapse of the 'Middle Kingdom'.

On the evidence of history there are thus two alternative denouements to attempts on the part of one civilization to devour and digest another by force. The evidence shows, however, that, even when the attempt is ultimately successful, there may be a period of centuries or even millennia before the result is assured; and this might incline twentieth-century historians to be chary of forecasting the outcome of the Western civilization's latter-day attempts to devour its contemporaries, considering how little time had elapsed since even the oldest of these attempts began, and how little had yet been seen of the unfolding story.

In the case of the Spanish conquest of the Middle American world, for example, it might well have been supposed that, when the alien substitute, in the shape of the Spanish viceroyalty of New Spain, had been supplanted by a Republic of Mexico, which sought and gained admission into the comity of Western states, the assimilation of the Middle American society into the body social of the Western society had become an irrevocably accomplished fact. Yet the Mexican Revolution of A.D. 1821 had been followed by the Revolution of A.D. 1910, in which the buried but hibernating indigenous society had suddenly bestirred itself, raised its head, and broken through the crust of culture deposited by Castilian hands on the grave into which the *conquistadores* had thrust the body which they believed themselves to have slain. This portent from Middle America raised the question whether the apparent cultural conquests of Western Christendom in the Andean world and elsewhere might not likewise prove, sooner or later, to have been no more than superficial and temporary.

The Far Eastern civilization in China, Korea, and Japan, which had succumbed to the influence of the West within the last century before the time of writing, was evidently far more potent than the Middle American had ever been; and, if the indigenous culture of Mexico was reasserting itself after four hundred years of eclipse, it would be rash to assume that the Far Eastern culture was destined to be assimilated either by the West or by Russia. As for the Hindu world, the inauguration of two successor-states of the British Rāj in A.D. 1947 might be interpreted as a peacefully accomplished counterpart of the Mexican Revolution of A.D. 1821, and at the time of writing it might be forecast that in this case, as in that, an act of political emancipation which had superficially set the seal on the process of Westernization by bringing the emancipated states into the comity of Western nations, might prove to have been the first step towards the cultural emancipation of a society that had been temporarily submerged by a Western tide.

The Arab countries, again, which had recently been gaining admission to the Western comity of nations as independent states, had been able to achieve this ambition in virtue of their success in shaking off an Ottoman political ascendancy, and an Iranic cultural veneer, by which they had been overlaid for four centuries. Was there any reason to doubt that the latent survival power of the Arabic culture would not assert itself, sooner or later, against the influence of the far more alien culture of the West?

The general effect of this survey of the ultimate consequences of cultural conversions is to confirm our conclusion that the sole sure beneficiary from the services afforded by a universal state is the internal proletariat. The benefits obtained by the external proletariat are always illusory, and those obtained by an alien civilization are apt to prove impermanent.

(3) THE SERVICEABILITY OF IMPERIAL INSTITUTIONS

Having now examined the effects of two general characteristics of universal states—their conductivity and their peace—we may go on to survey the services afforded to their beneficiaries by particular concrete institutions which they themselves deliberately create and maintain, but which are apt to find their historic mission in roles for which they had never been intended by their makers. Using the term institutions in a somewhat generalized sense we may take it to cover the following: communications; garrisons and colonies; provinces; capital cities; official languages and scripts; legal systems; calendars, weights and measures, and money; armies; civil services; citizenships. Each of these will now be passed in review.

Communications

Communications head the list because they are the master institution on which a universal state depends for its very existence.

They are the instrument not only of its military command over its dominions but also of its political control. These man-made imperial life-lines include much more than man-made roads, for the 'natural' highways provided by rivers, seas, and steppes are not practicable means of communication unless they are effectively policed. Means of transportation are also required. In most of the universal states so far known to History these means had taken the form of an imperial postal service, and the 'postmen'—if we may apply the familiar term to the officials of such a service, central and local—were very often also policemen. A public postal service seems to have been part of the machinery of the government of the Empire of Sumer and Akkad in the third millennium B.C. In the Achaemenian Empire, in the same part of the world two thousand years later, we find the same institutions raised to a higher level of organization and efficiency. The Achaemenian policy of utilizing the imperial communications system for maintaining the central government's control over the provinces reappears in the administration of the Roman Empire and of the Arab Caliphate.

It is really not surprising that similar institutions were to be found in universal states 'from China to Peru'. Ts'in She Hwang-ti, the revolutionary founder of the Sinic universal state, was a builder of roads radiating from his capital, and employed an elaborately organized inspectorate. The Incas, likewise, consolidated their conquests by means of roads. A message could travel from Cuzco to Quito, a distance of more than a thousand miles as the crow flies and perhaps half as much again by road, in as short a time as ten days.

Obviously the roads created and maintained by the governments of universal states could be used for all sorts of purposes for which they were not designed. The war-bands of the invading external proletariat would have extended their depredations much less rapidly in the latter days of the Roman Empire if that Empire had not unwittingly provided them with such excellent means of getting over the ground. But more interesting persons than Alaric are to be discerned on the road. When Augustus imposed the Roman Peace on Pisidia he was unconsciously paving the way for Saint Paul, on his first missionary journey, to land in Pamphylia and travel unmolested to Antioch-in-Pisidia, Iconium, Lystra, and Derbe. And Pompey had swept the pirates off the seas in order that Paul might make his momentous last voyage from Palestinian Caesarea to Italian Puteoli without having to brave man-made perils in addition to the ordeals of tempest and shipwreck.

The Roman Peace proved as propitious a social environment for

Paul's successors. In the latter part of the second century of the Roman Empire's existence, Saint Irenaeus of Lyons was paying an implicit tribute to the easy communications of the Empire when he extolled the unity of the Catholic Church throughout the Hellenic world. 'Having received this gospel and this faith', he writes, 'the Church, in spite of her dispersal throughout the World, preserves these treasures as meticulously as if she were living under one single roof.' Two hundred years later again, a disgruntled pagan historian, Ammianus Marcellinus, complains that 'crowds of prelates made use of the public post-horses for rushing to and fro on the business of these "synods", as they call them'.

Our survey[1] has brought to light so many cases in which a system of communications has been turned to account by unintended beneficiaries that we may regard this tendency as illustrating an historical 'law'; and in A.D. 1952 this conclusion raised a momentous question about the future of the Westernizing world in which the writer of this Study and his contemporaries were living.

By the year A.D. 1952 the initiative and skill of Western Man had been engaged for some four and a half centuries in knitting together the whole habitable and traversable surface of the planet by a system of communications, operated by a technique which was constantly accelerating its pace. The wooden caravels and galleons, rigged for sailing in the eye of the wind, which had enabled the pioneer mariners of Modern Western Europe to make themselves masters of all the oceans, had given way to mechanically propelled iron ships of relatively gigantic size; 'dirt tracks' travelled by six-horse coaches had been replaced by macadamized and concrete-floored roads travelled by automobiles; railways had competed with roads, and aircraft with all land-borne and water-borne conveyances. Concurrently, means of communication which did not require the physical transportation of human bodies had been conjured up and put into operation, in the shape of telegraphs, telephones, and wireless transmission—visual as well as auditory —by radio. Never before had so large an area been made so highly conductive to every form of human intercourse.

These developments foreshadowed the eventual unification, on the political level, of the society in which these technological portents had appeared. At the time of writing, however, the political prospects of the Western world were still obscure; for, even though an observer might feel certain that political unity would come about

---

[1] In the original work, of which this is an abridgement, Mr. Toynbee surveys the uses made of the communication systems of a large number of universal states.

in some form sooner or later, neither the date nor the manner of it could yet be divined. In a world which was still partitioned politically among sixty or seventy self-assertively sovereign parochial states, but which had already invented the atom bomb, it was manifest that political unity might be imposed by the familiar method of the 'knock-out blow'; and it was also probable that, if peace was thus to be imposed in this case, as it had been in so many others, by the arbitrary fiat of a single surviving Great Power, the price of unification by force, in terms of moral, psychological, social, and political (not to mention material) devastation, would be relatively still higher than it had been in other cases of the same kind. At the same time it was possible that this political unification might be achieved by the alternative method of voluntary co-operation. But, whatever solution might be found for this problem, it could be confidently predicted that the new world-wide network of communications would find its historic mission in the familiar ironic role of being turned to account by unintended beneficiaries.

Who would draw the largest benefits in this case? Hardly the barbarians of the external proletariat. Though we have already developed, and may again develop, Neo-barbarian Attilas, renegades of perverted civilization, in our midst, in the shape of Hitler and his like, our world-wide system has little to fear from the pitiable remnants of the genuine barbarians beyond the pale.[1] On the other hand, the extant higher religions, whose domains had been linked up with one another and with the dwindling tenements of pagan Primitive Man, had already begun to take advantage of their opportunities. Saint Paul, who had once ventured from the Orontes to the Tiber, had been eagerly venturing forth on broader seas than the Mediterranean. On board a Portuguese caravel he had rounded the Cape on his second journey to India,[2] and, farther afield again, through the Straits of Malacca, on his third journey to China.[3] Transhipping to a Spanish galleon, the indefatigable apostle had crossed the Atlantic from Cadiz to Vera Cruz, and the Pacific from Acapulco to the Philippines. Nor had Western Christianity been the only living religion to take advantage of Western communications. Eastern Orthodox Christianity, in the train of

[1] The Mau Mau movement in Kenya might be regarded as the most conspicuous protest of these latter at the moment of writing, A.D. 1954.

[2] Reckoning the Nestorian lodgement in Travancore as the first attempt of Christianity to convert India, and the Jesuit mission to the Court of Akbar as the second.

[3] Reckoning the seventh-century Nestorian lodgement at Si Ngan as the first attempt of Christianity to convert China; the thirteenth- and fourteenth-century Western Christian missions overland as the second; and the sixteenth-century Western Christian missions by sea as the third.

Cossack pioneers equipped with Western fire-arms, had been making the long trek from the River Kama to the Sea of Okhotsk. In nineteenth-century Africa, while Saint Paul, in the guise of the Scottish medical missionary David Livingstone, was preaching the gospel, healing the sick, and discovering lakes and waterfalls, Islam was also on the move. It was not inconceivable that the Mahāyāna might one day recollect its marvellous journey over a succession of royal roads from Magadha to Loyang and, in the strength of this buoyant memory, might turn such Western inventions as the aeroplane and the radio to as good account for its own work of preaching salvation as it had once turned the Chinese invention of the printing press.

The issues raised by this stimulation of missionary activities on a world-wide range were not just those of ecclesiastical geopolitics. The entry of established higher religions into new missionary fields brought up the question whether the eternal essence of a religion could be distinguished from its ephemeral accidents. The encounters of the religions with one another brought up the question whether, in the long run, they could live and let live side by side or whether one of them would supersede the rest.

The ideal of religious eclecticism had appealed to certain rulers of universal states—an Alexander Severus and an Akbar—who had happened to combine a sophisticated mind with a tender heart, and their experiments had proved entirely barren of result. A different ideal had inspired the pioneer Jesuit missionaries—a Francis Xavier and a Matteo Ricci—who were the first apostles of any religion to grasp the opportunities offered by the Modern Western technician's conquest of the high seas. These audacious spiritual pathfinders aspired to captivate for Christianity the Hindu and Far Eastern worlds, as Saint Paul and his successors had captivated the Hellenic world in their time; but—being endowed with an intellectual insight that matched their heroic faith—they did not fail to see that their enterprise could not succeed without fulfilling one exacting condition, and they did not shrink from accepting the consequences. They perceived that a missionary must convey his message in terms—intellectual, aesthetic, and emotional—that would appeal to his prospective converts. The more revolutionary the message in its essence, the more important it would be to clothe it in a familiar and congenial presentation. But this would require that the message should be stripped of the incompatible clothing in which the missionaries themselves happened to have inherited it from their own cultural tradition; and that, in turn, would demand of the missionaries that they should assume the responsibility of determining what was essence and what was accident in the traditional presentation of their religion.

The crux of this policy was that, in removing a stumbling-block from the path of the non-Christian societies that he was setting out to convert, the missionary would be placing another stumbling-block before the feet of his co-religionists; and on this rock the Early Modern Jesuit missions in India and China suffered shipwreck. They were the victims of jealousy on the part of rival missionaries and of conservatism at the Vatican. And yet this might prove to be not the end of the story.

If the local swaddling-clothes in which Christianity had been wrapped when it came into the world in Palestine had not been masterfully removed by Paul of Tarsus, the Christian artists of the Catacombs at Rome and the Christian philosophers of the divinity school at Alexandria would never have had their chance of presenting the essence of Christianity in terms of Greek vision and thought and thereby paving the way for the conversion of the Hellenic world. And, if, in the twentieth century of the Christian Era, Origen's and Augustine's Christianity could not divest itself of trappings acquired at those successive Syriac, Hellenic, and Western posting-stations at which it had once paused on its historic journey, it would not be able to take advantage of the worldwide opportunity opened up for every living higher religion at the time of writing. A higher religion that allows itself to become 'dyed in the wool' with the imprint of a temporary cultural environment condemns itself to become stationary and earth-bound.

But if Christianity were, after all, to take the other path, it might repeat in a latter-day *Oikoumenê* what it had once achieved in the Roman Empire. In the spiritual commerce that had been served by Roman means of communication, Christianity had drawn out of, and inherited from, the other higher religions and philosophies which it had thus encountered, the heart of what had been best in them. In a World materially linked together by the many inventions of Modern Western technique, Hinduism and the Mahāyāna might make no less fruitful contributions than Isis-worship and Neoplatonism had once made to Christian insight and practice. And, if, in a Western world too, Caesar's empire were to rise and fall—as his empire always had collapsed or decayed after a run of a few hundred years—an historian peering into the future in A.D. 1952 could imagine Christianity then being left as the heir of all the philosophies from Ikhnaton's to Hegel's and of all the higher religions as far back as the ever-latent worship of a Mother and her Son, who had started their travels along the King's Highway under the names of Ishtar and Tammuz.

Garrisons and Colonies

Plantations of loyal supporters of the imperial régime—who may be soldiers on active service, militiamen, discharged veterans, or civilians—are an integral part of any imperial system of communications. The presence, prowess, and vigilance of these human watchdogs provide the indispensable security without which roads, bridges, and the like would be of no use to the imperial authorities. The frontier posts are part of the same system, for frontier lines are always also lateral highways. But, besides planting garrisons for purposes of police or defence, a universal state may be moved to plant colonies for the more constructive purpose of repairing ravages inflicted by the devastating struggle for power during the anterior Time of Troubles.

It was this that was in Caesar's mind when he planted self-governing colonies of Roman citizens on the desolate sites of Capua, Carthage, and Corinth. In the course of the foregoing struggle for survival between the parochial states of the Hellenic world, the Roman Government of the day had deliberately made an example of Capua for her treacherous secession to Hannibal, and of Carthage for the crime of having almost defeated Rome herself, while Corinth had been arbitrarily singled out for the same treatment among the members of the Achaean League. Under the pre-Caesarian republican régime the conservative party had been stubbornly opposed to the restoration of these three famous cities, not so much from fear as from sheer vindictiveness, and the long-drawn-out controversy over their treatment became in due course the symbol of a wider issue. Was the *raison d'être* of Roman rule the selfish interest of the particular state which had established it, or did the Empire exist for the common weal of the Hellenic world of which it had become the political embodiment? Caesar's victory over the Senate was a victory for the more liberal, humane, and imaginative view.

This striking difference of moral character between the régime which Caesar inaugurated and that which he superseded was not a peculiar feature of Hellenic history. A similar change of attitude towards the use and abuse of power had accompanied the transition from a Time of Troubles to a universal state in the histories of other civilizations; but, though this historical 'law' may be discernible, it is subject to many exceptions. On the one hand we find Times of Troubles generating not only uprooted and embittered proletariats but also colonizing enterprises on a grand scale—as exemplified by the host of Greek city-states planted far and wide over the former domain of the Achaemenian Empire by

Alexander the Great. Conversely, the change of heart on the part of the dominant minority, which should be the psychological counterpart of the establishment of a universal state, is seldom so steadfast that it does not occasionally relapse into the brutal practices of the foregoing Time of Troubles. The Neo-Babylonian Empire, which stood on the whole for a moral revolt of the interior of the Babylonic world against the brutality of its Assyrian marchmen, lapsed into uprooting Judah, much as Assyria had uprooted Israel. It might be fanciful to claim a moral superiority for Babylon over Nineveh in this regard, on the score that Babylon's Judaic exiles were allowed to survive until Babylon's Achaemenian successor sent them home again, whereas Nineveh's victims, 'the Lost Ten Tribes', were liquidated and lost forever, except in the imaginations of British Israelites.

None the less, and in spite of exceptions, it remains broadly true that a relatively constructive and humane policy of colonization is one of the marks of universal states.

We have drawn a distinction between garrisons with a military or police purpose and colonies with a social or cultural purpose, but in the long run the distinction is one of purpose only and not of consequence. The installation of standing military garrisons along the frontiers and in the interior of a universal state by the empire-builders can hardly fail to bring civilian settlement in its train. The Roman legionaries, though debarred from contracting legal marriages during their term of active service, were permitted in practice to enter into permanent marital relations with concubines and to bring up families; and after their discharge they were able to convert a concubinate into legal marriage and legitimize their children. The Arab military *muhājirah* were actually allowed to bring their wives and children with them into the cantonments in which they settled. Thus Roman and Arab garrisons became the nuclei of civilian settlements, and the same must have been true of imperial garrison posts in all empires at all times.

But, besides arising as undesigned by-products of military establishments, civilian colonies were also planted as ends in themselves. For example, the north-east Anatolian districts in which the Achaemenidae had granted appanages to Persian barons were colonized by the 'Osmanlis with Albanian converts to Islam. In commercial centres in the heart of their dominions the 'Osmanlis settled civilian communities of refugee Sephardi Jews from Spain and Portugal. A long list could be cited of colonies founded by Roman Emperors as centres of civilization (Latinization or Hellenization as the case might be) in the more backward regions of their empire. One example out of many is Adrianople, the name of which to this day recalls the effort of a great Emperor of the second century to debarbarize the traditionally barbarous Thracians. The same policy was pursued by the Spanish empire-builders in Central and South America. These Spanish colonial city-states served as cells of an intrusive alien régime's administrative and judicial organization, and, like their Hellenic prototypes, they were economically parasitic.

'In the Anglo-American colonies the towns grew up to meet the needs of the inhabitants of the country: in the Spanish colonies the population of the country grew up to meet the needs of the towns. The primary object of the English colonist was generally to live on the land and derive his support from its cultivation; the primary plan of the Spaniard was to live in town and derive his support from the Indians or Negroes at work on plantations or in the mines. . . . Owing to the presence of aboriginal labour to exploit in fields and mines, the rural population remained almost entirely Indian.[1]

A type of internal colonization which is apt to become prominent in the last phase of the history of a universal state is the plantation of barbarian husbandmen on lands that have come to be depopulated either as the result of raids perpetrated by these barbarians themselves or as the result of some social sickness native to the decaying empire. A classic example is presented in the picture of a post-Diocletianic Roman Empire in the *Notitia Dignitatum*, which records the presence of a number of German and Sarmatian corporate settlements on Roman soil in Gaul, Italy, and the Danubian provinces. The technical term *laeti*, by which these barbarian settlers were known, is derived from a West German word denoting semi-servile resident aliens; and we may infer that they were descendants of defeated barbarian adversaries who had been rewarded or punished for past acts of aggression by being coerced or coaxed into becoming peaceful cultivators of the Promised Land which they had formerly devastated as raiders. They were cautiously planted in the interior and not in the neighbourhood of the frontier.

A survey of the garrisons and colonies established by the rulers of universal states, and a consideration of the arbitrary transferences of population that they involve, suggests that these institutions, whatever their merits in other contexts, must have intensified the process of pammixia and proletarianization, which we have already seen to be characteristic of Times of Troubles and universal states

[1] Haring, C. H.: *The Spanish Empire in America* (New York 1947, Oxford University Press), pp. 160 and 159.

alike. Permanent military garrisons installed on frontiers become 'melting-pots' in which the dominant minority fuses itself with both the external and the internal proletariat. The wardens of the marches and the opposing barbarian war-bands tend, with the passage of time, to become assimilated to one another, first in military technique and eventually also in culture. But, long before the dominant minority has been barbarized by contact on the frontier with the external proletariat, it will have been vulgarized by fraternization with the internal proletariat. For empire-builders seldom preserve either sufficient manpower or sufficient zest for the profession of arms to contemplate holding and defending their empire unaided. Their first recourse is to reinforce their armies by drawing recruits from subject peoples who have not lost their martial virtues. At a later stage they proceed to draw upon the barbarians beyond the pale as well.

For whose benefit does this process of pammixia and pro-letarianization chiefly operate? The most conspicuous beneficiaries are obviously the external proletariat; for the education which the barbarians acquire from the military outposts of a civilization—first as adversaries and later as mercenaries—enables them, when the empire collapses, to swoop across the fallen barrier and carve out successor-states for themselves; but we have already dwelt on the ephemeral character of these 'heroic age' achievements. The ultimate beneficiaries from the organized redistribution and inter-mixture of populations in the Roman and the Arab empires were Christianity in the one case and Islam in the other.

The military cantonments and frontier garrisons of the Umayyad Caliphate manifestly served Islam as invaluable *points d'appui* in that extraordinary deployment of latent spiritual forces by which Islam transfigured itself, and thereby transformed its mission, in the course of six centuries. In the seventh century of the Christian Era Islam had burst out of Arabia as the distinctive sectarian creed of one of the barbarian war-bands that were carving out successor-states for themselves in provinces of the Roman Empire. By the thirteenth century it had become a universal church providing shelter for sheep left without their familiar shepherds through the collapse of the 'Abbasid Caliphate at the dissolution of the Syriac civilization.

What was the secret of Islam's power to survive the death of its founder, the downfall of the primitive Arab empire-builders, the decline of the Arabs' Iranian supplanters, the overthrow of the 'Abbasid Caliphate, and the collapse of the barbarian successor-states that established themselves for their brief day on the Cali-phate's ruins? The explanation was to be found in the spiritual experience of the converts to Islam among the non-Arab subjects of the Caliphate in the Umayyad Age. Islam, which they had originally adopted mainly for reasons of social self-interest, struck roots in their hearts, and was taken by them more seriously than by the Arabs themselves. A religion which thus succeeded in winning loyalty in virtue of its intrinsic merits was not doomed to stand or fall with the political régimes which had successively sought to exploit it for non-religious purposes. This spiritual triumph was the more remarkable considering that such exploitation for political ends had proved fatal to other higher religions and that Islam had thus been placed in jeopardy not only by its founder's successors but by Muhammad himself, when he had migrated from Mecca to Medina and had become a brilliantly successful statesman instead of remaining a conspicuously unsuccessful prophet. In this *tour de force* of surviving the peril to which it had been exposed, through the tragic irony of history, by its own founder, Islam had borne witness, through the ages, to the spiritual value of the religious message which Muhammad had brought to Mankind.

Thus in the history of the Caliphate the carefully considered policy of the empire-builders in planting garrisons and colonies and regulating the transfer and intermingling of populations had the unintended and unexpected effect of expediting the career of a higher religion; and corresponding effects were produced by the same cause in the history of the Roman Empire.

In the first three centuries of the Roman Empire the most conspicuously active conductors of religious influences were the military garrisons along the frontiers, and the religions that were propagated the most rapidly along these channels were the Hellenized Hittite worship of the 'Iuppiter' of Dolichê and the Hellenized Syriac worship of the originally Iranian divinity Mithras. We can follow the transmission of these two religions from the Roman garrisons on the Euphrates to those on the Danube, on the German *limes*, on the Rhine, and on the Wall in Britain, and the spectacle recalls the contemporary journey that the Mahāyāna, in the last stage of its long trek from Hindustan round the western flank of the Tibetan Plateau, was making from the shores of the Tarim Basin to the shores of the Pacific along the chain of garrisons guarding the frontier of a Sinic universal state over against the Nomads of the Eurasian Steppe. In the next chapter of the story the Mahāyāna succeeded in penetrating from the north-western marches of the Sinic world into the interior and thereby becoming the universal church of the Sinic internal proletariat, and eventually one of the four principal higher religions

of a latter-day Westernizing world. The destinies of Mithraism
and of the worship of Iuppiter Dolichênus were more modest.
Bound up, as they had come to be, with the fortunes of the Roman
Imperial Army, these two military religions never recovered from
the blow dealt them by the army's temporary collapse in the middle
of the third century of the Christian Era; and, as far as they had
any permanent historical significance, it was as forerunners of
Christianity and as tributaries to the ever-growing stream of
religious tradition fed by the confluence of many waters in the
bed which Christianity dug for itself as it poured over the Roman
Empire along a different channel.

While Iuppiter Dolichênus and Mithras used the frontier
garrisons as their stepping-stones in their north-westward march
from the Euphrates to the Tyne, Saint Paul made a corresponding
use of colonies planted by Caesar and Augustus in the interior of
the Empire. On his first missionary journey he sowed seeds of
Christianity in the Roman colonies of Antioch-in-Pisidia and
Lystra; on his second in the Roman colonies of Troas, Philippi,
and Corinth. He was, of course, far from confining himself to such
colonies; for example he established himself for two years in the
ancient Hellenic city of Ephesus. Corinth, however, where he
stayed for eighteen months, played an important part in the life of
the Church in the post-Apostolic Age, and we may conjecture that
the prominence of the Christian community here was partly due
to the cosmopolitan character of the settlement of Roman freedmen
that had been planted there by Caesar.

The most signal example, however, of a Roman colony being
turned to Christian account is not Corinth but Lyons; for the
advance of Christianity from colony to colony did not come to a
stop when it had reached the metropolis, nor cease with the death
of Saint Paul. Planted in 43 B.C. on a carefully chosen site in the
angle formed by the confluence of the Rhone and the Saône, Lugdunum was a Roman colony not only in name but in fact; and this
settlement of Roman citizens of genuinely Italian origin on the
threshold of the vast tracts of Gallic territory that had been added
to the Empire by Caesar's conquests had been designed to radiate
Roman culture through this Gallia Comata, as it had been radiated
already through a Gallia Togata by the older Roman colony of
Narbonne. Lugdunum was the seat of the only Roman garrison
between Rome itself and the Rhine. Moreover, it was not only the
administrative centre of one of the three provinces into which
Gallia Comata had been divided; it was also the official meeting
place of 'the Council of the Three Gauls', where the representatives of sixty or more cantons assembled periodically round the

Altar of Augustus erected here by Drusus in 12 B.C. In fact, Lugdunum had been deliberately called into existence to serve important imperial purposes. Yet by A.D. 177 this Roman colony had come to harbour a Christian community of sufficient vitality to provoke a massacre; and here, as elsewhere, the blood of the martyrs was the seed of the Church. For it was as bishop of Lugdunum during the immediately following quarter of a century that Irenaeus—a Greek man of letters, possibly of Syrian origin—worked out the earliest systematic presentation of Catholic Christian theology.

Christianity in the Roman Empire, Islam in the Caliphate, and the Mahāyāna in the Sinic universal state each took advantage of the garrisons and colonies established by secular empire-builders for their own purposes; yet these unintended religious consequences of orderly redistributions of population were not so signal as those of Nebuchadnezzar's relapse into Assyrian methods of barbarism; for, in carrying Judah away captive, the Neo-Babylonian war-lord did not merely foster the progress of an existing higher religion but virtually called a new one into existence.

Provinces

Like the garrisons and colonies which the builders of universal states distribute over their dominions, the provinces into which they carve these dominions up have two distinct functions: the preservation of the universal state itself and the preservation of the society for whose body social a universal state provides the political framework. The histories of the Roman Empire and of the British Rāj in India could be adduced to show that the two main alternative functions of the political organization of a universal state are to maintain the supremacy of the empire-building Power and to fill a political vacuum arising in the body social of the disintegrating society through the destruction or collapse of its former parochial states.

The extent to which the founders of a universal state are tempted to resort to the devices of annexation and direct administration as measures of insurance against the danger of a resurgence of defeated rivals depends, no doubt, on the degree of the loyalty and regret that the abolished parochial states continue to evoke in the minds of their own former masters and subjects; and this, in turn, depends on the pace of the conquest and on the antecedent history of the society in whose domain the universal state has established itself. Victorious empire-builders have most reason to fear a violent undoing of their work when they have established their rule at one stroke, and when they have imposed it on a world of parochial states long accustomed to enjoy and abuse a status of sovereign independence.

In the Sinic world, for example, effective political unity was imposed for the first time by the empire-building state of Ts'in within a period of no more than ten years (230–221 B.C.). Within that brief span of time King Chêng of Ts'in overthrew the six other till then surviving kingdoms and thereby became the founder of a Sinic universal state, with the title of Ts'in She Hwang-ti. But he could not with equal rapidity extinguish the political self-consciousness of the former ruling elements, and the problem consequently confronting him has been dramatized by the historian Sse-ma Ts'ien in the form of a tournament of set speeches in the Imperial Council. By whatever processes the issue may have been fought out, it is certain that the radical policy prevailed and that in 221 B.C. Ts'in She Hwang-ti decided in favour of redistributing the whole territory of his newly established universal state into thirty-six military commands.

In taking this drastic step the Emperor was applying to the six parochial states which he had conquered the militaristic and non-feudal system that had also prevailed for a hundred years already in his own state of Ts'in. But the conquered states could hardly have been expected to like it, for Ts'in She Hwang-ti was a representative of that familiar figure in the histories of the establishments of universal states, a conquering marchman, and the ruling class in the conquered states regarded him much as fourth-century citizens of the Greek city-states regarded the Kings of Macedon—that is as being little better than a 'barbarian'. The peoples of the cultural centre of the Sinic world were naturally predisposed to idolize a culture of which they themselves were the principal exponents, and they had latterly been encouraged in this foible by the philosophers of the Confucian school, whose founder had diagnosed the social sickness from which the Sinic society had been suffering as being due to a neglect of the traditional rites and practices, and had prescribed as a sovereign remedy a return to the supposed social and moral order of the early Sinic Feudal Age. This canonization of a half-imaginary past had made little impression on the rulers and people of Ts'in, and the sudden imposition of the institutions of this uncultivated march-state roused violent resentment, to which Ts'in She Hwang-ti's only response was to take further repressive measures.

Such a policy invited an explosion, and the Emperor's death in 210 B.C. was followed by a general revolt resulting in the capture of the capital of the Ts'in Empire by one of the rebel leaders, Liu Pang; yet this victory of a violent reaction against the revolutionary work of the founder of the Sinic universal state did not, after all, result in a restoration of the *ancien régime*. Liu Pang was not a member of the dispossessed feudal nobility but a peasant, and he succeeded in founding an enduring régime because he did not attempt to re-establish either the anachronistic feudal order or Ts'in She Hwang-ti's revolutionary substitute for it. His policy was to feel his way gradually towards his predecessor's Caesarian goal through an Augustan semblance of compromise.

In the short interval between the collapse of the Ts'in Power in 207 B.C. and the general recognition of Liu Pang as sole master of the Sinic world in 202 B.C. the experiment of attempting to restore the *ancien régime* was tried by another rebel leader, Hsiang Yü, and proved unworkable. When, after this failure, Liu Pang made himself sole master of the Sinic world, his first act was to confer fiefs on his most deserving lieutenants, and he even left undisturbed such fief-holders of Hsiang Yü's régime as had managed to come to terms with him. But, one by one, the enfeofed generals were degraded and put to death, while other fief-holders were frequently transferred from one fief to another and were readily deposed without being given a chance of establishing any dangerously close relations with their temporary subjects. Meanwhile Liu Pang had taken effective measures for maintaining and increasing the pre-ponderance of the Imperial Power. In the upshot, Ts'in She Hwang-ti's ideal of a universal state controlled from the centre through a hierarchy of artificially mapped out units of local ad-ministration was translated into fact, once again, within a hundred years of Ts'in She Hwang-ti's death; and this time the achievement was definitive, because the Fabian statesmanship of Liu Pang and his successors had given the Imperial Government time to create the human instrument for lack of which the first Ts'in emperor's grandiose design had come to grief.

A centralized government cannot be operated without a profes-sional civil service, and the Han Dynasty, of which Liu Pang was the founder, succeeded in building up an efficient and acceptable civil service by entering into an alliance with the Confucian school of philosophy and weaning the Confucian philosophers from their former alliance with the old narrow military aristocracy of birth by opening the public service to a new and broader based aris-tocracy of cultural merit as measured by proficiency in the Con-fucian lore. The transition was made so gradually and was managed so skilfully that the new aristocracy inherited the old aristocracy's historic appellation—*chun tze*—without any overt recognition that a momentous social and political revolution was taking place.

Measured by the durability of his achievement, the founder of

the Han Dynasty may be accounted the greatest of all those statesmen whose careers have inaugurated a universal state. A Western
world, familiar with the similar but less remarkable achievement
of the Roman Augustus, is, apart from its specialists in Sinic history, barely aware of Liu Pang's historic existence. The historians
of an oecumenical society of some future age, with historic roots
in all the civilizations of the past, will presumably display a better
sense of proportion.

Having examined the significance of provincial organization in
the Sinic universal state, we have no space to consider other
examples. We pass at once to consider the services unconsciously
rendered by such provincial organizations to those for whose
benefit they were not primarily designed; and here again we will
limit ourselves to a single example, by recalling how the Christian
Church turned to its own account the provincial organization of
the Roman Empire.

In building up its body ecclesiastic, the Church availed itself of
the city states that were the cells of the Hellenic body social and
the Roman body politic, and, as the traditions of the Hellenic
civilization gradually died out, a city came to mean a town that
was the seat of a Christian bishop[1] instead of meaning a town
possessing institutions of civil self-government and chartered as a
municipality of the Roman Commonwealth. A local bishop whose
see was the centre of a Diocletianic Roman province came to be
recognized by the other bishops of the same province as their
superior. Such metropolitans or archbishops, in their turn, acknowledged as their primate the bishop whose see was the administrative
centre of one of those groups of provinces which in the Diocletianic system were called dioceses—a word which the Church
took over, but applied to the jurisdiction of a single bishop. Bishops,
metropolitans, and primates alike paid allegiance to regional
patriarchs who corresponded hierarchically to the Diocletianic
praetorian prefects. The Diocletianic prefecture of the East was
eventually divided between the four patriarchates of Alexandria,
Jerusalem, Antioch, and Constantinople, while the other three
prefectures were combined in the single vast but much more thinly
populated patriarchate of Rome.

This territorial organization of the Christian Church was not
called into existence by any emperor; it was built up by the Church
itself in days when the Church was an officially unrecognized and
fitfully persecuted institution. In virtue of this original independence of the secular régime whose provincial organization it had

---

[1] This was the usage in England until quite modern times. Cities were
'cathedral cities': other towns were 'boroughs'.

adapted to its own purposes, the structure could survive the breakdown of its secular counterpart. In Gaul, where a tottering imperial régime had sought to rehabilitate itself on a novel basis of local support by instituting periodic regional congresses of notables, the Church, after the Empire had faded out of existence, took its cue from this secular precedent by convening regional congresses of bishops.

On the medieval ecclesiastical map of France, for example, an historian could discern in the mosaic of bishoprics the boundaries of the city-states of Gallia Togata and the cantons of Gallia Comata, while the archbishoprics preserved the outlines of the Diocletianic subdivisions of the four Augustan provinces, Narbonensis, Aquitania, Lugdunensis, Belgica. Even the five patriarchates were all still in existence—four in Eastern Orthodox hands and one in Western Catholic hands—at the time when these lines were being written; and, though the areas of their circumscriptions, and the distribution and nationality of their ecclesiastical subjects, had undergone vast changes during the fifteen centuries since the Fourth Oecumenical Council, held at Calchedon (A.D. 451), their mortifying losses had been offset by gains that could never have been foreseen at the time when the patriarchates took shape.

Capital Cities

The seats of the central governments of universal states show a decided tendency to change their locations in course of time. Empire-builders usually begin by ruling their dominions from a seat of government suitable to themselves: either the established capital of their own fatherland (e.g. Rome) or some new site, on the fringe of the subjugated territories, easily accessible from the empire-builder's home country (e.g. Calcutta). But, as time goes on, the experience of imperial administration or the pressure of events is apt to lead either the original empire-builders or their successors who take their empire over after a temporary collapse, to adopt some new site commended by its convenience, not for the original empire-building Power, but for the empire as a whole. This new oecumenical outlook will, of course, suggest different new locations in different circumstances. If the chief consideration is administrative convenience, a central site with good communications is likely to be chosen. If the chief consideration is defence against some aggressor, the site chosen is likely to be one convenient for the deployment of strength on the threatened frontier.

We have seen that the founders of universal states are not always of the same origin. Sometimes they are representatives of a civilization which is foreign to the society for whose political needs they are providing. Sometimes they are barbarians who have become morally alienated from the civilization towards which they gravitate: in other words, an external proletariat. Sometimes, and indeed frequently, they are marchmen who have vindicated their claim to be members of a civilization by defending its borders against outer barbarians, before turning their arms against the interior of their own society and endowing it with a universal state. Lastly—and such cases seem to be rare—they may be neither aliens nor barbarians nor marchmen but 'metropolitans' from the interior of the society in question.

In universal states founded by aliens or barbarians or marchmen the capital will tend to move from the frontier towards the centre, though in the last-named case it may be held to the frontier by the fact that the marchmen have still to perform their original function. In universal states founded by 'metropolitans' the capital will naturally start in the centre, though it may be drawn to a frontier if a threat of aggression from a particular quarter becomes the government's most pressing concern. We must now offer illustrations of the rules which appear to regulate the location and migration of capitals.

The British Rāj in India is a conspicuous example of empire-building by aliens. Reaching India from overseas and coming there to trade with the inhabitants long before they ever dreamt of ruling them, the English established trading bases at Bombay, Madras, and Calcutta. The last-named became the first political capital because the East India Company happened to establish political dominion over two rich provinces in the hinterland of Calcutta a full generation before it made any comparable acquisitions elsewhere. Calcutta remained the capital of British India for more than a hundred years after the design of bringing all India under British rule had been conceived by Wellesley (Governor-General A.D. 1798–1805), and more than fifty years after that design had been carried into execution. But the gravitational pull of a politically unified sub-continent eventually proved strong enough to draw the seat of the British Indian central government from Calcutta to Delhi, which was a natural site for an empire including the basins of both the Indus and the Ganges.

Delhi was, of course, not only a natural site; it was also an historic one, having been from A.D. 1628 onwards the capital of the Mughals. The Mughals, like the British, had provided India with an alien universal state, coming into India, not overseas, but by way of the North-West Frontier. If they had anticipated the British example they might have established their first capital at Kābul. They did not do so, for reasons which a detailed examination of their history would explain. Delhi was not their first capital, but its predecessor, Agra, was a similarly central site.

If we take a glance at Spanish America we find that the empire-builders in Central America made their capital once and for all at Tenochtitlan (Mexico City)—a 'Delhi'—neglecting the possible claims of their port of entry, Vera Cruz—a 'Calcutta'. In Peru they pursued the opposite course, making their capital on the coast at Lima in preference to Cuzco, the old capital of the Incas on the inland plateau. The explanation is no doubt to be found in the fact that the Pacific coastlands of Peru were rich and important, whereas the Atlantic coastlands of Mexico were not.

The 'Osmanlis, the aliens who provided a universal state for the Eastern Orthodox Christian society, put up with a succession of makeshift capitals, first in Asia and then in Europe, until they had secured the peerless site of their Byzantine predecessors.

When the Mongol Khāqān Qubilāy (reigned A.D. 1259–94) achieved the conquest of the whole continental domain of the Far Eastern society he shifted his capital from Mongolian Qāraqorum to Chinese Peking. But, though Qubilāy's head dictated this move, his heart remained homesick for his ancestral pastures, and the semi-Sinified Mongol statesman indulged his unregenerate Nomad feelings by building himself a subsidiary residence at Chung-tu, a point on the south-eastern rim of the Mongolian Plateau, where the Steppe approached nearest to the new imperial city. But Peking remained the centre of government, and Chung-tu a holiday resort, though business had doubtless to be transacted there also some-times.

> 'In Xanadu did Kubla Khan
> A stately pleasure-dome decree.'

Perhaps we might equate Chung-tu with Simla, for, if Qubilāy sighed for his Steppe, British Viceroys certainly sighed for a temperate clime. We might even equate Chung-tu with Balmoral, for Queen Victoria's heart was as obviously in the Highlands as Qubilāy's was in the Steppe. We might go farther and imagine a nineteenth-century Chinese traveller describing the charms of Balmoral with an enthusiasm sufficient to inspire a twenty-fifth-century Chinese poet to enshrine Queen Victoria and her 'stately pleasure-dome' in a magical fragment of Chinese verse.

Seleucus Nicator, founder of one of the successor-states of the vast and ephemeral empire of Alexander the Great, furnishes a case of an empire-builder who was in two minds as to the location of his capital city, because he was in two minds as to the direction of his imperial ambitions. To begin with, he set his heart on winning, and in fact won, the rich Babylonian province of the former Achaemenian Empire and established a capital, Seleucia, on the right bank of the Tigris at the point where it comes nearest to the Euphrates. The site was admirably chosen, and Seleucia remained a great city and an important centre of Hellenic culture for more than five centuries following. Its founder, however, led astray by successful ventures at the expense of rival Macedonian generals farther west, shifted his centre of interest to the Mediterranean world and established his principal capital at Antioch in Syria, twenty miles from the mouth of the Orontes.[1] The result was that his successors wasted their energies in wars with the Ptolemies of Egypt and other Powers of the eastern Mediterranean and lost their Babylonian dominions to the Parthians.

All the above examples are taken from empires founded by representatives of alien Civilizations. We now pass on to consider the location of capitals in empires founded by barbarians.

The homeland of the Persian barbarians, whose conquests provided the Syriac society with a universal state in the form of the Achaemenian Empire, was mountainous, barren, and remote from the highways of human intercourse. According to the story with which Herodotus concludes his work, Cyrus the Great, who had created the Achaemenian Empire, deprecated a suggestion that the Persian people, now that they had become masters of the World, should evacuate their bleak highland homeland and settle in one of the more agreeable countries at their disposal. It is a good story, and we have already used it in an earlier part of this Study to illustrate the superiority of hard conditions for stimulating human enterprise. It is a matter of historical fact, however, that, more than a hundred years before Cyrus the Great overthrew his Median suzerain, one of his Achaemenian predecessors had transferred his seat of government from his ancestral highlands to the first piece of lowland territory of which he had gained possession. The place was called Anšan, and it was somewhere near Susa, though its exact location is still unknown. After the Achaemenian Empire was established, its seat of government migrated annually, according to the season, to and from several capitals with different climates, but Persepolis, Ecbatana, and even Susa (the Shushan of the Old Testament) may be regarded as, in the main, capitals of ceremony and sentiment, and for business purposes geographical convenience centred the affairs of the empire on Babylon, the capital of its lowland predecessor.

---

[1] One of many other Seleucias was also founded in this neighbourhood, to serve as the port of Antioch. From this Seleucia, as recorded in The Acts of the Apostles, Saint Paul set sail for Cyprus on his first missionary journey.

When the universal state that had been originally provided for the Syriac world by Persian empire-builders from the Iranian Plateau was eventually reconstituted, after nearly a thousand years of Hellenic intrusion, by Hijāzī barbarians from the rim of the Arabian Plateau, history repeated itself with emphasis. Thanks to the intuition of the discordant oligarchs of an oasis state in the Hijāz, who had invited the rejected prophet of a rival community at Mecca to make himself at home with them and try his hand at being their leader, in the hope that he would bring them the concord which they had failed to attain by themselves, Yathrib became, within thirty years of the Hijrah (Hegira), the capital of an empire embracing not only the former Roman dominions in Syria and Egypt but the entire domain of the former Sasanian Empire. Yathrib's title to remain the seat of government lay in the fact that this remote oasis state was the nucleus out of which the Muslim Arab World Empire had burgeoned with a rapidity strongly suggestive of divine intervention, and it was hallowed as Madīnat-an-Nabī, 'the City of the Prophet'. Medina remained the capital of the Caliphate *de jure*, at any rate until the foundation of Baghdad by the 'Abbasid Caliph Mansūr in A.D. 792, but, more than a hundred years before that date, the Umayyad Caliphs had shifted the capital *de facto* to Damascus.

We now pass to cases of universal states created by marchmen. In the long history of the Egyptiac civilization, political unity was conferred, or imposed, on the society no less than three times over by marchmen from the upper reaches of the Lower Nile, and on each occasion the aggrandizement of a march into a universal state was followed (though, on the third occasion, not immediately) by the transfer of the capital from an up-river site, Thebes (Luxor) or its equivalent, to a site more easily accessible for the main body of the population: to Memphis (Cairo) or its equivalent on the first two occasions, and on the third occasion to a frontier fortress near the militarily exposed north-eastern corner of the Nile Delta.

In Hellenic history the fortunes of Rome are reminiscent of those of Egyptiac Thebes. Rome won her spurs by taking over from the Etruscans the wardenship of the Hellenic world over against the Gauls, as Thebes had won hers by taking over from Al-Kāb the wardenship of the First Cataract of the Nile over against the barbarians of Nubia. Like Thebes, Rome afterwards turned her arms inwards and imposed political unity on the Hellenic society of which she was a member, and for many centuries she retained her position as capital of the empire that she had created, though it is conceivable that, if Mark Antony had had his way and the battle of Actium had gone differently, she might, in the same generation that had seen the completion of her main range of conquests, have lost her position as capital to Alexandria. Three centuries later, however, a variety of circumstances which cannot here be recorded led to the transfer of the capital of the now rapidly degenerating empire to the far superior site of Constantinople. The city on the Bosphorus had a long future ahead of it as a capital of successive universal states. The city on the Tiber, like Medina, had to resign itself to the role of becoming, in due course, the Holy City of a higher religion.

If Constantinople was a Second Rome, Moscow, in pre-Marxian times, often claimed to be the Third. We may now consider the competition between capitals in the universal state of the Russian Orthodox Christian civilization. Moscow, like Rome, started its career as the capital of a march state over against barbarians. As the threat from the Mongol Nomads retreated, Moscow found herself facing about and repelling attacks from her nearest neighbours in Western Christendom, the Poles and the Lithuanians. At a time when her future as a capital city might have seemed secure, however, she was suddenly deposed by the restless ambition of a Westernizing Czar, in favour of his new creation, Saint Petersburg, the foundations of which, on territory conquered from Sweden, were laid in A.D. 1703. Peter the Great, transferring his seat of government from far inland to a point which opened magic casements on the fairyland of what was, in his judgement, a much more technologically enlightened world, recalls Seleucus Nicator transferring himself from a remote 'oriental' Seleucia to Antioch on the Orontes. But, among other differences, this may be noticed. In abandoning his Seleucia for his Antioch, Seleucus, who was an alien empire-builder in south-western Asia, was deserting a new creation of his own, with no strong national sentiment attached to it, in favour of a site within a short day's journey of the Mediterranean, much nearer the heart of the Hellenic world. He was, in fact, turning homeward. In the Russian case, however, all the sentimental considerations were on the side of abandoned Moscow, and the chilly waterway towards the West on which the windows of Peter's new experimental capital opened, was a poor equivalent for the Hellenic World's Mediterranean. Saint Petersburg stood its ground for two hundred years. Then, with the Communist revolution, Moscow came into its own again, and the city of Saint Peter had to console itself with the new name of Leningrad.[1] It is

---

[1] There is something ridiculous about this topical name-changing. The editor of this abridgement remembers receiving, half a century ago, a letter from a friend who had recently returned to a French provincial town. He wrote:

curious to reflect that the fate of this Fourth Rome has been, in the matter of nomenclature, the reverse of that of the First. When Rome ceased to be the capital of a universal state it was in course of becoming what, in spite of Cavour and Mussolini, it still is: a Saint Peter's Burg or Holy City of Saint Peter.

Such have been the motives which have influenced the rulers of some of the universal states of history in the location of their capitals. When we pass on to the unintended uses that have been made of those capitals by others than the rulers and the dominant minorities surrounding them, we may start with the crudest, namely capture and pillage. That was the standard by which, according to an old story, Field-Marshal Blücher, the soldier of a Power rich only in its military prowess, is said to have measured the use of London as he passed down one of her richer streets when he was a guest of the Prince Regent after the battle of Waterloo. 'What plunder!' he is said to have exclaimed. One could make a long list of the sackings of capitals, and, if we estimated the results for the victorious plunderers, we should find, more often than not perhaps, that these Gargantuan feasts had been followed by a bout of indigestion. The Hellenic society of the fourth century B.C. and the Western society of the sixteenth century of the Christian Era were not only put to shame by the barbarism into which their militant apostles relapsed; they were also devastated by it. For a crime which primitive barbarians can commit with comparative impunity does not go unpunished in societies that have risen to a monetary economy. The rifling of the treasure houses of south-western Asia by the former and of the Americas by the latter put into sudden circulation an avalanche of bullion which produced a catastrophic inflation, and the sins of Macedonian plunderers at Persepolis and Spanish plunderers at Cuzco were expiated by Ionian artisans in the Cyclades and by German peasants in Swabia.

Let us pass on to less sordid themes. The capitals of universal states were obviously convenient stations for the radiation of all kinds of cultural influences. Higher religions found them service-able for their purpose. During the Babylonish captivity of Nebu-chadnezzar's deportees from Judah, the capital city actually served an embryonic higher religion as the incubator in which it found its soul by exchanging a parochial for an œcumenical outlook.

The seat of government of a universal state is indeed good ground for spiritual seeds to fall on, for such a city is an epitome of a wide world in a small compass. Its walls enfold representatives of all classes and of many nations, besides speakers of many languages,

'Since I was last here the anti-clericals have secured a majority on the Council and the Rue Jean-Baptiste has become the Rue Émile Zola.'

and its gates open on to highways leading in all directions. The same missionary can preach on the same day in the slums and in the palace; and, if he gains the Emperor's ear, he may hope to see the mighty machine of the Imperial administration placed at his disposal. Nehemiah's position in the Emperor's household at Susa gave him his opportunity of enlisting the patronage of Artaxerxes I for the temple-state at Jerusalem; and the Jesuit Fathers who sought and won a footing in the Imperial court at Agra and the Imperial court at Peking in the sixteenth and seventeenth centuries of the Christian Era dreamed of winning India and China for Catholicism by a Nehemian strategy.

Indeed, the historic mission of capital cities in the long run will often be found to lie in the religious field. The potent effect on the destinies of Mankind which the Sinic imperial city of Loyang was still exercising at the time when these lines were being written was not a consequence of her former political role as the seat of the Far Eastern Chóu Dynasty, and subsequently of the Posterior Han. Politically Loyang was 'one with Nineveh and Tyre'; but she was still exercising her potent effect in virtue of having been the nursery in which the seeds of the Mahāyāna were acclimatized to the Sinic cultural environment, and were thus enabled to sow themselves broadcast over the Sinic world. The desolate site of Qāraqorum, too, was still invisibly alive because, as an undesigned effect of this ephemeral Steppe city's meteoric political career in the thirteenth century of the Christian Era, she had brought missionaries of the Roman Catholic West face to face with Central Asian exponents of Nestorianism and Tibetan exponents of Lamaism.

To come nearer home, it was manifest, in 1952, that Peter and Paul, not Romulus and Remus or Augustus, were the authors of the 'eternal' significance of Rome; and Constantinople, the second and Christian Rome, having outrun all her manifestations as the capital of a universal state, owed such influence as she was still exercising in the World in virtue of her being the seat of a Patriarch who was still recognized by the ecclesiastical heads of the other Eastern Orthodox Churches, including the Church of Russia, as being *primus inter pares*.

Official languages and scripts

It can almost be taken for granted that a universal state will have provided itself with official media of mental communication, and that these will include not only languages transmitted *viva voce* but also some system of visual records. In nearly all cases the system of visual records had taken the form of a notation of the official language; and, though the Incas had succeeded in maintaining an almost totalitarian régime without the aid of any notational system beyond the wordless semantics of the *quipus*, this must be regarded as an exceptional *tour de force*.

There had been cases in which some single language and single script had driven all possible competitors off the field before the universal state had been established. In the Egyptiac 'Middle Empire', for example, the language and script were bound to be Classical Egyptian and hieroglyphic characters; in Japan under the Shogunate they were bound to be the Japanese language and the particular selection and usage of Chinese characters that had already been adopted in Japan; in the Russian Empire they were bound to be the Russian language and the Great Russian variety of the Slavonic version of the Greek alphabet. This simple situation has not, however, been the usual one. More often than not the empire-builders find themselves confronted, in this matter of official language and script, not with an accomplished fact to ratify, but with a difficult choice to make between a number of competing candidates.

In these circumstances most empire-builders had given official currency to their own mother tongue, and, if it had hitherto not been provided with a script, they had borrowed or invented one for the purpose. There had, indeed, been cases in which empire-builders had passed over their own mother tongue in favour of another language already current as a *lingua franca* in their dominions, or even in favour of a revived classical language. The most usual course, however, had been for empire-builders to give official currency to their own national language and script without granting them a monopoly.

These general propositions may now be illustrated in an empirical survey.

In the Sinic world the problem was solved in a characteristically drastic fashion by Ts'in She Hwang-ti. The founder of the Sinic universal state gave exclusive currency to the version of the Chinese characters that had been in official use in his own ancestral state of Ts'in, and thereby succeeded in arresting the tendency, which had gone far by the end of the foregoing Time of Troubles, for each of the Contending States to develop a parochial script only partially intelligible to the literati outside those parochial limits. Since the Sinic characters were 'ideograms' conveying meanings, and were not 'phonemes' representing sounds, the effect of Ts'in She Hwang-ti's act was to endow the Sinic society with a uniform visual language, which would continue—even if the spoken languages were to break up into mutually unintelligible dialects—

to serve as a means of œcumenical communication, for the small minority who could learn to read or write it—just as, in the Modern Western world, the Arabic numerals conveyed identical meanings on paper to peoples who, *viva voce*, called the numbers by different names. Yet, as this parallel indicates, Ts'in She Hwang-ti's standardization of Sinic characters would not have availed to avert a babel of tongues had not other forces been working in favour of uniformity in speech as well as in script.

The standardization of Sinic characters may have been anticipated by the unknown founder of the Minoan universal state. Though none of the scripts in use in the Minoan world had been deciphered at the time when this Study was written,[1] their sequence gave evidence of a revolutionary reform in the art of writing. At the transition from Middle Minoan II to Middle Minoan III two separate hieroglyphic scripts, which had made their appearance simultaneously at the beginning of the former period, were suddenly and completely superseded by a single new linear script (Linear A).[2] In the history of the Syriac society we know that Ts'in She Hwang-ti had a counterpart in the Umayyad Caliph 'Abd-al-Malik (reigned A.D. 685–705), who substituted the Arabic language and script for the Greek in the ex-Roman provinces of the Arab Caliphate, and for the Pehlavi in the ex-Sasanian provinces, as the official vehicle for the public records.

We may now pass on to some examples of the more frequent practice of providing a universal state with several official languages and scripts, including the empire-builders' own.

In the British Rāj in India the English mother tongue of the empire-builders was for certain purposes substituted for Persian, the official language bequeathed by the Mughals. In A.D. 1829, for instance, the British Indian Government made English the medium for its diplomatic correspondence and in A.D. 1835 the medium for higher education. But when, in A.D. 1837, the final step was taken in the deposition of Persian from its official status in British India, the British Indian Government did not introduce English for all the other purposes that Persian had previously served. In the

---

[1] Before this Abridgement of vols. vii–x was published, the Minoan 'Linear B' script had been deciphered by Messrs A. Ventris and I. Chadwick as a vehicle for the Greek language (see *The Journal of Hellenic Studies*, vol. lxxiii, pp. 84–103), and their interpretation had been immediately and almost unanimously recognized by other scholars.

[2] Linear A has not yet been deciphered by the time of writing in 1954. It had a wide currency throughout the Island of Crete, and the language conveyed in it is probably the pre-Greek Minoan (to whatever family of languages this may have belonged). The range of the later 'Linear B' script, now known to have conveyed the Greek language, was confined, in Crete, to Cnossos, but extended to several centres of the Mycenaean Civilization on the mainland.

conduct of judicial and fiscal proceedings, matters that personally concerned all Indians of every nationality, caste, and class, Persian was replaced, not by English, but by the local vernaculars; and the Sanskritized Hindi vernacular known as Hindustānī was actually manufactured by British Protestant missionaries to provide the Hindu population of Northern India with a counterpart of the Persianized Hindi vernacular, known as Urdu, which the Indian Muslims had already manufactured for themselves. This humane and politic decision to forbear from misusing political power by giving an exclusive currency to the foreign tongue of an alien empire-builder perhaps partially accounts for the remarkable fact that when, 110 years later, their descendants handed over their rāj to the descendants of their Indian subjects, it was taken as a matter of course, in both of the polyglot successor-states, that the English language would remain at least provisionally in use for the purposes which it had served under the British Rāj.

A contrast is offered by the abortive effort of the Emperor-King Joseph II (reigned 1780–90), one of the so-called enlightened despots of the Western world in the generation before the French Revolution, to impose the use of German on the non-German-speaking peoples of the Danubian Hapsburg monarchy. Though economic utility and cultural amenity told in favour of this political *Diktat*, Joseph's linguistic policy proved a disastrous failure, and evoked the first stirrings of those nationalist movements which, more than a hundred years later, were to tear the Hapsburg Empire to pieces.

The Turkish masters of the Ottoman Empire never embarked on the policy which was successfully applied in the Arab Caliphate and unsuccessfully in the Danubian Hapsburg Monarchy. The founders' native Turkish was the official language of imperial administration, but in the heyday of the Ottoman Power in the sixteenth and seventeenth centuries of the Christian Era the *lingua franca* of the Pādishāh's slave-household was Serbo-Croat and the *lingua franca* of the Ottoman navy Italian. Moreover, on the civil side, the Ottoman Government, like the British Indian Government, followed the policy of allowing its subjects to use languages of their own choice in communal affairs that were largely concerned with the private business of individuals.

A similar restraint was shown by the Romans in the imposition of Latin as an official language in provinces of their empire in which Greek was either the mother tongue or the established *lingua franca*. They contented themselves with making Latin the exclusive language of military command for units of the Imperial Army, wherever recruited and wherever stationed, and the principal

language of municipal administration for colonies of Latin origin
on Greek or Oriental ground. For other purposes they continued
to employ the Attic *koinê* wherever they found it already in official
use, and they made its official status conspicuous by giving it an
equal place, side by side with Latin, in the central administration
at Rome itself.

The Romans' forbearance towards the Greek language was something more than a tribute to the pre-eminence of Greek over Latin
as a medium of culture; it represented a signal victory of statesmanship over hybris in Roman souls; for, in the far-flung western
territories of the empire in which Greek was not in competition
with Latin, the triumph of Latin was sensational. So far from
having to impose its use on their subjects and allies outside the
range of the Greek language, the Romans were in the happy position of being able to enhance its attractiveness by treating its
official use as a privilege to be sued for. Nor did Latin win its
peaceful victories solely at the expense of languages that had never
been reduced to writing. In Italy it had to contend with sister
Italic dialects like Oscan and Umbrian, and with Illyrian dialects
like Messapian and Venetian, which had once been on a cultural
par with Latin—not to speak of Etruscan, freighted with the cultural heritage of its Anatolian homeland. In Africa it had to contend with Punic. In these contests Latin was invariably victorious.

An even more remarkable restraint was shown by the Sumerian
founders of 'the Realm of the Four Quarters' when they put the
upstart Akkadian language on a par with their own Sumerian.
Before this universal state came to an end, Akkadian had won the
day and Sumerian had become practically a dead language.

The Achaemenidae gave as modest a place in the government
of their empire to their Persian mother tongue as to their Persian
mother country. Darius the Great's account of his own acts on the
rock of Behistan, overhanging the Empire's great north-east road,
was transcribed in triplicate in three different adaptations of the
cuneiform script conveying the three diverse languages of the
three imperial capitals: Elamite for Susa, Medo-Persian for Ecbatana, and Akkadian for Babylon. But the winning language within
this universal state was none of the three thus officially honoured;
it was Aramaic, with its handier alphabetic script. The sequel
showed that commerce and culture may be more important than
politics in making a language's fortune; for the speakers of Aramaic
were politically of no account in the Achaemenian Empire. The
Achaemenian Government accepted a commercial *fait accompli* by
giving to Aramaic a belated official status, but the most remarkable
triumph of Aramaic was that its script succeeded in replacing the

cuneiform as the medium for conveying the Persian language in its post-Achaemenian phase.

In the Mauryan Empire the philosopher-emperor Açoka (reigned 273-232 B.C.) succeeded in reconciling the demands of impartial justice and practical convenience by employing a number of local vernaculars conveyed in two different scripts, the Brahmī and the Kharoshthī. This catholicity was prompted by the emperor's single-minded purpose of acquainting his peoples with the way of salvation revealed to Mankind by Açoka's master, Gautama. Similar motives induced the Spanish conquerors of the Empire of the Incas to allow the use of a Quichuan *lingua franca* for the propagation of the Catholic Faith among their American subjects.

If we now conclude by asking who were the beneficiaries, we shall find that official languages had been turned to account by restorers of the empires in which these languages had enjoyed official currency, by latter-day secular agencies of all kinds, and by the propagators of higher religions. The finding is, in this matter of languages and scripts, obvious enough not to need detailed illustration.

Of the languages mentioned in the course of our survey, none had a more remarkable after-history than Aramaic, which also owed less than most of them to the patronage of the rulers of the universal state in which its upward career began. On the overthrow of the Achaemenian Empire by Alexander it was brusquely deposed, in favour of the Attic *koinê*, from the official status that the Achaemenidae had conferred on it in their western dominions. Though thus deprived of imperial patronage, it completed, nevertheless, the process of cultural conquest which it had begun before receiving official patronage, by supplanting Akkadian on the east and Canaanite on the west as the living language of the entire Semitic-speaking population of 'the Fertile Crescent'.[1] It was, for example, the language in which Jesus must have conversed with his disciples. As for the Aramaic alphabet, it achieved far wider conquests. In A.D. 1599 it was adopted for the conveyance of the Manchu language on the eve of the Manchu conquest of China. The higher religions sped it on its way by taking it into their service. In its 'Square Hebrew' variant it became the vehicle of the Jewish Scriptures and liturgy; in an Arabic adaptation it became the alphabet of Islam; in its Syriac variant it served impartially the antithetical Christian heresies of Nestorianism and Monophysitism; in an Avestan adaptation of its Pehlavi variant it enshrined the sacred books of the Zoroastrian Church; in a Manichaean

---

[1] i.e. the stretch of fertile country round the north of the Arabian Desert from Egypt via Syria, Mesopotamia and Babylonia to the Persian Gulf.

adaptation it served an heresiarch whom Christians and Zoroastrians agreed in execrating; in a Kharoshthī variant it provided the Emperor Açoka with an instrument for conveying the teachings of the Buddha to his subjects in the former Achaemenian province in the Panjab.

Law

The field of social action which is the domain of Law divides itself into three great provinces: there is an administrative law that lays down the duties of subjects towards a government, and there are a criminal and a civil law, which are alike concerned with acts in which both parties are private persons. No government can, of course, be indifferent to administrative law, since the first concern of a government is to impose its authority and repress all acts of insubordination—from high treason to an omission to pay taxes—in which the subject may show himself recalcitrant to the government's will. The same considerations lead governments to concern themselves with the criminal law as well; for, though the criminal may not be directly or intentionally attacking the government, he is in fact interfering with it in its task of preserving order. In so far as they concern themselves with civil law, on the other hand, governments are acting for their subjects' benefit rather than for their own, and it is not surprising that there should be wide differences in the extent to which the governments of universal states have concerned themselves with law in this department.

In the domain of law, universal states are faced with a special problem which does not confront parochial states. Their territories include the subjects of a number of conquered parochial states which do not perish without leaving—in the domain of law as in other fields—legacies with which their destroyer and successor has to reckon. There had been at least one instance in which the empire-builders, in this case the Mongols, had been so inferior to their conquered subjects that they had found themselves unable to impose on them any part of their own ancestral law. The 'Osmanlis took firm control of administrative and criminal law, but took care to avoid interfering with the civil law of their various non-Turkish subject populations. In the Sinic world, on the other hand, Ts'in She Hwang-ti characteristically imposed an œcumenical uniformity of law at one stroke by decreeing that the legislation in force in his own ancestral kingdom of Ts'in should be applied throughout the territories of the six rival states which he had conquered and annexed, and his action had at least two Modern Western parallels. Napoleon introduced his newly minted codification of French law into all the Italian, Flemish, German, and

Polish territories of his empire, and the British Government of India introduced the Common Law of England—partly in its original form and partly in adaptations embodied in local legislation—throughout the Indian territories over which it established its direct rule.

The Romans were slower than the British or Napoleon or Ts'in She Hwang-ti in achieving uniformity of law in their empire. To live under Roman Law was one of the reputed privileges of Roman citizenship, and the progressive conferment of citizenship on the Empire's subjects was not carried to its completion till the promulgation of the Edict of Caracalla in A.D. 212. In the parallel history of the Caliphate the reign of Islamic Law was progressively extended by the conversion of non-Muslim subjects of the Caliphate to the empire-builders' religion.

In universal states in which a progressive standardization of the law had resulted in the attainment of approximate uniformity there had sometimes been a further stage in which a unified imperial law had been codified by the imperial authorities. In the history of Roman Law the first step towards codification was the 'freezing', in A.D. 131, of the *Edictum Perpetuum* which had hitherto been promulgated afresh by each successive Praetor Urbanus at the beginning of his year of office, and the final steps were the promulgation of the Justinianean Code in A.D. 529, and of the Institutes and Digest in A.D. 533. In the Sumeric 'Realm of the Four Quarters' an earlier code compiled under the Sumerian Emperors, ruling from Ur, appears to have been the basis of a later code promulgated by the Amorite restorer of the Empire, Hammurabi of Babylon, which was brought to light in A.D. 1901 by the Modern Western archaeologist, J. de Morgan.

As a rule the demand for codification reaches its climax in the penultimate age before a social catastrophe, long after the peak of achievement in jurisprudence has been passed, and when the legislators of the day are irretrievably on the run in a losing battle with ungovernable forces of destruction. Justinian himself had no sooner turned at bay against Fate and thrown up in her face the imposing barricade of his *Corpus Iuris* than he was driven by the Fury's relentless hounds to sprint on again in a paper-chase in which he was constrained to strew the course with the tell-tale sheets of his *Novellae*. Yet, in the long run, Fate is apt to deal kindly with the codifiers; for the mead of admiration which their outraged predecessors of a better period would certainly have refused to them has been offered to their ghosts by a posterity too remote, too barbarous, or too sentimental to be capable of arriving at a correct appraisal of their work.

Even this uncritically admiring posterity finds, however, that the consecrated codes cannot be applied until they have been translated, and when we say 'translated' we refer to a treatment much like that suffered by Shakespeare's Bottom, when Peter Quince exclaimed, 'Bless thee, Bottom! thou art translated', after seeing his friend provided with an ass's head. Justinian's reign was promptly followed by a deluge of Lombard, Slav, and Arab invasions; similarly, in the last phase of the Empire of Sumer and Akkad, Hammurabi's strenuous work of political and social reclamation on the Plains of Shinar was no less promptly waterlogged by the Kassite invasion from the hills. When Leo the Restorer and his successors, after a virtual interregnum of 150 years, set to work to rebuild a Byzantine Empire, they found apter materials in the Mosaic Law than in Justinian's *Corpus Iuris*, and in Italy the hope of the future lay not with the *Corpus Iuris* but with the Rule of Saint Benedict.

So the Code of Justinian died and was buried; but it came to life again, some four hundred years later, in the eleventh-century juristic renaissance at the university of Bologna. From this centre and from that time onwards it radiated its influence into the extremities and extensions of an expanding Western world, far beyond the ken of Justinian. Thanks to Bologna's capacity for intellectual 'cold storage' in the Dark Ages, a version of Roman Law was 'received' in Modern Holland, Scotland, and South Africa. In Orthodox Christendom the *Corpus Iuris* survived a less exacting ordeal of hibernating for three centuries at Constantinople, and re-emerged in the tenth century of the Christian Era as the Code with which the Macedonian Dynasty replaced the Mosaistic legislation of its eighth-century Syrian predecessors.

We will not pause to describe the infiltration of Roman Law into the custom of Teutonic barbarian states which had no future before them. Much more important and striking is its surreptitious and unavowed yet unmistakable infiltration into the Islamic law of the Arab conquerors of various ex-Roman provinces. The two elements that blended here were even more incongruous, and the result of their blending was the creation, not just of a parochial law for a barbarian state, but of an œcumenical law which was to serve the needs of a restored Syriac universal state and, after surviving the break-up of this political framework, was to govern and mould the life of an Islamic society that, after the fall of the Caliphate, was to continue to expand until, at the time of writing, its domain extended from Indonesia to Lithuania and from South Africa to China.

Unlike their Teutonic counterparts, the Primitive Muslim Arabs had been roughly shaken out of their archaic traditional way of life before they administered to themselves the additional shock of a sudden change of social environment by bursting out of the deserts and oases of Arabia into the fields and cities of the Roman and Sasanian empires. A long-continuing radiation of Syriac and Hellenic cultural influences into Arabia had produced a cumulative social effect which had declared itself dramatically in the personal career of the Prophet Muhammad; and his achievements had been so astonishing and his personality so potent that his oracles and acts, as recorded in the Qu'ran and the Traditions, were accepted by his followers as the source of law for regulating, not only the life of the Muslim community itself, but also the relations between Muslim conquerors and their at first many times more numerous non-Muslim subjects. The speed and sweep of the Muslim conquests combined with the irrationality of the accepted basis of the Muslim conquerors' new-laid law to create a most formidable problem. The task of extracting from the Qu'ran and the Traditions an œcumenical law for a sophisticated society was as preposterous as the demands for welling water in the wilderness which the Children of Israel are said to have addressed to Moses.

For a jurist in search of legal pabulum the Qu'ran was indeed stony ground. The chapters dating from the non-political Meccan period of Muhammad's mission, before the *Hijrah*, offered far less matter for a practical jurist than he would find in the New Testament, for they contain little beyond a spiritually crucial and unwearyingly reiterated declaration of the unity of God, and denunciations of polytheism and idolatry. The chapters afterwards delivered at Medina might look, at first sight, more promising; for at the *Hijrah* Muhammad achieved in his own lifetime a position not attained by any follower of Jesus till the fourth century of the Christian Era. He became the head of a state, and his utterances were henceforth mainly concerned with public business. Yet it would be at least as difficult to elicit a comprehensive system of law even from the Medinese *surahs* without extraneous reinforcement as it would be to perform the same juristic conjuring trick with the Epistles of Saint Paul.

In these circumstances the men of action who built the Arab Caliphate let theory take its chance and resorted to self-help. They found their way with the aid of common sense, analogy, consensus, and custom. They took what they wanted where they could find it, and, if the pious could suppose that it had come straight out of the Prophet's mouth, so much the better. Among the sources thus pillaged, Roman Law had an important place. In some cases they borrowed directly from this source in its

Syrian provincial version. More frequently, perhaps, Roman law reached Islam through the intermediary of the Jews.

The Jewish Law, which had had so long a history behind it already by the time of Muhammad's *Hijrah*, had originated, like the Islamic *Sharī'ah*, as the barbarian customary practice of Nomads who had broken out of the steppes of Northern Arabia into the fields and cities of Syria; and, for meeting the same emergency of an abrupt and extreme change of social environment, the primitive Israelites, like the primitive Arabs, had recourse to the existing law of a sophisticated society which they found in operation in the Promised Land.

While the Decalogue would appear to be a purely Hebrew product, the next piece of Israelite legislation, known to scholars as the Covenant Code,[1] betrays its debt to the Code of Hammurabi. This influx of a code of Sumerian law into legislation enacted at least nine centuries later in one of the local communities of a latter-day Syriac society testified to the depth and tenacity of the roots which the Sumeric civilization had struck in Syrian soil during the millennium ending in Hammurabi's generation. In the course of the near-millennium which followed, a bewildering variety of social and cultural revolutions had supervened, yet the Sumerian Law, embodied in Hammurabi's Code, had remained in force among the descendants of Hammurabi's Syrian subjects or satellites—and this in such vigour as to impress itself upon the callow legislation of the Canaanites' Hebrew barbarian conquerors.

In thus entering into the law of barbarians who happened to be incubators of a higher religion, the Sumerian Law, like the Roman Law, made a greater mark on history than when it was influencing barbarians whose destiny was the inglorious exit usual among their kind. At the time of writing, the Sumerian Law was still a living force in virtue solely of its Mosaic offprint. On the other hand, the Islamic *Sharī'ah* was neither the sole nor the liveliest carrier of the Roman Law at the same date. In the twentieth century of the Christian Era the chief direct heirs of Roman Law were the canons of the Eastern Orthodox and Western Catholic Christian churches. Thus, in the domain of law, as in other fields of social action, the master institution created by the internal proletariat was the universal state's principal beneficiary.

Calendars; Weights and Measures; Money

Standard measures of time, distance, length, volume, weight, and value are necessities of social life at any level above the primitive. Social currencies of these kinds are older than govern-

---

[1] Exod. xxxiv. 17–26, and, in a fuller statement, xx. 23 to xxiii. 33.

ments; they become matters of concern to governments as soon as these latter come into existence. The positive *raison d'être* of governments is to provide central political leadership for common social enterprises, and these cannot be operated without standard measures. Again, the negative *raison d'être* of governments is to ensure at least a modicum of social justice between their subjects, and, in most private issues of a 'business' kind, standard measures of some sort are involved. Standard measures thus concern governments of all kinds, but they are of particular concern to universal states; for these, by their nature, are confronted with the problem of holding together a far greater diversity of subjects than are usually found under the rule of a parochial state, and they have a special interest in the social uniformity that standard measures promote, if these are effectively enforced.

Of all standard measurements, a system of measuring time is the one for which a need is earliest felt, and the first necessity here is a measurement of the seasons of the year cycle. This calls for a harmonization of the three different natural cycles of the year, the month, and the day. The pioneer chronometrists quickly discovered that the ratios between these cycles are not simple fractions but surds; and the search for a *magnus annus*, in which these discrepant cycles would all start simultaneously and would then eventually come round again to their next simultaneous starting-point, led to an amazing application of astronomical mathematics in societies as early as the Egyptiac, the Babylonic, and the Mayan. Once embarked on this train of calculation, the budding astronomers were led on to take into account the cyclic movements not only of Sun and Moon but also of the planets and the 'fixed' stars, and their chronological horizon receded to a distance which is not easy to express and is still less easy to imagine—narrow-verged though it may seem to a latter-day cosmogonist in whose eyes our particular solar system is no more than one speck of star-dust in the Milky Way, and the Milky Way itself no more than one *ci-devant* nebula out of myriads of nebulae on their way from a flaming birth to a deathly incineration.

Short of the latest stage in the mental exploration of chronological magnitudes, the least common measure of the recurrent coincidences between the apparent movements of the Sun and those of a single one of the 'fixed stars' had generated the Egyptiac 'Sothic Cycle' of 1,460 years, and a recurrent common cycle of the Sun, the Moon, and five planets the Babylonic *Magnus Annus* of 432,000 years, while, in the stupendous Mayan Grand Cycle of 374,440 years, no less than ten distinct constituent cycles were geared together. This marvellously exact, though formidably complex, Mayan calendar was bequeathed by 'the Old Empire' of the Mayas to the affiliated Yucatec and Mexic societies.

Governments, like astronomers, find themselves concerned with computations in terms of years as well as with the articulation of the recurrent year-cycle; for the first concern of every government is to keep itself in existence, and the most naïve administration soon discovers that it cannot remain in business without keeping some permanent record of its acts. One method employed by governments was to date their acts by the names of the holders of some annual magistracy, such as the Roman consulate. Thus Horace, in one of his Odes, tells us that he was born *consule Manlio*, when Manlius was consul, which is as if a Londoner were reduced to dating his birth by the name of the City magnate who was Lord Mayor in his natal year. The inconvenience of such a system is obvious; no one could remember the names of all the consuls nor the order in which they came.[1]

The only satisfactory system is to choose some particular year as an initial date and to number the years subsequent to it. Classical examples were the eras starting from the Fascist occupation of Rome; from the establishment of the First French Republic; from the Prophet Muhammad's *Hijrah* from Mecca to Medina; from the establishment of the Gupta Dynasty in the Indic world; from the establishment of the Seleucid Empire's Hasmonaean successor-state in Judaea; from the triumphal re-entry of Seleucus Nicator into Babylon.

There were other cases in which eras had been reckoned from events of which the precise date was disputable. For example, there was no evidence that Jesus had in fact been born in the first year of a Christian Era that did not become current until the sixth century of that Era; there was no evidence that Rome had in fact been founded in 753 B.C., or that the Olympic Festival had first been celebrated in 776 B.C. Still less was there evidence that the World had been created on 7 October 3761 B.C. (according to the Jews), or on 1 September 5509 (according to the Eastern Orthodox Christians), or at 6 p.m. on the evening before 23 October, 4004 B.C. (according to the seventeenth-century Anglo-Irish chronologist, Archbishop Ussher).

[1] Similarly the clause 'suffered under Pontius Pilate', which occurs in both the 'Nicene' and the 'Apostles'' Creed used by Christian Churches, is a statement of a date rather than a charge against an individual. If the authors of the Creeds had wished to indulge in polemics, they would have imputed the crime to the Jews, whom Christians still hated, rather than to a representative of Imperial Rome, with which they had become reconciled. The point of 'suffered under Pontius Pilate' is the assertion that the Second Person of the Trinity had been an historical figure with a definite date, in contrast to the mythical figures of other religions, such as Mithras or Isis or Cybele.

In the two preceding paragraphs these eras have been listed in a descending order of the cogency of the evidence for the dates of the events selected; but, if we now resurvey the list from the standpoint of the relative success of these same eras in gaining a wide and lasting currency, we shall observe that the talisman by which their success or failure has been decided is the presence or absence of a religious sanction. In A.D. 1952 the Western Christian Era was in the ascendant all over the World, and its only serious rival was now the Islamic Era, though the Jews, with their usual persistence, still officially reckoned from their estimate of the date of the Creation. There is, in fact, a traditional association between the measurement of time by human intellects and the hold of religion over human souls. The persistence of this superstition in the inaccessible subconscious depths of the Psyche, even in societies that had attained a degree of sophistication at which astrology was professedly discredited, was attested by the rarity of the instances in which a rational reform of a calendar had succeeded in establishing itself. The French Revolution, whose rationalized codes of law went forth to the ends of the Earth and whose pedantically newfangled weights and measures—grammes and kilogrammes and milligrammes, metres and kilometres and millimetres—enjoyed a *succès fou*, was utterly defeated in its attempt to supersede a pagan Roman calendar which had been consecrated by the Christian Church. Yet the French Revolutionary Calendar was an attractive structure. The months had names which, divided by their terminations into four seasonal batches of three each, indicated the kind of weather which did, or at any rate ought to, occur in them, and each was cut to a uniform length of thirty days grouped in three ten-day weeks. The batch of five supernumerary days that made up the total of the ordinary (non-leap) year 'hardly marred the most sensible calendar ever invented—too sensible for a country which calls the tenth, eleventh, and twelfth months of the year October, November and December'.[1]

The Roman misnomers stigmatized in the passage quoted above had an explanation, which is to be found in the military history of the Roman Republic. The six months originally denoted in the Roman calendar by numerals, and not by the names of gods, had not, of course, been wrongly numbered when their names had been first bestowed upon them. Originally the Roman official year had begun on 1st March, a month named after the Roman god of war; and, so long as the Government's range of action extended no more than a few days' march from the capital, the newly elected magistrate, taking over his charge on 15th March, could take up the command

[1] Thompson, J. M.: *The French Revolution* (Oxford 1943, Blackwell), p. ix.

assigned to him in time for the spring campaigning season. When, however, the field of Roman military operations had expanded to lands beyond Italy, a magistrate appointed to one of these distant commands in March might find himself unable to get into action until the season was far advanced. Oddly enough, during the half-century following the Hannibalic War this calendrical drawback was not of practical significance, for the calendar itself had gone so wildly astray that the month which was supposed to herald the spring had drifted back into the previous autumn. For example, in the year 190 B.C., in which a Roman army defeated a Seleucid army on the Asiatic battlefield of Magnesia, the legions had arrived in good time for the simple reason that the official 15th March was actually 16th November in the preceding year, while in the year 168 B.C., in which another Roman army inflicted an equally decisive defeat on a Macedonian army at Pydna, the official 15th March had been actually the previous 31st December.

The Romans, one perceives, were already, between these two dates, beginning to correct their calendar. Unfortunately, the nearer that it approximated to astronomical correctitude the more apparent was its obsolescence as a military time-table. Accordingly, in 153 B.C., the day on which the annual magistrates were to enter on their term of office was shifted back from 15th March to 1st January; and, in consequence, January instead of March became the first month of the year. Astronomical improprieties continued until Julius Caesar was in a position to give dictatorial support to the conclusions of the astronomers and introduced a 'Julian' calendar which approximated so closely to correctitude that it stood for more than a millennium and a half. At the same time the first of the six numbered months, *Quinctilis*, was given his name and has become, in English, July. The following month in the following generation became August. After all, Julius and Augustus were officially Divus, and the intrusion of their names by the side of the gods already commemorated was not inappropriate.

The curious association of calendars with religions was illustrated by the subsequent history of the Julian calendar. By the sixteenth century of the Christian Era it was apparent that it had got ten days behindhand, and it was found possible, after the omission of ten days, to reduce its inaccuracy to an infinitesimal quantum by an alteration in the rule about centenary leap-years. In a sixteenth-century Western Christian society, even though the Age of Galileo was now treading on the heels of the Age of Saint Thomas Aquinas, it was felt that only the Pope could, as it were, press the button for the launching of a calendrical reform. Accordingly the amended calendar was inaugurated in the name of Pope Gregory

XIII in A.D. 1582. But in Protestant England the once revered Pope had now become merely the scandalous Bishop of Rome, from whose 'detestable enormities' the Second Prayer Book of King Edward VI had prayed that we might be delivered. The Elizabethan Prayer Book had omitted from the Litany this offensive petition, but the sentiment remained. The English and Scottish Governments held firmly to their ancient calendrical ways for another 170 years, thus inflicting upon future historians of that period the niggling nuisance of having to distinguish between N.S. and O.S. When at last Britain came into line with her Continental neighbours in 1752, the British public in a professedly rational eighteenth century appear to have made much more fuss than had been made by the Catholic world in the presumably less enlightened sixteenth century of the Christian Era. Was this because, where a calendar was concerned, an Act of Parliament was a poor substitute for *Vox Dei* in the guise of a Papal Bull?

When we pass from calendars and eras to weights and measures and money, we enter a province of the field of social currencies in which the rationalizing intellect holds sway uncensored by religious scruples. The French revolutionaries who failed so abjectly to implant their new secular calendar scored an œcumenical success with their new weights and measures.

A comparison of the respective fortunes of the French and the Sumeric new model metric systems suggests that the dazzling success of the French reformers' work was due to their judicious moderation. In reducing the bewilderingly variegated tables of the *Ancien Régime* to one single system of reckoning, they showed their practical good sense in irrationally following for this purpose the inconvenient decimal system which had been unanimously adopted by all branches of the Human Race, not on its merits but simply because the normal human being had ten fingers and ten toes. It was one of Nature's unkind practical jokes that she had furnished some of the tribes of her vertebrate brute creation with six digits apiece on each of the four limbs without endowing the possessors of this admirable natural abacus with the reasoning power to use it, while, in endowing the *Genus Homo* with reason, she had at the same time dealt out to it a niggardly allowance of appendages that added up only to tens and scores. It was unfortunate because, on a decimal count, the basic scale is divisible only by two and by five, while the lowest number divisible alike by two, three, and four is, in fact, twelve. The decimal notation was nevertheless inevitable because, by the time when any wits in any society had come to appreciate the intrinsic superiority of the number twelve, the decimal notation had become ineradicably entrenched in practical life.

The French reformers forbore to kick against these ten-pronged pricks, but their Sumerian predecessors had been less prudent. The Sumerian discovery of the virtues of the number twelve was a stroke of genius, and they took the revolutionary step of recasting their system of weights and measures on a duodecimal basis; but apparently they did not realize that, unless they could also achieve the further step of leading their fellow men to adopt a duodecimal notation for all purposes, the convenience of the duodecimal weights and measures would be more than offset by the inconvenience of having two incommensurable scales side by side. The Sumeric duodecimal system spread to the ends of the Earth, but during the last 150 years it has been fighting a losing battle against its youthful French competitor. Ur, like Oxford, has proved a 'home of lost causes'; though, to be sure, the cause of Ur is not quite lost so long as the English count 12 inches in the foot and 12 pennies in the shilling.[1]

As soon as it has come to be recognized that honest dealing is a matter of social concern and that any government worthy of the name must make the giving of false weight and measure a punishable offence, the invention of money lies just round the corner. Yet this corner can only be turned by the taking of certain precise successive steps, and the requisite combination of moves in fact remained unachieved until the seventh century B.C., though by that time the species of societies called civilizations had already been in existence for perhaps three thousand years.

The first step was the expedient of giving some particular commodities the function of serving as media of exchange, and thereby acquiring a second use independent of their intrinsic utility. But this step did not, in itself, lead on to the invention of money when the commodities selected were multifarious and not exclusively metallic. In the Mexic and Andean worlds, for example, by the time of the Spanish conquest, the substances known and coveted in the Old World as 'the precious metals' existed in quantities that seemed fabulous to the Spanish *conquistadores*, and the natives had long since learnt the art of extracting and refining these metals and using them for works of art; but they had not thought of using them as media of exchange, even though they had hit upon the notion of using for this purpose other special commodities—such as beans, dried fish, salt, and sea-shells.

In the commercially interwoven Egyptiac, Babylonic, Syriac, and Hellenic worlds the use of the precious metals as measures of

---

[1] The 24 hours of the day and the 60 minutes of the hour are also of Sumeric origin, and stand a better chance of indefinite survival. Even the French revolutionists did not try to decimalize the clock.

value, in units of conveniently weighable bars, had been current for hundreds or even thousands of years before the governments of certain Hellenic cities on the Asiatic coast of the Aegean Sea went beyond the existing practice of putting metallic media of exchange on a par with other commodities and thereby including them under the common rule that made it an offence at law to give false weight and measure. These pioneer city-states now took the two revolutionary steps of making the issue of these metallic units of value a government monopoly and of stamping this exclusive governmental currency with a distinctive official image and super-scription as a guarantee that the coin was an authentic product of the governmental mint, and that its weight and quality were to be accepted as being what they purported to be on the face of them.

Since the management of a coinage is evidently least difficult in a state with a minimum area and population, it was perhaps no accident that city-states should have been the laboratories in which the experiment was made. At the same time it is equally evident that the utility of a coinage increases with the enlargement of the area in which it is legal tender. Such a step forward was taken when, in the earlier decades of the sixth century B.C. the Lydian monarchy conquered all the Greek city-states along the western coast of Anatolia except Miletus, as well as the interior as far as the River Halys, and issued a coinage based on the local standard of the subjected Greek city-state Phocaea, which was given a general currency throughout the Lydian dominions. The most famous (and the last) of the Lydian kings was Croesus, who thus became and has remained a by-word for riches. More than half-way through the twentieth century of the Christian Era, it still comes more naturally to a Westerner's tongue to say 'as rich as Croesus' than to say 'as rich as'—Rothschild or Rockefeller or Ford or Morris or any other modern Western millionaire.

The last and decisive step was taken when the Kingdom of Lydia was incorporated, in its turn, in the vast Achaemenian Empire. Thenceforth the future of coined money was assured. The œcumenical Achaemenian gold 'archer' coins gave coinage an impetus that sped it on an almost ubiquitous course of conquest. Coined money was launched on its career in India by the Achae-menian annexation of the Punjab. The more distant Sinic world became ripe for adopting it after Ts'in She Hwang-ti's revolu-tionary empire-building had been salvaged thanks to being tem-pered by the tactful hands of Han Liu Pang. In 119 B.C. the Sinic Imperial Government had a brilliant intuition of the hitherto undiscovered truth that metal was not the only stuff of which money could be made.

'In the imperial park at Ch'ang Ngan the Emperor had a white stag, a very rare beast, which had no fellow in the Empire. On the advice of a minister the Emperor has this animal killed, and made a kind of treasury note out of its skin, which, he believed, could not be copied. These pieces of skin were a foot square, and were made with a fringed border and decorated with a pattern. Each piece was assigned the abitrary value of 400,000 copper coins. The princes, when they came to pay their respects to the Throne, were compelled to buy one of these pieces of skin for cash, and present their gifts to the Emperor upon it. The skin of the white stag was, however, a limited quantity, and the time soon came when this device ceased to supply the Treasury with much needed money.'[1]

The invention of currency notes did not become effectively applicable till it had been associated with the two Sinic inventions of paper and printing. Negotiable paper, in the form of cheques tallying with stubs retained by the Imperial Treasury, was issued by the T'ang Government in A.D. 807 and 809, but there is no evidence that the inscriptions on these cheques were printed. Printed paper money was certainly issued by the Sung Government in A.D. 970.

The invention of money undoubtedly proved beneficial to the subjects of the governments that issued it—in spite of the socially subversive fluctuations of inflation and deflation, and temptations to lend and borrow at usurious rates, which the invention brought in its train. But a greater benefit had assuredly accrued to the issuing governments themselves; for the issue of money is an *acte de présence* which brings a government into direct and constant contact with at least an active, intelligent, and influential minority of its subjects; and this monetary epiphany not only automatically fosters a government's prestige, but also gives it a magnificent opportunity for self-advertisement.

This effect of a coinage, even on the minds of a population under alien rule who resent the political yoke imposed upon them, is illustrated by a classic passage in the New Testament.

'They sent unto Him certain of the Pharisees and the Herodians, to catch Him in His words. And when they were come, they say unto Him: "Master, we know that thou art true, and carest for no man; for thou regardest not the person of man, but teachest the way of God in truth. Is it lawful to give tribute to Caesar, or not? Shall we give, or shall we not give?"

'But He, knowing their hypocrisy, said unto them: "Why tempt ye me? Bring me a penny, that I may see it." And they brought it, and He saith unto them: "Whose is this image and superscription?" And

[1] Fitzgerald, C. P.: *China; a Short Cultural History* (London 1935, Cresset Press), pp. 164–5.

they said unto him: "Caesar's." And Jesus answering said unto them: "Render to Caesar the things that are Caesar's, and to God the things that are God's."

'And they could not take hold of His words before the people, and they marvelled at His answer, and held their peace.'[1]

This automatic moral profit which the prerogative of issuing money yields, even in a formidably adverse political and religious environment, was of incomparably greater value to the Roman Imperial Government than any mere financial gains which the management of the mint might incidentally bring in. The Emperor's likeness on the coin gave the Imperial Government a certain status in the minds of a Jewish population which not only regarded Rome's dominion as illegitimate but treasured, as the second of the ten commandments believed to have been delivered to Moses by Yahweh, engraved on stone tablets by the Deity's own hand, the explicit injunction:

'Thou shalt not make unto thee any graven image, or any likeness of any thing that is in heaven above, or that is in the earth beneath, or that is in the water under the earth. Thou shalt not bow down thyself to them, nor serve them; for I the Lord thy God am a jealous God.'[2]

When in 167 B.C. the Seleucid king, Antiochus IV, Epiphanes had placed a statue of Olympian Zeus in the Holy of Holies of Yahweh's temple at Jerusalem, the horror and indignation of the Jews at seeing 'the abomination that maketh desolate'[3] 'standing where it ought not'[4] were so intense that they could not rest until they had thrown off every vestige of Seleucid rule. Again, when in A.D. 26 the Roman procurator Pontius Pilate smuggled into Jerusalem, draped and under cover of night, Roman military standards bearing the Emperor's image in medallions, the reaction of the Jews was so vehement as to compel Pilate to remove the offensive emblems. Yet these same Jews had schooled themselves meekly, not only to seeing but to handling, using, earning, and hoarding the abominable image on Caesar's coinage.

The Roman Government was not slow to perceive the value of an œcumenical coinage as an instrument of policy.

'From the middle of the first century onwards the Imperial Government had appreciated, as few governments have done before or since, not only the function of coinage as a mirror of contemporary life—of the political, social, spiritual, and artistic aspirations of the age—but also its immense and unique possibilities as a far reaching instrument

---

[1] Mark xii. 13–17. Cp. Matt. xxii. 15–21; Luke xx. 20–25.
[2] Exod. xx. 4, 5.
[3] Dan. xi. 31 and xii. 11.
[4] Mark xiii. 14.

of propaganda. Modern methods of disseminating news and modern vehicles of propaganda, from postage-stamps to broadcasting and the press, have their counterpart in the imperial coinage, where yearly, monthly—we might almost say, daily—novelties and variations in types record the sequence of public events and reflect the aims and ideologies of those who control the state.'[1]

Standing Armies

Universal states have differed very greatly in the extent to which they have required standing armies. A few seem to have been able to dispense with them almost entirely; others have found these expensive institutions a regrettable necessity, both mobile armies and stationary troops on garrison duty. The governments of such universal states have had to wrestle with the difficult and sometimes insoluble problems with which these always cumbrous and often dangerous institutions have confronted them. But these are matters which we cannot pause to explore. We will restrict ourselves in this section to one of the many subjects which might be brought under its title—one, however, that is perhaps the most interesting and the most important, and also the most closely aligned with the general argument of this chapter: namely the influence of the Roman Army on the development of the Christian Church.

The Christian Church was not, of course, the Roman Army's most obvious or most immediate beneficiary. The most obvious beneficiaries of all the armies of all disintegrating empires had been the aliens and barbarians enrolled in them. The later Achaemenids' recruitment of a mobile professional force of Greek mercenaries led to the conquest of the Achaemenian Empire by Alexander the Great. The enrolment of barbarians in the bodyguard of the 'Abbasid Caliphs and in the standing armies of the Roman Empire and the 'New Empire' of Egypt led to the establishment of Turkish barbarian rule in the Caliphate, Teutonic and Sarmatian barbarian rule in the western provinces of the Roman Empire, and Hyksos barbarian rule in Egypt. It is more surprising to see the mantle of an army descending upon a church—and the more so when the recipient of this inspiration is a church with an anti-military tradition.

In their conscientious objection to the shedding of blood, and consequently to the performance of military service, the Primitive Christians were at variance with Jewish tradition. They believed that the triumphal Second Coming of Christ was at hand, and that

[1] Toynbee, J. M. C.: *Roman Medallions* (New York 1944, The American Numismatic Society), p. 15.

they had been instructed to wait for it in patience. In striking contrast to the series of Jewish insurrections, first against Seleucid and then against Roman rule, during the three hundred years running from 166 B.C. to A.D. 135, the Christians never rose in armed revolt against Roman persecutors during the period of approximately equal length between the beginning of Jesus' mission and the conclusion of peace and alliance between the Roman Imperial Government and the Church in A.D. 313. As for service in the Roman Army, this was a stumbling-block for the Christians because it involved, not only the shedding of blood on active service, but also, among other things, the passing and execution of death sentences, the taking of the military oath of unconditional loyalty to the Emperor, the worship of the Emperor's genius and the offer of sacrifice to it, and the veneration of military standards as idols. Service in the army was, in fact, forbidden by successive Early Christian Fathers—by Origen, by Tertullian, and even by Lactantius in a work published after the conclusion of the Constantinian Peace.

It is significant that this ostracism of the Roman Army by the Christian Church broke down at a time when the Army was still being recruited by voluntary enlistment—indeed more than a hundred years before the issue was raised on the Roman Imperial Government's side through the reintroduction in practice of an always theoretically compulsory military service by Diocletian (reigned A.D. 283–305). Down to about the year A.D. 170 occasions for conflict over this issue were, it would seem, avoided. Christian civilians abstained from enlisting, while, if a pagan serving soldier became a convert, the Church tacitly acquiesced in his serving out his time and performing all the duties that the Army required of him. Possibly the Church justified herself for this laxity on the same ground on which she had from the first tolerated other anomalies, such as the continuance of slavery, even in cases where both master and slave were Christians; the inclusion of the Epistle to Philemon in the Sacred Canon is significant on this point. In the Church's expectation in this age, the time remaining before Christ's Second Coming was going to be so short that a soldier-convert might as well pass it under arms as a slave-convert in bondage.

In the third century of the Christian Era, when the Christians began to make their way in rapidly increasing numbers into the politically responsible classes of Roman society, partly by themselves rising in the world and partly by winning upper-class converts, they answered in practice the question raised for them by the social importance of the Roman Army without ever solving it in theory or waiting for the conversion of the state of which the army was an organ. In Diocletian's army the Christian contingent was already so large and so influential that the persecution of A.D. 303 was directed against Christianity in the army in the first instance. Indeed, it would appear that, in the western provinces, the percentage of Christians in the army was higher than the percentage in the civilian population.

Still more significant is the influence of the Army on the Church in the age when the ban on military service was still in force. War calls forth heroic virtues akin to those which the followers of an unpopular religion are called on to display, and many preachers of such religions had drawn upon the vocabulary furnished by the arts and implements of warfare, none more conspicuously than Saint Paul. In the Jewish tradition, which the Christian Church had retained as a treasured part of its own heritage, war was consecrated both in a literal and in a metaphorical sense. While, however, the Jewish martial tradition was a potent literary influence, the Roman martial tradition presented itself as a living and impressive reality. Baneful and hateful as the Roman Army of the Republic might have been in the cruel age of the Roman conquests and the still more cruel age of the Roman civil wars, the Army of the Empire, which lived on its pay instead of looting, and which was stationed on frontiers to defend civilization against the barbarians instead of infesting and devastating the civilized interior of the Hellenic world, came to win the involuntary respect, admiration, and even affection of Rome's subjects, as an œcumenical institution that ministered to their welfare and that was a legitimate object of pride.

'Let us observe', wrote Clement of Rome, about the year A.D. 95, in his First Epistle to the Corinthians, 'the conduct of the soldiers who serve our rulers. Think of the orderliness, the pliancy, the submissiveness with which they carry out their orders. Not all of them are legates or tribunes or centurions or options or officers of the grades below these. But each serving soldier in his own unit carries out the commands of the Emperor and the Government.'

In thus commending military discipline as an example to his Christian correspondents, Clement was seeking to establish order in the Church. Obedience, he was saying, is due from all Christians, not only to God but also to their ecclesiastical superiors. But in the evolution of the Christian Church's military imagery the 'soldier of God' was primarily the missionary. The missionary must disencumber himself from the impedimenta of civilian life, and has the same claim to be supported by his flock as the soldier has to receive his pay out of the contributions of the taxpayer.

Yet, whatever influence the Roman Army may have had on the development of the Church's institutions, it was less potent in that sphere than the influence of the Roman civil service, and the Army's example produced its principal effect on the Church in the sphere of ideals.

The Christian initiation-rite of baptism is equated by Saint Cyprian with the military oath (*sacramentum*) required of the recruit on enrolment in the Roman Army. Once enrolled, the Christian soldier must wage his warfare 'in accordance with the regulations'. He must eschew the unpardonable crime of desertion, and likewise the grave misdemeanour of 'dereliction of duty'. 'The pay of delinquency is death' is Tertullian's adaptation to military language of the phrase in Saint Paul's epistle to the Romans which appears as 'the wages of sin' in the Authorized English Version of the Bible. The ritual and moral obligations of the Christian life are equated by Tertullian with military 'fatigues'. In his terminology a fast is a stint of sentry-go, and the yoke which is easy, in the language of the Gospel according to Saint Matthew, is 'the Lord's light pack'. Moreover, the Christian soldier's faithful service is recompensed, on discharge, with 'God's gratuity'; and, short of receiving a gratuity, the soldier can look forward to drawing his rations as long as he gives satisfaction. The Cross is a military standard and Christ the commander-in-chief (*Imperator*). In fact, Baring-Gould's 'Onward, Christian Soldiers' and General Booth's 'Salvation Army' draw in word and in deed a parallel which goes back to the early days of the Church, but the army which originally suggested such a comparison was the non-Christian army which the Roman Empire had created and maintained for very different purposes.

Civil Services

Universal states have differed very greatly in the degree to which they have elaborated their civil services. At the upper end of the scale we find the Ottoman Government, which provided for its administrative needs by doing everything that human ingenuity could devise, and human determination accomplish, to produce a civil service that was to be no mere professional fraternity but a secular equivalent of a religious order, so rigorously segregated, so austerely disciplined, and so potently 'conditioned' as to be transfigured into a superhuman, or subhuman, race—as different from the ordinary run of human kind as a thorough-bred and broken-in horse, hound, or hawk is from the wild life that has been the breeder's and trainer's raw material.

A problem that often confronts the creators of civil services for universal states is, what use to make of the aristocracy that has often been lording it during the preceding Time of Troubles. There was, for example, an incapable aristocracy in Muscovy at the time when Peter the Great took her Westernization in hand, and a highly capable one in the Roman Empire at the date of the foundation of the Principate. Peter and Augustus each drew upon the aristocracy of his empire as material for the building of an œcumenical administrative structure, but their motives were different. While Peter tried to dragoon an old-fashioned nobility into becoming efficient administrators in the Western style, Augustus took the Senatorial Order into partnership, not so much because he needed their services as because he regarded this partnership as an insurance against his suffering the fate that his predecessor, Julius Caesar, had suffered at the hands of a gang of outraged members of the summarily deposed ex-ruling class. The antithetical problems that confronted Augustus and Peter the Great are the horns of a dilemma which is apt to catch the architect of an empire confronted with a pre-imperial aristocracy. If the aristocracy is capable, it will resent the emperor's service as being, for aristocrats, *infra dignitatem*. Conversely, if the aristocracy is incompetent, the dictator who employs it will find that the innocuousness of his tool is offset by the bluntness of its edge.

Pre-imperial aristocracies were not the only material that empire-builders required for the recruitment of their civil services. Such grandees, taken by themselves, would have constituted a corps of colonels without regiments. A middle class, consisting of lawyers and other professional men, would be required as the equivalents of the regimental officers, and a host of subordinates for the rank and file. Sometimes the builders of a universal state were in the fortunate position of being able to draw upon the services of a class that it had already called into existence to meet its own domestic needs. The character and achievements of the British Indian civil service can hardly be understood unless looked at against the background of an immediately preceding chapter of administrative history in the United Kingdom.

'The institution of factory inspection by the Act of 1833 was a stage in the development of a new kind of civil service. . . . Bentham's passion for substituting science for custom, his view of administration that it was a skilled business, had in this instance results that were wholly satisfactory. Under his inspiration England created a staff that brought to its work training and independence. Unlike the English Justice of the Peace, the new Civil Servant had knowledge: unlike the French *Intendant*, he was not a mere creature of a government. The English people learnt to use educated men on

terms that preserved their independence and their self-respect. . . .
For the moment, the chief occupation of this educated class was to
throw a searchlight on the disorder of the new [industrial] world.
Nobody can study the history of the generation that followed the passing of the Reform Bill without being struck by the part played by
lawyers, doctors, men of science and letters, in exposing abuses and
devising plans.'[1]

Such was the new fraternity of middle-class professional administrators which took passage to India. We shall find occasion
to consider both their achievement and their limitations in another
context in a later chapter.

The achievement of Augustus in calling a new civil service
into existence to answer the needs of the devastated, disorganized,
and weary world for which he made himself responsible had been
equalled, 150 years earlier, in the Sinic world by the work of Han
Liu Pang. Judged by the standard of endurance, indeed, the work
of this Sinic peasant far surpassed that of the Roman bourgeois
Octavian. Augustus's system went to pieces in the seventh century
after its creation, whereas Liu Pang's system lasted, with at least
a thread of continuity, down to A.D. 1911.

The defect of the Roman imperial civil service was its reflection
of the discord between the old senatorial aristocracy and the new
imperial dictatorship, which the Augustan compromise had glozed
over but had not healed. There were two rigidly segregated hier-
archies and two mutually exclusive careers in which the senatorial
and non-senatorial civil servants went their respective ways. This
schism was brought to an end in the third century of the Christian
Era by the elimination of the Senatorial Order from all posts of
administrative responsibility; but by this time the decay of local
civic self-government had so greatly swollen the volume of work
that Diocletian found himself compelled to make an inordinate
increase in the permanent establishment of the imperial civil
service. The social standard required from recruits was, in consequence, lowered. The contrast with the history of the Han
Dynasty's civil service is instructive. The opening of careers to
talent, irrespective of rank, prevailed from the first, when the
Emperor himself in 196 B.C., six years after his restoration of order,
issued an ordinance directing the provincial public authorities to
select candidates for the public service on a test of merit, and to
send them to the capital for establishment or rejection by the
officers of the central government.

[1] Hammond, J. L. and Barbara: *The Rise of Modern Industry* (London 1925,
Methuen), pp. 256–7.

This new Sinic civil service received its definitive form when Han Liu Pang's successor, Han Wuti (reigned 140 B.C.–87 B.C.), decided that the merit required of candidates should be proficiency in reproducing the style of the classical literature of the Confucian canon and in interpreting the Confucian philosophy to the satisfaction of the Confucian literati of the day. The Confucian school of the second century B.C., which was thus tactfully coaxed into partnership with the imperial régime, would have astonished Confucius himself, but even this dehydrated political philosophy was a more effective inspiration for a corporate professional way of life than the merely literary archaistic culture of the Hellenic world in the age of Diocletian. However pedantic it might be, it provided a traditional ethic which was lacking among the Roman counterparts of the Sinic civil servants.

While the Han Empire and the Roman Empire created their civil services out of their own social and cultural heritages, Peter the Great was debarred, by the very nature of his problem, from doing anything of the kind. In A.D. 1717–18 he established a number of Administrative Colleges to induct the Russians into new-fangled Western methods of administration. Swedish prisoners-of-war were roped in as instructors, and Russian apprentices sent to acquire a Prussian training at Königsberg.

Where, as in the Petrine Russian Empire, an imperial civil service is called into existence in conscious imitation of alien institutions, the need of special arrangements for training personnel is evident; but the need arises in some degree in all civil services. In the Incaic, Achaemenian, Roman, and Ottoman empires the Emperor's personal household was both the hub of the wheel of imperial government and the training school for the administrators themselves, and in a number of cases the educational function of the imperial household was provided for through the creation of a corps of 'pages' or, in workaday terms, apprentices. At the Inca Emperor's court at Cuzco there was a regular course of education, with tests at successive stages. In the Achaemenian Empire 'all Persian boys of noble birth', according to Herodotus, 'were educated at the Emperor's court, from the age of five to the age of twenty, in three things and three only: riding, shooting, and telling the truth'. The Ottoman court made provision for the education of pages in its early days at Brusa, and it was still treading this well-worn path when Sultan Murād II (reigned A.D. 1421–51) established a school for princes at Adrianople, which was the capital in his time. His successor, however, Sultan Mehmed II (reigned A.D. 1451–81), struck out a new line when he set about staffing his civil service, no longer with the sons of 'Osmanli

Muslim noblemen but with Christian slaves—including renegades and prisoners-of-war from Western Christendom as well as the 'tribute children' levied from the Pādishāh's own Eastern Orthodox Christian subjects. This peculiar institution has been described in an earlier part of this Study.

While the Ottoman Pādishāhs deliberately expanded their personal slave-household into an instrument for the government of a rapidly growing empire, actually to the exclusion of free 'Osmanlis, the Roman Emperors, though they found themselves compelled to make a similar use of Caesar's Household, took steps to limit the role of freedmen in the imperial administration. The freedmen's stronghold in the administration of the Roman Empire in the early days was the central government, in which five administrative offices in Caesar's Household had grown into imperial ministries; but, even in these posts, which were traditionally the freedmen's preserve, the freedmen became politically impossible as soon as they became conspicuous. The scandal caused by the spectacle of the freedmen-ministers of Claudius and Nero exercising unbridled power led, under the Flavian emperors and their successors, to the transfer of these key posts, one after another, to members of the Equestrian Order.

Thus in the history of the Roman civil service the equestrian, i.e. the commercial, class gained ground at the expense both of the slave underworld and the senatorial aristocracy, and its victory over its rivals was justified by the efficiency and integrity with which the equestrian civil servants performed their duties. This redemption of a class which, during the last two centuries of the republican régime, had risen to wealth and power by exploitation, tax-farming, and usury, was perhaps the most remarkable triumph of the Augustan imperial system. The British Indian civil servants were likewise recruited from a commercial class. They had originated as the employees of a trading company whose purpose had been pecuniary profit; one of their original incentives for taking employment far from home in an uncongenial climate had been the possibility of making fortunes by trading 'on the side' for their personal profit; and, when the East India Company was suddenly transformed, by a significantly easy military victory, into the sovereign, in all but name, of the richest province of the broken-down Mughal Empire, the Company's servants had, for a brief period, yielded to the temptation to extort monstrous pecuniary winnings for themselves with the same shamelessness as the Roman Equites had displayed over a much longer period. Yet in the British case, as in the Roman, a band of predatory harpies was converted into a body of public servants whose incentive was now no longer personal gain and who had learnt to make it a point of honour to wield enormous political power without abusing it.

This redemption of the character of the British administration in India was due in part to the East India Company's decision to educate their servants for bearing the new political responsibilities that had fallen on their shoulders. In A.D. 1806 the Company opened, at Hertford Castle, a college for probationer appointees to its administrative service which it moved, three years later, to Haileybury; and this college played an historic role during the fifty-two years of its existence. In 1853, on the eve of the transference of the Government of India from the Company to the Crown, Parliament's decision to recruit the service in future by competitive examination opened the door to candidates drawn from the wider field of such non-official institutions as the universities of the United Kingdom and the so-called 'public schools' from which the two ancient English universities were at that time mainly recruited. Haileybury College was closed in 1857, and, during the fifty-two years of its existence, Dr. Arnold of Rugby had come and gone, while all that he stood for had been broadcast throughout the public schools by like-minded masters. The average Indian civil servant during the latter half of the nineteenth century had acquired at school and university a training in exact scholarship, based on what were, for Westerners, the 'classical' languages and literatures, and a Christian outlook which was not less strong for being often somewhat vague and undogmatic. A not altogether fanciful parallel might be drawn between this moral and intellectual training and the education in the Sinic Confucian classics that was then still being demanded of a Chinese civil service which had been established twenty centuries earlier.

If we turn now to consider who had been the principal beneficiaries from the imperial civil services that universal states had called into existence for their own purposes, the most obvious beneficiaries were evidently those successor-states of these empires which had the intelligence to make use of such a precious legacy. From a list of these we should exclude the successor-states of the Roman Empire in the West. These learnt their lessons much less from the imperial civil service, which they disrupted, than from the Church to which they were converted; but, as we shall see, the Church itself had been a beneficiary of the Roman civil service, so that, even here, the legacy was partially transmitted at one remove. Without attempting a complete list of beneficiary successor-states, one can point, at the time of writing, to the recently formed Indian Union and Pakistan as beneficiaries of the British Indian civil service.

The most important beneficiaries, however, had been the churches. We have already noticed how the hierarchical organization of the Christian Church had been based on that of the Roman Empire. A similar basis was provided by the 'New Empire' of Egypt for the Pan-Egyptiac church under the Chief Priest of Amon-Re at Thebes and by the Sasanian Empire for the Zoroastrian church. The Chief Priest of Amon-Re was created in the image of the Theban Pharoah; the Zoroastrian Chief Mōbadh in the likeness of the Sasanian Shāhinshāh; and the Pope in the likeness of the post-Diocletianic Roman Emperor. Secular administrative corporations had, however, performed more intimate services for churches than the mere provision of an organizational last. They had also influenced their outlook and ethos, and in some cases these intellectual and moral influences had been conveyed, not merely by example, but by the translation of a person, in whom they had been incarnate, from the secular to the ecclesiastical sphere.

Three historic figures, each of whom gave a decisive turn to the development of the Catholic Church in the West, were recruits from the secular Roman imperial civil service. Ambrosius (lived *circa* A.D. 340–97) was the son of a civil servant who had reached the peak of his profession by attaining the office of praetorian prefect of the Gauls, and the future Saint Ambrose was following in his father's footsteps as governor of the province of Liguria and Aemilia when, in A.D. 374, to his consternation, he was dragged out of the rut of an assured official career and hustled into the episcopal see of Milan by a popular impetus that did not wait to ask his leave. Cassiodorus (lived *circa* A.D. 490–585) spent the first part of his very long life administering Roman Italy in the service of King Theodoric the Ostrogoth. In his later days he turned a rural property of his own in the toe of Italy into a monastic settlement that was the complement of Saint Benedict's foundation at Monte Cassino. Saint Benedict's school of monks broken in, by the love of God, to hard physical labour in the fields could not have done all that it did for a nascent Western Christian society if it had not been wedded, at the start, to a Cassiodoran school that was inspired by the same motive to perform the mentally laborious task of copying the pagan Classics and the works of the Fathers. As for Gregory the Great (lived *circa* A.D. 540–604), he abandoned the secular public service, after serving as *Praefectus Urbi*, in order to follow Cassiodorus's example by making a monastery out of his ancestral palace in Rome, and he was thereby led, against his expectation and desire, into becoming one of the makers of the Papacy. Each of these great civil servants found his true vocation in the service of the Church, and brought to the service of the Church aptitudes and traditions acquired in a civil service career.

Citizenships

Since a universal state usually arises in the first instance from the forcible union of a number of contending parochial states, it is apt to start life with a great gulf fixed between rulers and ruled. On the one side stands an empire-building community representing the survivors of a dominant minority after a protracted struggle for existence between the rulers of the competing local communities of the preceding age; on the other side lies a conquered population. It is also common form for the effectively enfranchised element to become, as time passes, a relatively larger fraction as a result of the admission of recruits from the subject majority. It had, however, been unusual for this process to go to the length of completely obliterating the initial division between rulers and ruled.

The outstanding exceptional case, in which a comprehensive political enfranchisement had been achieved—and this within a quarter of a century of the establishment of the universal state— was in the Sinic world. In the Sinic universal state established in 230–221 B.C., through the conquest of six other parochial states by their victorious competitor Ts'in, the supremacy of Ts'in was brought to an end when Hsien Yang, the capital of the Ts'in Power, was occupied by Han Liu Pang in 207 B.C. The political enfranchisement of the whole population of the Sinic universal state may be dated from 196 B.C. It need hardly be said that this political achievement could not change at one stroke the fundamental economic and social structure of the Sinic society. That society continued to consist of a mass of tax-paying peasants supporting a small privileged ruling class; but henceforth the avenue giving entry to this Sinic official paradise was genuinely open to talent, irrespective of social class.

The unifying effect produced by historical forces operating over a long period of time cannot, of course, be reproduced by a legislative act conferring uniform juridical status. The uniform status of Europeans, Eurasians, and Asiatics under the British Rāj in India, and of Europeans, Creoles, and 'Indians' in the Spanish Empire in the Indies, as subjects, in either case, of one Crown, did not have any appreciable effect in diminishing the social gulf between rulers and ruled in either of these polities. The classical instance in which an initial gulf was successfully obliterated by the gradual merger of a once privileged ruling minority in the mass of its former subjects is to be found in the history of the Roman Empire; and here, also, the substance of political equality was not communicated by the mere conferment of the juridical status of Roman citizen. After the promulgation of the Edict of Caracalla in A.D. 212 all free male inhabitants of the Roman Empire, with insignificant exceptions, were Roman citizens, but it still required the political and social revolution of the ensuing century to bring the realities of life into conformity with the law.

The ultimate beneficiary from the political egalitarianism towards which the Roman Empire was moving in the Age of the Principate,[1] and at which it arrived in the time of Diocletian, was of course the Catholic Christian Church. The Catholic Christian Church borrowed the Roman Empire's master idea of dual citizenship—a constitutional device that had solved the problem how to enjoy the advantages of membership of an œcumenical community without having to repudiate narrower loyalties or to cut local roots. In the Roman Empire under the Principate, which was the framework within which the Christian Church grew up, all citizens of the world-city of Rome (except the small number who actually lived in the metropolis) were also citizens of some local municipality that, though within the Roman body politic, was an autonomous city state with the traditional Hellenic form of city state self-government and the traditional hold of such a local motherland upon the affections of her children. On this Roman secular model a growing and spreading ecclesiastical community built up an organization and a corporate feeling that was simultaneously local and œcumenical. The Church to which a Christian gave his allegiance was both the local Christian community of a particular city and the Catholic Christian community in which all these local churches were embraced in virtue of a uniform practice and doctrine.

[1] i.e. the pre-Diocletianic Empire, founded by Augustus, who used the title Princeps, meaning 'Leader of the House' (i.e. the Senate).

VII
UNIVERSAL CHURCHES

XXVI. ALTERNATIVE CONCEPTIONS OF
THE RELATION OF UNIVERSAL
CHURCHES TO CIVILIZATIONS

(1) CHURCHES AS CANCERS

WE have seen that a universal church is apt to come to birth during a Time of Troubles following the breakdown of a civilization and to unfold itself within the political framework of the ensuing universal state. We have seen also, in the preceding part of this Study, that the principal beneficiaries of the institutions maintained by universal states have been universal churches; and it is therefore not surprising that the champions of a universal state, whose fortunes are on the wane, should dislike the spectacle of a universal church growing within its bosom. The church is therefore likely to be regarded, from the standpoint of the imperial government and its supporters, as a social cancer responsible for the decline of the state.

In the decline of the Roman Empire an indictment, which had been mounting up since the attack penned by Celsus near the end of the second century of the Christian Era, came to a head in the West when the Empire there was in its death agonies. An explosion of this hostile feeling was evoked in A.D. 416 in the heart of Rutilius Namatianus, a 'die-hard' pagan Gallic devotee of Imperial Rome, by the sad sight of desert islands colonized—or, as he would have said, infested—by Christian monks:

> 'Now, as we move, Capraria lifts itself
> Out of the sea; squalid the isle, and filled
> With men who shun the light; they dub themselves
> "Monks", with a Grecian name, because they wish
> To dwell alone, observed by none. They dread
> The gifts of Fortune, while her ills they fear.
> Who, to shirk pain, would choose a life of pain?
> What madness of a brain diseased so fond
> As, fearing evil, to refuse all good?'[1]

Before the end of his voyage Rutilius suffered the sadder sight of another island that had captivated a fellow countryman of his own.

[1] Rutilius Namatianus, C.: *De Reditu Suo*, Book I, lines 439–46, trans. by Dr. G. F. Savage-Armstrong (London 1907, Bell).

'The wave-girt Gorgon rises in mid-sea
'Twixt Pisa and Cyrnus one on either side.
I shun the cliffs, memorials as they are
Of late disaster; one of my own race
Here perished by a living death. For lately
A high-born youth of our own nation, one
Not lacking wealth or marriage-relatives,
Driven by madness, man and earth forsook
And, as a superstitious exile, sought
A shameful lurking-place. The ill-starred wretch
Deemed that the spark divine by squalor thrives,
And on his own life laid more cruel stripes
Than might the offended deities themselves.
Less potent is this sect than Circe's drugs?
Then bodies were transformed, but now men's minds.'[1]

Through these lines there breathes the spirit of a still pagan aristo-cracy who saw the cause of the ruin of the Roman Empire in the abandonment of the traditional worship of the Hellenic pantheon.

This controversy between a sinking Roman Empire and a rising Christian Church raised an issue that stirred the feelings not only of contemporaries directly concerned, but also of a posterity con-templating the event across a great gulf of time. In the statement 'I have described the triumph of Barbarism and Religion', Gibbon not only sums up the seventy-one chapters of his book in nine words but proclaims himself a partisan of Celsus and Rutilius. The cultural peak of Hellenic history, as he saw it, in the Antonine Age stood out clear across an intervening span of sixteen centuries which, for Gibbon, represented a cultural trough. Out of this trough the generation of Gibbon's grandparents in the Western world had tardily gained a footing on the upward slope of another mountain from which the twin peak of the Hellenic past was once again visible in its majesty.

This view, which is implicit in Gibbon's work, has been put clearly and sharply by a twentieth-century anthropologist who is a figure of comparable stature in his own field:

'The religion of the Great Mother, with its curious blend of crude savagery and spiritual aspirations, was only one of a multitude of similar Oriental faiths which in the later days of paganism spread over the Roman Empire, and by saturating the European peoples with alien ideals of life undermined the whole fabric of ancient civilisation.

'Greek and Roman society was built on the conception of the sub-ordination of the individual to the community, of the citizen to the state; it set the safety of the commonwealth, as the supreme aim of conduct, above the safety of the individual whether in this world or

[1] Ibid., lines 515–26.

in a world to come. Trained from infancy in this unselfish ideal, the citizens devoted their lives to the public service and were ready to lay them down for the common good; or, if they shrank from the supreme sacrifice, it never occurred to them that they acted otherwise than basely in preferring their personal existence to the interests of their country. All this was changed by the spread of Oriental religions which inculcated the communion of the soul with God and its eternal salvation as the only objects worth living for, objects in comparison with which the prosperity and even the existence of the state sank into insignificance. The inevitable result of this selfish and immoral doctrine was to withdraw the devotee more and more from the public service, to concentrate his thoughts on his own spiritual emotions, and to breed in him a contempt for the present life, which he regarded merely as a probation for a better and an eternal. The saint and the recluse, disdainful of earth and rapt in ecstatic contemplation of heaven, became in popular opinion the highest ideal of humanity, displacing the old ideal of the patriot and hero who, forgetful of self, lives and is ready to die for the good of his country. The earthly city seemed poor and contemptible to men whose eyes beheld the City of God coming in the clouds of heaven.

'Thus the centre of gravity, so to say, was shifted from the present to a future life, and, however much the other world may have gained, there can be little doubt that this one lost heavily by the change. A general disintegration of the body politic set in. The ties of the state and of the family were loosened: the structure of society tended to resolve itself into its individual elements and thereby to relapse into barbarism; for civilization is only possible through the active co-operation of the citizens and their willingness to subordinate their private interests to the common good. Men refused to defend their country and even to continue their kind. In their anxiety to save their own souls and the souls of others, they were content to leave the material world, which they identified with the principle of evil, to perish around them. This obsession lasted for a thousand years. The revival of Roman Law, of the Aristotelian philosophy, of ancient art and literature at the close of the Middle Ages marked the return of Europe to native ideals of life and conduct, to saner, manlier views of the world. The long halt in the march of civilization was over. The tide of Oriental invasion had turned at last. It is ebbing still.'[1]

It was still ebbing when the present lines were being written in 1948, and the present writer was wondering what the gentle scholar would have had to say, if he had been revising *The Golden Bough* for a fourth edition at that date, about some of the ways in which Europe's return 'to native ideals of life and conduct' had

---

[1] Frazer, Sir J. G.: *The Golden Bough: Adonis, Attis, Osiris: Studies in the History of Oriental Religion*, 2nd edn. (London 1907, Macmillan), pp. 251–3. In a footnote the author concedes that the spread of Oriental religion was not the only cause of the downfall of ancient civilization.

manifested itself during the forty-one years since the publication of this provocative passage. Frazer and his like-minded contemporaries had proved to be the last generation of Western neopagans of a rational and tolerant school which had first emerged in Italy in the fifteenth century of the Christian Era. By A.D. 1952 they had been swept off the field by demonic, emotional, violent-handed successors who had emerged out of the unplumbed deeps of a secularized Western society. The words of Frazer had been re-uttered by the voice of Alfred Rosenberg with a different ring. Yet the fact remains that Rosenberg and Frazer were both propounding an identical Gibbonian thesis.

We have already argued at length, in an early part of this Study, that the breakdown of the Hellenic society had in fact occurred long before it suffered the intrusion of Christianity or of any of the other Oriental religions which were Christianity's unsuccessful rivals. Our inquiries have already reached the conclusion that higher religions have never as yet been guilty of the deaths of any civilizations, yet this tragedy might still be a possibility. To get to the bottom of the issue we must carry our inquiry from the macrocosm into the microcosm, from the facts of past history to the abiding characteristics of human nature.

Frazer's contention is that the higher religions are essentially and incurably anti-social. When there is a shift in the focus of human interest from the ideals aimed at in the civilizations to those aimed at in the higher religions, is it true that social values, for which the civilizations claim to stand, are bound to suffer? Are spiritual and social values antithetical and inimical? Is the fabric of civilization undermined if the salvation of the individual soul is taken as being the supreme aim in life? Frazer answers these questions in the affirmative; and, if his answer were right, it would mean that human life was a tragedy without a catharsis. The writer of this Study believed that Frazer's answer was wrong, and that it was based on a misunderstanding of the nature both of higher religions and of human souls.

Man is neither a selfless ant nor an unsocial cyclops but a 'social animal', whose personality can be expressed and developed only through relations with other personalities. Conversely, Society is nothing but the common ground between one individual's network of relations and another's. It has no existence except in the activities of individuals who, for their part, cannot exist except in Society. Nor again is there a disharmony between the individual's relations with his fellow men and his relation with God. In the spiritual vision of Primitive Man there is manifestly a solidarity between the tribesman and his gods which, so far from alienating the tribesmen from each other, is the strongest of the social bonds between them. The workings of this harmony between Man's duty to God and his duty to his neighbour have been explored and illustrated at the primitive level by Frazer himself, and disintegrating civilizations had borne witness to it when they had sought a new bond for Society in the worship of a deified Caesar. Is the harmony converted into a discord by 'the higher religions', as Frazer contends? In theory and in practice alike the answer would appear to be in the negative.

On an *à priori* view (to start from that approach) personalities are not conceivable except as agents of spiritual activity; and the only conceivable scope for spiritual activity lies in relations between spirit and spirit. In seeking God, Man is performing a social act; and, if God's Love has gone into action in This World in the redemption of Mankind by Christ, then Man's efforts to make himself less unlike a God who created Man in His own image must include efforts to follow Christ's example in sacrificing himself for the redemption of his fellow men. The antithesis between trying to save one's own soul by seeking God and trying to do one's duty to one's neighbour is therefore false.

'Thou shalt love the Lord thy God with all thy heart and with all thy soul and with all thy mind. This is the first and great commandment. And the second is like unto it: Thou shalt love thy neighbour as thyself.'[1]

It is evident that, in the Church Militant on Earth, the good social aims of the mundane societies will be achieved much more successfully than they can ever be achieved in a mundane society which aims at these objects direct, and at nothing higher. In other words, the spiritual progress of individual souls in this life will in fact bring with it much more social progress than could be attained in any other way. In Bunyan's allegory, the Pilgrim could not find the 'wicket gate' which was the entrance to a life of good conduct until he had seen, far beyond it, the 'shining light' on the horizon.[2] And what we have here asserted in terms of Christianity could be translated into terms of all the other higher religions. The essence

[1] Matt. xxii. 37–39.
[2] No doubt the pilgrimage of Christian and his two companions in the First Part of *The Pilgrim's Progress* is a career of what we might call 'holy individualism'; but in the Second Part this imperfect conception is corrected, and we have a growing society of pilgrims not only travelling towards their spiritual goal but also rendering mundane social services to one another on the way. This contrast inspired Monsignor Knox's *jeu d'esprit* in which he develops the thesis that, though the First Part was the work of Bunyan the Puritan, the Second was the work of a Pseudo-Bunyan whose *nom de plume* concealed a devout Anglo-Catholic lady. Knox, Ronald A.: *Essays in Satire* (London 1928, Sheed and Ward), ch. vii: 'The identity of the Pseudo-Bunyan.'

of Christianity is the essence of the higher religions as a class, though in different eyes these different windows through which God's light shines into Man's soul may differ in the degree of their translucency or in the selection of the rays that they transmit.

When we pass from theory to practice, from the nature of the human personality to the record of history, our task of proving that, in fact, the men of religion have served the practical needs of society might seem to be too easy. If we were to cite a Saint Francis of Assisi, a Saint Vincent de Paul, a John Wesley, or a David Livingstone, we might be accused of proving what needs no demonstration. We will therefore cite a class of persons commonly regarded and derided as exceptions to the rule, a class of persons at once 'God-intoxicated' and 'anti-social', holy and ridiculous, qualifying for the cynic's jibe—'a good man in the worst sense of the word': namely the Christian anchorites, a Saint Antony in his desert or a Saint Symeon on his pillar. It is manifest that, in insulating themselves from their fellow men, these saints were entering into a far more active relation with a far wider circle than any that would have centred round them if they had remained 'in the World' and had spent their lives in some secular occupation. They swayed the World from their retreats to greater effect than the Emperor in his capital, because their personal pursuit of holiness through seeking communion with God was a form of social action that moved men more powerfully than any secular social service on the political plane.

'It has sometimes been said that the ascetic ideal of the East Roman was a barren withdrawal from the world of his day; the biography of John the Almsgiver may suggest why it was that the Byzantine in his hour of need turned instinctively for aid and comfort to the ascete in the full assurance of his sympathy and succour. . . . One of the outstanding features of early Byzantine asceticism is its passion for social justice and its championship of the poor and oppressed.'[1]

(2) CHURCHES AS CHRYSALISES

We have contested the view that churches are cancers eating away the living tissues of a civilization; yet we might still agree with Frazer's dictum, at the close of the passage quoted, that the tide of Christianity, which had flowed so strongly in the last phase of the Hellenic society, had been ebbing in these latter days, and that the post-Christian Western society that had emerged was of the same order as the pre-Christian Hellenic. This observation opens

[1] Dawes, E., and Baynes, N. H.: *Three Byzantine Saints* (Oxford 1948, Blackwell), pp. 198 and 197.

up a second possible conception of the relation between churches and civilizations, a view expressed by a Modern Western scholar in the following passage:

'The old civilization was doomed. . . . To the orthodox Christian, on the other hand, the Church stood, like Aaron, between the dead and the living, as a middle term between the things of the Next World and of This. It was the Body of Christ and therefore eternal; something worth living for and working for. Yet it was in the World as much as the Empire itself. The idea of the Church thus formed an invaluable fixed point round which a new civilization could slowly crystallize.'[1]

On this view universal churches have their *raison d'être* in keeping the species of society known as civilizations alive by preserving a precious germ of life through the perilous interregnum, between the dissolution of one mortal representative of the species and the genesis of another. A church would thus be part of the reproductive system of civilizations, serving as egg, grub, and chrysalis between butterfly and butterfly. The writer of this Study had to confess that he had been satisfied for many years with this rather patronizing view of the role of the churches in history;[2] and he still believed that this conception of them as chrysalises, unlike the conception of them as cancers, was true as far as it went; but he had come to believe that it was only a small part of the truth about them. It is, however, the part of the truth which we have now to examine.

If we cast our eye over the civilizations that were still alive in A.D. 1952, we shall see that every one of them had in its background some universal church through which it was affiliated to a civilization of an older generation. The Western and Orthodox Christian civilizations were affiliated through the Christian Church to the Hellenic civilization; the Far Eastern civilization was affiliated through the Mahāyāna to the Sinic civilization; the Hindu civilization through Hinduism to the Indic; the Iranic and Arabic through Islam to the Syriac. All these civilizations had churches for their chrysalises, and the various surviving fossils of extinct civilizations, which were discussed in an earlier part of this Study, were all preserved in ecclesiastical integuments: for example, the Jews and the

---

[1] Burkitt, F. C.: *Early Eastern Christianity* (London 1904, Murray), pp. 210–11.

[2] In a spiritually sensitive soul the same view may, of course, breed a mood of melancholy rather than complacency: 'As Classical Civilisation collapsed, Christianity ceased to be the noble faith of Jesus the Christ: it became a religion useful as the social cement of a world in dissolution. As such, it assisted at the rebirth of Western European Civilisation after the Dark Ages. It has endured to be the nominal creed of clever and restless peoples who are ceasing to give even lip-service to its ideals. As to its future, who can prophesy?' (Barnes, E. W.: *The Rise of Christianity* (London 1947, Longmans, Green), p. 336.)

Parsees. The fossils were, in fact, church-chrysalises which had failed to deliver their butterflies.

The process by which a civilization is affiliated to a predecessor will be found, in the survey of examples which follows, to be analysable into three phases which, from the standpoint of the chrysalis church, we may label 'conceptive', 'gestative', and 'parturient'. These three phases may also be roughly equated chronologically with the disintegration phase of the old civilization, the interregnum, and the genesis phase of the new civilization.

The conceptive phase of the affiliation process sets in when the church seizes the opportunities offered by its secular environment. One of the features of that environment is that the universal state will, inevitably, have put out of action many of the institutions and ways of life that gave vitality to the society in its growth phase and even in its Time of Troubles. The purpose of the universal state is tranquillity, but the ensuing sense of relief is soon tempered by a sense of frustration; for Life cannot preserve itself simply by bringing itself to a halt. In this situation a nascent church may make its own fortune by doing for a stagnant secular society the service that is now its most urgent need. It can open new channels for the baulked energies of Mankind. In the Roman Empire,

'The victory of Christianity over Paganism . . . furnished the orator with new topics of declamation and the logician with new points of controversy. Above all, it produced a new principle, of which the operation was constantly felt in every part of Society. It stirred the stagnant mass from the inmost depths. It excited all the passions of a stormy democracy in the listless population of an overgrown empire. The fear of heresy did what the sense of oppression could not do; it changed men, accustomed to be turned over like sheep from tyrant to tyrant, into devoted partisans and obstinate rebels. The tones of an eloquence which had been silent for ages resounded from the pulpit of Gregory. A spirit which had been extinguished on the plains of Philippi revived in Athanasius and Ambrose.'[1]

This is as true as it is eloquent, but its theme is the second, or 'gestative', phase. The first phase, the struggle preceding the victory, had given to ordinary men and women an exhilarating opportunity for making a supreme sacrifice, such as had been the glory and the tragedy of their ancestors in the days before the Roman Empire clamped down the dull peace of its universal state as an extinguisher on a Time of Troubles. Thus in the 'conceptive' phase the church receives into itself the energies that the state can no longer either liberate or utilize, and creates new

[1] Macaulay, Lord: 'History', in *Miscellaneous Writings* (London 1860, Longmans, Green, 2 vols.), vol. i, p. 267.

channels along which they can find vent. The 'gestative' phase that follows is marked by a vast increase in the church's range of action. It draws into its service men of mark who have failed to find scope for their talents in secular administration. A landslide sets in towards the rising institution, and its speed and scope is regulated by the pace at which the disintegrating society collapses. For example, in the disintegrating Sinic civilization the success of the Mahāyāna was much more complete in the Yellow River Basin, which was overrun by Eurasian Nomads, than in the Yangtse Basin, where they were longer held at bay. In the Hellenic world the landslide of the Latinized provincials towards Christianity in the fourth century coincided with the shift of the centre of government to Constantinople and the virtual abandonment of the western provinces. The same features could be illustrated from the progress of Islam in a disintegrating Syriac world and the progress of Hinduism in a disintegrating Indic world.

In the quaint but expressive imagery of Islamic mythology we may liken a church, in this heroic phase of its history, to the avatar of the Prophet Muhammad as a ram who sure-footedly crosses the bridge, narrow as a razor's edge, which is the only avenue of access to Paradise across the yawning gulf of Hell. Unbelievers, who hazard the adventure on their own feet, infallibly fall into the abyss; the only human souls that find their way across are those which, as a reward for their virtue or their faith, are permitted to cling to the ram's fleece in the conveniently portable shape of beatified ticks. When the crossing has been duly accomplished, the 'gestative' phase in the church's transmissionary service is succeeded by the 'parturient' phase. The roles of church and civilization are now reversed, and the church, which previously, in the 'conceptive' phase, had drawn vitality from an old civilization, and, in the 'gestative' phase, had navigated the course through the storms of the interregnum, proceeds to give out vitality to the new civilization conceived within its womb. We can watch this creative energy flowing out, under religious auspices, into secular channels on the economic and political, as well as the cultural, planes of social life.

On the economic plane, by far the most impressive existing legacy of a 'parturient' universal church to an emergent civilization was to be seen in the economic prowess of a contemporary Western world. By the time of writing, a quarter of a millennium had passed since a new secular society had completed a long-drawn-out process of extricating itself from the chrysalis of a Western Catholic Christian Church; yet the marvellous and monstrous apparatus of Western technology was still visibly a by-product of Western Christian monachism. The psychological foundation of this mighty material edifice was a belief in the duty and dignity of physical labour—*laborare est orare*. This revolutionary departure from the Hellenic conception of labour as vulgar and servile would not have established itself if it had not been hallowed by the Rule of Saint Benedict. On this foundation the Benedictine Order had planted the agricultural groundwork of Western economic life, and this groundwork had given the Cistercian Order a basis for the industrial superstructure which their intelligently directed activities had erected, until the cupidity that this monk-built Tower of Babel had aroused in the hearts of the builders' secular neighbours reached a pitch at which they could no longer keep their hands off it. A spoliation of the monasteries was one of the origins of a Modern Western capitalist economy.

As for the political sphere, we have watched, in an earlier part of this Study, the Papacy moulding a *Respublica Christiana* that promised to enable Mankind to enjoy simultaneously the benefits of parochial sovereignties and of a universal state without suffering the drawbacks of either. In giving, through ecclesiastical coronation, its blessing to the political status of independent kingdoms, the Papacy was bringing back into political life the multiplicity and variety that had been so fruitful in the growth stage of the Hellenic society, while the political disunity and dissension that had brought the Hellenic society to ruin were to be mitigated and controlled by the exercise of an overriding spiritual authority which the Papacy claimed as the ecclesiastical heir of the Roman Empire. The secular parochial princes were to dwell together in unity under the guidance of an ecclesiastical shepherd. After several centuries of trial and error this politico-ecclesiastical experiment miscarried, and the reasons for its miscarriage were discussed in an earlier part of this Study. Here we have only to take note of it as an illustration of the role of the Christian Church in its 'parturient' phase, and to observe the corresponding role played by the Brahman ecclesiastical fraternity in the political articulation of the nascent Hindu civilization. The Brahmans conferred legitimacy on Rajput dynasties in much the same way as the Christian Church rendered a like service to a Clovis or a Pepin.

When we pass to examine the Christian Church's political role in Orthodox Christendom and the Mahāyāna's in the Far East, we see the church's field of activity circumscribed in both these societies by the evocation of a ghost of the antecedent civilization's universal state—the Sui and T'ang renaissance of the Han Empire and the East Roman (Byzantine) renaissance of the Roman Empire in the main body of Orthodox Christendom. In the Far Eastern society the Mahāyāna found a new place for itself as one among a number of religions and philosophies existing side by side and catering for the spiritual needs of the same public. It continued unobtrusively to permeate the life of the Far Eastern society and contributed to the cultural conversion of Korea and Japan to the Far Eastern way of life. Its part here bears comparison with that played by the Western Catholic Church in the attraction of Hungary, Poland, and Scandinavia into the orbit of Western Christendom, and by the Eastern Orthodox Church in planting an offshoot of Orthodox Christian civilization in the soil of Russia.

When we pass from the political to the cultural contributions of 'parturient' churches to nascent civilizations, we find, for example, that the Mahāyāna, driven out of the political arena, reasserted itself effectively in the sphere of culture. Its enduring intellectual potency was part of the heritage of the Mahāyāna from the Primitive Buddhist school of philosophy. Christianity, on the other hand, started without any philosophical system of its own and found itself constrained to attempt the *tour de force* of presenting its faith in the alien intellectual terms of the Hellenic schools. In Western Christendom this Hellenic intellectual alloy became overwhelmingly dominant after it had been reinforced in the twelfth century by the 'reception' of Aristotle. The Christian Church made a notable contribution to the intellectual progress of the West by founding and fostering the universities, but it was in the sphere of the fine arts that the cultural influence of the Church made its greatest contribution; and this is a statement so obvious that it needs no illustration.

We have now completed our survey of churches in the role of chrysalises; but, if we were to climb to the bird's-eye viewpoint from which all the civilizations known to history are simultaneously visible in their relations with one another, we should not be slow to observe that the church-chrysalis is not the only medium through which one civilization can be affiliated to its predecessor. To take only one example: the Hellenic society was affiliated to the Minoan, but there is no evidence of a church developing within the Minoan world, and providing a church-chrysalis for the Hellenic society; and, though some rudimentary forms of higher religion were developed in the internal proletariats of some of the civilizations of the first generation (and may have developed, unknown to modern research, in others), it is plain that none of these rudiments got far enough to serve as efficient chrysalises for the civilizations which followed. A scrutiny of all available examples shows that *none* of the civilizations of the second generation—Hellenic, Syriac, Indic, &c.—was affiliated to its predecessor through the medium of a church; that *all* the known universal churches were developed within the disintegrating bodies social of civilizations of the second generation; that none of the civilizations of the third generation, though several of them are (and all of them may be) broken-down and disintegrating, shows any convincing evidence of producing a second crop of universal churches.

We have therefore an historical series which may be tabulated as follows:

Primitive societies.
Civilizations of the first generation.
Civilizations of the second generation.
Universal churches.
Civilizations of the third generation.

With this table in mind, we are now in a position to approach the question whether the churches are, or are not, something more than the reproductive conveniences of a particular generation of civilizations.

(3) CHURCHES AS A HIGHER SPECIES OF SOCIETY

(*a*) A NEW CLASSIFICATION

So far we have worked on the assumption that civilizations have been the protagonists in history and that the role of churches, whether as hindrances (cancers) or helps (chrysalises) has been subordinate. Let us now open our minds to the possibility that the churches might be the protagonists, and that the histories of the civilizations might have to be envisaged and interpreted in terms, not of their own destinies, but of their effect on the history of Religion. The idea may seem novel and paradoxical, but it is, after all, the method of approach to history employed in the collection of books that we call the Bible.

On this view we shall have to revise our previous assumptions about the *raison d'être* of civilizations. We shall have to think of the civilizations of the second generation as having come into existence, not in order to perform achievements of their own, nor in order to reproduce their kind in a third generation, but in order to provide an opportunity for fully-fledged higher religions to come to birth; and, since the genesis of these higher religions was a consequence of the breakdowns and disintegrations of the secondary civilizations, we must regard the closing chapters of their histories —chapters which, from their standpoint, spell failure—as being their title to significance. In the same line of thought, we shall have to think of the primary civilizations as having come into existence for the same purpose. Unlike their successors, these first civilizations failed to bring fully-fledged higher religions to birth. The rudimentary higher religions of their internal proletariats —the worship of Tammuz and Ishtar and the worship of Osiris and Isis—did not come to flower. Yet these civilizations accomplished their mission indirectly by giving birth to secondary civilizations, out of which the fully-fledged higher religions did eventually arise, and the rudimentary religious products of the first civilizations made their contribution in course of time to the inspirations of the higher religions produced by the second generation.

On this showing, the successive rises and falls of the primary and the secondary civilizations are examples of a rhythm—observed in other contexts—in which the successive revolutions of a wheel carry forward the vehicle which the wheel conveys. And, if we ask why the descending movement in the revolution of the wheel of civilization should be the means of carrying forward the chariot of Religion, we shall find the answer in the truth that Religion is a spiritual activity and that spiritual progress is subject to a 'law' proclaimed by Aeschylus in the two words πάθει μάθος—'we learn by suffering'. If we apply this intuition of the nature of spiritual life to a spiritual endeavour that culminated in the flowering of Christianity and her sister higher religions, the Mahāyāna, Islam, and Hinduism, we may discern in the passions of Tammuz and Attis and Adonis and Osiris a foreshadowing of the Passion of Christ.

Christianity had arisen out of spiritual travail that was a consequence of the breakdown of the Hellenic civilization; but this was the latest chapter of a longer story. Christianity had Jewish and Zoroastrian roots, and these roots had sprung from the earlier breakdowns of two other secondary civilizations, the Babylonic and the Syriac. The kingdoms of Israel and Judah, in which the wellsprings of Judaism were to be found, had been two of the many warring parochial states of the Syriac world; and the overthrow of these mundane commonwealths and the extinction of all their political ambitions were the experiences that had brought the religion of Judaism to birth and had evoked its highest expression in the elegy of the Suffering Servant,[1] composed in the sixth century B.C. during the last throes of the Syriac Time of Troubles, on the eve of the foundation of the Achaemenian Empire.

This was not, however, the beginning of the story, for the Judaic root of Christianity had a Mosaic root of its own, and this pre-prophetic phase of the religion of Israel and Judah had been the

[1] Various passages in Deutero-Isaiah, notably ch. 53.

outcome of a previous secular catastrophe, the break-up of the 'New Empire' of Egypt, into whose internal proletariat the Israelites had been, according to their own traditions, conscripted. These same traditions told that the Egyptiac episode in their history had been preceded by a Sumeric initiation, in which Abraham, having received a revelation from the One True God, had been led to extricate himself from the doomed imperial city of Ur, at some time during the disintegration of the Sumeric civilization. Thus the first step in the spiritual progress which was to culminate in Christianity was traditionally associated with the first instance known to historians of the collapse of a universal state. In this perspective Christianity could be seen to be the climax of a spiritual progress which had not merely survived successive secular catastrophes but had drawn from them its cumulative inspiration.

On this reading, the history of Religion appears to be unitary and progressive by contrast with the multiplicity and repetitiveness of the histories of civilizations; and this contrast in the time-dimension presents itself in the space-dimension as well; for Christianity and the other three higher religions surviving in the twentieth century of the Christian Era had a closer affinity among themselves than coeval civilizations had been apt to have with one another. This affinity was conspicuously close as between Christianity and the Mahāyāna, which shared the same vision of God as a self-sacrificing saviour. As for Islam and Hinduism, they too reflected insight into the nature of God which gave them a distinctive meaning and mission of their own. Islam was a reaffirmation of the unity of God against the apparent weakening of Christianity's hold on this important truth, and Hinduism reaffirmed the personality of God as an object of human devotion against an apparent denial of the existence of personality in the Primitive Buddhist system of philosophy. The four higher religions were four variations on a single theme.

But, if so, why was it that, at least in the religions of Judaistic origin, Christianity and Islam, Man's glimpse of the unity of revelation had been confined hitherto to a few rare spirits, whereas the ordinary outlook had been the opposite? In the official view of each of the Judaistic higher religions, the light that shone through its own private window was the only full light, and all its sister religions were sitting in twilight, if not in darkness. The same standpoint was maintained by each sect of each religion as against its sister sects; and this refusal of diverse denominations to recognize what they had in common and to admit each other's claims gave occasion for the agnostic to blaspheme.

When we ask the question whether this deplorable state of

affairs is likely to continue indefinitely, we have to remind ourselves what the word 'indefinitely' in this context implies. We have to remember, that is to say, that, unless the human race uses its newly found techniques to extinguish animal life on this planet, human history is still in its infancy, and is likely to continue for countless thousands of years. In the light of that prospect the notion of an indefinite continuance of the present state of religious parochialism becomes absurd. Either the various churches and religions will snarl each other out of existence until no more is left of any of them than was left of the Kilkenny cats at the end of their strictly similar activities, or else a unified human race will find salvation in a religious unity. We have now to see if we can envisage, however tentatively, what the nature of that unity might be.

Lower religions are, of their nature, local; they are the religions of tribes or parochial states. The establishment of universal states obliterates the *raison d'être* of these religions and establishes large areas within which religions, higher or other, compete for converts. Religion thus begins to become a matter of personal choice. We have seen, more than once already in this Study, how a variety of religions competed for the prize won by Christianity within the Roman Empire. What would be the outcome of a new outburst of simultaneous missionary activities in a single field—this time, on a world-wide range? The histories of corresponding activities within the frameworks of the Achaemenian, Roman, Kushan, Han, and Guptan empires showed that the outcome might be either of two alternatives. Either a single religion might prove victorious or the competing religions might reconcile themselves to living side by side, as in the Sinic and Indic worlds. The two denouements were not quite so different as they might appear, for a victorious religion had usually achieved its victory by taking over some of the leading features of its rivals. In the pantheon of a triumphant Christianity, the figures of Cybele and Isis had reasserted themselves in the transfiguration of Mary as the Great Mother of God, and the lineaments of Mithras and of Sol Invictus were visible in the militant presentation of Christ. Similarly, in the pantheon of a triumphant Islam, a banished God Incarnate had stolen back in the guise of a deified 'Alī, while a forbidden idolatry had reasserted itself in the Founder's own act of reconsecrating the fetish-worship of the Black Stone in the Ka'bah at Mecca. Nevertheless, the difference between the two alternative denouements is momentous; and ·the children of a twentieth-century Westernizing world could not be indifferent about the prospects in their own case.

Which was the more likely outcome? In the past, intolerance had prevailed when higher religions of Judaic origin had been in the field, while 'live and let live' had been the rule when the Indic ethos had been paramount. The answer in the present case might be determined by the nature of the adversaries whom the higher religions would find in their path.

Why did Christianity, after recognizing and proclaiming the Jewish insight that God is Love, readmit the incongruous Jewish concept of the Jealous God? This regression, from which Christianity had suffered grievous spiritual damage ever since, was the price that Christianity had paid for her victory in her life-and-death struggle with the worship of Caesar; and the restoration of peace through the Church's victory did not dissolve, but, on the contrary, confirmed, the incongruous association of Yahweh and Christ. In the hour of victory the intransigence of the Christian martyrs passed into the intolerance of the Christian persecutors. This early chapter of the history of Christianity was ominous for the spiritual prospects of a twentieth-century Westernizing world, because the worship of Leviathan, on which the early Christian Church had inflicted a defeat which had appeared to be decisive, had reasserted itself with the sinister emergence of a totalitarian type of state in which the Modern Western genius for organization and mechanization had been enlisted, with diabolic ingenuity, for the purpose of enslaving souls as well as bodies to a degree which had not been within the power of the worst-intentioned tyrants of the past. It looked as if, in a modern Westernizing world, the war between God and Caesar might have to be waged again; and it looked as if, in that event, the morally honourable yet spiritually perilous role of serving as a church militant would once again fall upon Christianity.

Christians born into the twentieth century of the Christian Era had therefore to reckon with the possibility that a second war with Caesar-worship might cost the Christian Church a second setback towards Yahweh-worship before she had recovered from the first. Yet, if they had faith to believe that, in the end, the revelation of God as Love incarnate in a suffering Christ would turn stony hearts into hearts of flesh, they might venture to peer into the prospects for Religion in a politically united world that would have been liberated by the Christian revelation from the worship of Yahweh as well as from the worship of Caesar.

When, towards the end of the fourth century of the Christian Era, the victorious Church began to persecute those who refused to join it, the pagan Symmachus entered a protest which contained the words: 'the heart of so great a mystery can never be reached by following one road only.' In this sentence the pagan came nearer to Christ than his Christian persecutors. Charity is the mother of insight, and uniformity is not possible in Man's approach to the

One True God, because human nature is stamped with the fruitful diversity which is the hallmark of God's creative work. Religion exists to enable human souls to receive the divine light, and it could not fulfil this purpose if it did not faithfully reflect the diversity of God's human worshippers. On this showing it might be surmised that the way of life offered, and the vision of God presented, by each of the living higher religions might prove to correspond to one of the major psychological types whose distinctive lineaments were gradually being brought to light by twentieth-century pioneers in this new field of human knowledge. If each of these religions did not genuinely satisfy some widely experienced human need, it is hardly conceivable that each of them should have succeeded in securing for such long periods the allegiance of so large a portion of the human race. In this light the diversity of the living higher religions would cease to be a stumbling-block and would reveal itself as a necessary corollary of the diversity of the Human Psyche.

If this view of the prospects of Religion were to carry conviction, it would open up a new view of the role of the civilizations. If the movement of the chariot of Religion was constant in its direction, the cyclic and recurrent movement of the rises and falls of civilizations might be not only antithetical but subordinate. It might serve its purpose, and find its significance, in promoting the chariot's ascent towards Heaven by periodic revolutions on Earth of 'the sorrowful wheel' of birth–death–birth.

In this perspective the civilizations of the first and second generations would clearly justify their existence, but the claims of those of the third generation would seem, at first sight, more dubious. The first generation had produced, in their decline, the rudiments of higher religions; the second generation had produced four fully-fledged representatives of the species which were still active at the time of writing. Such new religions as might conceivably be discerned among the productions of the internal proletariats of the third generation seemed, at the time of writing, to make a very poor showing; and, though, as George Eliot wrote, 'prophecy is the most gratuitous form of human error', one might run no great risk in forecasting that they would prove to be of no account in the long run. Perhaps the one conceivable justification for the existence of the Modern Western civilization, on the view of history that we are now presenting, was that it might perform for Christianity and her three living sister religions the service of providing them with a mundane meeting-ground on a world-wide scale, by bringing home to them the unity of their own ultimate values and beliefs, and by confronting them all alike with the challenge of a recrudescence of idolatry in the peculiarly vicious form of Man's corporate worship of himself.

(b) THE SIGNIFICANCE OF THE CHURCHES' PAST

The position taken in the previous section of this chapter is open to attack both from those who regard all religion as make-believe and wishful thinking, and from those who condemn the churches as always and entirely unworthy of the faiths which they profess. To deal with the former line of attack would be outside the scope of this Study of History; and, if we restrict ourselves to the latter, we shall heartily agree that our critic has plenty of material for his indictment. The leaders of the Christian Church, for example, at various times from the earliest to the most recent, might seem almost to have gone out of their way to deny their Founder by appropriating to themselves the priestcraft and pharisaism of the Jews, the polytheism and idolatry of the Greeks, and the legal-minded championship of vested interests which was the legacy of the Romans; and the other higher religions were not less vulnerable to criticism on similar lines.

Such failures might be explained, though not of course excused, by the quip of a witty Victorian bishop who, when asked why the clergy were such fools, replied, 'What can you expect? We have only the laity to draw on'. Churches are composed not of saints but of sinners, and the churches, like the schools, of any society at any time cannot be very much in advance of the society in which they live and move and have their being. But the adversary might return to the charge and rudely reply to our Victorian bishop that the selection that his church had made from that same laity was not of the cream but of the dregs. One of the charges constantly brought by politically-minded opponents against the Christian Church in the Modern Western world was that it had been a drag upon the wheels of progress.

'As a post-Christian Western civilization developed out of Western Christendom from the seventeenth century onwards, the Church, rightly fearing the spread of secularism and the reversion to neo-paganism, wrongly identified the Faith with the social system that was passing away. Thus, while conducting an intellectual rearguard action against "liberal", "modernist", and "scientific" errors, it incautiously fell into an attitude of political archaism, supporting feudalism, monarchy, aristocracy, "capitalism", and the *ancien régime* generally, and became the ally and often the tool of political reactionaries who were as anti-Christian as the common "revolutionary" enemy. Hence the unedifying political record of modern Christianity: in the nineteenth century it allied itself with monarchism and aristocracy in order to denounce liberal democracy; in the twentieth century it allies itself with liberal democracy in order to denounce totalitarianism. Thus it had seemed, ever since the French Revolution [always] to be one political phase behind the times. This, of course, is the gist of the Marxist criticism of Christianity in the Modern World. The Christian answer would perhaps be that, when the Gadarene swine of a disintegrating civilization are engaged in their headlong downward rush, it may be the Church's responsibility to keep in the rear of the herd and direct the eyes of as many as possible backwards up the slope.'[1]

Those to whom Religion was moonshine might merely be confirmed by these charges, and by many others which might be brought, in the standpoint which they had already adopted. On the other hand, those who, like the author of this Study, believed that Religion was the most important thing in life might be moved by this belief to take a very long view; to recall a past which, though relatively short, nevertheless faded into the mists of antiquity and to envisage a future which, unless cut short by race-suicide, committed with a hydrogen bomb or some other *chef-d'œuvre* of western technology, must be going to run to an almost inconceivably long tale of aeons.

(c) THE CONFLICT BETWEEN HEART AND HEAD

How were souls in search of God to disengage the essence of Religion from its accidents? How, in an *Oikoumenê* that was being united on a world-wide range, were Christians, Buddhists, Muslims, and Hindus to make further progress along this road? The only way open to these fellow seekers after spiritual light was the hard road along which their predecessors had arrived at the degree of religious enlightenment represented by the higher religions of the twentieth century of the Christian Era. By comparison with the stage embodied in primitive paganism, their relative enlightenment clearly represented a marvellous advance; but they could no longer rest on their predecessors' labours, because they were being racked by a conflict between heart and head which they could not leave unresolved, and which could be resolved only by a further spiritual move forward.

In order to resolve this conflict one had to understand how it had arisen, and fortunately the origin of the current conflict between heart and head was not obscure. It had been precipitated by the impact of Modern Western science on the higher religions, and it had overtaken them at a stage in their course when they were still carrying along with them a mass of ancient traditions which would,

[1] Comment given to the author by Mr. Martin Wight, and printed in *A Study of History*, vol. vii, p. 457.

by now, have been obsolescent in any view, even if the Modern scientific view had never come to light.

This was not the first instance of an encounter between Religion and Rationalism that was known to history. At least two previous instances were on record. To recall first the more recent of the two, we may remind ourselves that the four living higher religions had each encountered—and each, in this instance, had succeeded in coming to terms with—an older version of Rationalism in an earlier chapter of each religion's history. The now orthodox theology of each of them had been the product of an accommodation with an established secular philosophy which the rising religion had found itself unable to reject, or even to ignore, because this school of thought had governed the mental climate of a cultivated minority in the society that had at that time been the church's mission field. Christian and Islamic theology was a presentation of Christianity and Islam in terms of Hellenic philosophy, and Hindu theology was a presentation of Hinduism in terms of Indic philosophy, while the Mahāyāna was a school of Indic philosophy which had converted itself into a religion without ceasing to be a philosophy at the same time.

That was not, however, the first chapter in this story; for the philosophies, which were already hard-set systems of ideas at the time when the rising higher religions had to reckon with them, had once been dynamic intellectual movements; and in this youthful stage of life and growth—which was comparable to the growth-stage of Modern Western science—the Hellenic and Indic philosophies had had encounters with the pagan religions which the Hellenic and Indic civilizations had inherited from Primitive Man.

At first sight it might look as if these two precedents were re-assuring. If Mankind had survived two past encounters between Religion and Rationalism, was not that a good augury for the out-come of the current conflict? The answer was that, in the earlier of these two previous encounters, the current problem had not arisen, while in the later encounter it had received a solution which had been so efficacious for the purposes of its own time and place that it had survived to become the crux of the problem confronting a twentieth-century Westernizing world.

In the encounter between a dawning philosophy and a traditional paganism there had been no problem of reconciling Heart and Head because there had been no common ground on which the two organs could have come into collision. The pith of primitive religion is not belief but action, and the test of conformity is not assent to a creed but participation in ritual performances. Primitive religious practice is an end in itself, and it does not occur to the practitioners to look beyond the rites that they perform for a truth which these rites might convey. The rites have no meaning beyond the practical effect which their correct execution is believed to produce. Accordingly, when, in this primitive religious setting, philosophers arise who set out to make a chart of Man's environment in intellectual terms to which the labels 'true' and 'false' apply, no collision occurs so long as the philosopher continues to carry out his hereditary religious duties; and there can be nothing in his philosophy to inhibit him from doing this, because there is nothing in the traditional rites that could be incompatible with any philosophy. Philosophy and primitive religion encountered one another without colliding, and at least one conspicuous apparent exception to this rule takes on a different complexion under closer scrutiny. Socrates was not a philosophic martyr put to death by a persecuting paganism. An examination of the circumstances makes it clear that his judicial murder was an incident in the savage political strife between contending parties that followed the defeat of Athens in the Peloponnesian War. If the leader of the Athenian 'Fascists' had not been numbered among his pupils, Socrates would presumably have died as peacefully in his bed as did Confucius, his 'opposite number' in the Sinic pagan world.

A new situation arose when the higher religions came on the scene. These higher religions did, indeed, sweep up and carry along with them a heavy freight of traditional rites that happened to be current in the societies in which the new faiths made their first appearance; but this religious flotsam was not, of course, their essence. The distinctive new feature of the higher religions was that they based their claim to allegiance on personal revelations held to have been received by their prophets; and these deliveries of the prophets were presented, like the propositions of the philosophers, as statements of fact, to be labelled 'true' or 'false'. Therewith Truth became a disputed mental territory; henceforward there were two independent authorities, prophetic Revelation and philosophical Reason, each of which claimed sovereign jurisdiction over the intellect's whole field of action. Thus it became impossible for Reason and Revelation to live and let live on the auspicious precedent of the amicable symbiosis of Reason and Ritual. 'Truth', it now seemed, had two forms, each claiming an absolute and overriding validity, yet each at odds with the other. In this new and excruciating situation there were only two alternatives. Either the rival exponents of the two now coexisting forms of Truth must arrive at a compromise or they must fight it out until one party or the other had been driven off the field.

In the encounters between Hellenic and Indic philosophy on one side and Christian, Islamic, Buddhist, and Hindu revelation on the other, the parties had arrived at a peaceful accommodation in which Philosophy had tacitly consented to suspend the exercise of rational criticism against the deliveries of Revelation in exchange for being allowed to reformulate the prophets' messages in the sophists' language. We need not doubt that the compromise was made in good faith on both sides, but we can see that it contained no real solution of the problem of the relation between scientific and prophetic Truth. The would-be reconciliation of the two kinds of Truth in terms of the new mental discipline called Theology was no more than verbal, and the formulae consecrated in creeds were doomed to prove impermanent because they left the equivocal meaning of Truth as ambiguous as they had found it. This pseudo-solution of the second conflict had been handed down the generations to become more of a hindrance than a help towards the solution of the conflict of Religion and Rationalism in the present day Westernizing world. The true solution could not be found until it had been recognized that the same word 'Truth', when used by philosophers and scientists and when used by prophets, does not refer to the same realities but is a homonym for two different forms of experience.

The conflict had been bound to break out again sooner or later as a result of the compromise that we have described; for, when once the truth of Revelation had been formulated verbally in terms of the truth of Science, men of science could not for ever forbear to criticize a body of doctrine which purported to be scientifically true. On the other side Christianity, when once its doctrine had been formulated in rational language, could not refrain from claiming authority over provinces of knowledge which were Reason's legitimate domain; and, when, in the seventeenth century, a Modern Western science began to cast off the spell of Hellenic philosophy and to break new intellectual ground, the first impulse of the Roman Church was to issue an injunction against the aggression of an awakening Western intellect upon the Church's old Hellenic intellectual ally—as if a geocentric theory of astronomy had been an article of the Christian faith, and Galileo's correction of Ptolemy had been a theological error.

By the year A.D. 1952 this war between Science and Religion had been raging for three hundred years and the position of the ecclesiastical authorities had come to be much the same as that of the Governments of Great Britain and France after Hitler's destruction of the remnant of Czechoslovakia in March, 1939. For more than two hundred years the churches had been seeing Science capture from them one province after another. Astronomy, Cosmogony, Chronology, Biology, Physics, Psychology had each in turn been seized and reconstructed on lines incompatible with the established religious teaching, and no end of these losses was in sight. As some ecclesiastical authorities saw the situation, the only remaining hope for the churches lay in complete intransigence.

This 'die-hard' spirit had found expression in the Roman Catholic Church in the decrees of the Vatican Council of A.D. 1869–70 and in the anathema pronounced against Modernism in A.D. 1907. In the domain of the Protestant Churches of North America it had entrenched itself in the 'Fundamentalism' of 'the Bible Belt'. It was similarly manifested in the Islamic world in the militantly archaistic movements of Wahhabism, Idrisism, Sanusism, and Mahdism. Such movements were symptoms, not of strength, but of weakness. They made it look as if the higher religions were riding for a fall.

The prospect that the higher religions might irretrievably lose their hold upon the allegiance of Mankind boded evil; for Religion is one of the essential faculties of human nature. When people are starved of Religion, the desperate spiritual straits to which they then find themselves reduced can fire them to extract grains of religious consolation out of the most unpromising ores. The classical example of this was the astonishing metamorphosis by which the religion of the Mahāyāna had been conjured out of the forbiddingly impersonal philosophy that had been the first attempt of the disciples of Siddhārtha Gautama to formulate the message of the Buddha. In a Westernizing world in the twentieth century of the Christian Era the beginnings of a similar metamorphosis of the materialist philosophy of Marxism were perhaps discernible in Russian souls that had been deprived of their traditional religious sustenance.

When Buddhism had been converted from a philosophy into a religion, a higher religion had been the happy outcome, but, if the higher religions were to be driven from the field, it was to be feared that lower religions would occupy the vacuum. In several countries the converts to new mundane ideologies, Fascism, Communism, National Socialism, and the like, had been strong enough to seize control of governments and to impose their doctrines and practices by methods of ruthless persecution. But these flagrant examples of the recrudescence of Man's ancient worship of himself in the panoply of his corporate power gave no measure of the actual prevalence of the malady. The most serious symptom was that, in professedly democratic and professedly Christian countries, four-fifths of the religion of five-sixths of the population was, in practice, now the primitive pagan worship of the deified community concealed under the fine name of patriotism. Moreover, this corporate self-worship was far from being either the only *revenant* or the most primitive of these haunting ghosts; for all the surviving primitive societies and all the hardly less primitive peasantries of the non-Western civilizations, amounting to three-quarters of the living generation of Mankind, were being conscripted into the Western society's swollen internal proletariat; and, in the light of historical precedents, the ancestral religious practices through which this host of humble new recruits would continue to seek satisfaction for their own religious needs seemed likely to find their way into the empty hearts of the proletariat's sophisticated masters.

On this showing, a crushing victory of Science over Religion would be disastrous for both parties; for Reason as well as Religion is one of the essential faculties of human nature. During the quarter of a millennium ending in August 1914 the Western man of science had been buoyed up by the naïve conviction that he had only to go on churning out fresh discoveries, to ensure that the World would go on getting better and better.

> When men of science find out something more,
> We shall be happier than we were before.[1]

But the scientist's conviction was vitiated by two fundamental errors. He was mistaken in attributing the relative well-being of the eighteenth-century and nineteenth-century Western world to his own achievements; and he was mistaken in assuming that this recently achieved well-being was going to persist. It was not the Promised Land but the Waste Land that was just round the corner.

The truth is that the command over non-human nature, which Science has in its gift, is of almost infinitely less importance to Man than his relations with himself, with his fellow men, and with God. Man's intellect would never have had a chance of making Man the Lord of Creation if Man's pre-human ancestor had not been endowed with the capacity for becoming a social animal, and if Primitive Man had not risen to this spiritual occasion so far as to school himself in those rudiments of sociality that are the intellect's indispensable conditions for performing its co-operative and cumulative work. Man's intellectual and technological achievements have been important to him, not in themselves, but only in so far as they have forced him to face, and grapple with, moral

---

[1] Belloc, H.: *Electric Light*, a burlesque Newdigate Prize poem, the subject impertinently presumed to have been chosen by the authorities of the University of Oxford in, perhaps, the 1890's.

issues which otherwise he might have managed to go on shirking. Modern Science has thus raised moral issues of profound importance, but it has not, and could not have, made any contribution towards solving them. The most important questions that Man must answer are questions on which Science has nothing to say. This was the lesson that Socrates had sought to teach when he abandoned the study of Physical Science in order to seek communion with the spiritual power that informs and governs the Universe.

We are now in a position to see what is required of Religion. It must be prepared to surrender to Science every province of intellectual knowledge, including those traditionally within Religion's field, to which Science might succeed in establishing a title. Religion's traditional dominion over intellectual fields had been an historical accident, and she had been a gainer in so far as she had parted with her dominion over these fields, because the management of them was no part of her business, which is to lead Man towards his true end of worshipping God and entering into communion with Him. Religion has unquestionably gained by relinquishing to Science the intellectual provinces of Astronomy, Biology, and the rest of the lost provinces that we have already listed. Even the surrender of Psychology, painful as it seemed, might prove as beneficent as it was painful, because it might strip away from a Christian theology some of those anthropomorphic veils that had proved in the past to be the most tenacious of all the barriers between the Human Soul and its Maker. If it could succeed in doing this, Science, so far from depriving the Soul of God, would assuredly prove to have brought the Soul one step nearer towards the infinitely distant goal of its journey.

If Religion and Science could each acquire humility and retain self-confidence in the spheres in which, for each of them, self-confidence and humility were respectively in place, they might find themselves in a mood that would be propitious for a reconciliation; but a propitious state of feeling is not a substitute for action; and, if a reconciliation was to be achieved, the parties must seek it through some joint endeavour.

This had been recognized in the past by the parties to the encounters between Christianity and Hellenic philosophy and between Hinduism and Indic philosophy. In both these encounters a conflict had been arrested by the pacificatory act of giving theological expression to religious ritual and myth in philosophical terms; but, as we have seen, this line of action had, in both cases, been an aberration based on a false diagnosis of the relation between spiritual and intellectual truth. It had proceeded on the mistaken assumption that spiritual truth could be formulated in intellectual terms. In a twentieth-century Westernizing world the Heart and the Head would be well advised to take warning from this ultimately unsuccessful experiment.

Even if it were feasible to discard the classic theology of the four living higher religions and to substitute a newfangled theology expressed in terms of Modern Western Science, a successful achievement of this *tour de force* would merely be a repetition of a previous error. A scientifically formulated theology (if such could be conceived) would prove as unsatisfying and ephemeral as the philosophically formulated theologies which were hanging like millstones round the necks of Buddhists, Hindus, Christians, and Muslims in the year A.D. 1952. It would be unsatisfying because the language of the intellect is inadequate for conveying the insight of the Soul; and it would be ephemeral because it is one of the merits of the intellect that it is constantly shifting its ground and discarding its previous conclusions.

What then should the Heart and the Head do to be reconciled, in the light of their historic failure to build a common platform for themselves in the shape of theology? Was there any opening for a combined operation in a more promising direction? At the time when these words were being written the mind of Western Man was still obsessed by the mounting triumphs of Physical Science which had recently been crowned by the superb achievement of dissecting the structure of the atom. Yet, if it were true that a mile gained in the progress of Man's control over non-human nature is of less importance to him than an inch gained in the enhancement of his capacity to deal with himself, his fellow men, and God, then it was conceivable that, of all Western Man's achievements in the twentieth century of the Christian Era, the feat that would loom largest in retrospect might be the breaking of new ground in the field of insight into human nature. A gleam of light might be caught in a passage from the shrewd pen of a contemporary English poet.

> No more across the Ocean ships return
> Fresh from the ends of Earth, the globe astern,
> Homeward for Europe's tiny corner bound,
> Tense with the tidings of a world new-found . . .
> Yet, even so, in spite of every change,
> One world remains where Fancy still may range,
> Remote, mysterious-sea'd, uncertain-shored,
> And only recently by men explored,
> A world of phantom-shapes, fear-haunted mists,
> Sailed not by seamen but psychologists,

Without equator, latitude, or pole,
The veiled, vague chaos of the human soul.[1]

The sudden entry of the Western scientific mind into this realm of
Psychology had been, in part, a by-product of two world wars
waged with weapons capable of producing shattering effects on
the Psyche. Thanks to the unprecedented clinical experience thus
provided, the Western intellect had descried the subconscious
depths of the Psyche and, in the act, had acquired a new conception of itself as a will-o'-the-wisp hovering over the surface of this
unplumbed psychic abyss.

The Subconscious may be likened to a child, a savage, even a
brute beast, which is at the same time also wiser, more honest, and
less prone to error than the conscious self. It is one of those statically
perfect works of creation that are the Creator's stopping places,
whereas the conscious human personality is an infinitely imperfect
approximation towards a Being of an incommensurably higher
order, who is Himself the maker of both these diverse but inseparable organs of the Human Psyche. If Modern Western minds
were to have discovered the Subconscious merely to find in it a new
object for idolatrous worship, they would be placing a fresh
barrier between themselves and God instead of seizing a fresh
opportunity to draw nearer to Him. For undoubtedly there was an
opportunity here.

If Science and Religion could seize their opportunity of drawing
nearer to God by jointly seeking to comprehend God's protean
creature, the Psyche, in its subconscious depths as well as on its
conscious surface, what would be the rewards that they might
expect to win, if success were to crown such a joint endeavour?
The prize would indeed be splendid, for the Subconscious, not the
intellect, is the organ through which Man lives his spiritual life.
It is the fount of poetry, music, and the visual arts, and the channel
through which the Soul is in communion with God. In this en-
thralling voyage of spiritual exploration the first objective would
be to seek insight into the workings of the Heart; for 'the Heart has
its reasons which the Reason does not know'. The second objective
would be to explore the nature of the difference between rational
truth and intuitive truth, in the belief that each of them is genuine
Truth—each in its own sphere. The third objective would be to
seek to strike the underlying rock of fundamental Truth on which
rational and intuitive truth alike must be founded. And the final
objective, in striving to strike rock-bottom in the psychic cosmos,

[1] Skinner, Martyn: *Letters to Malaya III and IV* (London 1943, Putnam),
pp. 41 and 43.

would be to attain to a fuller vision of God the Dweller in the Innermost.

The warning, so unfortunately ignored by well-intentioned theologians, that 'it hath not pleased God to give His people salvation in dialectic',[1] is one of the refrains of the Gospels. 'Suffer little children, and forbid them not, to come unto me; for of such is the Kingdom of Heaven. . . . Except ye be converted and become as little children, ye shall not enter into the Kingdom of Heaven.' From the standpoint of the Reason, the Subconscious is indeed a childlike creature, both in its humble-minded attunedness to God, which the Reason cannot emulate, and in its undisciplined inconsequence, which the Reason cannot approve. Conversely, in the sight of the Subconscious, the Reason is a heartless pedant who has purchased a miraculous command over Nature at the price of betraying the Soul by allowing her vision of God to fade into the light of common day. Yet the Reason is not, of course, the enemy of God, any more than the realm of the Subconscious is, in truth, outside Nature's bounds. The Reason and the Subconscious alike are God's creatures: each has its appointed field and task, and they need not scandalize one another if they cease to trespass.

(d) THE PROMISE OF THE CHURCHES' FUTURE

If a generation born into the twentieth century of the Christian Era might look forward to a day when Heart and Head would have been reconciled, they might also hope to persuade Heart and Head to concur in a reading of the significance of the churches' past which would provide a starting-point for entering on the last stage of our inquiry into the relation between churches and civilizations. After having found that churches are not cancers, and that they are no more than incidentally chrysalises, we have been looking into the possibility that they may be a higher species of society. We cannot give our verdict on this issue without asking ourselves what light the churches' past may throw on the promise of their future; and here we have to remember first of all that, on the scale of historical time, the higher religions, and the churches in which they were embodied, were still exceedingly young. There is a hymn, popular in Victorian places of worship, which contains the verse

> Far down the ages now,
> Her journey well nigh done,
> The Christian Church pursues her way
> And longs to reach her home.

[1] Ambrose: *De Fide* Book I, ch. 5, § 42.

It is recorded of one incumbent that he instructed his congregation to alter the second line and sing 'Her journey just begun', and his action was entirely in accord with the facts of the case as understood by the writer of this Study. Civilizations were mere creatures of yesterday in comparison with the primitive societies, and the churches of the higher religions were less than half as old as the oldest civilizations.

What was the feature in a church, which differentiated it from both a civilization and a primitive society and which led us to classify churches as a distinct, and higher, species of the genus in which all these three types of society were embraced? The distinguishing mark of the churches was that they all had as a member the One True God. This human fellowship with the One True God, which had been approached in the primitive religions and had been attained in the higher religions, gave to these societies certain virtues not to be found in primitive societies or civilizations. It gave power to overcome the discord which was one of the inveterate evils of Human Society; it offered a solution of the problem of the meaning of history.

Discord is inveterate in human life because Man is the most awkward of all things in the World that Man is compelled to encounter; he is at one and the same time a social animal and an animal endowed with free will. The combination of these two elements means that, in a society consisting exclusively of human members, there will be a perpetual conflict of wills, and this conflict will be carried to suicidal extremity unless Man experiences the miracle of conversion. Man's conversion is necessary for Man's salvation because his free and insatiable will gives him his spiritual potency at the risk of alienating him from God. This risk will not have beset a pre-human social animal not blessed—or cursed— with a spiritual capacity for rising above the level of the Sub-conscious Psyche; for the Subconscious Psyche enjoys the same effortless harmony with God that its innocence assures to every non-human creature. This negatively blissful Yin-state was broken up when human consciousness and personality were created through a Yang movement in which 'God divided the light from the darkness'. Man's conscious self, which can serve as God's chosen vessel for the achievement of a miraculous spiritual advance, can also condemn itself to a lamentable fall, if its awareness of being made in God's image intoxicates it into idolizing itself. This suicidal infatuation, which is the wages of the sin of pride, is a spiritual aberration to which the Soul is perpetually prone in the unstable equilibrium which is the essence of human personality; and the Self cannot escape from itself by a spiritual retreat into the

Yin-state of *Nirvāna*. The recovered Yin-state in which salvation is to be found by Man is the peace not of nerveless self-annihilation but of taut-strung harmony. Psyche's task is to recapture a childlike virtue after having 'put away childish things'. The Self has to achieve its childlike reconciliation with God by the manful exertion of a God-given will to do the will of God and thereby evoke God's grace.

If this is Man's way of salvation, he has a rough road to tread; for the mighty act of creation which made him *homo sapiens* made it, by the same stroke, mortally hard for him to become *homo concors*; and a social animal that is *homo faber* must be co-operative if it is not to destroy itself.

In virtue of Man's innate sociality, every human society is potentially all-embracing. Down to the year A.D. 1952 no human society had ever yet become world-wide on every plane of social activity; but a secularized Modern Western civilization had latterly attained a virtual universality on the economic and technological plane without having achieved any comparable political or cultural success; and, after the shattering experience of two world wars, it was uncertain whether a political unification of the World could come to pass without the grimly familiar 'knock-out blow' that had been the traditional price of œcumenical unity in the histories of civilizations. In any case the unity of Mankind cannot be achieved by so coarse an expedient; it can be achieved only as an incidental result of acting on a belief in the unity of God and by seeing this unitary terrestrial society as a province of God's Commonwealth.

The great gulf fixed between the open society of the Commonwealth of God and the closed society exemplified in all the civilizations, and the spiritual leap without which this gulf cannot be crossed, had been pictured by a Modern Western philosopher:

'Man was designed for very small societies. That primitive societies were such is generally admitted, but it must be added that the primitive human soul continues to exist, concealed under habits without which civilizations could not have been created. . . . Civilized man differs from primitive mainly in the enormous mass of knowledge and of habits which he has acquired. . . . The natural man is buried under the acquired characteristics, but he is still there, practically unchanged. . . . It was a mistake to say "Drive out nature, she will return at the gallop", for you cannot drive her out. She is there all the time. Acquired characteristics are far from impregnating the organism and transmitting themselves hereditarily, as people used to suppose. . . . Repressed though it may be, primitive nature persists in the depths of the consciousness . . . it remains very much alive, in the most civilized societies. . . . Our civilized societies, different though they are from the kind of society for which we were originally intended, none the less resemble it in one essential respect. Both alike are closed societies. Vast though the civilizations may be in comparison with the petty groups for which we are adapted instinctively, they yet have the same characteristic of including some people and excluding others. Between the nation, however great it may be, and Humanity there is all the difference between the finite and the infinite, the closed and the open.

'Between the closed society and the open, the city and Humanity, there is a difference not just of degree, but of kind. The solidarity of a state is due primarily to its need to defend itself against other states; one loves one's fellow countrymen because one hates foreigners. That is primitive instinct, and it is still there beneath a superficial covering of civilization. We still feel a natural love for our relations and our neighbours, whereas love of Humanity is a cultivated taste. We reach the former direct, the latter only at second hand, for it is through God alone that Religion leads Man to love the Human Race; as also it is only through Reason that philosophers teach us the dignity of human personality, and the right of all men to be respected. Neither in the one case nor in the other do we reach the conception of Humanity by stages, by way of the family and the nation.'[1]

There can be no unity of Mankind without the participation of God; and, conversely, when the heavenly pilot is dropped, Man not only lapses into a discord which is at variance with his natural sociality; he is also tormented by a tragic crux which is inherent in his being a social creature, and which therefore presents itself the more sharply, the better he succeeds in living up to the moral requirements of his social nature, so long as he is seeking to play his part in a society of which the One True God is not a member. This crux is that the social action in which a human being fulfils himself immensely exceeds in its range, in both time and space, the limits of an individual's life on Earth. Thus History, seen solely from the standpoint of each individual human participant in it, is 'a tale told by an idiot, signifying nothing'. But this apparently senseless 'sound and fury' acquires spiritual meaning when Man catches in History a glimpse of the operation of the One True God.

Thus, while a civilization may be a provisionally intelligible field of study, the Commonwealth of God is the only morally tolerable field of action, and membership of this *Civitas Dei* on Earth is offered to human souls by the higher religions. Man's fragmentary and ephemeral participation in terrestrial history is indeed redeemed for him when he can play his part on Earth as the voluntary coadjutor of a God whose mastery of the situation gives a divine value and meaning to Man's otherwise paltry endeavours;

[1] Bergson, H.: *Les Deux Sources de la Morale et de la Religion* (Paris 1932, Alcan), pp. 24–28, 288, 293, 297.

and this redemption of History is so precious for Man that, in a secularized Modern Western world, a crypto-Christian philosophy of History had been retained by would-be ex-Christian rationalists.

'Because they put faith in the Bible and the Gospel, in the story of creation and in the announcement of the Kingdom of God, Christians were able to venture on a synthesis of the totality of History. All subsequent attempts of the same kind merely replaced the transcendent end that assured the unity of the mediaeval synthesis by various immanent forces that served as substitutes for God; but the enterprise remained substantially the same, and it was the Christians who first of all conceived it: namely, to provide the totality of History with an intelligible explanation, which shall account for the origin of Humanity and assign its end. . . .

'The whole Cartesian system is based on the idea of an omnipotent God who, in a way, creates Himself and therefore, *a fortiori*, creates the eternal truths, including those of mathematics, creates also the Universe *ex nihilo*, and conserves it by an act of continuous creation, without which all things would lapse back into that nothingness whence His will had drawn them. . . . Consider the case of Leibnitz. What would be left of his system if the properly Christian elements were suppressed? Not even the statement of his own basic problem—that, namely, of the radical origin of things and the creation of the Universe by a free and perfect God. . . . It is a curious fact, and well worth noting, that, if our contemporaries no longer appeal to the *City of God* and the Gospel as Leibnitz did not hesitate to do, it is not in the least because they have escaped their influence. Many of them live by what they choose to forget.'[1]

Finally, it is only in a society which worships the One True God that there can be a promise of exorcizing what, in an earlier part of this Study, was described as the perilousness of mimesis. The Achilles' heel in the social anatomy of a civilization is, as we have seen, its dependence on mimesis (imitation) as a 'social drill' for ensuring that the rank and file of Mankind shall follow their leaders. In the change-over from a Yin-state into a Yang-activity which takes place at the genesis of a civilization through a mutation in the character of a primitive society, the rank and file transfer their mimesis from their ancestors to the creative human personalities of the living generation; but the avenue thereby opened for a social advance may end in the gates of death, since no human being can be creative except within limits, and then no more than precariously; and, when an inevitable failure has bred an equally inevitable disillusionment, the discredited leaders are apt to resort to force in order to retain an authority that is morally

[1] Gilson, E.: *The Spirit of Mediaeval Philosophy*, English translation (London 1936, Sheed & Ward), pp. 390-1 and 14-17.

forfeit. In the *Civitas Dei* this peril is exorcized by a fresh transfer of mimesis—from the ephemeral leaders of mundane civilizations to a God who is the source of all human creativity.

This mimesis of God can never expose human souls that devote themselves to it to those disillusionments that are apt to attend the mimesis of even the most godlike human beings and that lead, when they arise, to the moral alienation of a restive proletariat from a now merely dominant minority. The communion between the Soul and the One True God cannot thus degenerate into the bondage of a slave to a despot, for in each of the higher religions, in diverse measure, the vision of God as Power is transfigured by the vision of Him as Love; and the presentation of this Loving God as a Dying God Incarnate is a theodicy which makes the Imitation of Christ immune against the tragedy inherent in any mimesis that is directed towards unregenerate human personalities.

XXVII. THE ROLE OF CIVILIZATIONS IN THE LIVES OF CHURCHES

(1) CIVILIZATIONS AS OVERTURES

IF the foregoing inquiry has convinced us that the churches embodying the higher religions are diverse approximations on Earth to one and the same *Civitas Dei*, and that the species of society of which this Commonwealth of God is the sole and unique representative is of a spiritually higher order than the species represented by the civilizations, we shall be encouraged to go farther in our experiment of inverting our original assumption that the role of civilizations is dominant in History and the role of churches subordinate. Instead of dealing with churches in terms of civilizations, we shall boldly make the new departure of dealing with civilizations in terms of churches. If we are looking for a social cancer we shall find it, not in a church which supplants a civilization, but in a civilization which supplants a church; and, if we have thought of a church as a chrysalis through which one civilization reproduces itself in another, we shall now have to think of the apparented civilization as being an overture to the epiphany of a church and of the affiliated civilization as being a regression from this higher level of spiritual attainment.

If we take, as a test case for the verification of this thesis, the genesis of the Christian Church, and cite the tenuous yet significant evidence afforded by the transference of words from a secular to a religious meaning and usage, we shall find this philological testimony supporting the view that Christianity is a religious theme with a secular overture, and that this overture consisted, not merely in the Roman political achievement of an Hellenic universal state, but in Hellenism itself, in all its phases and aspects.

The Christian Church is indebted for its very name to the technical term employed, in the city state of Athens, to denote the general assembly of the citizens for the transaction of political business; but, in thus borrowing the word *ecclesia*, the Church gave it a dual meaning which was a reflection of the political order of the Roman Empire. In Christian usage *ecclesia* came to mean both a local Christian community and the Church Universal.

When the Christian Church, local and universal, came to be articulated into the two religious classes of 'laity' and 'clergy', and when the 'clergy', in turn, came to be graded in a hierarchy of 'orders', the requisite terms were likewise borrowed from an existing secular Greek and Latin vocabulary. The 'laity' of the

Christian Church was designated by an archaic Greek word *laos* which denoted the people as distinct from those in authority over them. The 'clergy' took its name from a Greek word *Klêros*, whose general meaning of 'lot' had been specialized in a judicial sense to mean an allotted share of an inherited estate. The Christian Church adopted the word to mean the portion of the Christian community that God had allotted to Himself to serve Him as His professional priesthood. As for the 'orders' (*ordines*), they took their name from the politically privileged classes of the Roman body politic, the 'Senatorial Order' for example. The members of the highest order came to be known as 'overseers' (*episcopoi*, bishops).

The Christian Church's sacred book, in so far as it was not referred to as *ta biblia*—the Books—was designated by a term long since current in the vocabulary of the Roman inland revenue, *scriptura*. As for the two 'testaments', they were called *diathêkai* in Greek and *testamenta* in Latin because they were thought of as being the equivalent of legal instruments, or covenants, in which God had declared to Mankind, in two instalments, His 'will and testament' for the ordering of Human Life on Earth.

The training (*ascêsis*, hence 'ascetic') to which a spiritual élite in the early Christian Church subjected itself took its name from the physical training of athletes for the Olympian and other Hellenic games; and, when, in the fourth century, training to be an anchorite took the place of training to be a martyr, the action of this new-model Christian athlete, whose ordeal was to endure the solitude of the desert instead of facing the publicity of the criminal court and the amphitheatre, came to be designated by a Greek term, *anachorêtês*, originally applied to persons who had withdrawn from practical life, either to devote themselves to philosophical contemplation or as a protest against oppressive taxation. The word came to be applied to Christian enthusiasts, particularly in Egypt, who withdrew to the desert (the *erêmos*, whose denizen was an eremite or hermit) in search of communion with God and as a protest against mundane wickedness. When these solitaries (*monachoi*, monks), in defiance of the literal meaning of their name, took to living in disciplined communities, this creative contradiction in terms—a society of solitaries (*monastêrion*)—took its Latin name (*conventus*) from a word which, in the secular usage, had combined the two meanings of a quarter sessions and a chamber of commerce.

When the originally informal proceedings at the periodic meetings of each local church crystalized into a hard and fast ritual, this religious 'public service' (*leitourgia*, liturgy) took its name from the nominally voluntary expenditure which, in the Athenian Commonwealth of the fifth and fourth centuries B.C., had been euphemistically known by that honourable name to disguise the fact that they were virtually surtaxes. In this liturgy the crucial rite was a Holy Communion in which the worshippers achieved a living experience of their fellowship in and with Christ by partaking together of the 'sacrament' (*sacramentum*) of eating bread and drinking wine. This Christian sacrament took its name from a pagan Roman rite in which a new recruit was sworn in to membership in the Roman Army. The Holy Communion, which the sacrament consummated, took its name from a word which, both in its Greek form (*koinônia*) and its Latin translation (*communio*) had signified participation in any social concern, but, first and foremost, in a political community.

The evocation of a spiritual meaning out of a material one is an example of a process which, in an earlier part of this Study, we called 'etherialization' and have recognized as a symptom of growth. Our survey of the etherialization of the Greek and Latin vocabulary—which could easily be prolonged—suffices to indicate that Hellenism was an authentic *praeparatio evangelii* and that, in looking for the *raison d'être* of Hellenism in its service as an overture to Christianity, we have at any rate set our feet on a promising line of inquiry. On this showing, when the life of a civilization has served as an overture to the birth of a living church, the death of the precursor civilization may be regarded not as a disaster but as the proper conclusion of the story.

(2) CIVILIZATIONS AS REGRESSIONS

We have been trying to see how history looks if we break with our Modern Western habit of viewing the histories of churches in terms of the histories of civilizations and adopt, instead, the inverse standpoint, and this has led us to think of civilizations of the second generation as overtures to the living higher religions, and consequently to regard these civilizations, not as failures branded by their breakdowns and disintegrations, but as successes in virtue of their service in helping these higher religions to come to birth. On this analogy the civilizations of the third generation are presumably to be thought of as regressions from the higher religions that had arisen out of the preceding civilizations' ruins; for, if the mundane miscarriage of those now defunct civilizations ought to be judged to have been redeemed by its spiritual sequel, then the mundane achievement of the living civilizations in breaking out of their ecclesiastical chrysalises and setting out to live a new secular life of their own ought likewise to be judged on the criterion of its effect on the life of the Soul; and this effect has manifestly been an adverse one.

If we take as a test case the eruption of a Modern Western secular civilization out of the Medieval Western *Respublica Christiana*, we may find it illuminating to begin, on the lines of our inquiry in the first half of this chapter, by citing the evidence of words that had undergone a change of meaning and usage, and we may begin with the word cleric. Side by side with the 'clerk in holy orders' we have the humble secular clerk who in England performs minor office work and in America serves behind the counter in a store. 'Conversion', which once implied the turning of the Soul towards God, is now more familiar in such contexts as the conversion of coal into electric power or the conversion of a 5 per cent. into a 3 per cent. stock. We hear little of a 'cure of souls' but much of the 'cures' of the body performed by drugs; and 'holy day' has become holiday. All this betokens a linguistic dis-etherialization, which merely symbolizes a secularization of society.

'Frederick II had been the ward and pupil of the great Innocent, founder of the Church as a state. He was an intellectual man, and we need not wonder to find in his conception of the Empire a reflection of the Church. The whole Italian-Sicilian State, which the Popes coveted as their Patrimony of Peter, became, as it were, the Patrimony of Augustus for this gifted monarch, who sought to release the secular and intellectual powers that were fused into the spiritual unity of the Church and to build a new empire based on these. . . . Let us grasp the full significance of Frederick's Italian-Roman State: a mighty pan-Italian seignory, which for a short time united in one state Germanic, Roman, and Oriental elements—Frederick himself, Emperor of the World, being the Grand Signor and Grand Tyrant thereof, the last of these princes to wear the diadem of Rome, whose Caesarhood was not only allied with German kingship, like Barbarossa's, but with Oriental-Sicilian despotism. Having grasped this, we perceive that all the tyrants of the Renaissance, the Scala and Montefeltre, the Visconti, Borgia, and Medici, are, down to the tiniest features, the sons and successors of Frederick II, the diadochi of this "Second Alexander".'[1]

The list of Frederick of Hohenstaufen's 'successors' could be prolonged down to the twentieth century of the Christian Era, and the secular civilization of the Modern Western world may be regarded, in one of its aspects, as an emanation of his spirit. It would, of course, be absurd to pretend that, in the struggle between the Church and the secular princes, all the faults were on one side, but what we are concerned to observe here is that the monstrous birth

[1] Kantorowicz, E.: *Frederick the Second*, 1194–1250, English translation (London 1931, Constable), pp. 561–2, 493–4.

of a secular civilization out of the womb of a *Respublica Christiana* had been made practicable by the renaissance of the Hellenic institution of an 'absolute' state, in which religion had been a department of politics.

When a civilization of the third generation breaks its way out of a body ecclesiastic, is a renaissance of the 'apparented' civilization of the second generation an invariable and indispensable means to its accomplishment? If we look at the history of the Hindu civilization we shall find there no parallel resuscitation of the empire of the Mauryas or that of the Guptas; but, when we turn from India to China and look at the history of the Far Eastern civilization in its homeland, we do here find an unmistakable and striking counterpart to the revival of the Roman Empire in the Sui and T'ang revival of the Empire of the Han. The difference will be found in the circumstance that this Sinic renaissance of imperialism was far more successful than the Hellenic renaissance of a 'Holy Roman' Empire, and indeed more successful than the parallel Hellenic renaissance of a Byzantine Empire in the realm of the Eastern Orthodox Christian society. For the purpose of our present inquiry it is significant that the civilization of the third generation in whose history the renaissance of its predecessor had been carried to the greatest lengths should likewise have been the most successful in shaking itself free from the trammels of the church which its predecessor had brought to birth. The Mahāyānian Buddhism which had bidden fair to captivate a moribund Sinic world as thoroughly as a moribund Hellenic world had been captivated by Christianity had reached its zenith in the Far East at the nadir of the post-Sinic interregnum, but it had swiftly declined thereafter. On this showing, we must conclude that the renaissance of a dead civilization spells a regression from a living higher religion and that, the farther the revival is pushed, the greater the backsliding will be.

XXVIII. THE CHALLENGE OF
MILITANCY ON EARTH

IN the preceding chapter we observed that a secular civilization that breaks out of a body ecclesiastic is apt to win its way with the aid of elements from the life of the antecedent civilization, but we have still to see how the opportunity for this break-away arises; and evidently this 'beginning of evils' is to be looked for in some weak point, or false step, of the church at whose cost the eruption is achieved.

One formidable crux for a church is inherent in its *raison d'être*. A church is militant on Earth for the purpose of winning This World for the *Civitas Dei*, and this means that a church has to deal with secular as well as spiritual affairs and to organize itself on Earth as an institution. The gross institutional integument with which a church thus finds itself compelled to clothe its etherial nakedness, in order to do God's business in a recalcitrant environment, is incongruous with a church's spiritual nature; and it is not surprising to see disaster overtaking a terrestrial outpost of the Communion of Saints which, in This World, cannot do its spiritual work without being drawn into grappling with secular problems, which it has to attack with institutional tools.

The most celebrated tragedy of the kind is the history of the Hildebrandine Papacy, and in an earlier part of this Study we have observed how Hildebrand was dragged over the precipice by an apparently inevitable concatenation of causes and effects. He would not be a true servant of God if he did not throw himself into the struggle to reclaim the clergy from sexual and financial corruption; he could not reform the clergy unless he tightened up the organization of the Church; he could not tighten up the organization of the Church without arriving at a demarcation of the jurisdictions of church and state; and, since the functions of church and state were, in the feudal age, inextricably entangled, he could not arrive at a demarcation satisfactory to the Church without encroaching on the sphere of the state in a manner which the state was justified in resenting. Hence a conflict which began as a war of manifestoes and rapidly degenerated into a war of force, in which the resources of each side were 'money and guns'.

The tragedy of the Hildebrandine Church is a prominent example of spiritual regression precipitated by a church's becoming entangled in mundane affairs and committed to secular modes of action as an incidental consequence of its trying to do its own business. There is, however, another broad road leading to the same spiritually destructive worldliness. A church incurs the risk of falling into a spiritual regression in the very act of living up to its own standards. For the will of God is partially expressed in the righteous social aims of mundane societies, and these mundane ideals may be achieved all the more successfully by those who are aiming, not at these ideals as ends in themselves, but at something higher. Two classic examples of the working of this law were the achievements of Saint Benedict and those of Pope Gregory the Great. Both these saintly souls were bent upon the spiritual aim of promoting the monastic way of life in the West; yet, as a by-product of their spiritual work, these two unworldly men performed economic prodigies that were beyond the powers of secular statesmen. Their economic achievement would be praised by Christian and Marxian historians alike; yet, should these praises become audible to Benedict and Gregory in an Other World, these saints would assuredly recall, with a pang of misgiving, their Master's saying: 'Woe unto you when all men shall speak well of you'; and their misgiving would certainly turn to anguish if they were enabled to revisit This World and to see with their own eyes the ultimate moral consequences of the eventual economic effects of their immediate spiritual endeavours during their life on Earth.

The disconcerting truth is that the incidental material fruits of the spiritual labours of the *Civitas Dei* are not only certificates of its spiritual success; they are also snares in which the spiritual athlete may be trapped more diabolically than an impetuous Hildebrand is ruined by entanglement in politics and war. The thousand years of monastic history between the times of Saint Benedict and the pillaging of ecclesiastical institutions in the so-called 'Reformation' is a familiar story, and it is unnecessary to believe all the allegations of Protestant and anti-Christian writers. The quotation which follows is taken from the work of a modern writer who is above suspicion of anti-monastic bias, and it may be noted that his description does not refer to what is commonly regarded as the latest and worst period of pre-Reformation monasticism.

'The gulf which appeared between abbot and convent was largely caused by the accumulation of wealth. As time went by, the estates of the monasteries became so enormous that the abbot found himself almost fully occupied in the administration of his lands and in the various responsibilities which these entailed. A similar process of division of estates and duties was taking place at the same time among the monks themselves. . . . Each monastery was divided into what were practically separate departments, each with its own income and its own special responsibilities. . . . As Dom David Knowles says: "Save in monasteries such as Winchester, Canterbury, and Saint Albans, where strong intellectual or artistic interests existed, business of this kind was the career that absorbed all the talent of the house.' . . . For such as had administrative gifts, but were not blessed with any property on which to exert them, the monasteries, with their vast estates, offered much scope.'[1]

Yet the monk who has degenerated into a successful man of business does not exemplify the most deadly form that spiritual regression can take. The worst temptation that lies in wait for the citizens of the *Civitas Dei* in This World is neither to plunge into politics nor to slide into business but to idolize the terrestrial institution in which a Church Militant on Earth is imperfectly though unavoidably embodied. If *corruptio optimi* is *pessima*, an idolized church is the one idol that is more pernicious than the idolized human ant-heap that men worship as Leviathan.

A church is in danger of lapsing into this idolatry in so far as she lapses into believing herself to be, not merely a depository of truth, but the sole depository of the whole truth in a complete and definitive revelation of it; and she is specially prone to set her feet on this descent of Avernus after she has suffered some heavy blow, and particularly if the stroke has been struck by members of her own household. The classic example had been the Counter-Reformational Tridentine Roman Catholic Church, as non-Catholics saw her. For four hundred years already, down to the time of writing, she had been standing on guard, in a posture that was as rigid as her vigilance was unrelaxing, massively armoured with the helmet of the Papacy and the breastplate of the hierarchy, and continually presenting arms to God in the recurrent rhythm of an exacting liturgy. The subconscious purpose of this heavy institutional panoply was to outlast the very toughest of the contemporary secular institutions of This World. In the twentieth century of the Christian Era a Catholic critic could argue with force, in the light of four hundred years of Protestant history, that a Protestant impatience of even the lighter equipment of pre-Tridentine Catholicism had been premature. Yet that verdict, even if cogent, would not prove either that the casting off of impedimentā would always be a mistake or that the Tridentine multiplication of them had not also been an error.[2]

---

[1] Moorman, J. R. H.: *Church Life in England in the Thirteenth Century* (Cambridge 1945, University Press), pp. 279–80, 283, 353.

[2] The foregoing paragraph, together with all the rest of this Part of 'The Study of History', was submitted in typescript to the author's friend, Mr. Martin Wight, and the full version of the book reproduces a number of comments by him, including the following: 'A Roman Catholic critic would reply to you here, in words that you so often quote, "Respice finem". The whole of the foregoing passage is anticipation: it has not yet come true. Is it not the fact that the Roman

We have now laid our finger on some of the causes of regression from higher religions to vain repetitions of secular civilizations, and in each case we have found that the calamity is precipitated, not by a *saeva necessitas* or by any other external force, but by an 'Original Sin' which is innate in terrestrial human nature. But, if regressions from higher religions are effects of Original Sin, are we driven to conclude that such regressions are inevitable? If they are, this would mean that the challenge of militancy on Earth was so prohibitively severe that no church would ever be capable of standing up to it in the long run; and that conclusion, in turn, would drive us back towards the view that the churches are good for nothing better than to serve as ephemeral chrysalises for vainly repetitive civilizations. Is this the last word? Before we resign ourselves to a suggestion that God's inflowing light is doomed to be perpetually overwhelmed by an uncomprehending darkness, let us cast our eyes back once again over the series of spiritual illuminations brought into the World by the epiphanies of the higher religions; for these chapters of past spiritual history may prove to be auguries of spiritual recovery from the regressions to which a Church Militant is prone.

We have noticed that the successive milestones in Man's spiritual advance which are inscribed with the names of Abraham, Moses, the Prophets, and Christ all stand at points where a surveyor of the course of secular civilization would report breaks in the road and breakdowns in the traffic; and the empirical evidence has given us reason to believe that this coincidence of high points in Man's religious history with low points in his secular history may be one of the 'laws' of Man's terrestrial life. If so, we should expect to find, also, that the high points in secular history coincide with low points in religious history, and that the religious achievements that accompany mundane declines are therefore not merely spiritual advances but also spiritual recoveries. They are, of course, presented as recoveries in the traditional version of the story.

Church is incomparably more vigorous and influential in the twentieth century than at any time since the Council of Trent? Whereas in 1870 it inscribed the Infallibility of the Pope among its dogmas, at the apparent nadir of its fortunes, as an act of defiance, in 1950 it was able still further to scandalize a secular Western world by adding the dogma of the Assumption of the Virgin as an act of self-confidence. Is it not equally likely, at the time of writing, that the Roman Church in its Tridentine panoply will be the only Western institution capable of challenging and withstanding the neo-pagan totalitarian Communist state, and is not this borne out by the particular fear and hatred with which Moscow regards the Vatican? If this be so, the figure of the dinosaur's carapace will be less apt than that of a long and successfully sustained siege, and the Tridentine phase of Catholic history may appear in retrospect like the Churchillian phase of British history from the fall of France to D-Day. You prejudge the outcome. "Respice finem."¹

The call of Abraham, for example, is presented in Hebrew legend as a sequel to a defiance of God by the self-confident builders of the Tower of Babel. The mission of Moses is presented as a move to rescue God's Chosen People from a spiritually unpropitious enjoyment of the fleshpots of Egypt. The Prophets of Israel and Judah were inspired to preach repentance from the spiritual back-slidings into which Israel had lapsed when he made a material success of the exploitation of the 'land flowing with milk and honey' which Yahweh had provided for him. The Ministry of Christ, whose Passion, as a secular historian sees it, is fraught with all the anguish of an Hellenic Time of Troubles, is presented in the Gospels as an intervention of God Himself for the purpose of ex-tending to the whole of Mankind a covenant previously made by God with an Israel whose descendants had alloyed their spiritual heritage with a Pharisaic formalism, a Sadducaean materialism, an Herodian opportunism, and a Zealot fanaticism.

On this showing, four outbursts of spiritual illumination had been sequels to spiritual eclipses, besides having been accompani-ments of mundane disasters, and we may surmise that this is no chapter of accidents. We observed in an earlier part of this Study that physically hard environments are apt to be nurseries of mun-dane achievements, and, on this analogy, it is to be expected that spiritually hard environments will have a stimulating effect on religious endeavour. A spiritually hard environment would be one in which the Soul's aspirations are choked by material prosperity. A miasma of worldly prosperity, which stupefies the mass, might well provoke spiritually sensitive and strenuous souls into a de-fiance of the charms of This World.

Would a return to religion in the world of the twentieth century of the Christian Era mark a spiritual advance, or would it be an abject attempt at an impossible evasion of the hard facts of life as we know it? Our answer to this question will partly depend on our estimate of the possibilities of spiritual growth.

We have already touched upon the probability that the world-wide expansion of a secular Modern Western civilization would translate itself into political form at no distant date through the establishment of a universal state which would fulfil at last the ideal of a polity of this species by embracing the entire surface of the planet in a commonwealth that would have no physical fron-tiers. In the same context we considered the possibility that, within such a framework, the respective adherents of the four living higher religions might come to recognize that their once rival systems were so many alternate approaches to the One True God along avenues offering diverse partial glimpses of the Beatific Vision. We threw out the idea that, in this light, the historic living churches might eventually give expression to this unity in diversity by growing together into a single Church Militant. Supposing that this were to happen, would it mean that the Kingdom of Heaven would then have been established on Earth? In the Western World of the twentieth century of the Christian Era this was an inevitable question, because some kind of earthly paradise was the goal of most of the secular ideologies. In the writer's opinion, the answer was in the negative.

The manifest reason for a negative answer is exhibited by the nature of Society and the nature of Man. For Society is nothing but the common ground between the fields of action of personalities, and human personality has an innate capacity for evil as well as for good. The establishment of such a single Church Militant as we have imagined would not purge Man of Original Sin. This World is a province of the Kingdom of God, but it is a rebellious province, and, in the nature of things, it will always remain so.

VIII
HEROIC AGES

XXIX. THE COURSE OF THE TRAGEDY

(1) A SOCIAL BARRAGE

WHEN a growing civilization breaks down through the deterioration of an attractively creative into an odiously dominant minority, one of the results is the estrangement of its former proselytes in the once primitive societies round about, which the civilization in its growth stage was influencing in divers degrees by the effect of its cultural radiation. The ex-proselytes' attitude changes from an admiration expressing itself in mimesis to a hostility breaking out into warfare, and this warfare may have one or other of two alternative outcomes. On a front on which the local *terrain* offers the aggressive civilization the possibility of advancing up to a natural frontier in the shape of some unnavigated sea or untraversed desert or unsurmounted mountain range, the barbarians may be decisively subjugated; but, where such a natural frontier is absent, geography is apt to militate in the barbarians' favour. Where the retreating barbarian has open to him, in his rear, an unlimited field of manœuvre, the shifting battle-front is bound, sooner or later, to arrive at a line at which the aggressive civilization's military superiority will be neutralized by the handicap of the ever-lengthening distance of the front from the aggressor's base of operations.

Along this line a war of movement will change into a static war without having reached any military decision, and both parties will find themselves in stationary positions in which they will be living side by side, as the creative minority of the civilization and its prospective proselytes were living before the breakdown of the civilization set them at variance with one another. But the psychological relation between the parties will not have reverted from hostility to its previous creative interplay, and there will have been no restoration, either, of the geographical conditions under which this cultural intercourse once took place. In the growth stage, the civilization gradually shaded off into a surrounding barbarism across a broad threshold which offered the outsider an easy access to an inviting vista within. The change from friendship to hostility has transformed this conductive cultural threshold (*limen*) into an insulating military front (*limes*). This change is the geographical expression of the conditions that generate an heroic age.

An heroic age is, in fact, the social and psychological consequence of the crystallization of a *limes;* and our purpose now is to trace this sequence of events. A necessary background to this undertaking is, of course, a survey of the barbarian war-bands that had breasted divers sections of the *limites* of divers universal states, and a survey of this kind has already been attempted in an earlier part of this Study, in the course of which we have noted the distinctive achievements of these war-bands in the fields of sectarian religion and epic poetry. In our present inquiry this foregoing survey can be drawn upon for purposes of illustration without having to be recapitulated.

A military *limes* may be likened to a forbidding barrage across a no longer open valley—an imposing monument of human skill and power setting Nature at defiance, and yet precarious, because a defiance of Nature is a *tour de force* on which Man cannot venture with impunity.

'The Arab-Muslim tradition relates that once upon a time there was to be seen in the Yaman a colossal work of hydraulic engineering known as the dam or dyke of Ma'rib, where the waters descending from the eastern mountains of the Yaman collected in an immense reservoir and thence irrigated an immense tract of country, giving life to an intensive system of cultivation and thereby supporting a dense population. After a time, the tradition goes on to relate, this dam broke, and, in breaking, devastated everything and cast the inhabitants of the country into a state of usch dire distress that many tribes were compelled to emigrate.'[1]

This story has served to account for the initial impulse behind an Arab Völkerwanderung that eventually swept out of the Arabian Peninsula with an impetus which carried it across the Tien Shan and the Pyrenees. Translated into a simile it becomes the story of every *limes* of every universal state. Is this social catastrophe of the bursting of the military dam an inevitable tragedy or an avoidable one? To answer this question we must analyse the social and psychological effects of the barrage-builders' interference with the natural course of relations between a civilization and its external proletariat.

The first effect of erecting a barrage is, of course, to create a reservoir above it; but the reservoir, however large, will have its limits. It will never cover more than a fraction of even its own catchment basin. There will be a sharp distinction between the submerged tract immediately above the barrage and a region at the back of beyond which is left high and dry. In a previous context we have already observed the contrast between the effect of a *limes*

[1] Caetani, L.: *Studi di Storia Orientale,* vol. i (Milan 1911, Hoepli), p. 266.

on the life of barbarians within its range and the undisturbed torpidity of primitive peoples in a more distant hinterland. The Slavs continued placidly to lead their primitive life in the Pripet Marshes throughout the span of two millennia which first saw the Achaean barbarians convulsed by their proximity to the European land-frontier of 'The thalassocracy of Minos' and then saw the Teuton barbarians going through the same experience as a result of their proximity to the European land-frontier of the Roman Empire. Why are the barbarians in the 'reservoir' so exceptionally upset? and what is the source of a subsequent access of energy which has enabled them invariably to break through the *limes*? We may find answers to these questions if we follow out our simile in terms of its geographical setting in Eastern Asia.

Let us suppose the imaginary dam that symbolizes a *limes* in our simile to have been built astride some high valley in the region actually traversed by the Great Wall within the latter-day Chinese provinces of Shinsi and Shansi. What is the ultimate source of that formidable body of water pressing in ever-increasing volume upon the dam's up-stream face? Though the water must manifestly all have come down-stream from above the dam, its ultimate source cannot lie in that direction, for the distance between the dam and the watershed is not great, and behind the watershed stretches the dry Mongolian Plateau. The ultimate source of supply is, in fact, to be found, not above the dam but below it, not on the Mongolian Plateau but in the Pacific Ocean, whose waters have been transformed by the sun into vapour and carried by an east wind until, condensed by cold air, they fall as rain into the catchment basin. The psychic energy that accumulates on the barbarian side of the *limes* is derived only in an inconsiderable measure from the trans-frontier barbarians' own exiguous social heritage; the bulk of it is drawn from the vast stores of the civilization which the barrage has been built to protect.

How is this transformation of psychic energy brought about? The transformation process is the decomposition of a culture and its recomposition in a new pattern. Elsewhere in this Study we have compared the social radiation of culture to the physical radiation of light, and here we must recall the 'laws' at which we arrived in that context.

The first law is that an integral culture ray, like an integral light ray, is diffracted into a spectrum of its component elements in the course of penetrating a recalcitrant object.

The second law is that the diffraction may also occur, without any impact on an alien body social, if the radiating society has already broken down and gone into disintegration. A growing civilization can be defined as one in which the components of its culture—the economic, the political, and the 'cultural' in the stricter sense—are in harmony with one another; and, on the same principle, a disintegrating civilization can be defined as one in which these three elements have fallen into discord.

Our third law is that the velocity and penetrative power of an integral culture. ray are averages of the diverse velocities and penetrative powers which its economic, political, and 'cultural' components display when, as a result of diffraction, they travel independently of each other. The economic and political components travel faster than the undiffracted culture; the 'cultural' component travels more slowly.

Thus, in the social intercourse between a disintegrating civilization and its alienated external proletariat across a military *limes*, the diffracted radiation of the civilization suffers a woeful impoverishment. Practically all intercourse is eliminated except what is economic and political—trade and war; and of these the trade, for various reasons, comes to be more and more restricted and the warfare to be more and more inveterate. Under these sinister auspices, such selective mimesis as occurs takes place on the barbarians' own initiative. They show their initiative in imitating those elements which they accept in a manner which will disguise the distasteful source of what has been imitated. Examples both of recognizable adaptations and of virtually new creations have been given already in an earlier part of this Study. Here we need only recall that the 'reservoir' barbarians are apt to borrow the higher religion of an adjoining civilization in the form of a heresy (for example, the Arian heretical Christianity of the Goths), and the Caesarism of an adjoining universal state in the form of an irresponsible kingship, resting not on tribal law but on military prestige, while the barbarian capacity for original creation is displayed in heroic poetry.

(2) THE ACCUMULATION OF PRESSURE

The social barrage created by the establishment of a *limes* is subject to the same law of Nature as the physical barrage created by the construction of a dam. The water piled up above the dam seeks to regain a common level with the water below it. In the structure of a physical dam the engineer introduces safety-valves in the form of sluices, which can be opened or closed as circumstances require, and this safeguarding device is not overlooked by the political engineers of a military *limes*, as we shall see. In this case, however, the device merely precipitates the cataclysm. In the maintenance of a social dam the relief of pressure by a regulated release of water is impracticable; there can be no discharge from the reservoir without the undermining of the dam; for the water above the dam, instead of rising and falling with the alternations of wet and dry weather, is, in the nature of the case, continuously on the rise. In the race between attack and defence, the attack cannot fail to win in the long run. Time is on the side of the barbarians. The time, however, may be long drawn out before the barbarians behind the *limes* achieve their break-through into the coveted domain of the disintegrating civilization. This long period, during which the spirit of the barbarians has been profoundly affected, and distorted, by the influence of the civilization from which they have been barred out, is the necessary prelude to an 'heroic age', in which the *limes* collapses and the barbarians have their fling.

The erection of a *limes* sets in motion a play of social forces which is bound to end disastrously for the builders. A policy of non-intercourse with the barbarians beyond is quite impracticable. Whatever the imperial government may decide, the interests of traders, pioneers, adventurers, and so forth will inevitably draw them beyond the frontier. A striking illustration of this tendency among the marchmen of a universal state to make common cause with the barbarians beyond the pale is afforded by the history of the relations between the Roman Empire and the Hun Eurasian Nomads who broke out of the Eurasian Steppe towards the end of the fourth century of the Christian Era. Though the Huns were unusually ferocious barbarians, and though their ascendancy along the European *limes* of the Roman Empire was ephemeral, a record of three notable cases of fraternization has survived among the fragmentary remnants of contemporary accounts of this brief episode. The most surprising of these cases is that of a Pannonian Roman citizen named Orestes, whose son Romulus Augustulus was to achieve an ignominious celebrity as the last Roman Emperor in the West; this same Orestes was for a time employed by the celebrated Hun warlord Attila as his secretary.

Of all the goods which passed outwards across the ineffectively insulating *limes*, weapons of war were perhaps the most significant. The barbarians could never have attacked effectively without the use of the weapons forged in the arsenals of civilization. On the North-West Frontier of the British Indian Empire from about 1890 onwards, 'the influx of rifles and ammunition into tribal territory . . . completely changed the nature of border warfare';[1] and, while the transfrontier Pathans' and Baluchīs' earliest source

---

[1] Davies, C. C.: *The Problem of the North-West Frontier, 1890–1908* (Cambridge 1932, University Press), p. 176.

of supply of up-to-date Western small-arms was systematic robbery from the British Indian troops on the other side of the line, 'there would . . . have been little cause for apprehension, had it not been for the enormous growth of the arms traffic in the Persian Gulf, which, both at Bushire and [at] Muscat, was at first in the hands of British traders'[1]—a striking example of the tendency for private interests of the empire's subjects in doing business with the transfrontier barbarians to militate against the public interest of the imperial government in keeping the barbarians at bay.

The transfrontier barbarian is not, however, content simply to practise the superior tactics which he has learnt from an adjoining civilization; he often improves upon them. For example, on the maritime frontiers of the Carolingian Empire and of the Kingdom of Wessex, the Scandinavian pirates turned to such good account a technique of ship-building and seamanship which they had acquired, perhaps, from the Frisian maritime marchmen of a nascent Western Christendom that they captured the command of the sea and, with it, the initiative in the offensive warfare which they proceeded to wage along the coasts and up the rivers of the Western Christian countries that were their victims. When, pushing up the rivers, they reached the limits of navigation, they exchanged one borrowed weapon for another and continued their campaign on the backs of stolen horses, for they had mastered the Frankish art of cavalry fighting as well as the Frisian art of navigation.

In the long history of the war-horse, the most dramatic case in which this weapon had been turned by a barbarian against the civilization from which he had acquired it was to be found in the New World, where the horse had been unknown until it had been imported by post-Columbian Western Christian intruders. Owing to the lack of a domesticated animal which, in the Old World, had been the making of the Nomad stockbreeder's way of life, the Great Plains of the Mississippi Basin, which would have been a herdsman's paradise, had remained the hunting-ground of tribes who followed their game laboriously on foot. The belated arrival of the horse in this ideal horse-country had effects on the life of the immigrant and the life of the native which, while in both cases revolutionary, were different in every other respect. The introduction of the horse on to the plains of Texas, Venezuela, and Argentina made Nomad stockbreeders out of the descendants of 150 generations of husbandmen, while at the same time it made mobile mounted war-bands out of the Indian tribes of the Great Plains beyond the frontiers of the Spanish viceroyalty of New Spain and

[1] Ibid., p. 177.

of the English colonies that eventually became the United States. The borrowed weapon did not give these transfrontier barbarians the ultimate victory, but it enabled them to postpone their final discomfiture.

While the nineteenth century of the Christian Era saw the prairie Indian of North America turn one of the European intruder's weapons against its original owner by disputing with him the possession of the Plains with the aid of the imported horse, the eighteenth century had already seen the forest Indian turn the European musket to account in a warfare of sniping and ambuscades which, with the screening forest as the Indian's confederate, had proved more than a match for contemporary European battle-tactics, in which close formations, precise evolutions, and steady volleys courted destruction when unimaginatively employed against adversaries who had adapted the European musket to the conditions of the American forest. In days before the invention of fire-arms, corresponding adaptations of the current weapons of an aggressive civilization to forest conditions had enabled the barbarian denizens of the Transrhenane forests of Northern Europe to save a still forest-clad Germany from the Roman conquest that had overtaken an already partially cleared and cultivated Gaul, by inflicting on the Romans a decisively deterrent disaster in the Teutoburger Wald in A.D. 9.

The line along which the military frontier between the Roman Empire and the North European barbarians consequently came to rest for the next four centuries carries its own explanation on the face of it. It was the line beyond which a forest that had reigned since the latest bout of glaciation was still decisively preponderant over the works of *Homo Agricola*—works which had opened the way for the march of Roman legions from the Mediterranean up to the Rhine and the Danube. Along this line, which happened, un-fortunately for the Roman Empire, to be just about the longest that could have been drawn across Continental Europe, the Roman Imperial Army had henceforward to be progressively increased in numerical strength to offset the progressive increase in the military efficiency of the transfrontier barbarians whom it was its duty to hold at bay.

On the local anti-barbarian frontiers of the still surviving paro-chial states of a Westernizing world which, at the time of writing, embraced all but a fraction of the total habitable and traversable surface of the planet, two of the recalcitrant barbarians' non-human allies had already been outmanœuvred by a Modern Western industrial technique. The Forest had long since fallen a victim to cold steel, while the Steppe had been penetrated by the motor-car and the aeroplane. The barbarian's mountain ally, however, had proved a harder nut to crack, and the highlander rear-guard of Barbarism had been displaying, in its latest forlorn hopes, an impressive ingenuity in turning to its own advantage, on its own *terrain*, some of the latter-day devices of an industrial Western military technique. By this *tour de force* the Rīfī highlanders astride the theoretical boundary between the Spanish and French zones of Morocco had inflicted on the Spaniards at Anwal in A.D. 1921 a disaster comparable with the annihilation of Varus's three legions by the Cherusci and their neighbours in the Teutoburgerwald in A.D. 9, and had made the French Government in North-West Africa rock on its foundations in A.D. 1925. By the same sleight of hand the Mahsūds of Waziristan had baffled repeated British attempts to subdue them during the ninety-eight years between A.D. 1849, when the British had taken over this anti-barbarian frontier from the Sikhs, and A.D. 1947, when they disencumbered themselves of a still unsolved Indian North-West Frontier problem by bequeathing this formidable legacy to Pakistan.

In A.D. 1925 the Rīfī offensive came within an ace of cutting the corridor which linked the effectively occupied part of the French Zone of Morocco with the main body of French North-West Africa; and, if the Rīfīs had succeeded in an attempt which failed by so narrow a margin, they would have put in jeopardy the whole of the French Empire on the southern coast of the Mediterranean. Interests of comparable magnitude were at stake for the British Rāj in India in the trial of strength between the Mahsūd barbarians and the armed forces of the British Indian Empire in the Waziristan campaign of A.D. 1919–20. In this campaign, as in the Rīfī warfare, the barbarian belligerent's strength lay in his skilful adaptation of Modern Western arms and tactics to a *terrain* that was unpropitious for their use on the lines that were orthodox for their Western inventors. The elaborate and costly equipment which had been invented on the European battlefields of the war of A.D. 1914–18, in operations on level ground between organized armies, was much less effective against parties of tribesmen lurking in a tangle of mountains.[1]

In order to defeat, even inconclusively, transfrontier barbarians who have attained the degree of military *expertise* shown by the Mahsūds in A.D. 1919 and by the Rīfīs in A.D. 1925, the Power behind

---

[1] Similarly, veterans of the Peninsular War of A.D. 1808–14, employing the tactics that had defeated again and again the armies of Napoleon, were routed with ridiculous ease at New Orleans in A.D. 1814 by the 'frontiersman's' methods employed against them by Andrew Jackson.

the threatened *limes* has to exert an effort that—measured in terms either of manpower or of equipment or of money—is quite disproportionate to the slender resources of its gadfly opponents to which this ponderous counter-attack is the irreducible minimum of effective response. Indeed, what Mr. Gladstone in A.D. 1881 called 'the resources of civilization'[1] could be almost as much of a hindrance as a help in warfare of this kind, for the mobility of British Indian forces was impaired by the multitude of the gadgets on which it depended for the assertion of its superiority. Again, if the British Indian forces were hindered by their too-muchness from striking rapidly and effectively, the Mahsūds presented too little to strike at. The purpose of a punitive expedition is to punish, but how was one to punish such people as these? Reduce them to destitution? They were destitute already; they took this state of life for granted, even if they did not enjoy it. Their lives were already—in the terms of Thomas Hobbes's description of the 'State of Nature'—solitary, poor, nasty, brutish, and short. It was hardly possible to make them more solitary, poorer, nastier, more brutish, and shorter; and, if it were possible, could one be sure that they would greatly care? We are here reaching a point that has been made in a different context in an earlier part of this Study— that a primitive body social recovers more easily and rapidly than a body social enjoying high material civilization. It is like the humble worm which, when cut in half, takes no notice and carries on as before. But we must return from the Rīfīs and Mahsūds, who have failed—so far—to carry through to a successful conclusion their assaults upon civilizations, and resume our examination of the process of the tragedy in cases where it has gone through to its Fifth Act.

The *crescendo* of frontier warfare, which produced this progressive change in the balance of military power, progressively weakens the civilization involved by putting its monetary economy under the strain of an ever-increasing burden of taxation. On the other hand, it merely stimulates the military appetite of the barbarians. If the transfrontier barbarian had remained an unmodified primitive man, a much greater proportion of his total energies would have been devoted to the arts of peace and a correspondingly greater coercive effect would have been produced upon him by the punitive destruction of the products of his pacific labours. The tragedy of a hitherto primitive society's moral alienation from the neigh-

---

[1] 'The resources of civilization are not exhausted', said Mr. Gladstone in the House of Commons, meaning thereby that British administration would in the long run prove too much for Nationalist agitation and crime in Ireland. He was wrong. Forty years later 'civilization' admitted its exhaustion, and signed the Treaty establishing the Irish Free State.

bouring civilization is that the barbarian has neglected his former peaceful productivity in order to specialize in the art of border warfare, first in self-defence but afterwards as an alternative and more exciting method of earning his living—to plough and reap with sword and spear.

This striking inequality in the material consequences of border warfare for the two belligerents is reflected in the great and growing inequality between them in *moral*. For the children of a disintegrating civilization, the interminable border warfare spells the burden of an ever-increasing financial charge. For the barbarian belligerents, on the other hand, the same warfare is not a burden but an opportunity, not an anxiety but an exhilaration. In this situation it is not surprising that the party which is both author and victim of the *limes* should not resign himself to his doom without trying the last expedient of enlisting his barbarian adversary on his own side. We have already examined the consequences of this policy in an earlier part of this Study, and here we need only recall our previous finding, that this expedient for averting the collapse of a *limes* actually precipitates the catastrophe which it was designed to forestall.

In the history of the Roman Empire's struggle to arrest an inexorable inclination of the scales in favour of the transfrontier barbarians, the policy of enlisting barbarians to keep their fellow barbarians at bay defeated itself—if we are to believe a hostile critic of the Emperor Theodosius I's administration—by initiating the barbarians into the Roman art of war and at the same time apprising them of the Empire's weakness.

'In the Roman forces, discipline was now at an end, and all distinction between Roman and barbarian had broken down. The troops of both categories were all completely intermingled with one another in the ranks; for even the register of the soldiers borne on the strength of the military units was now no longer being kept up to date. The [barbarian] deserters [from the transfrontier barbarian war-bands to the Roman Imperial Army] thus found themselves free, after having been enrolled in Roman formations, to go home again and send off substitutes to take their place until, at their own good time, they might choose to resume their personal service under the Romans. This extreme disorganization that was thus now prevalent in the Roman military formations was no secret to the barbarians, since—with the door thrown wide open, as it had been, for intercourse—the deserters were able to give them full intelligence. The barbarians' conclusion was that the Roman body politic was being so grossly mismanaged as positively to invite attack.'[1]

When such well-instructed mercenaries change sides *en masse*,

---

[1] Zosimus: *Historiae*, Book IV, chap. xxxi, §§ 1–3.

it is no wonder that they are often able to give the *coup de grâce* to a tottering empire; but we have still to explain why they should be moved, as they so frequently have been, to turn against their employers. Does not their personal interest coincide with their professional obligation? The regular pay they are now drawing is both more lucrative and more secure than the plunder that they used to snatch on occasional raids. Why, then, turn traitor? The answer is that, in turning against the empire that he has been hired to defend, the barbarian mercenary is indeed acting against his own material interests, but that in doing so he is not doing anything peculiar. Man seldom behaves primarily as *homo economicus*, and the traitor mercenary's behaviour is determined by an impulse stronger than any economic considerations. The plain fact is that he hates the empire whose pay he has taken; and the moral breach between the two parties cannot be permanently mended by a business deal which is not underwritten by any real desire, on the barbarian's side, to share in the civilization that he has undertaken to guard. His attitude towards it is no longer one of reverence and mimesis, as was that of his ancestors in happier days when the same civilization was still in its attractive growth stage. The direction of the current of mimesis has, indeed, long since been reversed, and, so far from the civilization's retaining prestige in the barbarian's eyes, it is the barbarian who now enjoys prestige in the eyes of the representative of civilization.

'Early Roman history has been described as the history of ordinary people doing extraordinary things. In the Later Empire it took an extraordinary man to do anything at all except carry on a routine; and, as the Empire had devoted itself for centuries to the breeding and training of ordinary men, the extraordinary men of its last ages—Stilicho, Aëtius, and their like—were increasingly drawn from the Barbarian world.'[1]

(3) THE CATACLYSM AND ITS CONSEQUENCES

When the barrage bursts, the whole body of water that has been accumulating above the dam runs violently down a steep place into the sea, and this release of long-pent-up forces produces a threefold catastrophe. In the first place, the flood destroys the works of Man in the cultivated lands below the broken barrage. In the second place, the potentially life-giving water pours down to the sea and is lost without ever having served Man for his human purposes. In the third place, the discharge of waters empties the

---

[1] Collingwood, R. G., in Collingwood, R. G., and Myres, J. N. L.: *Roman Britain and the English Settlements*, 2nd edn. (Oxford 1937, Clarendon Press), p. 307.

reservoir, leaving its shores high and dry and thus dooming to death the vegetation which had been able to strike root there. In short, the waters which were fructifying so long as the barrage held, make havoc everywhere, in the lands that they lay bare as well as in the lands that they submerge, so soon as the bursting of the barrage releases them from the control which the presence of the barrage had imposed upon them.

This episode in Man's contest with Physical Nature is an apt simile of what happens on the collapse of a military *limes*. The resulting social cataclysm is a calamity for all concerned; but the incidence of the devastation is unequal and the reverse of what might have been expected, for the principal sufferers are not the ex-subjects of the defunct universal state but the ostensibly triumphant barbarians themselves. The hour of their triumph proves to be the occasion of their discomfiture.

What is the explanation of this paradox? It is that the *limes* had served not only as a bulwark of civilization but also as a providential safeguard for the aggressive barbarian himself against demoniacally self-destructive forces within his own bosom. We have seen that the proximity of a *limes* induces a malaise among the transfrontier barbarians within range of it because their previously primitive economy and institutions are disintegrated by a rain of psychic energy, generated by the civilization within the *limes*, that is wafted across a barrier which is itself an obstacle to the fuller and more fruitful intercourse characteristic of the relations between a growing civilization and the primitive proselytes beyond its open and inviting *limen*. We have also seen that, so long as the barbarian is confined beyond the pale, he succeeds in transmuting some, at least, of this influx of alien psychic energy into cultural products—political, artistic, and religious—which are partly adaptations of civilized institutions and partly new creations of the barbarian's own. In fact, so long as the barrage holds the psychological disturbance to which the barbarian is being exposed is being kept within bounds within which it can produce a not wholly demoralizing effect; and this saving curb is provided by the existence of the very *limes* which the barbarian is bent on destroying; for the *limes*, so long as it holds, supplies a substitute, in some measure, for the discipline of which Primitive Man is deprived when the breaking of his cake of primitive custom converts him into a transfrontier barbarian. The *limes* disciplines him by giving him tasks to perform, objectives to reach, and difficulties to contend with that constantly keep his efforts up to the mark.

When the sudden collapse of the *limes* sweeps this safeguard away, the discipline is removed and at the same time the barbarian is called upon to perform tasks which are altogether too difficult for him. If the transfrontier barbarian is a more brutal, as well as a more sophisticated, being than his primitive ancestor, the latter-day barbarian who has broken through the frontier and carved a successor-state out of the derelict domain of the defunct empire becomes much more demoralized than before. While the *limes* still stood, his orgies of idleness spent in consuming the loot of a successful raid had to be paid for with the hardships and rigours of defence against the punitive expedition that his raid was bound to provoke; with the *limes* broken down, orgies and idleness could be prolonged with impunity. As we observed in an earlier part of this Study, the barbarians *in partibus civilium* condemned themselves to the sordid role of vultures feeding on carrion or maggots crawling in a carcass. If these comparisons appear too brutal, we may liken the hordes of triumphant barbarians running amok amid the ruins of a civilization which they cannot appreciate to the gangs of vicious adolescents who had escaped the controls of home and school and were among the problems of overgrown urban communities in the twentieth century of the Christian Era.

'The qualities exhibited by these societies, virtues and defects alike, are clearly those of adolescence. . . . The characteristic feature . . . is emancipation—social, political, and religious—from the bonds of tribal law. . . . The characteristics of heroic ages in general are those neither of infancy nor of maturity. . . . The typical man of the Heroic Age is to be compared rather with a youth. . . . For a true analogy we must turn to the case of a youth who has outgrown both the ideas and the control of his parents—such a case as may be found among the sons of unsophisticated parents who, through outside influence, at school or elsewhere, have acquired knowledge which places them in a position of superiority to their surroundings.'[1]

One of the results of the decadence of primitive custom among primitive-turned-barbarian peoples is that the power formerly exercised by kindred-groups is transferred to the *comitatus*, a body of individual adventurers pledged to personal loyalty to a chief. So long as a civilization maintained within its universal state a semblance of authority, such barbarian war-lords and their *comitatus* could, on occasion, perform with success the service of providing buffer states. The history of the Salian Frankish guardians of the Roman Empire's Lower Rhenish frontier from the middle of the fourth to the middle of the fifth century of the Christian Era may be adduced as one of many examples of this state of affairs. But the fates of successor-states established by barbarian con-

[1] Chadwick, H. M.: *The Heroic Age* (Cambridge 1912, University Press), pp. 442–4.

querors in the interior of an extinct universal state's former domain show that this coarse product of a jejune barbarian political genius was quite unequal to the task of bearing burdens and solving problems that had already proved too much for the statesmanship of an œcumenical Power. A barbarian successor-state blindly goes into business on the strength of the dishonoured credits of a bankrupt universal state, and these boors in office hasten the advent of their inevitable doom by a self-betrayal through the outbreak, under stress of a moral ordeal, of something fatally false within; for a polity based solely on the fickle loyalty of a gang of armed desperadoes to an irresponsible military leader is morally unfit for the government of a community that has made even an unsuccessful attempt at civilization. The dissolution of the primitive kingroup in the barbarian *comitatus* is swiftly followed by the dissolution of the *comitatus* itself in the alien subject population.

The barbarian trespassers *in partibus civilium* have, in fact, condemned themselves to suffer a moral breakdown as an inevitable consequence of their trespass, yet they do not yield to their fate without a spiritual struggle that has left its traces in their literary records of myth and ritual and standards of conduct. The barbarians' ubiquitous master-myth describes the hero's victorious fight with a monster for the acquisition of a treasure which the unearthly enemy is withholding from Mankind. This is the common *motif* of the tales of Beowulf's fight with Grendel and Grendel's mother; Siegfried's fight with the dragon; and Perseus' feat of decapitating the Gorgon and his subsequent feat of winning Andromeda by slaying the sea-monster who was threatening to devour her. The *motif* reappears in Jason's outmanœuvring of the serpent-guardian of the Golden Fleece and in Herakles' kidnapping of Cerberus. This myth looks like a projection, on to the outer world, of a psychological struggle, in the barbarian's own soul, for the rescue of Man's supreme spiritual treasure, his rational will, from a demonic spiritual force released in the subconscious depths of the Psyche by the shattering experience of passing, at one leap, from a familiar no-man's-land outside the *limes* into the enchanted world laid open by the barrier's collapse. The myth may, indeed, be a translation into literary narrative of a ritual act of exorcism in which a militarily triumphant but spiritually afflicted barbarian has attempted to find a practical remedy for his devastating psychological malady.

In the emergence of special standards of conduct applicable to the peculiar circumstances of an heroic age we can see a further attempt, from another line of approach, to set moral bounds to the ravages of a demon that has been let loose in the souls of barbarian lords and masters of a prostrate civilization by the fall of the material barrier of the *limes*. Conspicuous examples are the Achaeans' Homeric *Aidôs* and *Nemesis* ('Shame' and 'Indignation') and the Umayyads' historic *Hilm* (a studied self-restraint).

'The great characteristic of [*Aidôs* and *Nemesis*], as of Honour generally, is that they only come into operation when a man is free: when there is no compulsion. If you take people . . . who have broken away from all their old sanctions and select among them some strong and turbulent chief who fears no one, you will first think that such a man is free to do whatever enters his head. And then, as a matter of fact, you find that, amid his lawlessness, there will crop up some possible action which somehow makes him feel uncomfortable. If he has done it, he 'rues' the deed and is haunted by it. If he has not done it, he 'shrinks' from doing it. And this, not because anyone forces him, nor yet because any particular result will accrue to him afterwards, but simply because he feels *Aidôs*. . . .

'*Aidôs* is what you feel about an act of your own; *Nemesis* is what you feel for the act of another. Or, most often, it is what you imagine that others will feel about you. . . . But suppose no one sees. The act, as you know well, remains νεμεσητόν—a thing to feel *Nemesis* about: only there is no one there to feel it. Yet, if you yourself dislike what you have done, and feel *Aidôs* for it, you inevitably are conscious that somebody or something dislikes or disapproves of you. . . . The Earth, Water, and Air [are] full of living eyes: of *theoi*, of *daimones*, of *kêres*. . . . And it is they who have seen you and are wroth with you for the thing which you have done.'[1]

In a post-Minoan heroic age, as depicted in the Homeric Epic, the actions that evoke feelings of *Aidôs* and *Nemesis* are those implying cowardice, lying, and perjury, lack of reverence, and cruelty or treachery towards the helpless.

'Apart from any question of wrong acts done to them, there are certain classes of people more αἰδαῖοι, objects of *Aidôs*, than others. There are people in whose presence a man feels shame, self-consciousness, awe, a sense keener than usual of the importance of behaving well. And what sort of people chiefly excite this *Aidôs*? Of course there are kings, elders and sages, princes and ambassadors: αἰδοῖοι βασιλῆες, γέροντος, and the like: all of them people for whom you naturally feel reverence, and whose good or bad opinion is important in the World. Yet . . . you will find that it is not these people, but quite others, who are most deeply charged, as it were, with *Aidôs* . . . before whom you feel still more keenly conscious of your unworthiness, and whose good or ill opinion weighs somehow inexplicably more in the last account: the disinherited of the Earth, the injured, the helpless, and, among them the most utterly helpless of all, the dead.'[2]

[1] Murray, Gilbert: *The Rise of the Greek Epic*, 3rd edn. (Oxford 1924, Clarendon Press), pp. 83–84. [2] Ibid., pp. 87–88.

THE COURSE OF THE TRAGEDY

In contrast to *Aidôs* and *Nemesis*, which enter into all aspects of social life, *Hilm* is a *vertu des politiques*.[1] It is something more sophisticated than *Aidôs* and *Nemesis*, and consequently less attractive. *Hilm* is not an expression of humility;

'its aim is rather to humiliate an adversary: to confound him by presenting the contrast of one's own superiority; to surprise him by displaying the dignity and calm of one's own attitude. . . . At bottom, *Hilm*, like most Arab qualities, is a virtue for bravado and display, with more ostentation in it than real substance. . . . A reputation for *Hilm* can be acquired at the cheap price of an elegant gesture or a sonorous *mot* . . . opportune above all in an anarchic *milieu*, such as the Arab society was, where every act of violence remorselessly provoked a retaliation. . . . *Hilm*, as practised by [Mu'āwiyah's Umayyad successors], facilitated their task of giving the Arabs a political education; it sweetened for their pupils the bitterness of having to sacrifice the anarchic liberty of the Desert in favour of sovereigns who were condescending enough to draw a velvet glove over the iron hand with which they ruled their empire.'[2]

These masterly characterizations of the nature of *Hilm*, *Aidôs*, and *Nemesis* show how nicely adapted these standards of conduct are to the peculiar circumstances of the Heroic Age; and, if, as we have intimated already, the Heroic Age is, intrinsically, a transient phase, the surest signs of its advent and its recession are the epiphany and the eclipse of its specific ideals. As *Aidôs* and *Nemesis* fade from view, their disappearance evokes a cry of despair. 'Pain and grief are the portion that shall be left for mortal men, and there shall be no defence against the evil day.'[3] Hesiod is harrowed by his illusory conviction that the withdrawal of these glimmering lights that have sustained the children of the Dark Age is a portent of the onset of perpetual darkness; he has no inkling that this extinguishing of the night-lights is a harbinger of the return of day. The truth is that *Aidôs* and *Nemesis* reascend to Heaven as soon as the imperceptible emergence of a nascent new civilization has made their sojourn on Earth superfluous by bringing into currency other virtues that are socially more constructive though aesthetically they may be less attractive. The Iron Age into which Hesiod lamented that he had been born was in fact the age in which a living Hellenic civilization was arising out of a dead Minoan civilization's ruins; and the 'Abbasids, who had no use for the

[1] Lammens, S. J., Père H.: *Études sur la Règne du Calife Omaiyade Mo'âwia Ier* (Bayrut 1908, Imprimerie Catholique; Paris 1908, Geuthner), p. 81, n. 2. The quotations from this book have been made with the permission of the publishers.
[2] Ibid., pp. 81, 87, 103.
[3] Hesiod: *Works and Days*, lines 197–200.

Hilm that had been their Umayyad predecessors' *arcanum imperii*, were the statesmen who set the seal on the Umayyad's *tour de force* of profiting by the obliteration of the Syrian *limes* of the Roman Empire in order to reinaugurate the Syriac universal state.

The demon who takes possession of the barbarian's soul as soon as the barbarian's foot has crossed the fallen *limes* is indeed difficult to exorcise, because he contrives to pervert the very virtues with which his victim has armed himself. One might well say of *Aidôs* what Madame Roland said of Liberty: 'What crimes have been committed in thy name!' The barbarian's sense of honour 'roars like a rapacious beast that never knows when it has had its fill'.[1] Wholesale atrocities are the outstanding features of the Heroic Age, both in history and in legend. The demoralized barbarian society in which these dark deeds are perpetrated is so familiar with their performance and so obtuse to their horror that the bards whose task it is to immortalize the memory of the war-lords do not hesitate to saddle their heroes and heroines with sins of which they may well have been innocent, when a blackening of their characters will magnify their prowess. Nor is it only against their official enemies that the Heroes perform their appalling atrocities. The horrors of the Sack of Troy are surpassed by the horrors of the family feud of the House of Atreus. 'Houses' thus divided against themselves are not likely to stand for long.

A sensationally sudden fall from an apparent omnipotence is, indeed, the characteristic fate of an heroic-age barbarian Power. Striking historical examples are the eclipse of the Huns after the death of Attila, and that of the Vandals after the death of Genseric. These and other historically attested examples lend credibility to the tradition that the wave of Achaean conquest likewise broke and collapsed after engulfing Troy, and that a murdered Agamemnon was the last Pan-Achaean war-lord. However widely these war-lords might extend their conquests, they were incapable of creating institutions. The fate of the empire of even so sophisticated and comparatively civilized a war-lord as Charlemagne provides a dramatic illustration of this incapacity.

(4) FANCY AND FACT

If there is truth in the picture presented in the preceding chapter, the verdict on the Heroic Age can only be a severe one. The mildest judgement will convict it of having been a futile

---

[1] Grönbech, V.: *The Culture of the Teutons* (London 1931, Milford, 3 vols. in 2), vols. ii–iii, p. 305.

escapade, while sterner judges will denounce it as a criminal out-
rage. The verdict of futility makes itself heard through the mellow
poetry of a Victorian man of letters who had lived on to feel the
frost of a neo-barbarian age.

> Follow the path of those fair warriors, the tall Goths
> from the day when they led their blue-eyed families
> off Vistula's cold pasture-lands, their murky home
> by the amber-strewen foreshore of the Baltic sea,
> and, in the incontaminat vigor of manliness
> feeling their rumour'd way to an unknown promised land,
> tore at the ravel'd fringes of the purple power,
> and trampling its wide skirts, defeating its armies,
> slaying its Emperor, and burning his cities
> sack'd Athens and Rome; untill supplanting Caesar
> they ruled the world where Romans reigned before:—
> Yet from those three long centuries of rapin and blood,
> inhumanity of heart and wanton cruelty of hand,
> ther is little left. . . . Those Goths wer strong but to destroy;
> they neither wrote nor wrought, thought not nor created;
> but, since the field was rank with tares and mildew'd wheat,
> their scything won some praise: Else have they left no trace.[1]

This measured judgement, delivered across a gulf of fifteen
centuries, could hardly have satisfied an Hellenic poet who was
bitterly conscious of still living in a moral slum made by barbarian
successors of the 'thalassocracy of Minos'. Criminality, and not
mere futility, is the burden of Hesiod's indictment against a post-
Minoan heroic age that, in his day, was still haunting a nascent
Hellenic civilization. His judgement is merciless.

'And Father Zeus made yet a third race of mortal men—a Race of
Bronze, in no wise like unto the Silver, fashioned from ash-stems,
mighty and terrible. Their delight was in the grievous deeds of Ares and
in the trespasses of Pride ($\H{v}\beta\rho\iota\varsigma$). No bread ever passed their lips, but
their hearts in their breasts were strong as adamant, and none might
approach them. Great was their strength and unconquerable were the
arms which grew from their shoulders upon their stalwart frames. Of
bronze were their panoplies, of bronze their houses, and with bronze
they tilled the land (dark iron was not yet). These were brought low by
their own hands and went their way to the mouldering house of chilly
Hades, nameless. For all their mighty valour, Death took them in his
dark grip, and they left the bright light of the Sun.'[2]

In Posterity's judgement on the overflowing measure of suffering

---

[1] Bridges, Robert: *The Testament of Beauty* (Oxford 1929, Clarendon Press),
Book I, lines 535-55.
[2] Hesiod: *Works and Days*, lines 143-55.

which the barbarians bring on themselves by their own criminal follies, this passage in Hesiod's poem might have stood as the last word, had not the poet himself run on as follows:

'Now when this race also had been covered by Earth, yet a fourth race was made, again, upon the face of the All-Mother, by Zeus son of Cronos—a better race and more righteous, a divine race of men heroic, who are called demigods, a race that was aforetime on the boundless Earth. These were destroyed by evil War and dread Battle—some below Seven-Gate Thebes in the land of Cadmus, as they fought for the flocks of Oedipus, while others were carried for destruction to Troy in ships over the great gulf of the sea, for the sake of Helen of the lovely hair. There verily they met their end and vanished in the embrace of Death; yet a few there were who were granted a life and a dwelling-place, apart from Mankind, by Zeus son of Cronos, who made them to abide at the ends of the Earth. So there they abide, with hearts free from care, in the Isles of the Blessed, beside the deep eddies of Ocean Stream—happy heroes, for whom a harvest honey-sweet, thrice ripening every year, is yielded by fruitful fields.'[1]

What is the relation of this passage to the one which immediately precedes it, and indeed to the whole catalogue of races in which it is imbedded? The episode breaks the sequence of the catalogue in two respects. In the first place the race here passed in review, unlike the preceding races of gold, silver, and bronze and the succeeding race of iron, is not identified with any metal; and, in the second place, all the other four races are made to follow one another in a declining order of merit. Moreover, the destinies of the three preceding races after death are consonant with the tenour of their lives on Earth. The Race of Gold 'became good spirits by the will of great Zeus—spirits *above* the ground, guardians of mortal men, givers of wealth'. The inferior Race of Silver still 'gained among mortals the name of blessed ones *beneath* the ground—second in glory; and yet, even so, they too are attended with honour'. When we come, however, to the Race of Bronze, we find that their fate after death is passed over in ominous silence. In a catalogue woven on this pattern we should expect to find the fourth race condemned after death to suffer the torments of the damned; yet, so far from that, we find at least a chosen few of them transported after death to Elysium, where they live, above ground, the very life that had been lived by the Race of Gold.

Manifestly the insertion of a Race of Heroes between the Race of Bronze and the Race of Iron is an afterthought, breaking the poem's sequence, symmetry, and sense. What moved the poet to make this clumsy insertion? The answer must be that the

[1] Hesiod: *Works and Days*, lines 156–73.

picture here presented of a Race of Heroes was so vividly impressed on the imagination of the poet and his public that a place had to be found for it. The Race of Heroes, is, in fact, the Race of Bronze described over again, in terms, not of sombre Hesiodic fact, but of glamorous Homeric fancy.

In social terms the Heroic Age is a folly and a crime, but in emotional terms it is a great experience, the thrilling experience of breaking through the barrier which has baffled the barbarian invaders' ancestors for generations, and bursting out into an apparently boundless world that offers what seem to be infinite possibilities. With one glorious exception, all these possibilities turn out to be Dead Sea fruit; yet the sensational completeness of the barbarians' failure on the social and political planes paradoxically ministers to the success of their bards' creative work, for in art there is more to be made out of failure than out of success; no 'success story' can achieve the stature of a tragedy. The exhilaration generated by the Völkerwanderung, which breaks down into demoralization in the intoxicated souls of the men of action, inspires the barbarian poet to transmute the memory of his heroes' wickedness and ineptitude into immortal song. In the enchanted realm of this poetry the barbarian *conquistadores* achieve vicariously the splendour that eluded their grasp in real life. Dead history blossoms into immortal romance. The fascination exercised by heroic poetry over its latter-day admirers deludes them into vizualizing what was in fact a sordid interlude between the death of one civilization and the birth of its successor as—what we have called it, not without intentional irony, in the terminology of this Study—an Heroic Age, an Age of Heroes.

The earliest victim of this illusion is, as we have seen, the poet of a 'Dark Age', which is the 'Heroic Age's' sequel. As is manifest in retrospect, this later age has no reason to be ashamed of a darkness which signifies that the barbarian incendiaries' bonfires have at last burnt themselves out; and, though a bed of ashes smothers the surface of the flame-scarred ground, the Dark Age proves to be creative, as the Heroic Age certainly was not. In the fullness of time, new life duly arises to clothe the fertile ash-field with shoots of tender green. The poetry of Hesiod, so pedestrian when set beside that of Homer, is one of these harbingers of a returning spring-time; yet this honest chronicler of the darkness before the dawn is still so bedazzled with a poetry inspired by the recent nocturnal incendiarism that he takes on faith, as historical truth, an imaginary Homeric picture of a Race of Heroes.

Hesiod's illusion seems strange, considering that, in his picture of the Race of Bronze, he has preserved for us, side by side with his reproduction of an Homeric fantasy, a merciless exposure of the barbarian as he really is. Yet, even without this clue, the heroic myth can be exploded by detonating the internal evidence. The Heroes turn out to have lived the evil lives and died the cruel deaths of the Race of Bronze, and Valhalla likewise turns out to be a slum when we switch off all the artificial lights and scrutinize by the sober light of day this poetic idealization of turbulent fighting and riotous feasting. The warriors who qualify for admission to Valhalla are in truth identical with the demons against whom they have exercised their prowess; and, in perishing off the face of the Earth by mutual destruction, they have relieved the World of a pandemonium of their own making and have achieved a happy ending for everyone but themselves.

Hesiod may have been the first, but he was by no means the last, to be beguiled by the splendours of barbarian epic. In a supposedly enlightened nineteenth century of the Christian Era we find a philosopher-mountebank launching his myth of a salutary barbarian 'Nordic Race' whose blood acts as an elixir of youth when injected into the veins of an 'effete society'; and we may still be cut to the heart as we watch the lively French aristocrat's political *jeu d'esprit* being keyed up into a racial myth by the prophets of a demonic German Neobarbarism. Plato's insistence that poets should be banished from his Republic gains a vivid significance as we trace the line of cause and effect between the authors of the Sagas and the founders of the Third Reich.

Yet there have been occasions when the barbarian interloper has performed, after all, a humble service for Posterity. At the transition from the civilizations of the first generation to those of the second, the interloping barbarians did in some cases provide a link between the defunct civilization and its newborn successor, as, in the subsequent transition from the second generation to the third, a link was provided by the chrysalis-churches. The Syriac and Hellenic civilizations, for instance, were thus linked with an antecedent Minoan civilization through this Minoan society's external proletariat, and the Hittite civilization stood in the same relation to an antecedent Sumeric civilization, and the Indic civilization to an antecedent Indus culture (if, in fact, this last had a life of its own that was independent of the Sumeric civilization). The modesty of the service thus performed is brought out by comparing it with the role of the chrysalis-churches. While the internal proletariat that builds churches, like the external proletariat that breeds war-bands, is the offspring of a psychological secession from a disintegrating civilization, the internal proletariat obviously acquires and hands on to future generations a far richer heritage of the past. This becomes obvious if we compare the debt of the Western Christian civilization to the Hellenic with the debt of the Hellenic civilization to the Minoan. The Christian Church was hellenized to saturation-point; the Homeric poets knew next to nothing of Minoan society: they present their Heroic Age *in vacuo*, with no more than a casual reference to the mighty carcass on which the bard's vulture-heroes—'sackers of cities' as they are proud to call themselves—are making their carrion-feasts.

On this showing, the service of the Achaeans and the other barbarians of their generation who played the same transmissive role might seem to dwindle to vanishing-point. What did it really amount to? Its reality becomes evident when we compare the destinies of those civilizations of the second generation that were affiliated to predecessors by this tenuous barbarian link with the destinies of the rest of the secondary civilizations. Any secondary civilization not affiliated through its predecessor's external proletariat must have been affiliated through its predecessor's dominant minority. These are the only alternatives, since no chrysalis-churches came out of the rudimentary higher religions of the internal proletariats of the primary civilizations.

We have, then, two groups of civilizations of the second generation, those affiliated to their predecessors through external proletariats and those affiliated through their predecessors' dominant minorities, and in other respects also these two groups stand at opposite poles. The former group are so distinct from their predecessors that the very fact of affiliation becomes dubious. The latter are so closely linked with their predecessors that their claims to separate existence may be disputed. The three known examples of the latter group are the Babylonic, which may be regarded either as a separate civilization or as an extension of the Sumeric, and the Yucatec and the Mexic, which are similarly related to the Mayan. Having sorted out these two groups, we may go on to observe another difference between them. The group of supra-affiliated secondary civilizations (or dead trunks of primary civilizations) all failed, where civilizations of the other group—the Hellenic, the Syriac, the Indic—succeeded; none of the super-affiliated civilizations gave birth, before its own expiry, to a universal church.

If we call to mind our conclusion that our serial order of chronologically successive types of society is at the same time an ascending order of value, in which the higher religions would be the highest term so far attained, we shall now observe that the barbarian chrysalises of civilizations of the second generation (but not those of the third) would have to their credit the honour of having participated in the higher religions' evolution. The proposition can be conveyed most clearly by means of the following table:

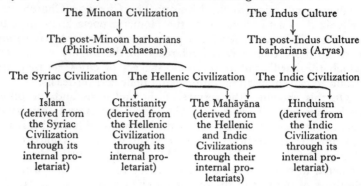

The Minoan Civilization		The Indus Culture
↓		↓
The post-Minoan barbarians (Philistines, Achaeans)		The post-Indus Culture barbarians (Aryas)

The Syriac Civilization	The Hellenic Civilization		The Indic Civilization
↓	↓	↓	↓
Islam (derived from the Syriac Civilization through its internal proletariat)	Christianity (derived from the Hellenic Civilization through its internal proletariat)	The Mahāyāna (derived from the Hellenic and Indic Civilizations through their internal proletariats)	Hinduism (derived from the Indic Civilization through its internal proletariat)

NOTE: 'THE MONSTROUS REGIMENT OF WOMEN'

THE Heroic Age might have been expected to be a masculine age *par excellence*. Does not the evidence convict it of having been an age of brute force? And, when force is given free rein, what chance can women have of holding their own against the physically dominant sex? This *a priori* logic is confuted, not only by the idealized picture presented in heroic poetry, but also by the facts of history.

In the Heroic Age the great catastrophes are apt to be women's work, even when the woman's role is ostensibly passive. If Alboin's unsatisfied desire for Rosamund was the cause of the extermination of the Gepidae, it is credible that the sacking of Troy was provoked by the satisfaction of Paris's desire for Helen. More commonly the women are undisguisedly the mischief-makers whose malice drives the heroes into slaying each other. The legendary quarrel between Brunhild and Kriemhild, which eventually discharged itself in the slaughter in Etzel's Danubian hall, is all of a piece with the authentic incidents of the quarrel between the historic Brunhild and her enemy Fredegund, which cost the Merovingian successor-state of the Roman Empire forty years of civil war.

The influence of women over men in the Heroic Age was not, of course, exhibited solely in the malevolence of goading their menfolk into fratricidal strife. No women left deeper marks on history than Alexander's mother, Olympias, and Mu'āwīyah's mother Hind, both of whom immortalized themselves by their lifelong moral ascendancy over their redoubtable sons. Yet a list of Gonerils, Regans, and Lady Macbeths, culled from the records of authenticated history, could be indefinitely prolonged. There are perhaps two lines of explanation of this phenomenon, one sociological and the other psychological.

The sociological explanation is to be found in the fact that the Heroic Age is a social interregnum in which the traditional habits of primitive life have been broken up, while no new 'cake of custom' had yet been baked by a nascent civilization or a nascent higher religion. In this ephemeral situation a social vacuum is filled by an individualism so absolute that it overrides the intrinsic differences between the sexes. It is remarkable to find this unbridled individualism bearing fruits hardly distinguishable from those of a doctrinaire feminism altogether beyond the emotional range and the intellectual horizon of the women and men of such periods. Approaching the problem on the psychological side, it may be suggested that the winning cards in the barbarians' internecine struggles for existence are not brute force but persistence, vindictiveness, implacability, cunning, and treachery; and these are qualities with which sinful human nature is as richly endowed in the female as in the male.

If we ask ourselves whether these women who exercise their 'monstrous regiment' in the inferno of the Heroic Age are heroines or villainesses or victims, we shall arrive at no clear answer. What is plain is that their tragic moral ambivalence makes them ideal subjects for poetry; and it is not surprising that, in the epic legacy of a post-Minoan heroic age, one of the favourite *genres* should have been 'catalogues of women', in which the recital of one legendary virago's crimes and sufferings called up the legend of another, in an almost endless chain of poetic reminiscence. The historic women whose grim adventures echo through this poetry would have smiled, with wry countenances, could they have foreknown that a reminiscence of a reminiscence would one day evoke *A Dream of Fair Women* in the imagination of a Victorian poet. They would have felt decidedly more at home in the atmosphere of the third scene in the first act of *Macbeth*.

IX

CONTACTS BETWEEN CIVILIZATIONS IN SPACE

XXX. AN EXPANSION OF THE FIELD OF STUDY

THE initial working hypothesis of this Study of History was that the historic civilizations are so many intelligible fields of study; and, if this had proved to hold good for all phases of their histories, our task would now be completed. Actually, however, we have found that, though a civilization proves to be an intelligible unit so long as we are considering its genesis, growth, and breakdown, it ceases to be so in the phase of its disintegration. We cannot understand this last phase of a civilization's history without extending our mental range of vision beyond its bounds and taking account of the impact of external forces. To mention only a single conspicuous example, the Roman Empire provided an Hellenic cradle for a Syriac-inspired Christianity.

The importance of the part played in the geneses of higher religions by encounters between different civilizations is illustrated by one of the commonplaces of historical geography. When we mark down the birthplaces of the higher religions on a map, we find them clustering in and round two relatively small patches of the total land-surface of the Old World—on the one hand the Oxus–Jaxartes Basin and on the other hand Syria, using that term in its broader sense to cover an area bounded by the North Arabian Steppe, the Mediterranean Sea, and the southern escarpments of the Anatolian and Armenian plateaux. The Oxus–Jaxartes Basin was the birthplace of the Mahāyāna, in the form in which it spread over the Far Eastern world, and, before that, perhaps, of Zoroastrianism. In Syria, Christianity acquired at Antioch the form in which it spread from there over the Hellenic world, after having made its first appearance as a variety of Pharisaic Judaism in Galilee. Judaism and the sister religion of the Samaritans arose in Southern Syria. The Monothelete Christianity of the Maronites and the Hākim-worshipping Shi'ism of the Druses both came to birth in Central Syria. This geographical concentration of the birthplaces of higher religions becomes still more conspicuous when we extend our horizon to take in adjacent regions. The Hijāzī prolongation of Syria southwards along the highlands fringing the Red Sea contains the birthplace of a Christian heresy which became the new religion of Islam, and, when we similarly extend the radius of our observation of the Oxus–Jaxartes Basin, we sight the birthplace of the Mahāyāna in its first appearance in the basin of the Indus, and the birthplace of primitive Buddhism, and also of post-Buddhaic Hinduism, in the middle basin of the Ganges.

What is the explanation? When we look into the characteristics of the Oxus–Jaxartes Basin and of Syria and compare them with each other, we find that each of them had been endowed by Nature with the capacity for serving as a 'round-about', where traffic coming in from any point of the compass could be switched to any other point of the compass in any number of alternative combinations. On the Syrian roundabout, routes converged from the Nile Basin, from the Mediterranean, from Anatolia with its South-East European hinterland, from the Tigris–Euphrates Basin, and from the Arabian Steppe. On the Central Asian roundabout, similarly, routes converged from the Tigris–Euphrates Basin via the Iranian Plateau, from India through the passes over the Hindu Kush, from the Far East via the Tarim Basin, and from an adjacent Eurasian Steppe that had taken the place, and inherited the conductivity, of a now desiccated 'Second Mediterranean', whose former presence there was attested by its fragmentary survival in the Caspian Sea, the Sea of Aral, and Lake Balkash.

The role for which Nature had thus designed these two potential traffic centres had actually been played by each of them again and again during the five or six thousand years since the emergence of the earliest civilizations. Syria had been the scene of encounters, in successive periods, between the Sumeric and Egyptiac civilizations; between the Egyptiac, Hittite, and Minoan civilizations; between the Syriac, Babylonic, Egyptiac, and Hellenic civilizations; between the Syriac, Orthodox Christian, and Western Christian civilizations; and, in a final bout of contacts, between the Arabic, Iranic, and Western civilizations. The Oxus–Jaxartes Basin had similarly been the scene of encounters in successive periods between the Syriac and Indic civilizations; between the Syriac, Indic, Hellenic, and Sinic civilizations; and between the Syriac and Far Eastern civilizations. As a result of these encounters, each of these two peculiarly 'numeniferous' (religion-bearing) regions had been included in the universal states of a number of different civilizations, and the exceptionally active intercourse between civilizations in these two areas explains the extraordinary concentration, within their limits, of the birthplaces of higher religions.

On the strength of this evidence, we may venture to propound a 'law' to the effect that, for a study of the higher religions, the minimum intelligible field must be larger than the domain of any single civilization, since it must be a field in which two or more civilizations have encountered each other. Our next step will be to take a wider survey of those encounters that, in certain historic instances, have had the effect of bringing higher religions to birth.

The encounters in question are contacts in the space-dimension between civilizations which, *ex hypothesi*, must be contemporaries with each other; but before passing on to this, the subject of the present Part of this Study, we may remark that civilizations have had contacts with each other in the time-dimension also, and this of two kinds. One kind of contact in time is the apparentation-and-affiliation relation between successive civilizations, a subject which has been with us throughout this Study. The other is a relation between a grown-up civilization and the 'ghost' of its long-dead predecessor. We may call encounters of this type renaissances, from the name invented by a French writer in the nineteenth century of the Christian Era to describe a particular example—by no means the only example—of this historical phenomenon. These Encounters of Civilizations in Time will be reserved for the following Part of this Study.

XXXI. A SURVEY OF ENCOUNTERS BETWEEN CONTEMPORARY CIVILIZATIONS

(1) A PLAN OF OPERATIONS

IN setting out to make a survey of encounters between contemporary civilizations, we are confronted with a formidably intricate maze of history, and we shall be well advised, before plunging into the thicket, to look for a favourable point of entry. The number of civilizations that we originally located on our cultural map was twenty-one; and, if the progress of archaeological discovery were to warrant us in regarding the Indus culture as a separate society from the Sumeric civilization, and the Shang culture as a civilization antecedent to the Sinic, this change in our reckoning would raise our total muster to twenty-three. It is obvious, however—even when we allow for the fact that two civilizations with no contemporaneous overlap cannot have had an encounter of the kind with which we are here concerned—that the number of encounters between contemporary civilizations might enormously exceed, and in fact does greatly exceed, the number of the civilizations themselves. We have, as we have often already observed, three generations of civilizations. If the first generation had all died simultaneously, and the second likewise, the weave of encounters in the space-dimension would be simplified. We should have to consider, let us say, the mutual encounters of A, B, C, D, and E, civilizations of the first generation, without allowing for the possibility that any of these had had encounters with F, G, H, I, and J, civilizations of the second generation; but, of course, it is not so. Though the Sumeric civilization may have submitted to being decently interred before it could encounter any lusty youngster of the second generation, that Tithonus of the first generation, the Egyptiac civilization, behaved very differently.

There was one factor which, until 'modern' times, caused the number of actual encounters between contemporary civilizations in space to fall mercifully short of the mathematically possible maximum; the space itself might be so great, or of such a nature, as to forbid mutual encounter. There were, for example, no encounters between the civilizations of the Old World and the New World before the mastering of the technique of oceanic navigation by the Western Christian civilization in the 'modern' chapter of its history (*circa* A.D. 1475–1875). This achievement is an historical landmark, and it may give us our clue to finding a point of entry into the historical maze that we have undertaken to explore.

When, in the course of the fifteenth century of the Christian Era, West European mariners did master the technique of oceanic navigation, they thereby won a means of physical access to all the inhabited and habitable lands on the face of the planet. In the lives of all other societies the impact of the West gradually came to be the paramount social force. As Western pressure on them increased, their lives were turned upside down. The Western society alone appeared at first to remain unaffected, in its own life, by the havoc that it was thus making of the rest of the World; but, within the lifetime of the writer of this Study, one of the encounters between the West and its contemporaries had come to darken the horizon of the Western society itself.

The dominating role in Western affairs that had thus come to be played by a collision between the West and a foreign body social was a novel feature in recent Western history. From the failure of the second Ottoman assault on Vienna in A.D. 1683 down to the defeat of Germany in the General War of A.D. 1939–45, the West as a whole had been so overwhelmingly superior in power to the rest of the World that the Western Powers had virtually nobody to reckon with outside their own circle. This Western monopoly of power came to an end, however, in 1945, for, from that date onwards, for the first time since 1683, one of the protagonists in power politics was once again a Power of a non-Western complexion.

There was, it is true, an ambiguity in the relation of both the Soviet Union and the Communist ideology to the Western civilization. The Soviet Union was the political heir of a Petrine Russian Empire which had become a voluntary convert to the Western way of life at the turn of the seventeenth and eighteenth centuries of the Christian Era and had participated thereafter in the Western game on a tacit understanding that the proselyte would abide by the accepted Western rules. Communism, again, was, in origin, like Liberalism and Fascism, one of the secular ideologies that had arisen in the Modern West as substitutes for Christianity. And thus, from one point of view, the competition between the Soviet Union and the United States for the hegemony of the World, and between Communism and Liberalism for the allegiance of Mankind, might still be regarded as a domestic issue within the household of the Western society. From another point of view, however, the Soviet Union could be looked upon, like its Petrine predecessor, as a Russian Orthodox Christian universal state clinging to life in a Western dress which it had adopted as a convenience and a disguise. From the same angle of vision, Communism could be looked upon as an ideological substitute for Eastern Orthodox Christianity, chosen in preference to Liberalism because Liberalism was a Western orthodoxy, whereas Communism, though of Western origin, was in Western eyes an abominable heresy.

However that might be, it was unquestionable that a sharp re-accentuation of the anti-Western tendency in Russian feeling and thought had been one of the consequences of the Russian Communist Revolution of A.D. 1917, and that the emergence of the Soviet Union as one of two surviving rival World Powers had reintroduced a cultural conflict into a political arena which, for some 250 years previously, had been reserved for domestic political quarrels between Powers of the same cultural complexion. It is also to be observed that, in thus re-engaging in their struggle against Westernization after having apparently long since given up the battle for lost, the Russians were setting an example which, within 31 years had already been followed by the Chinese and which might well be followed, in time, by the Japanese, Hindus, and Muslims, and even by societies that had become so deeply dyed with a Western colour as the main body of Orthodox Christendom in South-Eastern Europe and the three submerged pre-Columbian civilizations of the New World.

These considerations suggest that a scrutiny of the encounters between the Modern West and the other living civilizations might prove to be a convenient point of departure. The next set of encounters to be examined would then naturally be those of Western Christendom in its earlier, so-called Medieval, period with its neighbours in that age. Thereafter our plan would be to single out, among civilizations now extinct, those which had made an impact on their neighbours comparable with that of the West on its contemporaries, without committing ourselves to examine every single encounter which a meticulous examination of history might discover.

Before starting on this plan of operations, however, we have to determine the date at which the 'modern' chapter of Western history begins.

Non-Western observers would date its beginning from the moment when the first Western ships made a landfall on their coasts; for, in non-Western eyes, *Homo Occidentalis*, like Life itself according to one scientific hypothesis, was a creature of marine origin. Far Eastern scholars, for example, when they set eyes on their first specimens of Western humanity in the Ming Age, labelled the new arrivals 'South-Sea Barbarians', on the evidence of their immediate provenance and their apparent level of culture. In this and other encounters, the ubiquitous Western mariners went through a series of rapid metamorphoses in their victims' bewildered eyes. At their first landing they looked like harmless marine animalculae of a previously unknown breed; soon they revealed themselves to be savage sea-monsters; and eventually they proved to be predatory amphibians as mobile on dry land as in their own element.

From the Modern West's own point of view, its modernity had begun at the moment when Western Man thanked not God but himself that he had outgrown his 'medieval' Christian discipline. This hopeful discovery had been made first in Italy, and it so happened that the generation which saw the Italianization of the Transalpine majority of Western peoples was the same as that which saw the conquest of the ocean by the Western peoples of the Atlantic seaboard. With these two historic landmarks in view we may confidently place the beginning of the Modern chapter of Western history in the last quarter of the fifteenth century.

When we come to consider the results of the encounters between the Modern West and the rest of the World, we shall find, however, that the period of four and a half centuries that has elapsed since the opening of the drama is inconveniently short and that we are dealing with an unfinished story. This becomes at once apparent if we turn our attention back to an earlier story of the same kind. If we measure off the history of the impact of the Modern West on its contemporaries down to the time of writing against the history of the impact of the Hellenic civilization on the Hittite, Syriac, Egyptiac, Babylonic, Indic, and Sinic societies, and if, for the purposes of this chronological comparison, we equate Alexander's crossing of the Hellespont in 334 B.C. with Columbus's crossing of the Atlantic in A.D. 1492, the 460 years that bring us down to A.D. 1952 in the Modern Western record will bring us, on the other record, down only to the year A.D. 126, which is only a few years later than the date of the correspondence between the Emperor Trajan and his high commissioner Pliny, on the subject of the treatment of the obscure sect of the Christians in the province of Bithynia and Pontus. Who, at that date, could have guessed the subsequent triumph of Christianity? This historical parallel indicates how utterly the future might be hidden in A.D. 1952 from the mental vision of a Western student of the impact of the West on the rest of the World.

At the time of writing in the twentieth century of the Christian Era, the encounter between Hellenism and its contemporaries had long since been over, so that it was possible for the historian to follow the story from beginning to end; but where was that end to be found? The searcher for it did not have to probe farther back in time from his own day than the twelfth century of the Christian Era, when both the Far Eastern world and the Syriac world were reacting to the impact of Hellenism with a vigour that left no room for doubt. In the Far Eastern world the visual arts were then still being inspired by Hellenic influences, and in the Syriac world Aristotelian philosophy and science were then still stimulating Oriental thinkers through the medium of the Arabic language.

Such considerations, which could be indefinitely elaborated and fortified by examples from other sources, are a reminder of the 'wise saw' that the writing of contemporary history is impossible. It is, however, at the same time one of those impossible things that historians quite rightly refuse to refrain from attempting; and hereupon, with our own eyes open and with due warning given to the reader, we enter upon the particular field of this 'impossible' undertaking which is the task immediately ahead of us.

(2) OPERATIONS ACCORDING TO PLAN

(a) ENCOUNTERS WITH THE MODERN WESTERN CIVILIZATION

(i) *The Modern West and Russia*

The establishment of the Russian Orthodox Christian universal state through the incorporation of the Republic of Novgorod with the Grand Duchy of Muscovy was achieved in the eighth decade of the fifteenth century and is thus practically coincident with the opening of the 'modern' chapter of Western history. The 'Western Question', however, was already familiar to Russian minds before that date, for in the fourteenth and fifteenth centuries Polish and Lithuanian rule had been extended over large stretches of the original patrimony of Russian Orthodox Christendom. In the course of the sixteenth, seventeenth, and eighteenth centuries the Western civilization's hold over the Russian populations in Poland and Lithuania—these two kingdoms were united in A.D. 1569—was strengthened by the ecclesiastical union of a part of the subject Russian Orthodox Christian community with the Roman Catholic Church. The landowning aristocracy was to a large extent converted by Jesuit missionaries, while a considerable part of the peasantry became members of a Uniate Church, which was allowed to retain most of its traditional rites and discipline. The 'irrepressible conflict' between Muscovy and the West over the allegiance of these White Russian and Ukrainian populations that had then been segregated from their fellow Russian Eastern Orthodox Christians continued until the end of the General War of A.D. 1939–45, when, willy-nilly, the last remnants of them were once again brought within the Russian fold.

This originally Russian but latterly semi-Westernized border-land had not, however, been the principal field in which the encounter between Russia and the Modern West had been taking place; for the Polish reflection of the Modern Western culture was too dim to impress itself deeply on Russian souls. In the crucial encounter the principals on the Western side had been those maritime peoples on the Atlantic coast who had taken over from the Italians the leadership of the Western world. This dominant group had come to include Russia's immediate neighbours along the east coast of the Baltic; but, though the German barons and *bourgeoisie* of the Baltic provinces exercised an influence on Russian life out of proportion to their numbers, the influence of the Atlantic peoples, filtering through ports of entry which the Imperial Russian Government deliberately opened to receive it, was to count for much more.

In this intercourse the plot of the drama was dictated by a perpetual interplay between the technological prowess of the West and the determination of Russian souls to preserve their spiritual independence. The Russian conviction of the uniqueness of Russia's destiny had found expression in the belief that the mantle of Constantinople—the 'Second Rome'—had fallen on Russia's shoulders. Moscow's assumption of the role of a unique repository and citadel of Christian Orthodoxy had culminated in the establishment of an autocephalous Patriarchate of Moscow in A.D. 1589, at the very moment when the Russian domain, already much reduced by Medieval Western encroachments, was beginning to be threatened by the opening triumphs of Modern Western technology.

To this challenge there were three diverse Russian responses. One was a totalitarian 'Zealot' reaction which found its typical exponents in the fanatical sect of the Old Believers. The second response was the thorough-going 'Herodianism' which found an exponent of genius in Peter the Great. The Petrine policy was to convert the Russian Empire from an Orthodox Christian universal state into one of the parochial states of a Modern Western world. In acquiescing in the Petrine policy the Russians were resigning themselves to being, after all, like other nations and implicitly renouncing Moscow's pretension to the unique destiny of being the citadel of Orthodoxy: the one society pregnant, as the Old Believers maintained, with the future hopes of Mankind. Though the Petrine policy was adopted with apparent success for over two hundred years, it never won the Russian people's whole-hearted support. The ignominious collapse of Russia's military effort during the General War of A.D. 1914–18 offered lurid evidence that, after having been tried for more than two hundred years, the

Petrine policy of Westernization had not only been un-Russian but had also been unsuccessful; it had not 'delivered the goods', and in these circumstances a long-suppressed insistence on the uniqueness of Russia's destiny reasserted itself through the Communist revolution.

Russian Communism was an attempt to reconcile this irrepressible sense of Russian destiny with the ineluctable necessity of coping with Modern Western technological prowess. This adoption of a Modern Western ideology, even though an ideology in rebellion against current Western Liberalism, was a paradoxical way of reasserting, against the Modern West, Russia's pretension to be the heir to a unique heritage. Lenin and his successors divined that a policy of fighting the West with a selection of its own weapons could not hope to succeed if the weapons were conceived of in purely material terms. The secret of the amazing success of the Modern West had lain in a masterly co-operation of the spiritual with the temporal arm. The breaches blown by the blast of Modern Western technology had opened a passage for the spirit of Modern Western Liberalism. If Russia's reaction against the West was to succeed, she must appear as the champion of a faith that could contend on equal terms with Liberalism. Armed with this faith Russia must compete with the West for the spiritual allegiance of all the living societies that were neither Western nor Russian in their native cultural traditions; and—not content with that—she must have the audacity to carry the war into the enemy's camp by preaching the Russian faith in the West's own homeland. This is a subject to which we shall inevitably return in a later part of this Study.

(ii) *The Modern West and the Main Body of Orthodox Christendom*

The reception of Modern Western culture in the main body of Orthodox Christendom was coeval with its reception in Russia. In both cases the Westernizing movement set in towards the close of the seventeenth century of the Christian Era; in both cases the movement marked a revulsion from a previously long sustained attitude of hostility; and, in both cases again, one cause of this change of attitude in Orthodox Christian souls was an antecedent psychological change in the West, from an intolerant religious fanaticism to an irreligious tolerance, reflecting the profound disillusionment of Western souls which was an aftermath of the West's so-called religious wars. On the political plane, however, these two separate Orthodox Christian Westernizing movements followed different courses.

Both the Orthodox Christian societies were, at the date in question, clamped together in universal states, but, whereas the Russian universal state was an indigenous production, that of the main body of Orthodox Christendom had been imposed upon it from outside by the Ottoman Turks. Thus in Russia the Westernizing movement was designed to strengthen the existing Imperial Government and was launched from above downwards by a revolutionary genius who was also Czar, whereas, in the Ottoman Empire, the Westernizing movements aspired ultimately to recapture political independence for Serbs, Greeks, and other subject Orthodox Christian peoples by subverting the Ottoman Power, and were launched from below upwards, not by princes performing acts of state, but through the enterprise of private individuals.

The seventeenth-century revolution in the attitude of Orthodox Christians towards the West signified an even greater change in Serb and Greek than in Russian hearts, if one compares the respective degrees of their previous hostility to the West. In the thirteenth century of the Christian Era the Greeks had reacted violently against the so-called Latin Empire imposed upon them for half a century by the 'Franks' of the Fourth Crusade. In the fifteenth century they had repudiated the union of the Orthodox and Catholic Churches, achieved on paper at the Council of Florence in A.D. 1439, though this union appeared to offer them their only chance of Western support against the Turkish invader. They preferred the Pādishāh to the Pope. As late as A.D. 1798 the Greek press at Constantinople published a statement from the Patriarch of Jerusalem in which he told his readers that

'when the last emperors of Constantinople began to subject the Oriental Church to Papal thraldom, the particular favour of Heaven raised up the Ottoman Empire to protect the Greeks against heresy, to be a barrier against the political power of the Western nations, and to be the champion of the Orthodox Church'.[1]

This exposition of a traditional 'Zealot' thesis was, however, a parting shot in a losing cultural battle which had taken its decisive turn more than a hundred years before. The date of the beginning of this transfer of the Orthodox Christians' cultural allegiance from their Ottoman masters to their Western neighbours is proclaimed by the psychologically significant index of changes in fashions of dress; and this sartorial testimony is corroborated by evidence in the cultural field. In the seventh decade of the seventeenth century, Ottomanization was still the goal of the ra'īyah's social ambition, as was observed at the time by the shrewd secretary of the English Embassy at Constantinople, Sir Paul Rycaut:

[1] Finlay, G.: A History of Greece, B.C. 146 to A.D. 1864 (Oxford 1877, Clarendon Press, 7 vols.), vol. v, pp. 284–5.

'It is worth a wise man's observation how gladly the Greeks and Armenian Christians imitate the Turkish habit, and come as near to it as they dare; and how proud they are when they are privileged upon some extraordinary occasion to appear without their Christian distinction.'[1]

On the other hand, Demetrius Cantemir, the Ruman Orthodox Christian grandee who was appointed Prince of Moldavia by the Porte in A.D. 1710 and deserted to the Russians in the following year, is represented in a contemporary portrait wearing a bagwig, coat and waistcoat, and rapier. Such changes in dress were, of course, outward signs of corresponding changes in cast of mind. Cantemir, for example, could read and write Latin, Italian, and French, and the Phanariot Greek Orthodox Christians in the Turkish service were valued by their Turkish employers in the eighteenth century on account of their knowledge of Western ways of life, in an age when the Ottoman Government found itself having to employ wily diplomatists to deal with Western Powers that it could no longer simply defeat in battle.

The sufferings of the Orthodox Christian subjects of the Ottoman Porte in the eighteenth century were largely due to the misgovernment into which the Empire lapsed on its way to dissolution. By contrast, the onset of religious scepticism in Western Christendom was accompanied there by an advance in administrative efficiency and a dawn of political enlightenment. The Catholic Hapsburg Monarchy now ceased to persecute its non-Catholic subjects, and its Serb Orthodox Christian subjects—refugees from the Ottoman Empire settled in ex-Ottoman territories conquered by the Hapsburg Monarchy in Hungary—became the psychologically conductive medium through which the Modern Western culture penetrated the Serb people as a whole. Another channel of Western cultural influence ran through Venice, which, for four and a half centuries preceding the year A.D. 1669, had been in occupation of the Greek Orthodox Christian island of Crete and had for shorter periods ruled parts of Continental European Greece. Another Westernizing force was the Western diplomatic corps in Constantinople, who took advantage of the classic Ottoman principle of non-territorial autonomy for all communities within the Empire to create miniature *imperia in imperio* in which they reigned not only over their own nationals resident in the Ottoman Empire but also over Ottoman subjects who had become their official protégés. Yet another channel was opened up by the Greek

---

[1] Rycaut, Sir P.: *The Present State of the Ottoman Empire* (London 1668, Starkey & Brome), p. 82.

commercial communities which came to be established in the Western world as far afield as London, Liverpool, and New York. The Modern Western influence that thus radiated into the main body of Orthodox Christendom through these overland and maritime channels was playing upon a society that was living under an alien universal state. Thus the attempt to adopt a Modern Western way of life was made on the educational plane before being extended to the political. The academic work of an Adhamándios Korais in Paris and of a Vuk Karadžic in Vienna preceded the insurrections of a Qāra George and a Miloš Obrenovic.

At the opening of the nineteenth century of the Christian Era it might safely have been forecast that the European territories of the Ottoman Empire would undergo some kind of Westernizing transformation, but the form which that transformation would take was then still obscure. In the course of the century ending in A.D. 1821 the Phanariot Greek entourage of the Œcumenical Patriarch had transmuted their old dream of raising from the dead the East Roman ghost of the Roman Empire into a new dream of solving the Western Question on the political plane by converting the Ottoman Empire, as Peter the Great had converted the Russian Empire, into a replica of such contemporary Western multi-national 'enlightened monarchies' as the Danubian Hapsburg Monarchy; and this ambitious Phanariot Greek aspiration was fostered by an encouraging series of progressive political successes.

In making the Œcumenical Patriarch the official head of all the Eastern Orthodox Christian ra'iyah of an expanding Ottoman Empire, the Sultan had given this Constantinopolitan prelate political authority over Christian peoples that had never been under the rule of any Constantinopolitan Emperor since the Arab conquest of Syria and Egypt in the seventh century of the Christian Era; and in the seventeenth and eighteenth centuries the political power of the Phanar had been further extended by the action of their free Muslim fellow subjects. During the hundred years following the death, in A.D. 1566, of Suleymān the Magnificent, the free Muslims had compelled the Pādishāh's slave-household to take them into partnership in the Government of the Ottoman Empire, and they had followed up this political victory by taking the Greek ra'iyah into partnership with themselves. The creation of the offices of Dragoman of the Porte and Dragoman of the Fleet, with a view to employing Ottoman Greek ability in the service of the Empire, had been followed by further measures in favour of the Greeks at the expense of the non-Greek Orthodox Christian ra'iyah.

In the half-century preceding A.D. 1821 the Phanariot Greeks might have fancied that they had within their reach an ascendancy in the Ottoman Empire of the kind that the contemporary King-Emperor Joseph II had been working to secure for the Germans in the Danubian Hapsburg Monarchy. By this time, however, the Phanariots' ascendancy had been undermined by the repercussions of revolutionary events in the West. Enlightened Monarchy had been abruptly supplanted by Nationalism as the dominant Western political idea, and the non-Greek Orthodox Christian *ra'īyah* of the Ottoman Empire foresaw no satisfaction for their own awakening nationalist aspirations in the substitution of a Phanariot Greek for a Turkish Muslim domination—as the Rumanian population of the Danubian Principalities showed when in A.D. 1821, after 110 years of local experience of Phanariot Greek rule, they made a fiasco of Hypsilandi's raid by turning a deaf ear to this Greek's summons to them to rally to him as fellow members of an Orthodox Christian community that was to liberate itself from Ottoman rule by taking up arms under Phanariot Greek leadership.

The frustration of the Phanariots' 'Great Idea' was an intimation that a multi-national Orthodox Christian population in the Ottoman Empire, which had set its heart on adopting a Western way of life, would have to sort itself out into a patchwork of parochial states, Greek, Ruman, Serb, Bulgar, Albanian, and Georgian, on the pattern of France, Spain, Portugal, and Holland, in each of which a particular language, instead of a particular religion, would be the shibboleth uniting 'fellow countrymen' and distinguishing them from 'foreigners'. But at the beginning of the nineteenth century the outlines of this exotic Modern Western pattern were hard to discern. At that date there were few districts in the Ottoman Empire whose population was even approximately homogeneous in linguistic nationality, and also few which possessed even the rudiments of statehood. The radical reconstruction of the political map, in order to make it conform to a revolutionary Modern Western design, spelled misery for millions of human beings, and the suffering inflicted became more widespread and more intense as the procrustean operation was successively performed on territories and populations that were less and less amenable to being organized politically on a nationalistic basis. The horrible story extends from the extermination of the Ottoman Muslim minority in the Morea by Greek nationalists in A.D. 1821 to the wholesale flight of a Greek Orthodox Christian minority from Western Anatolia in A.D. 1922.

The Orthodox Christian national states that had come into existence in these untoward circumstances and on this petty scale could not, of course, indulge, like a Westernizing Russian Empire, in the ambition of playing, *vis-à-vis* the Modern West, the role of the East Roman Empire *vis-à-vis* a Medieval Western Christendom. Their feeble energies were absorbed in local disputes over small parcels of territory and their bitterest animosities were those which they harboured against each other. In relation to the outside world they found themselves in a situation not unlike that of their predecessors during the centuries immediately preceding the establishment of the *Pax Ottomanica*. In that age Greeks, Serbs, Bulgars, and Rumans had been confronted by a choice between domination by their Medieval Western fellow Christians and domination by the 'Osmanlis. In a post-Ottoman Age the alternatives that confronted them were incorporation into a secular Modern Western body social or subjection, first to a Petrine, and thereafter to a Communist, Russia.

In A.D. 1952 a majority of these non-Russian Orthodox Christian peoples were actually under Russia's military and political control. The only exceptions were Greece—where the Russians had been worsted in an undeclared war-after-the-war between the Soviet Union and the United States in which the combatants on each side had been Greek proxies of the foreign belligerents—and Jugoslavia, which had thrown off a post-war Russian hegemony and had accepted American aid. In the states under Russian domination, however, it was apparent that even an indirect exercise of Russian power was odious to all but a small minority of Communists who were governing these countries as the Soviet Government's agents.

This recalcitrance against a Russian ascendancy was an old story which could be illustrated from the history of Russia's relations with Rumania, Bulgaria, and Serbia in the nineteenth century, at dates long previous to the Communist Revolution in Russia. On the morrow of the Russo-Turkish War of A.D. 1877–8, for example, Russia had looked forward to exercising a paramount influence over a Serbia whom she had just rescued from defeat by Turkish armies; over a Rumania to whom she had just presented the Dobruja; and, above all, over a Bulgaria whom she had just called into existence, *ex nihilo*, by the sheer force of Russian arms. But the sequel proved, as had been proved many times before and in many different places, that there is no such thing as gratitude in international politics.

This anti-Russian feeling in non-Russian Orthodox Christian countries might seem at first sight surprising at a time when Orthodox Christianity was still the established religion of the Russian state and when the 'Old Slavonic' dialect still provided a common liturgical language for the Russian, Rumanian, Bulgarian, and Serbian Orthodox Churches. Why did Pan-Slavism and Pan-Orthodoxy prove of so little avail to Russia in her dealings with these peoples, to whom she had also given such effective help in their struggles to extricate themselves from Ottoman toils?

The answer appears to be that the Ottoman Orthodox Christians had fallen under the spell of the West, and that, in so far as Russia attracted them at all, it was not because she was Slav nor because she was Orthodox but because she was a pioneer in the enterprise of Westernization on which they too had set their hearts. But, the closer their acquaintance with Russia, the more alive did these non-Russian Westernizing peoples become to the superficiality of a Petrine Russia's Western veneer. 'Scratch a Russian and you will find a Tartar.' A good deal of documentary evidence could be produced to show that Russian cultural prestige among Ottoman Christians had stood highest in the Age of Catherine the Great (reigned A.D. 1762–96) and that thereafter it had tended to decline, as Russian interference in the affairs of the Ottoman Empire increased and as Russian characteristics came to be more familiar to the 'oppressed Christian peoples' of whom Russia had sought to constitute herself the champion.

(iii) *The Modern West and the Hindu World*

The circumstances in which the Hindu world encountered the Modern West were in some points remarkably similar to those in which the main body of Orthodox Christendom underwent the same experience. Each of these civilizations had already entered into its universal state, and in each case this régime had been imposed by alien empire-builders who were children of the Iranic Muslim civilization. In Mughal India, as in Ottoman Orthodox Christendom, the subjects of these Muslim rulers were feeling the attraction of their masters' culture at the time when the Modern West appeared above their horizons, and in both regions they subsequently transferred their allegiance to this later-risen star, as the West manifestly increased and the Islamic society declined in potency. But these points of similarity throw into relief some no less striking points of difference.

For example, when the Ottoman Orthodox Christians turned towards the West, they had to overcome a traditional antipathy resulting from their unfortunate experience of an encounter with that civilization in its preceding Medieval phase. The Hindus, on the other hand, in their corresponding cultural reorientation, had no such unhappy memories to live down; for the encounter between the Hindu world and the West, which began when da Gama made his landfall at Calicut in A.D. 1498, was virtually the first contact that had ever occurred between these two societies.

Moreover, this difference in the antecedents is overshadowed by a far more important difference in the sequel. In the history of Orthodox Christendom the alien universal state remained in the hands of its Muslim founders until it went into dissolution, whereas the empire which the feeble successors of the Timurid Mughal war-lords failed to hold together was reconstituted by British business men, who stepped into Akbar's shoes when they became aware that the framework of law and order in India, without which no Westerner could carry on his business there, was going to be restored by the French if the British did not forestall these rivals by doing the work themselves. Thus the Westernization of the Hindu world entered on its critical stage in a period in which India was under Western rule; and, in consequence, the reception of the Modern Western culture was initiated in India, as in Russia, from above downwards, and not from below upwards as in Ottoman Orthodox Christendom.

In this situation the Brahman and Banya castes of the Hindu society, between them, succeeded in playing the part in Hindu history for which, in non-Russian Orthodox Christian history, the Phanariot Greeks had made an unsuccessful bid. Under all political régimes in India one of the prerogatives of the Brahmans had been to serve as ministers of state. They had played this part in the Indic world before playing it in the affiliated Hindu society. The Mughals' Muslim forerunners and the Mughals themselves in their turn had found it convenient to follow the example of the Hindu states which they were supplanting. Brahman ministers and minor officials in the service of Muslim rulers made this alien rule less odious to Hindus than it would otherwise have been, and the British Rāj, in its turn, followed the example of the Mughal Rāj, while British economic enterprise opened up corresponding opportunities for the Banyas.

As a consequence of the transfer of the government of India to British hands, the British policy of making English, instead of Persian, the official language of the imperial administration, and giving Western literature a preference over Persian and Sanskrit literature as a medium of higher education, had as great an effect on Hindu cultural history as was made on Russian cultural history by the Westernizing policy of Peter the Great. In both cases a veneer of Western life came into vogue through the fiat of an œcumenical autocratic government. High-caste Hindus acquired a Western education because the Government had ruled that this education should be the key to entry into the British Indian public service. The Westernization of Indian business and government called into existence in India two Western liberal professions, the University Faculty and the Bar, and in a Westernized business world based on private enterprise the most profitable openings could not be made a monopoly for European British subjects.

It was inevitable that this new element in the Hindu society should aspire, as in Ottoman Orthodox Christendom the Phanariot Greeks had aspired, to take over the œcumenical empire under which they were living from the alien hands by which it had been built, and to turn it into one of the parochial states of a Westernizing world on the constitutional pattern prevalent at the time. At the turn of the eighteenth and nineteenth centuries the Phanariots had dreamed of turning the Ottoman Empire into an eighteenth-century enlightened monarchy. At the turn of the nineteenth and twentieth centuries the Westernizing political leaders of the Hindu world paid homage to a change in Western political ideals by setting themselves the far more difficult task of turning the British Indian Empire into a democratic Western national state. At a date less than five years after the completion of the transfer of the Government of India from British to Indian hands on the 15th August, 1947, it was still far too early to forecast the outcome of this enterprise; but it was already possible to say that Hindu statesmanship had been more successful than foreign well-wishers could have dared to hope in its efforts to salvage as much as possible of the political unity which had been perhaps the most precious British gift to the Indian sub-continent. Many British observers of the trend of events had foretold that the downfall of the British Rāj would be followed by a 'Balkanization' of the whole sub-continent. The forecast had proved to have been mistaken, though unity was marred, from the Hindu standpoint, by the secession of Pakistan.

The Indian Muslims' motive in insisting upon the creation of Pakistan was a fear arising from a consciousness of weakness. They had not forgotten how, in the eighteenth century of the Christian Era, the Mughal Rāj had failed to maintain with the sword a dominion which the sword alone had won; and they were aware that, by the same arbitrament, the greater part of the Mughals' former domain would have become the prize of Marāthā and Sikh Hindu successor-states if British military intervention had not given the course of Indian political history a different turn. They also knew that, under the British Rāj, they had again allowed themselves to be outstripped by the Hindus in a phase of the perennial conflict between these two communities in which a British arbiter had decreed that the pen should be substituted for the sword as the instrument with which the competition was to be conducted.

For these reasons the Indian Muslims insisted in A.D. 1947 on having a separate successor-state of their own, and the consequent partition threatened to reproduce the tragic consequences that had followed from the partition of the Ottoman Empire in the previous century. The attempt to sort out geographically intermingled communities into territorially separate national states led to the drawing of frontiers that were execrable from the administrative and economic points of view. Even at this price, huge minorities were left on the wrong sides of the dividing lines. There was a panic flight of millions of refugees who abandoned their homes and property, were harried by embittered adversaries in the course of a terrible trek, and arrived destitute in unfamiliar country in which they had to start their lives afresh. Worse still, there was one section of the border between India and Pakistan where an undeclared war ensued for the possession of Kashmir. By the year A.D. 1952, however, effective efforts had been made by Indian statesmen, at both Delhi and Karachi, to save India from following the dreadful Ottoman course to the bitter end. Thus, at the time of writing, Indian prospects were on the whole encouraging from a short-term political point of view: and, if the impact of the Modern West still threatened the Hindu world with serious perils, these were to be looked for not so much on the political surface of life as in its economic subsoil and its spiritual depths, and were perhaps likely to take some time in coming to a head.

The obvious perils of Westernization which the Hindu world had to apprehend were two. In the first place, the Hindu and Western civilizations had hardly any common cultural background; and, in the second place, the Hindus who had mastered the intellectual content of an exotic Modern Western culture were a tiny minority perched on the backs of a vast mass of ignorant and destitute peasants. There was no ground for supposing that the process of Western cultural penetration would stop at that level, and there were strong grounds for forecasting that, when it began to leaven the peasant mass beneath, it would also begin to produce there some novel and revolutionary effects.

The cultural gulf between the Hindu society and the Modern West was no mere diversity; it was an outright contradiction; for the Modern West had fabricated a secular version of its cultural heritage from which religion was eliminated, whereas the Hindu society was and remained religious to the core—so much so, indeed, as to be open to the charge of 'religiosity' if, as that pejorative word implies, there can in truth be such a thing as an excessive concentration on Man's most important pursuit. This antithesis between a passionately religious and a deliberately secular outlook on life cut deeper than any diversity between one religion and another; and in this point the Hindu, the Islamic, and the Medieval Western Christian cultures were more in accord with each other than any of them were with the secular culture of the Modern West. On the strength of this common religiousness it had been possible for Hindus to become converts to Islam and to Roman Catholic Christianity without subjecting themselves to intolerable spiritual tension, as was manifest in the Muslims of Eastern Bengal and in the Roman Catholics of Goa.

This proven ability of Hindus to make their way on to alien cultural ground by a religious approach was significant, because, if religiosity was their civilization's chief distinguishing mark, its next most conspicuous feature was aloofness. This aloofness had, no doubt, been overcome in the intellectual compartment of their spiritual life by those Hindus who had acquired a secular Modern Western education and had thereby qualified for playing a part in the reconstruction of the political and economic sides of Indian life on a Modern Western basis. But the recruits of this unhappy intelligentsia performed their useful services at the cost of a schism in their own souls. This Hindu intelligentsia bred by the British Rāj remained aloof in their hearts from the Western ways with which their minds had become familiar; and this discord produced a deep-seated spiritual malaise that could not be cured by the political panacea of obtaining independence for an Indian national state organized on the Western pattern.

The unyielding spiritual aloofness of Western-educated Hindu minds had been matched by an accentuated spiritual aloofness in the souls of the Western rulers with whom the Hindu intelligentsia had had to do business under the British Rāj. Between the year A.D. 1786, in which Cornwallis had assumed the governor-general-ship with a mandate to reform the administration and the year A.D. 1858, which saw the completion of the transfer of British political authority from the East India Company to the Crown, there was a profound, and on the whole untoward, change in the attitude of the European-born British ruling class in India towards their Indian-born fellow subjects.

In the eighteenth century the English in India had followed the customs of the country, not excluding the custom of abusing power, and had been on familiar terms of personal intercourse with the Indians whom they cheated and oppressed. In the course of the nineteenth century they achieved a notable moral rally. The intoxication with suddenly acquired power which had disgraced the first generation of English rulers in Bengal was successfully overcome by a new ideal of moral integrity, which required the English civil servant in India to regard his power as a public trust and not as a personal opportunity. But the moral redemption of the British administration was accompanied by a waning of personal intercourse between English residents in India and their Indian neighbours, until the all too humanly Indianized English 'nabob' of the bad old days had been transformed into the professionally irreproachable and personally unapproachable British civil servant who said goodbye in A.D. 1947 to an India to which he had dedicated his working life without making her his home.

Why was it that the former free-and-easy personal relations died away so unluckily in an age when the loss of their beneficent influence could least well be afforded? No doubt the change was due to a number of causes. In the first place, the latter-day British official in the Indian Civil Service might fairly plead that his aloofness was the inevitable price of his moral integrity in the discharge of his duties. How could a man be expected to act professionally as a god without also maintaining a godlike aloofness in his social relations? Another, and less estimable, cause of the change was perhaps the pride inspired by conquest; for by A.D. 1849, and indeed by A.D. 1803, the military and political power of the British in India had become sensationally stronger than it had been in the eighteenth century. The operation of these two causes has been analysed acutely by a twentieth-century English student of the history of Indo-British social and cultural relations.

'As the [eighteenth] century drew to its close, a change in the social atmosphere gradually came about. The frequency of . . . "reciprocal entertainments" decreased, the formation of intimate friendships with Indians ceased. . . . The higher posts of the Government were filled with appointments from England; its designs became more imperial and its attitude more haughty and aloof. The gulf which Mussulman nawābs and English bons viveurs, diplomatic pandits and English scholars had for a time bridged over began ominously to widen again. . . . A "superiority complex" was forming which regarded India not only as a country whose institutions were bad and people corrupted, but one which was by its nature incapable of ever becoming any better. . . .

'It is one of the ironies of Indo-European relations in India that the purging of the administration coincided with the widening of the racial gulf. . . . The days of corrupt Company officials, of ill gotten fortunes, of oppression of ryots, of zenanas and of illicit sexual connexions, were also the days when Englishmen were interested in Indian culture, wrote Persian verses, and foregathered with pandits and maulvis and nawābs on terms of social equality and personal friendship. The tragedy of Cornwallis . . . was that in uprooting the acknowledged evils of corruption he upset the social balance without which mutual understanding was impossible. . . . Cornwallis . . . made a new governing class by his exclusion of all Indians from the higher governmental posts. Corruption was stamped out at the cost of equality and cooperation. In his own mind, as in the commonly accepted view, there was a necessary connexion between the two measures; "Every native of Hindustan", he said, "I verily believe, is corrupt." . . . He thought English corruption could be solved by reasonable salaries, and did not stop to consider that the advantage of Indian goodwill made it at least worth trying as a remedy for Indian corruption also. He never thought of creating an Indian imperial bureaucracy on the model of Akbar's mansabdars, which, by special training, proper salaries and the encouragement of equal treatment, promotion and honours, might have been bound to the Company as the Moghul officials were bound to the Emperor.'[1]

A third cause of estrangement was the speeding-up of communications between India and England, which made it feasible for British people to travel frequently to and fro and to remain psychologically domiciled in a home on English ground. But there was perhaps a fourth cause more potent than all of the rest, of which the Englishman in India was the victim and not the originator. An Indian who had resented the latter-day English resident's aloofness might feel more charitably towards the intruder if he were to recollect that, for perhaps as long as three thousand years before the advent of the English in India, the sub-continent had been saddled with the institution of Caste; that the Hindu society had accentuated an evil which it had inherited from its Indic predecessor; and that after the departure of the English, as before their arrival, the people of India were still afflicting themselves with a social evil of their own making. Looked at in the long perspective of Indian history, the aloofness which the English developed during the 150 years of their Rāj could be diagnosed as a mild attack of an endemic Indian malady.

While the aggravating effect of a latter-day English aloofness might be relieved by the termination of the British Rāj, the ameliorative effect of British administration on the condition and expectations of the Indian peasantry was a British legacy which might prove a mill-stone round the necks of the British civil servants' Hindu successors.

Under the *Pax Britannica* the natural resources of the subcontinent had been eked out in divers ways: by the building of railways, by irrigation, and, above all, by able and conscientious administration. By the time of the departure of their English

---

[1] Spear, T. G. P.: *The Nabobs: a Study of the Social Life of the English in Eighteenth-Century India* (London 1932, Milford), pp. 136, 137, and 145.

rulers, the Indian peasantry had perhaps become just sufficiently alive to the material achievements of Modern Western technology and to the political ideals of a Christian-hearted Modern Western democracy to begin to question both the justice and the necessity of their own ancestral indigence. But at the same time an Indian peasantry that was beginning to dream these dreams had been doing its worst to prevent their realization by continuing to breed up to the limits of subsistence, with the result that the addition to India's food supply, which had been produced by British enterprise, had gone, not towards improving the peasant's individual lot, but towards increasing the peasantry's numbers. The population of an undivided India had risen from about 206,000,000 in A.D. 1872 to 338,119,154 in A.D. 1931 and 388,997,955 in A.D. 1941, and the flood was still rising. How were the Hindu successors of the British to handle a political legacy which already allowed no margin for incompetence in the administration of the stewardship which they had taken over?

The traditional cure for over-population was to allow famine, pestilence, civil disorder, and war to reduce the population again to a figure at which the survivors would once more find themselves able to lead their traditional life at their customary low standard; and Mahatma Gandhi, in his single-minded quest for Indian independence, had willed for her the same Malthusian end, without willing the necessary barbaric means. He had divined that mere political independence might prove an illusory emancipation if India still remained entangled in the economic tendrils of a Westernized world; and he unerringly laid his axe to this economic banyan tree's technological root by launching his campaign for the abandonment of the use of machine-made cotton goods. The complete failure of his campaign was a proof that by this time India was inextricably entangled in the economic life of a Westernized world.

If and when India's population problem reached a crisis which even politicians could not ignore, Hindu statesmen responsible for the government of India would find themselves constrained by the moral atmosphere of a Westernizing world to strive for a humane rather than a Gandhi-Malthusian solution. If the policies pursued by such Western-minded Hindu statesmen should fail, there could be little doubt that a rival Russian panacea would force its way on to India's national agenda; for Communist Russia, like Westernizing India, had inherited the problem of a depressed peasantry from her cultural past, and, unlike India, she had already responded to this challenge on lines of her own. These Communist lines might be too ruthless and too revolutionary for either the

Indian peasantry or the Indian intelligentsia to be able to follow them with any zest; but, as an alternative to the still grimmer fate of old-style depopulation there was the possibility that, in an evil day, a Communist programme might find its way on to the Government of India's agenda.

(iv) *The Modern West and the Islamic world*

At the opening of the modern chapter of Western history two sister Islamic societies, standing back to back, blocked all the overland lines of access from the domains of the Western and Russian societies to other parts of the Old World. The Arabic Muslim civilization was still, at the close of the fifteenth century, holding an Atlantic seaboard in Africa from the Straits of Gibraltar to Senegal. Western Christendom was thus cut off from Tropical Africa overland, while waves of Arab influence were breaking upon the Dark Continent not only along its northern frontier in the Sudan out of the Sahara but also along its east coast, 'the Sawāhil', out of the Indian Ocean. That Ocean had indeed become an Arab lake, to which the Venetian trading partners of the Egyptian middlemen had no access, while Arab shipping was not only plying up and down the African shore from Suez to Sofala but had also found its way across to Indonesia, captured the archipelago from Hinduism for Islam, and pushed on eastwards to plant an outpost in the Western Pacific by converting the pagan Malay inhabitants of the Southern Philippines.

At the same date the Iranic Muslim civilization held what seemed to be an even stronger strategic position. The 'Osmanli empire-builders had occupied Constantinople, the Morea, Qāramān, and Trebizond; and had turned the Black Sea into an Ottoman lake by the seizure of the Genoese colonies in the Crimea. Other Turkish-speaking Muslim peoples had extended the domain of Islam from the Black Sea to the middle course of the Volga; and, behind this western front, the Iranic world extended south-eastwards to the north-western Chinese provinces of Kansu and Shensi, and over Iran and Hindustan to Bengal and the Deccan.

This massive Islamic road-block was a challenge which evoked a correspondingly energetic response from pioneer communities in the two blockaded Christian societies.

In Western Christendom the peoples of the Atlantic seaboard invented in the fifteenth century a new type of ocean-going sailing-ship, three-masted and square-rigged, with a sprinkling first of lateen and later of fore-and-aft sails, which was capable of keeping the sea for months on end without putting into port. In such vessels Portuguese mariners, who had made their trial runs in deep-sea navigation by discovering Madeira *circa* A.D. 1420 and the Azores in A.D. 1432, succeeded in outflanking the Arab seafront on the Atlantic by rounding Cape Verde in A.D. 1445, reaching the Equator in A.D. 1471, rounding the Cape of Good Hope in A.D. 1487–8, landing at Calicut on the west coast of India in A.D. 1498, seizing command of the Straits of Malacca in A.D. 1511, and pushing into the Western Pacific to show their flag at Canton in A.D. 1516 and on the coast of Japan in A.D. 1542–3. In a flash the Portuguese had snatched out of Arab hands the 'thalassocracy' of the Indian Ocean.

While the eastward-faring Portuguese pioneers in a sudden oversea expansion of the Western world were thus outflanking an Arabic Muslim world on the south, eastward-faring Cossack river-boatmen were as suddenly and sweepingly extending the borders of the Russian world by outflanking an Iranic Muslim world on the north. The way was opened for them by the Muscovite Czar Ivan IV when he conquered Qāzān in A.D. 1552; for Qāzān had been the Iranic Muslim world's north-eastern bastion, and after its fall there was no obstacle except forest and frost, which were the Nomad-fighting Cossacks' familiar allies, to prevent these pioneers of a Russian Orthodox Christendom from passing the Urals and working their way eastwards along the Siberian waterways until they were brought to a halt by stumbling in A.D. 1638 on the Pacific Ocean and, on the 24th March, 1652, on the north-eastern marches of the Manchu Empire. In reaching these new frontiers, an expanding Russian world had outflanked not only the Iranic world but the whole of the Eurasian Steppe.

Thus, in the course of little more than a century, an Islamic world, into which the Iranic and Arabic societies had coalesced, had been not only outflanked but completely encircled. By the turn of the sixteenth and seventeenth centuries the noose was round the victim's neck. Yet the suddenness with which the Islamic world had been caught in this potential stranglehold was not so extraordinary as the length of time that was to elapse before either the Muslims' adversaries or the Muslims themselves were to become sufficiently alive to the situation to be moved to take action—on the Western and the Russian side, action to pounce on an apparently helpless prey, and, on the Muslim side, action to escape from apparently desperate straits. In A.D. 1952 Dār-al-Islām was in essentials intact, having been shorn only of a few outlying provinces. The central core, from Egypt to Afghanistan and from Turkey to the Yaman, was free from alien political rule or even control. By that date Egypt, Jordan, the Lebanon, Syria, and 'Irāq had all re-emerged from beneath a flood of British and

French imperialism which had submerged them successively in A.D. 1882 and in the course of the General War of A.D. 1914–18, and the residual threat to the heart of the Arabic world was now coming, not from the Western Powers, but from the Zionists.

The clues to an understanding of the Muslim peoples' approach to 'the Western Question' are to be found in three circumstances. At the time when the impact of the Modern Western culture became the dominant problem of their lives, the Muslim peoples—like the Russians and unlike the Ottoman Orthodox Christians at the corresponding crises in their histories—were still politically their own masters; they were also the heirs of a great military tradition which was the warrant of the Islamic civilization's value in its own children's eyes; and the sudden demonstration of their latter-day military decadence by the unanswerable logic of defeat in battle was as surprising to them as it was humiliating.

The Muslims' complacency over their historic military prowess was so deeply ingrained that the lesson implicit in the turn of the military tide against them, after their failure before Vienna in A.D. 1683, had not yet made any appreciable impression on them when, nearly a hundred years later, this lesson was on the point of being driven home. When, after the outbreak of war between the Ottoman Empire and Russia in A.D. 1768, the Turks were told that the Russians intended to bring into action against them a navy that had been built in the Baltic, they obstinately refused to believe that there was a through route by water between the Baltic and the Mediterranean until the fleet in question actually arrived. Similarly, thirty years later, when the Mamlūk war-lord Murād Bey was warned by a Venetian business man that Napoleon's seizure of Malta might be the prelude to a descent on Egypt, he burst out laughing at the absurdity of the idea.

In the Ottoman world at the turn of the eighteenth and nineteenth centuries, as in the Russian world a century earlier, the aftermath of defeat by a Modern Western war-machine was a Westernizing movement from above downwards, beginning with a remodelling of the armed forces; but there was at least one point of capital importance in which the Ottoman and the Petrine policies diverged. Peter the Great divined, with the insight of genius, that a policy of Westernization must be 'all or nothing'. He saw that, in order to make a success of it, he must apply it not only to the military but to every department of life; and though, as we have seen, the Petrine régime in Russia never succeeded in Westernizing more than the urban superstructure of life and ultimately paid the penalty for its failure to leaven the rural mass by forfeiting its mandate to Communism, the eventual arrest of

Peter's cultural offensive, short of the complete attainment of his objectives, was due not so much to failure of vision on his part as to a lack of sufficient driving power in the Russian administrative machine. In Turkey, on the other hand, for a century and a half running from the outbreak of the Russo-Turkish War in A.D. 1768 till after the close of the First World War in A.D. 1918, the unwilling converts to a policy of Westernizing the Ottoman fighting forces continued, in despite of successive painful exposures of their fallacy, to hug the illusion that, in adopting elements from an alien culture, it was possible to pick and choose. The judgement on all the successive doses of Westernization that the 'Osmanlis administered to themselves, with wry faces, in the course of that period, is the damning verdict: 'Each time too little and too late.' It was not till 1919 that Mustafā Kemāl and his companions launched out unreservedly, in Petrine fashion, on a policy of wholehearted Westernization.

The Westernized Turkish national state of Mustafā Kemāl's creation looked, at the time of writing, like a successful achievement. Nothing like it, however, had as yet been achieved in other parts of the Islamic world. The Westernization of Egypt carried through in the second quarter of the nineteenth century of the Christian Era by the Albanian adventurer Mehmed 'Alī, though much more thorough than anything attempted or achieved by Turkish sultans in the same century, turned rotten under his successors and proved in the upshot to be a Western-Islamic hybrid exhibiting some of the worst features of both the original and the imitated civilization. The attempt of Amānullah of Afghanistan to ape Mustafā Kemāl in the much more intractable field of his own semi-barbarian kingdom was an experiment which may be regarded, according to inclination, as a tragedy or as a comedy, but which in either case cannot escape being pronounced a failure.

In the World as it was half-way through the twentieth century of the Christian Era, however, the success or failure of such parochial experiments as that of Amānullah was not going to decide the future of the Islamic world. In the immediate future, at any rate, the Islamic world's prospects would depend upon the issue of a trial of strength between a Western and a Russian world which encircled the Islamic world between them. To these combatants the Islamic world's importance had been enhanced, since the invention of the internal combustion engine, both as a source of key commodities and as a channel of key communications.

The Islamic world embraced the homelands of three out of the four primary civilizations of the Old World; and the agricultural wealth which those now extinct societies had once wrested from the previously intractable valleys of the Lower Nile, the Tigris–Euphrates, and the Indus had been increased in Egypt and the Panjab, and had been partially restored in 'Irāq, by the application of Modern Western methods of water-control. The principal addition, however, to the Islamic world's economic resources had been made by the discovery and utilization of subterranean deposits of mineral oil in regions that had never been of any outstanding agricultural value. The natural 'gushers' which, in a pre-Islamic age, had been turned to religious account by Zoroastrian piety to keep alight a perpetual flame in honour of the holiness of Fire, had been noted down in A.D. 1723 by the prospector's eye of Peter the Great as a potential economic asset; and, though some 150 years had still to pass before an intuition of genius was confirmed by a commercial exploitation of the Baku oilfield, fresh discoveries in rapid succession thereafter showed that Baku was only a link in a golden chain stretching south-eastwards through 'Irāqī Kurdistan and Persian Bakhtiyaristan into once reputedly valueless territories in the Arabian Peninsula. The results of the ensuing scramble for oil produced a tense political situation, since Russia's slice of the cake in the Caucasus and the Western Powers' slices in Persia and the Arab countries were within point-blank range of each other.

This tension was increased by the revival of the Islamic world's importance as a node of œcumenical communications. The shortest routes between Russia and a circum-Atlantic Western world on the one side and India, South-East Asia, China, and Japan on the other all traversed Islamic ground, waters, or air; and on the route-map, as on the oil-map, the Soviet Union and the West were at dangerously close quarters.

(v) *The Modern West and the Jews*

Whatever might be the ultimate verdict of Mankind on Western civilization in the Modern chapter of its history, it was manifest that Modern Western Man had branded himself by the commission of two crimes of indelible infamy. One was the shipping of Negro slaves from Africa to labour on plantations in the New World; the other was the extermination of a Jewish diaspora in its European homeland. The tragic issue of the encounter between the Western world and Jewry was the consequence of an interplay between Original Sin and a particular conjunction of social circumstances. Our task is to elucidate the latter.

Jewry, in the form in which it collided with Western Christendom, was an exceptional social phenomenon. It was a fossilized relic of a civilization that was extinct in every other shape. The Syriac parochial state of Judah, from which Jewry was derived, had been one of a number of Hebrew, Phoenician, Aramaean, and Philistine communities; but whereas Judah's sister communities had lost their identity as well as their statehood as a result of fatal injuries which the Syriac society had sustained from successive collisions with its Babylonic and Hellenic neighbours, the same challenges had stimulated the Jews to create for themselves a new mode of corporate existence in which they had managed to survive the loss of their state and their country by preserving their identity as a diaspora (dispersion) among an alien majority and under alien rule. This exceptionally successful Jewish reaction was not, however, unique; for the Jewish diaspora in the Islamic and Christian worlds had an historical counterpart in the Parsee diaspora in India, which was another fossilized relic of the same Syriac society.

The Parsees were survivors of Iranian converts to the Syriac civilization who had given that society its universal state in the shape of the Achaemenian Empire. The Parsee, like the Jewish, community was the monument of a victorious will to outlive the loss of state and country; and the Parsees, too, had suffered this loss as a result of successive collisions between the Syriac world and neighbouring societies. Like the Jews during the three centuries ending in A.D. 135, the Parsees' Zoroastrian forefathers had sacrificed themselves in an unsuccessful effort to eject an intrusive Hellenism, and the penalty for failure, which had been inflicted on the Jews by the Roman Empire, had been inflicted on the Zoroastrian Iranians in the seventh century of the Christian Era by Primitive Muslim Arab invaders. In these similar crises of their histories the Jews and the Parsees had preserved their identity by improvising new institutions and specializing in new activities. They had found in the elaboration of their religious law a new social cement and had survived the disastrous economic consequences of being uprooted from the land of their fathers by developing in exile a special skill in commerce and other urban business in place of a husbandry which these landless exiles were no longer able to pursue.

Nor were these Jewish and Parsee diasporas the only fossils that an extinct Syriac society had left behind it. Anti-Hellenic Christian heresies of the period between the foundation of Christianity and the foundation of Islam had produced 'fossils' in the shape of the Nestorian and Monophysite churches. Nor was the Syriac society the only one from which communities that had lost their statehood and had been uprooted from the soil had succeeded in surviving through a combination of ecclesiastical discipline with business enterprise. Under an alien Ottoman régime a subjugated Greek Orthodox Christian community had been partially uprooted from the soil and had responded with changes in their social organization and their economic activities that carried them far along the road towards becoming a diaspora of the same type as those already mentioned.

Indeed, the millet system in the Ottoman Empire was merely an organized version of a communal structure of society which had grown up spontaneously in the Syriac world after the Syriac state-system had been pulverized and the Syriac peoples inextricably intermingled by the assaults of Assyrian militarism. The consequent re-articulation of society into a network of geographically intermingled communities in place of a patchwork of geographically segregated parochial states had been inherited from the Syriac society by its Iranic and Arabic Muslim successors, and had subsequently been imposed by 'Osmanli Iranic Muslim empire-builders on a prostrate Orthodox Christendom.

In this historical perspective it is manifest that the Jewish diaspora encountered by Western Christendom was far from being a unique social phenomenon. On the contrary it was a specimen of a type of community that had become the standard type throughout an Islamic world over which, as well as over Western Christendom, the Jewish diaspora was spread. So it may well be asked whether the peculiar social setting of the tragic encounter between Jewry and Western Christendom may not be found to consist in peculiarities on the Western side at least as much as on the Jewish side; and, when we put this question we can see that the course of Western history was indeed peculiar in three respects that are all relevant to the history of Jewish-Occidental relations. In the first place, the Western society articulated itself into a patchwork of geographically segregated parochial states. In the second place, it gradually transformed itself from an ultra-rural society of peasants and landlords into an ultra-urban society of artisans and bourgeois. In the third place, this nationalist-minded and middle-class-minded latter-day Western society emerged from the relative obscurity of its medieval chapter and came rapidly to overshadow all the rest of the World.

The inner connexion between Antisemitism and the Western Christian ideal of a homogeneous community embracing all the inhabitants of a particular territory reveals itself in the history of the Jewish diaspora in the Iberian Peninsula.

As soon as the gulf between the Roman and Visigothic communities had been bridged by the conversion of the latter, from

Arian to Catholic Christianity, in A.D. 587, tension began to arise in Visigothia between the unified Christian community and the consequently more conspicuously peculiar Jewish millet. The accentuation of this tension is registered in a series of anti-Jewish enactments that presents a painful contrast to the simultaneously increasing humanity of Visigothic legislation for protecting slaves against their masters. Both the morally ascending and the morally descending series of enactments are evidence of the influence of the Church on the state. In these circumstances the Jews eventually conspired with their co-religionists in North Africa to procure the intervention of the Muslim Arabs. No doubt the Arabs might have come without this invitation. Anyway, they came; and there ensued in the Peninsula five hundred years of a Muslim régime (A.D. 711–1212) under which an autonomous Jewish diaspora was not a 'peculiar people'.

The social effect of the Arab conquest of the Iberian Peninsula was indeed to make the Jewish community at home there again by re-establishing the horizontally articulated structure of society which the conquerors brought with them from their Syriac world. But the well-being of the Jewish diaspora in the Peninsula did not outlive the Muslim Power's collapse, for the Medieval Catholic Christian barbarian conquerors of the Andalusian Umayyad Caliphate's domain were dedicated to the ideal of a homogeneous Christian commonwealth, and between A.D. 1391 and A.D. 1497 the Jews were compelled either to go into exile or to profess conversion to Christianity.

The ideal of communal homogeneity, which was the political motive of the peculiar inhospitality of Western Christendom to the Jewish strangers in its midst, was reinforced in course of time by economic and social developments.

The birthplace of the Western society was an outlying tract of the Hellenic world where the urban culture of Hellenism had failed to strike root. The superstructure of urban life that had been erected in the western provinces of the Roman Empire on primitive agricultural foundations had proved an incubus instead of a stimulus; and, after this exotic Roman-built superstructure had collapsed under its own weight, the West sank back to the same low economic level at which it had lain before Hellenism had attempted to seed itself beyond the Appennines or across the Tyrrhene Sea. This peculiar economic handicap had two consequences. In the first stage, Western Christendom was invaded by a Jewish diaspora which found an opening for making a livelihood in the West by providing a rustic society with that minimum of commercial experience and organization without which even

Ruritania could not live, but which Ruritania could not as yet provide out of her own resources. In the second stage the Western Christian Gentiles were inspired with an ambition to become their own Jews by mastering the lucrative Jewish arts.

In the course of ages a more and more demonic concentration of Western Gentile will-power on this Jewish economic objective came to reap a sensational reward. By the twentieth century of the Christian Era even the eastern rearguard of the Western peoples' column of route in their long march towards the goal of economic efficiency was going through a metamorphosis that had been achieved a thousand years earlier by the North Italian and Flemish pioneers of a movement which could be called with equal appropriateness either modernization or 'Judaization'. In Western history the sign of the attainment of this social modernity was the emergence of an Antonio class who were capable of doing the whole of Shylock's work for themselves and were consequently eager to eject him.

This economic quarrel between Jews and Western Gentiles ran through three acts. In the first act the Jews were as unpopular as they were indispensable, but the ill-treatment which they incurred was kept within bounds by the inability of their Gentile persecutors to get on economically without them. The second act opened, in one Western country after another, as soon as a nascent Gentile *bourgeoisie* had acquired sufficient experience, skill, and capital of its own to feel itself capable of usurping the local Jews' place. At that stage—which England reached in the thirteenth, Spain in the fifteenth, and Poland and Hungary in the twentieth century of the Christian Era—the Gentile bourgeois used their newly won power to secure the expulsion of their Jewish rivals. In the third act, a now well-established Gentile *bourgeoisie* had become such past-masters in Jewish economic arts that their traditional fear of succumbing to Jewish competition no longer constrained them to forgo the economic advantage of re-enlisting Jewish ability in the service of their Gentile national economy. In this spirit the Tuscan Government allowed crypto-Jewish refugees from Spain and Portugal to settle at Leghorn in and after A.D. 1593; Holland had already opened her doors to them since A.D. 1579; and England, who had felt strong enough to expel her Jews in A.D. 1290, felt strong enough to let them in again in A.D. 1655.

This economic enfranchisement of the Jews in the Modern age of Western history was rapidly followed by a social and political enfranchisement which was the consequence of the contemporary religious and ideological revolutions in Western Christendom. The Protestant Reformation broke the hostile front of a united

Catholic Church, and in seventeenth-century England and Holland refugee Jews received a welcome as victims of these Protestant countries' Roman Catholic enemies. Subsequently the Jews in general shared the benefits of the growth of toleration in Catholic and Protestant countries alike. By A.D. 1914 the official emancipation of the Jews on all planes of human activity was a long since accomplished fact in all provinces of the Modern Western world outside those territories of the now extinct United Kingdom of Poland–Lithuania which had been annexed to the Russian Empire. At this stage the Jewish problem might have been thought to be finding a solution in a fusion of the Jewish and Christian communities with each other through a union that was voluntary on both sides. But such hopes were falsified. What had looked like a drama in three acts with a happy ending soon entered on a fourth act which was more horrifying than anything that had preceded it. What had gone wrong?

One lesion was the survival of a psychological barrier between Western Gentiles and Jews after the juridical barriers between them had been officially removed. There was still an invisible ghetto within which the Western Gentile continued to confine the Jew, and the Jew, on his side, continued to segregate himself from the Western Gentile. Within an officially united society the Jew still found himself in various subtle ways an excluded person, while the Gentile found himself still faced by a freemasonry among Jews who were eager to claim, without being willing to accord, the benefits that ought to have accrued equally to all members of a united society. Both parties continued to observe a double standard of behaviour—a higher standard for dealing with members of its own crypto-community and a lower standard for dealing with nominal fellow citizens on the other side of a supposedly no longer existent social pale—and this new coat of hypocrisy embalming the old vice of inequity made either party more contemptible, as well as less formidable, in the other party's eyes, and thereby made the situation more exasperating, as well as less onerous, for both parties.

The precariousness of the relations between the two communities was revealed by the recrudescence of Antisemitism wherever there was an appreciably rapid increase in the numerical ratio of the Jewish to the Gentile ingredient in the local population. This tendency was discernible by A.D. 1914 in London and New York as a result of Jewish immigration since A.D. 1881 from ex-Polish-Lithuanian territories of the Russian Empire under pressure of Russian persecution; and after A.D. 1918 it became virulent in German Austria and in the German Reich as a result of further Jewish immigration from Galicia, 'Congress Poland', and the easterly provinces of 'the Pale' during the First World War. This German Antisemitism was not the least potent of the forces that carried the German National Socialists to power. The subsequent 'genocide' of the Jews carried out by the German National Socialists need not be enlarged upon here. The facts are as notorious as they are appalling, and constitute an exhibition of wickedness on a national scale to which history perhaps afforded no parallel up to date.

Modern Western Nationalism attacked the Jewish diaspora in the Western world on two flanks simultaneously. It led the Western Jews by its attractiveness at the same time as it drove them by its pressure to invent a nationalism of their own which might be described as a collective form of Westernization, in contrast to the individual form of Westernization associated, for the Jews, with the preceding age of nineteenth-century Liberalism. Like the Westernizing ideal of turning the individual Jew into a Western bourgeois of Jewish religion, the alternative ideal of concentrating the Jewish diaspora, or a part of it, in a parochial nation-state, with an exclusively and homogeneously Jewish population, was evidence that the emancipation of Western Jewry had been real enough to expose them to the influence of current Western ideals. At the same time, Zionism, on the testimony of its founder, Theodor Herzl himself, was also evidence of an anxiety lest the avenue of individual assimilation should be closed against them again by a Nationalism that, among Western Gentiles, was now following fast on Liberalism's heels. It is perhaps no accident that Jewish Zionism and German neo-Antisemitism should have arisen successively in the same geographical zone, namely the German-speaking territories of the pre-1918 Austrian Empire.

Of all the sombre ironies of history none throws a more sinister light on human nature than the fact that the new-style nationalist Jews, on the morrow of the most appalling of the many persecutions that their race had endured, should at once proceed to demonstrate, at the expense of Palestinian Arabs whose only offence against the Jews was that Palestine was their ancestral home, that the lesson learnt by Zionists from the sufferings which Nazis had inflicted on Jews was, not to forbear from committing the crime of which they themselves had been the victims, but to persecute, in their turn, a people weaker than they were. The Israeli Jews did not follow in the Nazis' footsteps to the extent of exterminating the Palestinian Arabs in concentration camps and gas chambers; but they did dispossess the majority of them, to the number of more than half a million, of the lands which they and their fathers had occupied and cultivated for generations, and of the property that they were unable to carry with them in their flight, and thereby they reduced them to destitution as 'displaced persons'.

One result of the Zionist experiment was to prove a point made in an earlier part of this Study, namely that the 'Jewish' characteristics which Western Gentiles had long associated with the Jews in their midst were the result of the peculiar circumstances of the Jewish diaspora in the Western world and not of any peculiar inherited racial endowment. The paradox of Zionism was that, in its demonic effort to build a community that was to be utterly Jewish, it was working as effectively for the assimilation of Jewry to a Western Gentile world as the individual Jew who opted for becoming a Western bourgeois 'of Jewish religion' or a Western bourgeois agnostic. The historic Jewry was a diaspora, and the distinctively Jewish êthos and institutions—a meticulous devotion to the Mosaic law and a consummate virtuosity in commerce and finance—were those which the diaspora, in the course of ages, had wrought into social talismans endowing this geographically scattered community with a magic capacity for survival. Latter-day Jewish Westernizers, of the Liberal and of the Zionist school alike, were breaking with this historic past; and Zionism's breach was much the more drastic of the two. In deserting the diaspora collectively in order to build up a new nation settled on the land, after the manner of the Modern Western Protestant Christian pioneers who had created the United States, the Union of South Africa, and the Commonwealth of Australia, the Zionists were assimilating themselves to a Gentile social milieu; and, in so far as they were inspired by their own Scriptures, the inspiration came neither from the Law nor from the Prophets but from the narratives in the Books of Exodus and Joshua.

In this spirit they set out defiantly and enthusiastically to turn themselves into manual labourers instead of brain-workers, into country-folk instead of city-dwellers, into producers instead of middlemen, into agriculturists instead of financiers, into warriors instead of shopkeepers, into terrorists instead of martyrs. In their new roles, as in their old roles, they displayed an astonishing toughness and resiliency; but what the future had in store for the Israelis, as the Palestinian Jews now called themselves, only the future would show. The surrounding Arab peoples appeared to be determined to expel the intruder from their midst; and these Arab peoples in 'the Fertile Crescent' far outnumbered the Israelis; yet, for the time, at any rate, their superiority in numbers was far more than offset by their inferiority in energy and efficiency.

Moreover, all questions had now come to be world questions.

On which side would the Soviet Union and the United States eventually find their Middle Eastern interests to lie? That was the question; and, so far as the Soviet Union was concerned, the answer was difficult to forecast. So far as the United States was concerned, the determining factor in her Palestinian policy up to date had been the immense disparity in numbers, wealth, and influence between the Jewish and the Arab element in her population. Compared with the American Jews, the American Arabs were an almost negligible quantity, even when account had been taken of those of Lebanese Christian origin. The Jewish contingent in the American citizen body wielded a political power that was disproportionate to its numbers; for they were concentrated in New York City, and, in the competition for votes in American domestic politics, this was a key city in a key state. But the calculations of cynical Gentile American politicians were not, as some equally cynical observers professed to believe, the complete explanation of the far-reaching support that the United States Government had given to Israel in the critical years just after the end of the Second World War. This policy was a reflection, not merely of cold domestic political calculations, but also of disinterested and idealistic, though perhaps ill-informed, public feeling. Americans found themselves able to enter into the sufferings of Jews in Europe at Nazi hands because other Jews were familiar human figures in their everyday life. There were no familiar Arabs to bring the Palestinian Arabs' sufferings home to them; and 'the absent are always in the wrong'.

(vi) *The Modern West and the Far Eastern and Indigenous American Civilizations*

The living civilizations whose encounters with the Modern West we have been surveying up to this point had all of them had experience of the Western society before they began to be affected by its impact in its modern phase. This is true even of the Hindu society, though its contacts had been comparatively slight. By contrast, the existence of the West was quite unknown in the Americas, and all but unknown in China and Japan, down to the moment when the Modern Western pioneer navigators reached their shores. In consequence the emissaries of the West were received at first without suspicion, and what they brought had the charm of novelty. In the event, however, the two stories took sharply different turns. The American civilizations were as unsuccessful as the Far Eastern civilizations were successful in coping with a difficult situation.

The Spanish conquerors of the Middle American and Andean worlds immediately overwhelmed their ill-equipped and unsuspecting victims by force of arms; they virtually exterminated those elements of the population that were the repositories of the indigenous cultures; they substituted themselves as an alien dominant minority, and they reduced the rural population to the status of an internal proletariat of the Western Christian society by putting their labour at the disposal of Spanish economico-religious *entrepreneurs* on the understanding that these planter-missionaries would make it a part of their business to convert their human flocks to the Roman Catholic form of Christianity. Even so, it could not be regarded as certain, at the time of writing, that the indigenous cultures would not in some form eventually re-emerge, as the Syriac society had re-emerged and reconstituted itself after a thousand years of Hellenic domination.

The two Far Eastern societies in China and Japan, on the other hand, survived the deadly peril to which they were exposed by their initial ignorance. They managed to weigh the Western civilization in the balance, find it wanting, make up their minds to cast it out, and muster the necessary force for putting into effect a considered policy of virtual non-intercourse. But this, as it turned out, was not the end of the story. In breaking off relations with the West in the form in which the West had first presented itself, the Chinese and Japanese had not disposed of their 'Western Question' once for all. A rebuffed West subsequently transformed itself, and then reappeared on the East Asian scene, now offering its technology instead of its religion as its principal gift, and the Far Eastern societies now found themselves confronted with a choice of either mastering this newfangled Western technology for themselves or else succumbing to it.

In this Far Eastern drama the Chinese and Japanese behaved alike in some ways and in other ways diversely. A striking point of likeness was that, in the second act, the reception of a secularized Modern Western culture was initiated in both China and Japan from below upward. The Manchu Empire in China and the Tokugawa Shogunate in Japan failed, alike, to seize the initiative, in contrast with the Petrine Czardom in Russia. In the next scene of this act, however, Japan, unlike China, went over to the Petrine method. On the other hand, in the first act, that is to say in the sixteenth-century encounters, the two Far Eastern societies had taken different courses from the outset. In their tentatively accorded and subsequently revoked reception of the Modern Western culture in its sixteenth-century and seventeenth-century religious phase the initiative had come throughout from above downwards in China and from below upwards in Japan.

If one were to plot the reactions of the two Far Eastern societies to the Modern West over the last four centuries in the form of graphs one would find that the Japanese curves were much sharper than the Chinese. The Chinese never went to such lengths as the Japanese either in surrendering themselves to the Western culture on either occasion or in insulating themselves from it during the intervening period of xenophobia.

By the turn of the sixteenth and seventeenth centuries a Japan whose political unification was still incomplete had come to be perilously exposed to the danger of having political unity imposed on her from abroad by the ruthless hands of alien *conquistadores*. The Spanish conquest of the Philippines in A.D. 1565–71 and the Dutch conquest of Formosa in A.D. 1624 were object lessons of the fate that might befall Japan. By contrast, the vast sub-continent of China had nothing very serious to fear from the advent of the Western pirates of that age. Such unmechanized sea-raiders, however annoying they might be, were not potential conquerors. The dangers that gave serious cause for anxiety to a Chinese Imperial Government at that time were those of overland invasion from the Eurasian Steppe; and after the Ming Dynasty had been supplanted by the vigorous semi-barbarian Manchus in the course of the seventeenth century, a recurrence of danger from the interior of the Continent did not present itself for another two hundred years.

This difference in the geographico-political situations of China and Japan goes far to explain why it was that in China the repression of Roman Catholic Christianity was postponed till the end of the seventeenth century and was the outcome not of political apprehensions but of a theological controversy—in contrast with the promptness and the ruthlessness of the suppression of Roman Catholic Christianity in Japan and the final cutting of all but one solitary Dutch thread in the nexus between Japan and the Western world. The succession of blows delivered by a newly established Japanese central Government began with Hideyoshi's ordinance of A.D. 1587 decreeing the banishment of all Western Christian missionaries and culminated in the ordinances of A.D. 1636–9 forbidding Japanese subjects to travel abroad and Portuguese subjects to reside in Japan.

In Japan, as in China, the abandonment of the policy of insulation came from below upwards and was inspired by a hunger to taste the fruits of Modern Western scientific knowledge. Many of the pioneers of the movement suffered martyrdom for their faith in technology in the proscriptions of A.D. 1840–50, immediately before the so-called 'Opening of Japan' in A.D. 1853. In Japan the movement was wholly secular. On the other hand, the corresponding nineteenth-century movement in China was associated with the activities of Protestant Christian missionaries who accompanied British and American salesmen here, as their Portuguese forerunners in Japan had been accompanied by Roman Catholic Christian missionaries, and in China this Protestant missionary influence continued. Sun Yat-sen, the founder of Kuomintang, was the son of a convert to Protestant Christianity, and another Protestant Christian Chinese family played a paramount part in the Kuomintang's subsequent history in the persons of Madame Sun Yat-sen, her sister Madame Chiang Kai-shek, and their brother T. V. Soong.

The Japanese and the Chinese Westernizing movements were both confronted with the formidable task of having to liquidate and replace a well-established indigenous œcumenical régime, but the Japanese Westernizers were more alert, prompt, and efficient than the Chinese. Within fifteen years of the appearance of Commodore Perry's squadron in Japanese territorial waters in A.D. 1853, they had not only overthrown the Tokugawa régime, which had failed to rise to the occasion; they had also achieved the far more difficult task of installing in its place a new régime capable of putting into operation a comprehensive Westernizing movement from above downwards. The Chinese took 118 years to accomplish even the negative half of this task. The arrival of Lord Macartney's Embassy at Peking in A.D. 1793 was no less illuminating a demonstration of the enhanced potency of the West than the arrival of Commodore Perry's squadron in Yedo Bay sixty years later; yet in China the overthrow of the *ancien régime* did not follow till A.D. 1911 and was then replaced, not by an effective Westernizing new order, but by an anarchy which the Kuomintang failed to overcome during the quarter of a century (A.D. 1923–48) which this would-be Liberal Westernizing movement had at its disposal.

The difference can be measured by the degree of Japan's military superiority over China during the fifty years running from the outbreak of the Sino-Japanese War of 1894–5.[1] During that half-century China was militarily at Japan's mercy; and though, in the last round of this struggle, an effective conquest of the whole of China proved to be beyond Japan's resources, it was equally evident that, if the Japanese war-machine had not been shattered by the United States, the Chinese would never have been able, unaided, to wrest back out of Japanese hands the captured ports, industrial areas, and railways that were the keys to the Westernization of China.

[1] A *Punch* cartoon, apropos of this war, entitled 'Jap the Giant-Killer', illustrates the amiably frivolous attitude of the British public at the time.

By the opening of the second half of the twentieth century, however, the Japanese hare and the Chinese tortoise had arrived almost simultaneously at the same disastrous goal. Japan was lying passive under the military occupation of the greatest of the Western Powers while China had passed, by way of revolution, out of anarchy into its antithesis in the shape of the iron control of a Communist régime. Whether we regard this as Western or anti-Western (a point already discussed in this Study), it was in any case an alien ideology from the standpoint of the Far Eastern culture.

What was the explanation of this uniformly disastrous ending of the first phase of the second encounter between these two Far Eastern societies and the Modern West? In both China and Japan the disaster had its root in an unsolved problem common to Asia and Eastern Europe, which has come to our attention already in considering the impact of the West upon the Hindu world. What was to be the effect of the Western civilization's impact on primitive peasant populations which had been accustomed for ages to breed up to the limits of bare subsistence, and which were now being inoculated with a novel discontent, but had not yet begun to face the fact that possibilities of economic betterment could be realized only at the price of an economic, a social, and, above all, a psychological revolution? In order to tap the bounty of Amalthea's horn, these hide-bound peasants would have to revolutionize their traditional methods of land-utilization and sytems of land tenure, and would also have to regulate the number of their births.

It had been possible to stabilize the political and economic life of Japan under the Tokugawa Shogunate—as far as it had been stabilized during that period—because there had been a basis of demographic stability underpinning it. Population had been kept stationary at about thirty millions by a variety of means, which had included abortion and infanticide. When this régime was liquidated, an unnaturally frozen Japanese body social thawed out, and population began to leap up. Unlike the changes on the political and economic planes, the resumption of unrestricted breeding was not due to Western influence but was simply a reversion to the traditional habits of a peasant society which had been put under restraint, by a psychological *tour de force*, in the glacial atmosphere of the Tokugawa Age. Contemporary Westernization did, however, accentuate the demographic effect of this relapse into primitive habits by lowering the death-rate.

In these circumstances Japan had either to expand or explode, and the only practicable forms of expansion were either to persuade the rest of the World to trade with her or to conquer additional territory, resources, and markets by force of arms from existing owners who were militarily too weak to defend their property against a militarily Westernized Japan's aggression. The history of Japanese foreign policy from A.D. 1868 to A.D. 1931 is a history of oscillations between these alternatives. The gradual effect of a world-wide accentuation of economic nationalism in converting the Japanese people to the militarist alternative was clinched by the terrible experience of the economic blizzard which descended on Wall Street in the autumn of A.D. 1929 and then swept over the rest of the World. Almost exactly two years later, Japan launched at Mukden, on the night of 18th–19th September 1931, her great venture in aggression which ended with V–J Day, A.D. 1945.

Since the Chinese were not cooped up in a cluster of relatively small islands but sprawled over an enormous subcontinent the population problem had not presented itself as urgently nor been tackled as ruthlessly in China as in Japan. It was none the less equally serious on a rather longer view, and the responsibility for dealing with it had now come to rest on the shoulders of Chinese Communist dictators. This ideological conquest of China by Communism was the latest move in a Russian assault on the main body of the Far Eastern society that had been in progress for some three hundred years. We will not dwell on its earlier stages. In the nineteenth century, in a period before Japan had been seriously reckoned as a competitor, Russia and the Western Powers had appeared as rival aggressors nibbling at the carcass of a moribund Chinese Empire. At this stage the question had seemed to be whether Hong Kong and Shanghai would prove to be for British imperialism in China the growing-points that Bombay and Calcutta had been for British imperialism in India. On the other hand Russia had acquired sovereignty over Vladivostok in 1860 and a lease of the much more central and important Port Arthur in 1897. It had been Japan who had nipped this Russian effort in the bud in the epoch-making Russo-Japanese war of A.D. 1904–5. The end of the First World War had again seen Russia apparently dissolved in anarchy, while Japan had drawn exorbitant profits as a more or less sleeping partner in the victorious Western coalition. However, where Russian Czardom had failed, Russian Communism succeeded, for reasons which, in one shape or another, we have so often encountered in this Study—reasons which are reducible to such platitudinous paradoxes as the copy-book maxim which tells us that the pen is mightier than the sword. Marx's secular gospel of Communism gave Russia a psychological appeal which naked Czarism had not been able to make. Hence the Soviet Union could command in China—as elsewhere—a formidable 'fifth column'. If a now Communist Russia furnished the tools, or some of them, her Chinese admirers could be relied on to do her job for her.

(vii) *Characteristics of the Encounters between the Modern West and its Contemporaries*

The most significant conclusion that suggests itself as arising out of a comparison of the encounters that we have now described is that the word 'modern' in the term 'Modern Western civilization' could be given a more precise and concrete connotation by being translated 'middle class'. Western communities had become 'modern' as soon as they had produced a *bourgeoisie* capable of becoming the predominant element in Society. We think of the new chapter of Western history that opened at the end of the fifteenth century as being 'modern' because it was at that time that, in the more advanced Western communities, the middle class began to take control. It follows that, during the currency of the Modern Age of Western history, the ability of aliens to become Westernized depended on their capacity for entering into the middle-class Western way of life. When we examine examples, already noted, of Westernization from below upwards, we find that, in the pre-existing social structure of Greek Orthodox Christian, Chinese, and Japanese life, for example, there were already middle-class elements through which the Westernizing leaven worked. On the other hand, in cases where the process of Westernization proceeded from above downwards, the autocrats who set themselves to Westernize their subjects by fiat could not wait for an unforced process of evolution to provide them with authentic middle-class agents of indigenous origin but were constrained to provide themselves with an artificial substitute for a home grown middle class by manufacturing an intelligentsia.

The intelligentsias thus called into existence in Russia and in the Islamic and Hindu worlds were, of course, successfully imbued by their makers with a genuine tincture of Western middle-class qualities. The Russian case suggests, however, that this tincture might prove ephemeral. For the Russian intelligentsia, which had originally been called into existence by the Petrine Czardom to bring Russia into the middle-class Western fold, had revolted in its heart against both the Czardom and the Western bourgeois ideal, long before the revolutionary explosion of A.D. 1917. It was possible that what had happened in Russia might happen elsewhere to other intelligentsias as well.

In the light of this anti-bourgeois turn which the Russian intelligentsia had already taken, it was perhaps worth pausing to look into the likenesses and the differences between the non-Western intelligentsias and the Western middle class whose role they had been commissioned to play in a non-Western environment.

One common feature of their histories was that both had come from beyond the pale of the societies in which they had established themselves. We have seen that the Western society, when it first emerged from the Dark Ages, was an agrarian society in whose life urban pursuits were so exotic that some of them were practised originally by an alien Jewish diaspora, until a Gentile middle class was called into being by the Gentiles' aspiration to become their own Jews.

Another experience that was common to the Modern Western middle class and the contemporary intelligentsias was that both had won their eventual dominance by revolting against their original employers. In Great Britain, Holland, France, and other Western countries, the middle class had come into power by stepping into the shoes of monarchies whose patronage had inadvertently made the middle class's fortune.[1] Similarly, in non-Western polities of the Late Modern Age, the intelligentsia had come into power by successfully revolting against Westernizing autocrats who had deliberately called them into existence. If we take a synoptic view of this common episode in the histories of Petrine Russia, the latter-day Ottoman Empire, and the British Rāj in India, we shall see that the revolt of the intelligentsia not only occurred in all three cases but came to a head in each case after the lapse of approximately the same length of time. In Russia the abortive Decembrist Revolution of A.D. 1825, which was the Russian intelligentsia's declaration of war on the Petrine system, broke out 136 years after Peter's effective advent to power in A.D. 1689. In India, political 'unrest' began to reveal itself towards the end of the nineteenth century, rather less than 140 years after the establishment of British rule in Bengal. In the Ottoman Empire, the Committee of Union and Progress overthrew Sultan 'Abd-al-Hamid II in A.D. 1908, 134 years after the Porte had first been impelled, by the shock of defeat in the Russo-Turkish War of A.D. 1768–74, to begin training an appreciable number of its Muslim subjects in the Modern Western art of war.

But these points of likeness are offset by at least one signal difference. The Modern Western middle class was an indigenous element in the society that it came to dominate; it was, in a psychological sense, 'at home' there. By contrast, the intelligentsias suffered from the double handicap of being both *novi homines* and

---

[1] It was, for example, a commonplace of English history that the powers given to the Commons by the Tudors were used by them against the Stuarts.

exotics. They were products and symptoms, not of natural growth, but of their own societies' discomfiture in collisions with an alien Modern West. They were symbols not of strength but of weakness. The intelligentsias, for their part, were sensitively aware of this invidious difference. The social service that they had been created to perform made them aliens in the society for which they performed it. Their intuition of the thanklessness of their task conspired with an inexorable nervous strain arising from the inherent contractions in their social situation to breed in them a smouldering hatred of a Western middle class which was both their sire and their bane, their cynosure and their bugbear; and their excruciatingly ambivalent attitude towards this pirate sun, whose capitivated planets they were, is poignantly conveyed in Catullus' elegiac couplet:

> Odi et amo: quare id faciam, fortasse requiris.
> nescio, sed fieri sentio et excrucior.[1]

The intensity of an alien intelligentsia's hatred of the Western middle class gave the measure of its foreboding of its inability to emulate Western middle-class achievement. The classic instance, up to date, in which this embittering prescience had been justified, was the Russian intelligentsia's catastrophic failure, after the first of the two Russian revolutions in A.D. 1917, to carry out its fantastic mandate to transform the wreck of the Petrine Czardom into a parliamentary constitutional state in the nineteenth-century Western style. The Kerensky régime was a fiasco because it was saddled with the task of making bricks without straw: of making a parliamentary government without having a solid, competent, prosperous, and experienced middle class to draw on. By contrast, Lenin succeeded because he set himself to create something which would meet the situation. His All-Union Communist Party was not, indeed, a thing entirely without precedent. In Iranic Muslim history it had been anticipated in the slave-household of the Ottoman Pādishāh, in the Qyzylbash fraternity of devotees of the Safawīs, and in the Sikh Khālsā that had been called into being by a decision to fight the Mughāl ascendancy with its own weapons. In these Islamic and Hindu fraternities the êthos of the Russian Communist Party is already unmistakably discernible. Lenin's claim to originality rests on his having reinvented this formidable political instrument for himself and on his priority in applying it to the special purpose of enabling a non-Western society to hold its own against the Modern West by mastering the latest devices

[1] I hate you and I love you: perhaps you ask why. I do not know, but that is how I feel, and it tortures me.

of Western technology while at the same time eschewing the West's current orthodox ideology.

The success of Lenin's single-party type of dictatorial régime is proved by the number of its imitators. Passing over those imitators who professed and called themselves Communists, we need only point to the régime established by Mustafā Kemāl Atatürk for the masterful regeneration of Turkey; to the Fascist régime of Mussolini in Italy; and to the National Socialist régime of Hitler in Germany. Of these three non-Communist single-party régimes, the new order in Turkey has been unique in having succeeded in transforming itself into a two-party régime, on Liberal Western lines, by a peaceful transition instead of paying the price of a catastrophe.

(b) ENCOUNTERS WITH MEDIEVAL WESTERN CHRISTENDOM

(i) The Flow and Ebb of the Crusades

The term 'Crusades' is commonly confined to those Western military expeditions which, at Papal instigation and with Papal blessings, set forth to win, to support, or to win again, a Christian kingdom at Jerusalem. We here use the term in a much wider sense to cover all the warfare of Western Christendom on its frontiers in the Medieval chapter of its history, against Islam in Spain as well as in Syria, against the rival Christendom of the East Roman Empire, and against pagan barbarians on the north-eastern frontier. All this warfare may well be called Crusading, for the warriors consciously, and not entirely hypocritically, thought of themselves as extending or defending the frontiers of a Christendom. We may surmise that Chaucer would approve the extended use of the term. The Knight—'a very parfit gentil knight'—who figures first in the gallery of pen-portraits presented in his *Prolog* to the Canterbury Tales, was a veteran who might well in his youth have fought at Crécy and Poitiers, but it never occurs to his creator to connect him with such family quarrels between local Western states. Instead, he is portrayed as having fought all round the frontiers of Western Christendom from 'Gernade' (Granada) to 'Ruce' and 'Pruce' and 'Lettow' (Russia and Prussia and Lithuania), and, though Chaucer does not actually call him a Crusader, he clearly thinks of him as a warrior who had been engaged in distinctively Christian warfare. Our concern at present, before going on to analyse the impact of an aggressive Western Christendom on the other civilizations concerned, is to give some idea of the general course of these medieval wars of expansion.

The medieval outbreak of the Western society in the eleventh century of the Christian Era was as surprisingly abrupt as its modern outbreak at the turn of the fifteenth and sixteenth centuries, and the eventual collapse of the medieval Western adventure came as swiftly as its initial success. An intelligent observer from, say, China, who had made his way to the other end of the Old World in the middle years of the thirteenth century of the Christian Era, would have been as unlikely to foresee that the Western intruders were on the verge of being expelled from Dār-al-Islām and 'Romania' (the Orthodox Christian domain of the East Roman Empire) as he would have been—had he arrived on the scene three hundred years earlier—to foresee that these same two worlds were on the verge of being attacked and overrun by the hitherto apparently backward and uncultivated natives of the western extremity of the cultivated visitor's *Oikoumenē*. As soon as he had learnt to distinguish the two Hellenistic Christian societies from each other and from a Syriac society in process of conversion to the all but Christian heresy of Islam, he would probably have come to the conclusion that, of these three competitors for the control of the Mediterranean Basin and its hinterlands, Orthodox Christendom had the best prospects and Western Christendom the worst.

On the divers tests of comparative standing in wealth, education, administrative efficiency, and success in war, Orthodox Christendom would assuredly have come out at the top of our mid-tenth-century observer's list and Western Christendom at the bottom. Western Christendom was then an agrarian society in which urban life was exotic and coin a rare currency, whereas in contemporary Orthodox Christendom there was a money economy based on a prosperous commerce and industry. In Western Christendom only the clergy was literate, whereas in Orthodox Christendom there was a highly educated lay governing class. Western Christendom had relapsed into anarchy after the failure of Charlemagne's abortive new Roman Empire there, whereas the new Roman Empire created by Leo Syrus in the same eighth century in Eastern Orthodox Christendom was still flourishing and was beginning to reconquer the lands that the original Roman Empire had lost in the seventh century to the Primitive Muslim Arab conquerors.

After the tide of Muslim conquest had begun to recede on land, it had continued for a time to advance at sea; and both the Christendoms had been roughly handled in the ninth century by Maghribī[1]

[1] The Maghrib, meaning, in Arabic, 'the West', is the Islamic name for the north-western shoulder of Africa—consisting of the latter-day Tunisia, Algeria, and Morocco. This 'Africa Minor' is virtually an island; for the Sahara Desert insulates it from Tropical Africa ('Africa Proper') more effectively than the Mediterranean Sea insulates it from Europe.

Muslim buccaneers. Orthodox Christendom had, however, responded to their challenge by reconquering Crete from them, whereas no similar response is recorded from Western Christendom. On the contrary, the Muslim raiders were then still pushing inland from the Riviera and infesting the Alpine passes.

A more penetrating vision than we can demand of our hypothetical Chinese observer might, no doubt, have discerned some underlying realities. It might have discerned deadly weaknesses beneath the imposing surface of Orthodox Christendom. It might have noticed that Western Christendom, which had made such a poor showing in the Mediterranean, had put up a valiant fight, in other quarters, against its Scandinavian and Magyar barbarian assailants. Even against the Muslims, the Western Christian frontier had already begun its long slow advance in the Iberian Peninsula. Tenth-century Western Christendom, unlike either of its rivals, was a civilization in the growth stage. Its spiritual citadel was monasticism, and the tenth-century Cluniac rejuvenation of the Benedictine way of monastic life was the archetype of all subsequent Western social reforms, religious and secular.

Yet these signs of vitality in a tenth-century Western Christendom seem hardly adequate to account for the amazing outburst of Western energy in the eleventh century, an outburst in which an outbreak of aggression against two neighbouring societies was one of the less creative and less admirable episodes. The Western Christians followed up their feat of converting the Scandinavian colonists of Normandy and the Danelaw by bringing within their fold the Scandinavian war-bands in their native lairs, as well as the barbarians of Hungary and Poland. The Cluniac reform of monastic life led to the Hildebrandine reform of the whole ecclesiastical system under Papal leadership. An acceleration of the advance in the Iberian Peninsula was paralleled by a conquest of the East Roman Empire's dominions in Southern Italy and of the Muslims mastery of Sicily, and by a threatening—though as it turned out, abortive—thrust across the Adriatic towards the East Roman Empire's heart. A climax came with the First Crusade (A.D. 1095–9), which established, at the expense of Islam, a chain of Western Christian principalities in Syria from Antioch and Edessa (beyond the Euphrates) to Jerusalem and Azla (at the head of the Gulf of Aqaba, which opens into the Red Sea).

The eventual collapse of this Medieval Western Christian ascendancy in the Mediterranean Basin would have been no less surprising to our Far Eastern observer if he could have resurveyed the scene 150 years after the First Crusade. By then the Western aggressors had lost practically all their exposed outposts in Syria.

In the Iberian Peninsula, on the other hand, the Muslim domain had been reduced to a mere enclave round Granada, and the Westerners had consoled themselves for their losses in Syria by assaulting and conquering the European dominions of the East Roman Empire. A Frankish prince was usurping the place and name of Roman Emperor in Constantinople. Far away to the east a great Mongolian Empire .had arisen, and Western Christian visionaries had conceived a dream of taking Islam in the rear by converting the rulers of this new World Power to the Western form of the Christian religion. Papal missionaries had made the long journey to Qārāqorum. Marco Polo would soon be on his way to the court of 'Kubla Khan'.

Nothing came of it; and, very soon after the date that we have assigned to our imaginary Chinese observer, the ramshackle edifice of the 'Latin Empire' at Constantinople collapsed (A.D. 1261). The Greek Orthodox Christian Empire was restored, though the future here was to belong not to the Greeks but to the Ottoman Turks. Western Christendom now diverted its aggressive energies to its north-eastern frontier. The Teutonic Knights decamped from Syria and sought their fortunes on the Vistula at the expense of the pagan Prussians, Letts, and Ests. Only in the Iberian Peninsula, Southern Italy, and Sicily had the advance made at the beginning of the medieval period been increased and maintained right down to the end of it. The attempt of a Medieval Western Christendom to extend its frontiers southwards and eastwards to include all the lands that had once belonged to its Hellenic parent had failèd. If one considers the material resources of Medieval Western Christendom in wealth and population and intelligence, any other result was hardly to be expected.

(ii) *The Medieval West and the Syriac World*

When the Medieval Western Christians launched their assault on the Syriac world in the eleventh century of the Christian Era, they found its inhabitants divided in their communal allegiance between Islam and a variety of Christian heresies—Monophysitism, Nestorianism, and others—which represented pre-Islamic attempts of Syriac souls to de-Hellenize Christianity. In the first period after the Arab conquest, Islam had been the distinctive religion of these victorious barbarians, much as Arianism had been the religion of most of the Teutonic conquerors of various provinces of the Roman Empire. Throughout the period between the Muslim conquest in the eighth century and the First Crusade at the end of the eleventh there was, for a variety of reasons, a steady drift towards Islam among these subject peoples, but it was by no means

complete at the end of that period. The effect of the Crusades
was to convert this drift into a landslide. The new-born Islamic
societies, Arabic and Iranic, arose out of the ruins of the dead
Syriac world.

Considering that Muslims and Christians ranked officially as
'unbelievers' in each other's eyes, and that the champions of these
two fanatically exclusive-minded Judaic religions were chronically
at war, we may marvel at the degree of mutual respect which their
fighting men came to feel for one another, and at the amount and
importance of the cultural nourishment which Medieval Western
Christendom imbibed through a Syriac channel in which the spirit
and technique of an Arabic poetry were conveyed to them in
a Romance language by Provençal troubadours, and the ideas of
an Hellenic philosophy in the Arabic language through Muslim
scholars.

In the realm of the sword the sympathy between the warriors in
the two opposing camps arose from the discovery of an unexpected
affinity. On the battlefields of Andalusia the Andalusian Muslims
and the transfrontier Iberian Christian barbarians sometimes felt
a closer kinship with one another than the Iberian Christians felt
with their co-religionists from beyond the Pyrenees, or the Iberian
Muslims with their co-religionists from North Africa. On the
battlefields of Syria the Turkish barbarians who had become converts to Islam in the act of overrunning the dominions of the
Caliphate were not unsympathetic adversaries for the contemporary
Christian knights who, in degree of civilization, were not far above
their barbarian ancestors who had become Christians in the act of
overrunning the Roman Empire. Indeed the Normans, who were
the spearhead of the Frankish offensive, were as recent converts
from barbarism as the Saljūqs.

In the realm of the pen the Crusaders' temporary conquests in
Syria, and, still more, their lasting conquests in Sicily and Andalusia, at the expense of Dār-al-Islām, became so many transmitting
stations through which the spiritual treasures of a moribund Syriac
world were communicated to a Medieval Western Christendom.
The genial atmosphere of religious tolerance and intellectual
curiosity, which temporarily captivated the Western Christian
conquerors of Palermo and Toledo in virtue of its contrast to their
own traditional fanaticism, was native to an early Islam; but the
cultural treasures which, in this propitious environment, Western
minds consented to receive from Muslim and Jewish hands during
the next two centuries were of Hellenic as well as Syriac origin.
The Syriac society was not the creator but was merely the carrier
of authentic and apocryphal works of Aristotle which were made

accessible to twelfth-century Western schoolmen by being translated into Latin out of Arabic.

In mathematics, astronomy, and medicine the Syriac-speaking
Nestorian Christian pupils of the Hellenes and the Arabic-speaking
Muslim pupils of the Nestorians had not only preserved and
mastered the achievements of their Hellenic predecessors but had
also taken lessons in an Indic school and had gone on to achieve
original work of their own. In these fields a Medieval Western
Christendom took over from contemporary Muslim men of science
the results of Muslim research, together with the so-called 'Arabic'
system of mathematical notation which the Muslims had acquired
from India; and, when we raise our eyes from the intellectual to
the poetic plane, we shall see that the treasure that was acquired
from the Andalusian Muslim representatives of a dying Syriac
culture was a native Arab achievement which was to inspire all the
subsequent achievements of a Western school of poetry down to
the end of the Western civilization's Modern Age—if it was true
that the ideas and ideals, as well as the versification and rhyming,
of this Western school's Provençal troubadour pioneers could be
traced back to an Andalusian Muslim source.

The Modern West had gone far beyond its Muslim heritage in
the field of science, yet the impact of the Syriac civilization on the
youthfully impressionable imagination of a Medieval Western
Christendom was still being visually proclaimed in the realm of
architecture by 'Gothic' buildings which—in confutation of the
absurd nickname which had been conferred upon them by
eighteenth-century antiquaries—bore on their face a patent certi-
ficate of derivation from models still extant in the ruins of Armenian
churches and Saljūq caravanserais. In the twentieth century the
cities of Western Europe were still dominated by 'Gothic' cathedrals
which had superseded their Romanesque predecessors as the result
of a medieval Western architectural revolution precipitated by the
architectural impact of the Syriac world.

(iii) *The Medieval West and Greek Orthodox Christendom*

These two Christendoms found it more difficult to come to
terms with one another than with their Muslim neighbours. The
discord was a consequence of the historical fact that the Hellenic
civilization had given birth to two daughter societies; for, on the
morrow of their simultaneous emergence, towards the close of the
seventh century of the Christian Era, some five hundred years
before the final breach between them in the tragic years A.D. 1182-
1204,[1] these two societies had already become alienated by a

---

[1] The three atrocious acts that made the breach irreparable were the massacre

diversity of êthos and a conflict of interests. The conflict of interests came to a head in a struggle for predominance in South-Eastern Europe and Southern Italy, a struggle embittered by their rival claims to be the sole legitimate heir of a Christian universal church, a Roman Empire, and an Hellenic civilization.

The political conflict was apt to be masked under the form of ecclesiastical controversies. For example, when in the eighth century the Roman See took sides, in a quarrel in Eastern Orthodox Christendom over image worship, against the iconoclastic policy of the East Roman Imperial Government, it was declaring, on behalf of the people of the remaining fragments of the East Roman Empire in Central Italy, a political decision to look beyond the Alps, to the grandfather and subsequently to the father of Charlemagne, for military assistance against the Lombards which it had failed to obtain from Constantinople. When, midway through the eleventh century, rival movements for liturgical uniformity issuing from Rome and Constantinople came into collision, the conflict which led to the schism of A.D. 1054 was at the same time a political contest for the allegiance of ecclesiastical subjects of the Papacy in Southern Italy who were political subjects of the East Roman Empire. On neither occasion, however, was the breach between the two societies made absolute.

At the time of the First Crusade, forty years after the latter of these two ecclesiastico-political conflicts, the reigning East Roman Emperor Alexius I Comnenus, on whom the passage of the Crusaders through his dominions inflicted extreme political anxiety and personal discomfort, is credited by his daughter the historian Anna Comnena with a scrupulous reluctance to authorize his troops to shed their fellow Christians' blood. One of the motives attributed by Anna to Alexius for his policy of sending East Roman forces to convoy the Crusaders across Anatolia is a concern to save them from being cut to pieces by the Turks. This wry-faced forbearance towards the Crusaders practised by Alexius (reigned A.D. 1081–1118) was to be transformed in the attitude of his grandson, the Emperor Manuel I (reigned A.D. 1145–80), into a positive passion for Frankish comrades and customs; and there were prelates on both sides, as well as secular statesmen on the East Roman side, who were concerned to avert a breach between the two Christendoms.

Why was it, then, that a breach between the two Christendoms

of Frankish residents in the East Roman Empire in A.D. 1182, the sack of Salonica by an avenging Norman expeditionary force in A.D. 1185, and the sack of Constantinople by a Franco-Venetian expeditionary force in A.D. 1204 ('the Fourth Crusade').

came to pass, after all, in the years A.D. 1182–1204, and thereafter widened until, in the fifteenth century, the Eastern Orthodox Christians opted for political submission to the Turk in preference to accepting the Western Christian Pope's ecclesiastical supremacy? No doubt on that occasion the Roman terms were severe, but the ultimate cause of the catastrophe is perhaps to be found in a progressive divergence between the two cultures which had begun to show itself seven hundred or even a thousand years earlier. An aggravating circumstance was the sudden, unexpected, and sensational reversal, in the eleventh century, of the two Christian societies' relative strengths and prospects, to which we have called attention in the previous section of this chapter.

One of the consequences of this political and economic reversal of fortunes was that, thenceforth, either party presented an insufferable appearance in the other's eyes. In the sight of the Eastern Orthodox Christians the Franks were *parvenus* cynically exploiting a brute force which a freak of fortune had conferred upon them; in the sight of the Franks the Byzantines were mandarins whose overweening pretensions were neither justified by merit nor backed by force. To the Greeks the Latins were barbarians; to the Latins the Greeks were on the way to becoming 'Levantines'.

Out of the copious Greek and Latin literature illustrating the Franks' and Byzantines' mutual dislike we must be content to cite a few illuminating passages from one representative spokesman on either side. As evidence of the Franks' prejudice against the Byzantines we may quote a report by the Lombard Bishop Liutprand of Cremona on a mission to the East Roman Imperial Court which he carried out on behalf of the West Roman Emperor Otto II in A.D. 968–9. As evidence of Byzantine prejudice against the Franks we may quote the Greek princess-historian Anna Comnena, who became disagreeably well acquainted with the Franks both before and during the First Crusade.

Bishop Liutprand's official anxieties in the difficult diplomatic mission entrusted to him were aggravated by his personal disgust with all the incidental details of daily life in the Orthodox Christendom of his day. The palace assigned to him was always either too hot or too cold, and in these odious apartments he and his suite were kept isolated by security police. He was swindled by the tradesmen. The wine was undrinkable and the food uneatable. The poverty-stricken Greek bishops were uniformly inhospitable. The beds were as hard as stone and had neither mattress nor pillow. On his departure he took a schoolboy's revenge on his hosts by scrawling on the walls and table of his palace a screed of abusive Latin hexameters in which he recorded his joy at seeing the last of 'that once opulent and flourishing but now famine-stricken, per-jured, lying, deceitful, rapacious, covetous, miserly, empty-headed city'.

Liutprand's conversations with the Emperor Nikiphóros and his ministers were enlivened on both sides by vituperative sallies. His most telling shot was that 'it was the Greeks who bred heresies and the Westerners who killed them'. True enough, no doubt; for the Greeks were intellectuals, and had been for centuries applying their brains to the minutiae of theology with disastrous results, whereas the Latins were men of law with no patience for that sort of nonsense. At a state banquet on the 7th June, 968, the in-flammatory word 'Romans', which was claimed by both Empires, kindled into flame the perpetually smouldering resentment between the representatives of the two Christendoms.

'Nikiphóros refused to give me a chance of replying to him, and added insultingly: "You are not Romans; you are Lombards!" He wanted to go on, and motioned to me to be silent, but I lost my temper and took the floor. "It is a notorious historical fact," I declared, "that Romulus, after whom the Romans are called, was a fratricide and a son of a whore—born, I mean, out of lawful wedlock—and that he set up an Alsatia for defaulting debtors, fugitive slaves, murderers, and perpe-trators of other capital offences. He harboured these criminals, collected a crowd of them, and called them Romans. This is the fine aristocracy from which your emperors, or κοσμοκράτορες as you call them, are descended. But we—and by 'us' I mean us Lombards, Saxons, Frenchmen, Lorrainers, Bavarians, Swabians, Burgundians—we despise the Romans so utterly that, when we lose our tempers with our enemies, the one word 'Roman!' is all that we have to utter, because, in our parlance, this single bad name embraces the whole gamut of meanness, cowardice, avarice, decadence, untruthfulness, and all the other vices."'[1]

In provoking Liutprand to lose his temper the Emperor had stung his Latin guest into proclaiming his sense of solidarity with his Teutonic-speaking fellow Westerners in a common antipathy against all 'Romans'. In a later and more genial conversation Nikiphóros used the word 'Franks' to include both Latins and Teutons, and this usage had been justified by Liutprand's revealing outburst. Though Liutprand was a Latin of the Latins in his intellectual culture—well versed, as he was, in the Latin version of the classical Hellenic literature—a common Hellenic cultural background had not bred in his heart any feeling of affinity with the contemporary Greek heirs of the same culture. Between this tenth-century Italian and these tenth-century Greeks a great gulf

---

[1] *Liutprandi Relatio de Legatione Constantinopolitanâ*, ch. 12.

was already fixed, whereas there was no gulf of the kind between Liutprand and his Saxon employers.

All that we have cited throws, admittedly, quite as much light on the personality of Liutprand as on anything more important, and his coarse caricature of the Emperor's personal appearance, if we were to quote it, would throw still more. The Lombard bishop was a man of coarse fibre, and, if the Byzantine pearls cast before him were only imitation pearls, in establishing the fact he simultaneously stamps himself as an unmistakably genuine swine. The measure of the Byzantine society's superiority over the contemporary Franks is given by the contrast between Liutprand's *Relatio* and Anna Comnena's objective and discriminating portrait of the Norman adventurer Bohemund, a blond beast whose pugnacity, treachery, and ambition had given her imperial father much more trouble than the Emperor Nikiphóros had ever given to Liutprand and his Saxon imperial employers. A minute description of the physique of this magnificent specimen of Nordic Man—'whose build reproduced the proportions of the canon of Polycleitus'—is prefaced by Anna with a generous encomium:

'The like of him was not to be seen in all Romania. There was not a barbarian or a Hellene who could measure up to him. He was not only a marvel to behold; he was a legendary figure whose mere description took your breath away.'

The sting of this outburst of feminine eloquence was located in its tail.

'Nature had given him an outlet through his heroic nostrils for the mighty spirit boiling up from his heart—for it must be confessed that there was something attractive about the man's countenance, though the effect of this was marred by the intimidating impression which the whole ensemble conspired to convey. The mercilessness of a beast of prey was writ large over the whole man . . . ; it was betrayed by something about his look . . . and also by his laugh, which smote on other people's ears like a lion's roar. His spiritual and physical complexion was such that ferocity and lust were always rampant in him, and both these passions were perpetually seeking vent in war.'

This fascinating delineation of one of the arch-Franks of Anna's day is almost equalled in vividness by a panorama of Frankdom in the mass which she introduces as an overture to her account of the descent of the First Crusade upon Orthodox Christendom.

'Intelligence of the approach of innumerable Frankish armies gave the Emperor Alexius considerable anxiety. He was only too familiar with the Franks' uncontrollable impetuosity, fickleness of mind, and suggestibility, and with the other inveterate characteristics, primary and secondary, of the Western Barbarians (Κελτοί). He was likewise familiar with the insatiable covetousness that has made these barbarians a by-word for the light-heartedness with which they take any excuse for tearing up treaties. This was the Franks' standing reputation, and it was completely confirmed by their acts. . . . The event proved to be even more portentous and more fearful than the anticipations. It turned out that the entire West, including all the tribes of the barbarians living between the west coast of the Adriatic and the Straits of Gibraltar, had started a mass migration and was on the march, bag and baggage, for Asia through the intervening parts of Europe.'

The most sorely trying of the afflictions which the Emperor Alexius suffered from the passage of the First Crusade was the unlimited call which these unwelcome and obtusely inconsiderate visitors made upon the precious time of a hard-worked administrator.

'From crack of dawn, or at least from sunrise, Alexius made it his practice to sit on the imperial throne and to let it be known that every Western Barbarian who desired an audience with him could have unrestricted access to his presence every day in the week. His motives were the immediate one of wishing to give them the opportunity of presenting their requests and the ulterior one of using the divers opportunities that conversation with them would offer to him for influencing them in the direction of his own policy. These Western Barbarian barons have some awkward national characteristics—an impudence, an impetuosity, a covetousness, a lack of self-control in indulging any lust that seizes them, and, last but not least, a garrulousness—for which they hold the World's record; and they showed a typical lack of discipline in their abuse of the Emperor's accessibility.

'Each baron brought with him into the imperial presence as many retainers as he fancied, and one followed at another's heels, and a third at the second's heels, in a continuous queue. Worse still, when they held the floor they did not set themselves any time-limit for their talk, such as the Attic orators used to have to observe. Each Tom, Dick, and Harry took just as much time as he chose for his talk with the Emperor. Being what they were—with their inordinately wagging tongues and their entire lack of respect for the Emperor, lack of sense of time, and lack of sensitivity to the indignation of the officials in attendance—they none of them thought of leaving any time over for those behind them in the queue; they just went on talking and making demands interminably.

'The volubility and mercenariness and banality of the Western Barbarians' talk are, of course, notorious to all students of national characters; but first-hand experience has given a more thorough education in the Western Barbarians' character to those who have had the misfortune to be present on these occasions. When dusk descended on the proceedings, the unfortunate Emperor—who had laboured through the live-long day without a chance of breaking his fast—would rise from his throne and make a motion in the direction of his private apartments;

but even this broad hint did not avail to extricate him from being pestered by the Barbarians. They would go on jockeying for priority with one another—and this game was played not only by those who were still left in the queue; those who had already had their audience during the day would now keep on coming back and bringing up one pretext after another for speaking to the Emperor again, while the poor man was being kept on his feet and was having to put up with this babel of chatter from the swarm of Barbarians thronging round him. The affability with which this one devoted victim kept on responding to the interpellations of the multitude was a sight to see, and the unseasonable chatter had no end to it; for, whenever one of the chamberlains tried to shut the Barbarians up, he would find himself shut up, instead, by the Emperor, who was aware of the Franks' proneness to lose their tempers and was afraid of some trifling provocation producing an explosion that might inflict the gravest injury on the Roman Empire.'

A mutual antipathy of this intensity might have been expected to rule out any possibility of mutual cultural influences; yet the Crusades bore fruit in Franco-Byzantine, as well as in Franco-Muslim, interchanges of cultural goods.

After acquiring from the Muslims a philosophic and scientific abstract from the corpus of Hellenic literature translated into Arabic, the Medieval Western Christians tardily completed their Hellenic library by acquiring in their original tongue all the 'classics' that had been preserved. The cultural debt of the East to the West was of a more unexpected order. The thirteenth-century Frankish conquerors of Constantinople and the Morea rendered to their Greek victims the same unintentional but signal literary service that the contemporary Mongol conquerors of China likewise inadvertently performed for the Chinese. In China the temporary dethronement of the Confucian litterati gave a belated opportunity for a submerged popular literature in the living vernacular language to rise to the surface of Chinese social life, where it had never been allowed to make this shocking display of its vitality under the culturally repressive rule of Confucian-minded civil servants who were the incurably devoted slaves of the ancient Sinic classics. In a barbarian-ridden Orthodox Christendom the same cause produced the same effect on a minor scale, in the flowering of a popular lyric and epic poetry. The Moreot Frankish author of *The Chronicle of the Morea* expressed himself in a native Greek accentual verse, entirely free from classical shackles, and foreshadowing the Greek verse of the early nineteenth century.

The most momentous of all the gifts exchanged between a Medieval Western Christendom and a contemporary Eastern Orthodox Christendom was the political institution of the absolute authoritarian state as embodied in the East Roman Empire and communicated to the West as a going concern in the Western successor-state which eleventh-century Norman swords had carved out of the East Roman Empire's former domain in Apulia and Sicily. This became a cynosure of all Western eyes—whether they beheld it with admiration or with aversion—when it was embodied in the person of Frederick II Hohenstaufen; for this *Stupor Mundi*, besides inheriting through a Norman mother the Kingdom of Sicily, was also West Roman Emperor and withal a man of genius. The later fortunes of this Leviathan Absolutism down to its 'totalitarian' manifestations in the twentieth century of the Christian Era have been traced already on an earlier page of this Study.

(c) ENCOUNTERS BETWEEN CIVILIZATIONS OF THE FIRST TWO GENERATIONS

(i) *Encounters with the Post-Alexandrine Hellenic Civilization*

In a post-Alexandrine Hellenic view of Hellenic history the generation of Alexander marked a break with the past and the beginning of a new era as sharply as, in a Modern Western view of Modern Western history, the transition to a 'modern' from a 'medieval' age was marked by a conjuncture of striking new departures at the turn of the fifteenth and sixteenth centuries of the Christian Era. In both these new chapters of history the most obvious ground for a depreciation of the past by comparison with the present was the consciousness of a sudden increase in power, including both power over other human beings, manifested by military conquests, and power over physical nature, manifested in geographical explorations and scientific discoveries. The Macedonian feat of overthrowing the Achaemenidae was as exhilarating as the Spanish feat of overthrowing the Incas. But that was not all. If either a Hellene of the third century B.C. or a Westerner of the sixteenth century of the Christian Era had been asked to describe the sensations by which his consciousness of a new era was sustained, he would probably have given less weight to his sense of an enhancement of his society's material power than to his sense of an expansion of its mental horizon. In the sensation produced by the discovery of a hitherto fabulous India, to which the Macedonians made their way by opening up a continent and the Portuguese by mastering the Ocean, the sense of power was qualified and enhanced, on both occasions, by a sense of wonder at the revelation of a marvellous alien world. In the sensation produced in the Hellenic world by the scientific discoveries of Aristotle and his successors, and in the Western world by the 'renaissance' of the Hellenic culture, the sense of power arising from new knowledge was likewise qualified by a sense of impotence in face of the reminder of Man's relative ignorance which every addition to Man's understanding of the Universe is apt to bring with it.

The parallel between the two epochs can be carried farther. We know that the impact of the Modern West has been world-wide and we might unthinkingly assume that in this respect the post-Alexandrine Hellenic civilization cuts a comparatively poor figure. But it is not so. The post-Alexandrine Hellenic civilization was ultimately encountered by the Syriac, the Hittite, the Egyptiac, the Babylonic, the Indic, and the Sinic societies; in fact, by every single society in process of civilization that was contemporaneously extant in the Old World.

But now we have to take note of an important point of difference. In studying the impact of the Modern West on its contemporaries, we have found occasion to distinguish between an Early Modern Age, in which the West was radiating its entire culture, including its religion, and a Late Modern Age in which the West was radiating a secular extract of its culture, from which the religious element had been eliminated. There is no corresponding division of chapters in the post-Alexandrine history of the radiation of Hellenism; for, by comparison with the West, Hellenism was intellectually precocious. Hellenism had started with a poor endowment in the sphere of religion, and had emerged from its religious chrysalis a full century before the opening of the Alexandrine Age.

In this Hellenic crisis of spiritual emancipation a disgust at the light-hearted immorality of the barbarian pantheon of Olympus, and a revulsion from the spiritually deeper, but also darker, stratum of religious life that was tapped by the 'chthonic' cults of blood and soil, were quickly overborne by an unsatisfied hunger for spiritual food. When the triumphal progress of their military and intellectual conquests brought the post-Alexandrine Hellenes into contact with full-blooded non-Hellenic religions, the emotion that this experience evoked in Hellenic hearts had more in it of a wistful envy for the privileged possessors of a pearl of great price than of contempt for the dupes of a fraudulent priestcraft. The Hellenic world became uncomfortably aware of the fact that it was suffering from a religious vacuum. This receptive attitude of the post-Alexandrine Hellenic conquerors towards the religions of societies which Hellenism had taken captive on the intellectual as well as the military plane was one cause of the momentous religious consequences of an aggressive Hellenic impact on six other societies. We must take the measure of a post-Alexandrine Hellen-ism's flow and ebb if we are to see its religious consequences in their historical setting.

The first objective of the Macedonian and Roman military aggressors was the economic exploitation of their victims; yet their profession of the nobler aim of propagating Hellenic culture was not insincere, as was proved by the extent of its translation from words into deeds. The Hellenic conquerors' master instrument for the fulfilment of their promise to impart the spiritual wealth of the Hellenic culture was the founding on non-Hellenic ground of city-states out of which a nucleus of Hellenic citizen-colonists was to radiate the light of Hellenism. This policy was inaugurated on the grand scale by Alexander himself and was pursued thereafter, for some four and a half centuries, by his Macedonian and Roman successors down to the Emperor Hadrian.

This more or less benevolent propagation of Hellenic culture by Hellenic conquerors is not, however, so remarkable as its spontaneous imitation by non-Hellenes, with the consequence that post-Alexandrine Hellenic culture made peaceful conquests of ground never occupied by Hellenic armies, or, if occupied, rapidly relinquished by them in the ebbing of the Alexandrine tide which followed Alexander's death. The cultivation of Hellenic art in the Kushan successor-state of a Bactrian Greek Empire astride the Hindu Kush in the last century B.C. and the first century of the Christian Era, and the cultivation of Hellenic science and philosophy in the Sasanian and 'Abbasid successor-states of a Seleucid Greek Empire, had to wait for its harvest until the experience of Hellenic military conquest had not only come but had gone. Similarly the Syriac world did not begin to show a spontaneous interest in Greek science and philosophy till it had begun to shake itself loose from Hellenic domination by providing itself with a Christianity of its own in the shape of the Nestorian and Monophysite heresies and with a literary medium of its own in the shape of the Syriac language.

The peaceful penetration of Hellenic culture into regions never trodden by Hellenic conquerors teaches the same lesson as Hellenism's posthumous artistic and intellectual triumphs after the ebb of its military dominion; and this Hellenic lesson is illuminating for the general study of encounters between contemporary civilizations. That light was visible to students of history in the generation of the writer of this Study because they happened to know the whole story—in contrast to the state of their knowledge of current encounters with the Modern West, in which a flood of detailed information, out of all proportion to the meagre surviving records of Hellenic history, was abruptly cut short, in the middle of the story, by the iron curtain of Man's ignorance of the future.

Whether the impotence of force in the cultural commerce between contemporaries was one day to be illustrated in Modern Western history, as it had already been revealed in post-Alexandrine Hellenic history, was a question still unanswered in A.D. 1952; and this enigmatic mark of interrogation served to remind the student that those historical events that were for him the least remote, the best documented, and the most familiar were also therefore the least illuminating for the purpose of his inquiry into the general course and character of human affairs. The more remote and less fully documented history of the encounters with an Hellenic society promised to teach him more about this, and, in particular, more about the outcome of encounters between civilizations on the religious plane.

To the twentieth-century Western historian it was evident that, by his day, the spontaneous acceptance of Hellenic art in a fifth-century Sinic world and of Hellenic science and philosophy in a ninth-century Syriac world had gone the same way as the feats of Macedonian and Roman armies. The artistic and intellectual, like the military and political, transactions between a post-Alexandrine Hellenism and its contemporaries were by this time a closed account. On the other hand, the continuing impact of the results of these encounters on the life of Mankind in the twentieth century was proclaimed by the allegiance of an overwhelming majority of the living generation of Mankind to one or other of four religions —Christianity, Islam, the Mahāyāna, and Hinduism—whose historical epiphanies could be traced back to episodes in a now extinct Hellenism's encounters with now extinct Oriental civilizations; and, if the future course of human affairs were to vindicate an intuition that the universal churches embodying the higher religions were an apter vehicle than civilizations were for helping human beings to make their pilgrim's progress towards the goal of human endeavours, it would follow that the encounters with a post-Alexandrine Hellenism shed a light which the encounters with the Modern West did not shed upon the main theme of any general study of history.

(ii) *Encounters with the Pre-Alexandrine Hellenic Civilization*

The drama in which the pre-Alexandrine Hellenic society was the protagonist was performed in the same Mediterranean theatre that, some eighteen hundred years later, was to be the scene of a play in which a Medieval Western Christendom was to take the principal part; and in both performances there were three actors on the stage. The two rivals of a pre-Alexandrine Hellenism were the sister Syriac society and the fossilized remnant of a prematurely shattered Hittite society which had preserved its existence in the fastnesses of the Taurus. In the competition between these parties for the dominion of the Mediterranean Basin the Syriac society was represented by the Phoenicians and the Hittite by the seafarers who, in the overseas territories in which they won a footing, became known in Greek as Tyrrhenians and in Latin as Etruscans to their Hellenic rivals.

In this three-cornered contest, which opened in the eighth century B.C., the prizes were the shores of the Western Mediterranean, whose culturally backward natives were no match for any of the three rival intruding societies; the shores of the Black Sea opening on to the Great Western Bay of the Eurasian Steppe, which gave access in turn to the arable belt of Black Earth along the Steppe's north-western fringe; and the long since intensively cultivated land of Egypt, whose civilization had reached a point of decrepitude at which it was no longer able to keep one alien neighbour at bay without enlisting the services of another.

In the struggle for these prizes the Hellenes enjoyed several advantages over both their competitors.

Their most manifest advantage was geographical. The Hellenic base of operations in the Aegean was closer to the Western Mediterranean, and much closer to the Black Sea, than the Etruscan and Phoenician bases at the eastern extremity of the Mediterranean were to either of these objectives. Then, the Hellenes possessed another advantage in the head of population which had accumulated as a result of a victory of the Lowlands over the Highlands in the preceding chapter of Hellenic history. The consequent pressure of population on the means of subsistence in Hellas gave the Hellenes' expansion an explosive force and stimulated them to follow up the establishment of trading posts overseas by making this new world into a Magna Graecia through a rapid and intensive settlement of Hellenic agricultural colonists on the land. Our scanty evidence gives the impression that neither the Etruscans nor the Phoenicians had a comparable amount of manpower to dispose of in this age; and it is at any rate clear that neither of them in fact emulated the Hellenic achievement of making a new world their own by colonizing it.

The third advantage enjoyed by the Hellenes was, like the first, a result of their geographical situation. The opening of the Mediterranean competition between these three rivals happened to coincide in date with the opening of the last and worst bout of Assyrian militarism, to which the Phoenicians and Etruscans on the Asiatic mainland were exposed, while the Hellenes were fortunate in living far enough to the west to be exempt from it.[1]

[1] Similarly, in the seventeenth century of the Christian Era, the insular

Considering these handicaps, it is remarkable that the Phoenicians and Etruscans should have done as well as they did. In the race for the Black Sea they were, as one would expect, entirely defeated. The Black Sea became an Hellenic lake; and, in the period of quiescence on the Steppe after the eruption of the Cimmerian and Scythian Nomads, the Hellenic masters of the Black Sea and the Scythian masters of the Great Western Bay of the Eurasian Steppe entered into a profitable commercial partnership in which the cereal harvests raised by the Scythians' sedentary subjects on the Black Earth were exported overseas to feed Hellenic urban populations in the Aegean Basin in exchange for Hellenic luxury goods designed to suit the Royal Scythians' taste.

In the Western Mediterranean the struggle lasted longer and went through many vicissitudes, but here also it ended in an Hellenic victory.

Even in the shorter race for Egypt, which was the one goal out of the three where the advantage of geographical proximity did not lie with the Hellenes, the seventh century saw the Hellenes again carry off the prize, by supplying the Egyptian Government of the Pharaoh-Liberator Psammetichus I with the Ionian and Carian 'brazen men from the sea' whom he enlisted for the task of expelling the Assyrian garrisons from the Lower Nile Valley in the years 658–651 B.C.

Towards the middle of the sixth century B.C. it looked as if the Hellenes had not only won their maritime competition for the Mediterranean Basin but were also in a fair way to inheriting the Assyrians' continental empire in South-West Asia. Nearly half a century before Psammetichus's Hellenic mercenaries had turned the Assyrians out of Egypt, Sennacherib had been incensed by an audacious insurrection of interloping Hellenic 'brazen men from the sea' on the Cilician coast of his dominions; and it looks as if the Assyrian Empire's Neo-Babylonian successor-state followed the example of Egypt in hiring Hellenic mercenaries, if we may assume that other Hellenic soldiers of fortune served in Nebuchadnezzar's bodyguard besides a Lesbian Antimenidas, whose name and record happen to have been saved from oblivion by the accident of his having been a brother of the poet Alcaeus. Alexander's conquest of the Achaemenian Empire was preceded and foreshadowed by the wholesale employment of Hellenic mercenaries by the Achaemenidae themselves. It might have seemed as if

English enjoyed an advantage over their Continental Dutch competitors for transoceanic trade by reason of the fact that the Dutch were exposed, as the English were not, to the military onslaughts of Hapsburg and Bourbon continental empire-builders.

an 'Alexander' could have stepped on to the stage of history two centuries in advance of his actual date. But in truth the stage was set, not for a phantom precursor of Alexander, but for an actual Cyrus.

The Hellenes' sixth-century prospects in Egypt and South-west Asia were blotted out within the twenty years or so that elapsed between Cyrus's conquest of the Lydian Empire *circa* 547 B.C. and his successor Cambyses' conquest of Egypt *circa* 525 B.C. Cyrus's stroke, which substituted an outlandish Persian for a familiar Lydian suzerainty over the Hellenic city-states along the western seaboard of Anatolia, was the sharper as well as the more surprising of the two; but Cambyses' conquest of Egypt dealt the Hellenes a further double blow; it depreciated the military prestige of the 'brazen men' and it placed Greek commercial interests in Egypt at the mercy of Persian goodwill. Moreover, these Hellenic reverses were accentuated by the no less signal and sudden benefits which the Persian empire-builders conferred on the Syrophoenicians.

The same Achaemenian policy which allowed the Jews to return from their Babylonian captivity and to construct a politically insignificant temple-state round their ancestral city, Jerusalem, gave the Syrophoenician cities along the coast not merely autonomy for themselves but a dominion, under Achaemenian suzerainty, over other Syrian communities which placed them on at least a par with the most powerful city-states of the Hellenic world. Economically, their gains were even more striking; they found themselves partners in a commonwealth which stretched away inland from their Syrian shore of the Mediterranean Sea to the almost fabulously distant north-eastern outposts of *Homo Agricola* on the Sogdian dry shore of the Great Eurasian Steppe.

Meanwhile there had arisen in the west a Phoenician colony which had surpassed in wealth and power the Syrian city from which it sprang, much as, in the twentieth century of the Christian Era, the chief Trans-Atlantic 'colony' of the Modern West had surpassed the European states from which its citizens had emigrated. Carthage took the lead in the Phoenician counter-offensive which, from an Hellenic standpoint, might be called the First Punic War, had that name not been annexed by a much later act in the same long-drawn-out drama. The result was indecisive, but it may be said that, before the end of the sixth century B.C., the expansion of the Hellenic world had been arrested on all sides by a combination of the threatened members of competing societies, and it might have been expected that, after this, the hitherto mobile eastern and western frontiers between an Hellenic and a Syriac world would settle down along the lines that the Achaemenian and Carthaginian empire-builders had drawn.

Yet this equilibrium was upset almost as soon as the fifth century B.C. had begun: we are on the threshold of one of the most famous wars of history. How was the historian to account for this surprisingly unhappy denouement? An Hellenic student of human affairs would have found the cause of the calamity in some act of hybris, the pride that goes before a fall, the madness with which the Gods inflict those whom they wish to destroy; and a Modern Western inquirer might refrain from contesting this supernatural explanation while pushing his inquiries farther on a merely human level.

The human cause of the renewal of the conflict was an error in Achaemenian statesmanship; and this error was a miscalculation into which empire-builders are prone to fall when they have made sensationally wide and rapid conquests over populations that have proved easy game because their spirit has already been broken by previous harrowing experiences. In such circumstances the empire-builders are apt to attribute their success entirely to their own prowess, without recognizing their debt to forerunners whose ruthless ploughshares have broken the soil before the eventual empire-builders' arrival on the scene to reap their easy harvest; and an overweening self-confidence, bred by this mistaken belief in their own invincibility, then leads them on to court disaster by rashly attacking still unbroken peoples whose spirit and capacity for resistance takes them by surprise. This is the story of the disaster suffered in Afghanistan in A.D. 1838–42 by British conquerors of the derelict domain of a broken-down Mughal Rāj in India, who had light-heartedly assumed that the unscathed highlanders of Eastern Iran would submit themselves as tamely as the stricken population of a sub-continent whose demoralizing experience of five centuries of alien rule had been crowned by the agony of a century of anarchy.

Probably Cyrus had imagined that he was bequeathing to his successors a definitive north-west frontier when he had completed his conquest of the Lydian dominions by subjugating the Asiatic Greek communities that had previously acknowledged the suzerainty of Lydia. Yet Apollo's warning to King Croesus of Lydia that, if he crossed the River Halys, he would destroy a Great Power might have been addressed to Croesus's conqueror Cyrus, while he paused on the opposite bank of the same river, with no less prescience on a rather longer view; for, in conquering the Lydian Empire, Cyrus was unwittingly bequeathing to his successors an entanglement with the Hellenic world which was eventually to be the death of the Achaemenian Empire.

Cyrus had got rid of an unsatisfactory river-frontier with Lydia (the River Halys) by extending his dominion over a conquered Lydia to the coast of Anatolia; Darius reckoned that he would get rid of an unsatisfactory sea-frontier with an independent remnant of Hellas by bringing the whole of Hellas under his sovereignty. After the last embers of Hellenic revolt in Asia had been stamped out in 493 B.C., he immediately started operations against Hellas-in-Europe. The upshot was the series of historic defeats—which twentieth-century Western heirs of Hellas still remembered as historic victories—at Marathon, Salamis, Plataea, and Mycale.

In retorting to the revolt of his Hellenic subjects in Asia by resolving to conquer their kinsmen and accomplices in Europe, Darius had converted a seven-years-long insurrection (499–493 B.C.) into a fifty-one-years-long war (499–449 B.C.), by the end of which the Achaemenidae had to reconcile themselves to the loss of their West Anatolian seaboard. During the same period a Carthaginian attack on the Hellenes in Sicily had ended in an even greater catastrophe for the aggressor, and this Hellenic victory in the West on land was followed by another at sea when the Etruscans attacked the Campanian outpost of the Hellenic world at Cumae, on the west coast of Italy, a little to the west of Naples.

Thus matters stood at the fatal date 431 B.C., which saw the outbreak of a fratricidal conflict between Hellene and Hellene, the Atheno-Peloponnesian War. The warfare thus begun within the bosom of the Hellenic society spelled its breakdown; for it dragged on, with brief truces, until a settlement was dictated in 338 B.C. by King Philip of Macedon. The Hellenic civil war obviously presented both the Carthaginians and the Achaemenidae with an irresistible temptation to take advantage of their Hellenic rivals' apparently suicidal mania. In yielding to this temptation the Carthaginians achieved little, but the Persians considerable, success. But their success did not profit them long; for one result of the fratricidal warfare in Hellas was to make the Hellenes past-masters in the art of war; and the Achaemenian and Carthaginian empires were swept away as soon as the new Hellenic weapons were turned by Macedonian and Roman war-lords against the Hellenic world's hereditary enemies.

Thus the military and political aggression of the Hellenic society against its neighbours entered on the wider scope which was surveyed in the previous chapter; but there was also a cultural plane of action on which enduring pacific conquests were made by the Hellenic civilization before, as well as after, the generation of Alexander the Great.

The natives of Sicily, who did their utmost to resist Greek conquest by force of arms, were at the same time voluntarily adopting the language, religion, and art of their Greek assailants. Even in the 'barred zone' behind the Carthaginian 'wooden curtain', within which no Hellenic merchant was allowed to penetrate, the Carthaginians imported Greek products which were more attractive than anything that they themselves could produce—much as the government of Napoleonic France, after having made a show of excluding British merchandise by a Berlin Decree, surreptitiously imported British boots and great-coats for the use of the Napoleonic armies.

The Hellenization of the peoples of the western provinces of the Achaemenian Empire had been started long before that empire had come into existence, by the radiation of Hellenic culture from the Asiatic Greek cities through the Kingdom of Lydia. Croesus figures in the pages of Herodotus as an enthusiastic Hellenizer. But a pre-Alexandrine Hellenism's most fruitful cultural conquests were made among the Etruscans and other non-Hellenic peoples along the west coast of Italy. The Etruscans had become Hellenes by adoption before they came under the rule of Roman empire-builders who had acquired much of their own Hellenism at second hand from their Etruscan neighbours.

The Hellenization of Rome was, of course, the most important cultural conquest that the Hellenes ever achieved at any stage of their history; for the Romans, whatever their origin, took up a task that had proved beyond the power of the Etruscan settlers on the West Italian coast to the north of them and the Greek settlers on the West Italian coast to the south of them and the Massilian pioneers of Hellenism near the delta of the Rhone. After the Italiot Greeks had succumbed to an Oscan, and the Etruscans to a Celtic, barbarian counter-offensive, the Romans carried a Latinized Hellenism over the Appennines, the Po, and the Alps till they had planted it right across the Continental European hinterland of the Mediterranean, from the delta of the Danube to the mouths of the Rhine and, across the Straits of Dover, in Britain.

(iii) *Tares and Wheat*

Our survey of encounters between contemporaries[1] has made us aware that the only fruitful results of these encounters are the works of peace, and most mournfully aware that these creatively peaceful interchanges are rare indeed by comparison with the stultifying and disastrous conflicts that are apt to arise when two or more diverse cultures come into conflict with one another.

[1] Sections concerning encounters with the Syriac society and encounters with the Egyptiac society in the age of the Late Kingdom have been omitted in this Abridgement.

If we scan the field once more, we shall observe in the intercourse between the Indic and the Sinic civilizations one instance of a peaceful interchange which seems as fruitful as it seems at first sight free from the blight of violence. The Mahāyāna was transmitted from the Indic to the Sinic world without the two societies ever falling into war with one another; and the peacefulness of the intercourse which produced this historic effect was advertised in the traffic of Buddhist missionaries from India to China and of Buddhist pilgrims from China to India both by the sea route through the Straits of Malacca and by the land route across the Tarim Basin from the fourth to the seventh century of the Christian Era. However, when we consider the land route, which was the more frequented of the two, we find that it was opened up, not by Indic or Sinic men of peace, but by Bactrian Greek pioneers of an intrusive Hellenic society and by these Greeks' Kushan barbarian successors, and that it was created by these men of war for purposes of military aggression—by the Greeks against the Indic Mauryan Empire and by the Kushans against the Sinic Han Empire.

If we are in search of an instance of a spiritually fruitful encounter between contemporaries in which there is no evidence of any concomitant military conflict, we shall have to look farther back into the past than the age of the civilizations of the second generation to a time before the Egyptiac civilization had been galvanized by the shock of the Hyksos invasion into an unnatural prolongation of an already complete term of life. In that preceding age, from the turn of the twenty-second and twenty-first centuries to the turn of the eighteenth and seventeenth centuries B.C., an Egyptiac universal state in the shape of the Middle Kingdom and a Sumeric universal state in the shape of the Empire of Sumer and Akkad had been living side by side, and alternating in the exercise of a control over the Syrian land-bridge between them, without, so far as is known, ever falling into a clash of arms. This apparently peaceful contact was, however, apparently also sterile, and we must peer farther back still to find what we are looking for.

In the investigation of so early a chapter in the histories of civilizations the knowledge accumulated by Modern Western archaeological discovery still left the twentieth-century historian groping in an historical twilight; yet, subject to this caution, we may recall our tentative finding that the worship of Isis and Osiris, which came to play so vital a part in Egyptiac spiritual life, was a gift from a disintegrating Sumeric world where the heart-rending yet heart-consoling figures of the Sorrowing Wife or Mother and her Suffering Husband or Son had made their earliest epiphany under the names of Ishtar and Tammuz. If it be indeed true that a worship which was the harbinger of all other higher religions was transmitted from the society in which it had first arisen to the children of a contemporary civilization without the strife and bloodshed by which so many of the subsequent encounters between contemporaries were to be marred, we may have caught here one glimpse of the bow in the cloud that lowers over the histories of those contacts between civilizations in which the parties to the encounter have met one another in the flesh.

XXXII. THE DRAMA OF ENCOUNTERS
BETWEEN CONTEMPORARIES

(1) CONCATENATIONS OF ENCOUNTERS

THE discovery that encounters between contemporary societies may present themselves, not singly, but in concatenations[1] was made in the fifth century B.C. by Herodotus, when he set himself to give an account of the then recent conflict between the Achaemenian Empire and the independent Hellenic city-states in Continental European Greece. He divined that, to make his story intelligible, he must place it in the setting of its historical antecedents, and, viewing it from this angle, he perceived that the Graeco-Persian conflict was the latest episode in a causally related succession of collisions of the same character. The victim of an aggression is not content simply to defend himself; if his defence is successful he passes over into a counter-offensive. No doubt the earlier 'acts' of the Herodotean drama appear to the sophisticated modern reader as more amusing than enlightening, for their plot is an alternating series of abductions of a succession of too attractive young women. The Phoenicians start the feud (as one would expect in the Hellenic version of the story) by abducting Hellenic Io; the Hellenes retaliate by abducting Phoenician Europa; the Hellenes then abduct Colchian Medea; the Trojans abduct Hellenic Helen, and the Hellenes retaliate by besieging Troy. This was all very foolish, 'since it was obvious that these women would not have got themselves abducted if they had not so desired', and in any case Paris must have failed to bring his lady home; for it was also obvious that the Trojans would have surrendered her, had they been in a position to do so, rather than undergo a ten years' siege. At least, this is how the legends emerge from a cold douche of the rationalism which is one of Herodotus' many endearing characteristics. Anyhow, at the making of the Trojan War by the Greeks, Ares replaces Aphrodite as the presiding deity in the proceedings; and, however sceptical we may be about the series of abductions, it must be agreed that Herodotus showed profound insight in regarding a Graeco-Phoenician encounter as an earlier act in the concatenation which included the Graeco-Persian War.

We need not recapitulate our own view of this particular con-

---

[1] The word concatenation is often loosely used, and it may be helpful to the reader who knows no Latin to be told that *catēna* means a chain, and that a concatenation of events is therefore a series in which one incident leads on to another.

catenation down to the Persian Wars, but will proceed at once to trace the chain of offensives and counter-offensives onwards into post-Herodotean times, and to see where it will lead us.[1]

The sensational defeat of the Persian invasions of Greece was only the first instalment of the penalty that this act of aggression drew down on the heads of its perpetrators. The ultimate nemesis was Philip of Macedon's decision to turn the tables by conquering the Achaemenian Empire; and Alexander the Great, who was as sensationally successful in executing his father's political testament as Xerxes had been sensationally unsuccessful in executing that of his father Darius, opened the first act in a new drama. The destruction of the Achaemenian Empire in the fourth century B.C. by Alexander, and of the Carthaginian Empire in the third century B.C. by Rome, gave the Hellenic society a dominion over its neighbours which far exceeded the most ambitious dreams of sixth-century Hellenic adventurers who had sailed as traders to Tartessus or had served as mercenaries in Egypt or Babylon. But this portentous career of post-Alexandrine Hellenic aggression duly evoked a reaction on its Oriental victims' part; and the eventual success of this reaction tardily restored a long-upset equilibrium when, a thousand years after Alexander's passage of the Dardanelles, the undoing of his work was completed by Primitive Muslim Arabs who, in a series of lightning campaigns, liberated all the once-Syriac territories, from Syria to Spain inclusive, that, at the opening of the seventh century of the Christian Era, had still been under the rule of the Roman Empire or its Visigothic successor-state.

The re-establishment of a Syriac universal state in the shape of an Arab Caliphate which embraced the former domains of both the Achaemenian and the Carthaginian empires might have terminated this concatenation of encounters. Unfortunately the Arab avengers of a Syriac society that had been the victim of Hellenic aggression were not content to evict the aggressor from territories on which he had trespassed. They proceeded to repeat Darius's error of passing over into the counter-offensive without having the excuse of finding themselves poised on an untenable frontier that must be moved forward if it was not to be set back. The Arabs crossed the natural frontier of the Taurus to besiege Constantinople in A.D. 673–7 and again in A.D. 717; they crossed the natural frontier of the Pyrenees to invade France in A.D. 732, and in the next century the natural frontier of the sea to conquer Crete and Sicily and Apulia and to establish bridgeheads on the

[1] Some further remarks of Herodotus' theory will be found in the NOTE at the end of this part: p. 238.

Mediterranean coast of Western Christendom from the Rhone to the Garigliano. These wanton aggressions incurred their nemesis in due course.

The explosive reaction of a Medieval Western Christendom whose latent energies had been fired by the Muslim aggressions of the eighth and ninth centuries of the Christian Era found expression in the Crusades, and these in turn provoked the counter-reaction that was to be expected on the part of their victims. The efforts of Saladin, and of other champions of Islam before and after him, evicted the Frankish Crusaders from Syria, and the 'Osmanlis completed the Greek Orthodox Christians' unfinished work of evicting them from 'Romania' as well. When the Ottoman Emperor Mehmed II the Conqueror (reigned A.D. 1451–81) had done his life work of providing an Islamic universal state for a disintegrating Greek Orthodox world, yet another opportunity of breaking off the conflict at a point of equilibrium was offered— and was rejected. Just as the Arabic Muslims of the eighth and the ninth century had intruded on Western Christendom where they had no occasion, in France and Italy and elsewhere, and thereby provoked an energetic but ultimately unsuccessful Medieval Western counter-offensive in the shape of the Crusades, so, in the sixteenth and seventeenth centuries of the Christian Era, the Turkish Muslims also intruded where they had no occasion, pushing up the Danube towards the homelands of the West. This time the Western reaction took a more original and more portentous form.

The envelopment of Western Christendom by the horns of the Ottoman crescent came near enough to success to persuade the Westerners to cut their losses in the Mediterranean *cul-de-sac* and reinvest their energies in embarking on a conquest of the Ocean which was to make them the masters of the World; and this staggeringly successful response by the West seemed, to an observer situated midway through the twentieth century of the Christian Era, to be evolving a counter-response, or perhaps several counter-responses. We have come a long way from the abductions of Io and Europa, and the end is not yet.

(2) DIVERSITIES OF RESPONSE

Our survey of encounters, and, more clearly still, perhaps, our survey of the concatenation of encounters which we have taken as an illustration of that type of series, suggests that, in each encounter, there is apt to be an assailant on one side and a victim of assault on the other. However, since these terms imply a moral judgement, it may be better to use the morally neutral terms, agent and reagent; or, to employ terms with which an earlier part of this Study has made us familiar, the party that challenges and the party that responds to the challenge. It is now our purpose to consider and classify the kinds of reaction or response that have been evoked in societies thus challenged.

It is of course conceivable that the original agent's assault may be so overwhelming that the assaulted party may be subjugated, or even annihilated, without offering any effective resistance. This had no doubt been the fate of many primitive societies which had had the misfortune to encounter civilizations. They had gone, as the dodo went on the arrival of Modern Western Man on Mauritius. Others, more or less fortunate than the dodo, were eking out an inconspicuous existence, interesting to anthropologists, in human 'zoos' or reserves. But our concern is with civilizations, and we have already seen reason to doubt whether any civilization, even the fragile and apparently irretrievably broken civilizations of Middle and Andean America, had even suffered this fate. After a long death-in-life they might arise again, as the Syriac society had reappeared and had resumed its life-story after a thousand years of submergence under the incubus of the Hellenic society.

In surveying the alternative types of reaction by an assaulted civilization, we will begin with those that are retorts in kind to the action by which they have been evoked, and the most conspicuous form of a retort in kind is the reply to force by force. For example, the Hindu and Orthodox Christian victims of an aggressive Iranic Muslim militarism retorted by turning militant themselves. This was the Sikhs' and the Marāthās' retort to the Mughals, and the Greek and Serb nationalists' retort to the 'Osmanlis. History is crowded with examples in which a militarily inferior party has retorted in kind by mastering its assailants' military technique. The Russian Czar Peter the Great is said to have remarked, after his army had suffered an ignominious defeat at Narva at the hands of Charles XII of Sweden: 'This man will teach us how to beat him.' Whether he actually said such words or not is of no importance because the facts speak for themselves; and the facts are that Charles taught, and Peter learnt, and Charles was beaten.

The Communist successors of the Petrine régime had gone one step further than Peter. Not content to master the industrial and military techniques of a Germany and a United States who had been Russia's successive Western enemies in and after the Second World War, the Russian Communists created a new form of warfare in which the old-fashioned method of fighting by physical force was to be replaced by a spiritual combat in which the master weapon would be 'ideological' propaganda. The instrument of propaganda, which Communism brought into action as a new weapon in the arena of mundane power politics, was not created by its new employers *ex nihilo*. It had been fashioned first by the missionaries of the higher religions, and had been adapted next by a Modern Western society of shopkeepers to the purposes of salesmanship.

While the Communist propaganda could hardly improve on the practice of contemporary Western commercial advertising in the lavishness of its outlay and the painstakingness of its 'market research', it aimed at, and achieved, results that were both different and more important. It showed itself capable of re-awakening a long dormant enthusiasm in spiritually starved Western souls that were so hungry for the bread without which Man shall not live that they swallowed the word which Communism gave them without pausing to ask whether this was God's word or Antichrist's. Communism called upon post-Christian Man to cure himself of a 'childish' nostalgia for a 'justly' discredited other-worldly utopia by transferring his allegiance from a 'non-existent' God to a very present Human Race to whose service he could devote all his powers by working for the attainment of an Earthly Paradise. The 'cold war', in fact, was a response on the plane of propaganda to a challenge on the plane of physical armaments, and this was not the first response on a non-military plane that the old-fashioned military challenge had evoked.

The 'spiritual' response of Communist Russia became less spiritually impressive to the Westerner when he reminded himself—if he needed the reminder—that this ideological propaganda was only an ancillary weapon in the armoury of an imperialistic Power that had already armed itself to the teeth with the weapons of physical force. We pass on to cases in which the use of force as a retort to force was wholly discarded, and here also it would be a mistake to attribute any moral superiority. In such cases it would usually be found either that an adequate display of force was out of the question or that force had been tried and had failed.

A striking example of a pacific response to a military challenge is furnished by the encirclement of the Babylonic world by the Syriac society in the Achaemenian Age as a result of a cultural conversion of Iranian barbarians who had become rulers of a universal state. The missionaries of the Syriac culture who had thus defeated their Babylonic conquerors in a captivation of Iranian souls were neither military nor merchant adventurers: they were 'displaced persons' who had been deported by Assyrian or Babylonian war-lords with the object of making it once and for all impossible for them to re-establish their beloved Israel's or Judah's military and political power; and their conquerors' calculation had proved correct as far as it had gone. The reaction by which the Babylonic militarists' Syriac victims eventually wrested the initiative out of their oppressors' hands had been quite beyond the oppressors' purview. The oppressors had so utterly failed to reckon with the possibility of any retort on the cultural plane that, with their own hands, they had planted their victims in a cultural mission-field which these exiles would never have visited if they had not been posted there by force against their wills.

In thus exerting itself to impress its cultural influence on the Gentiles among whom it had been scattered abroad, a Syriac diaspora was moved by a concern to preserve its communal identity. In the histories of the Jewish and other *déracinés* the same concern was more apt to express itself in the opposite policy of self-isolation; and self-isolation in reply to molestation is another variety of the type of reaction which operates on a different plane from the action to which it is a rejoinder. This policy of 'isolationism' presents itself in its simplest form when practised by a society whose habitat happens to be a physical fastness. An insular Japanese society, in its first encounter with a pre-industrialized West, had reacted to Portuguese intruders in this way, and the same response was successfully made at about the same time to the same intruders by the Abyssinians in their mountain fastness. The plateau of Tibet likewise provided an almost inaccessible fastness for a Tantric Mahāyānian fossil of an extinct Indic society. But none of these feats of physical isolationism, aided by geographical factors, can compare in historical interest with the psychological isolationism which was a diaspora's retort to the same threat to its survival; for a diaspora had to face this threat in geographical circumstances which, so far from aiding it, placed it at the mercy of its neighbours.

Such an isolationism is a strictly negative proceeding, and, wherever it has met with any measure of success, it will usually be found to have been accompanied by other reactions of a more positive order. In the life of a diaspora, its psychological self-isolation would prove impossible if those who practised it did not, at the same time, develop on the economic plane a special efficiency in the exploitation of such economic opportunities as had been left open to them. An almost uncanny aptitude for economic specialization and a meticulous observance of jots and tittles of a traditional law are a diaspora's two main devices for providing itself with artificial substitutes for impregnable frontiers or military prowess.

The device of replying to force by a retort on the cultural plane has also been used by societies that have been hard hit by the impact of an alien Power without having been reduced to the desperate straits of a diaspora. The Orthodox Christian *ra'īyah* of the ʿOsmanlis and the Hindu *ra'īyah* of the Mughals both succeeded in turning the tables on these men of the sword by a counterstroke with the pen. The Muslim conquerors of India and Orthodox Christendom allowed the mirage of their past military triumphs to blind them to the realities of the next chapter of history, in which their kingdom was being divided and given to the Franks. The *ra'īyah* foresaw the coming triumph of the West and adapted themselves to the new order.

But all these non-violent responses to the challenge of force that have so far been passed in review are, of course, eclipsed by the supremely pacific and at the same time supremely positive response of creating a higher religion. The impact of an Hellenic society on its Oriental contemporaries was answered in this fashion by the epiphany of Cybele-worship, Isis-worship, Mithraism, Christianity, and the Mahāyāna; and a military impact of the Babylonic society on the Syriac evoked the epiphany of Judaism and Zoroastrianism. This religious type of response, however, carries us beyond the limits of our present inquiry into the divers ways in which one civilization may respond to a challenge delivered by another; for, when an encounter between two civilizations thus gives occasion for a higher religion to make its appearance, the entry of this new actor signifies the opening of a new play with a different cast and plot.

XXXIII. THE CONSEQUENCES OF ENCOUNTERS BETWEEN CONTEMPORARIES

(1) AFTERMATHS OF UNSUCCESSFUL ASSAULTS

THE effect of an encounter between contemporary civilizations is apt to be a disturbing one for both parties, even in the most favourable circumstances, as when a civilization in its growth stage successfully repels an assault. The classic example here is the effect on the Hellenic society of its repulse of the assault delivered by the Achaemenian Empire.

The first perceptible social effect of this military triumph was to give Hellenism a stimulus to which it responded by bursting into flower in every field of activity. Yet, within fifty years, the political outcome of this same encounter came to a climax in a disaster which Hellas first failed to avert and then failed to retrieve; and the root of her post-Salaminian political disaster was the same sudden brilliant emergence of Athens which had likewise been the root of the post-Salaminian outburst of Hellenic cultural achievement.

We have noticed elsewhere in this Study that, in the age preceding the Great Persian War, Hellas had accomplished an economic revolution through which she had enabled herself to maintain a growing population within a no longer expanding domain by substituting a new economic régime of specialization and interdependence for an old one in which each single Hellenic city-state had been an economically autonomous unit. In this economic revolution Athens had played the decisive part; but the new economic régime could not be maintained unless it could be housed within the framework of a new political régime of the same order. Before the close of the sixth century B.C. some form of political unification had thus become the Hellenic world's most urgent social need, and it had looked as if the solution would be found, not by the Athens of Solon and Peisistratus, but by the Sparta of Chilon and Cleomenes.

Unhappily, in the crisis with which Hellas was confronted by Darius' fateful resolve to bring European as well as Asiatic Hellas under Achaemenian rule, Sparta left it to Athens to play the beau role, with the result that a Hellas in need of salvation through unity was afflicted with a pair of rival saviours of approximately equal potency. The upshot was the Atheno-Peloponnesian War, and all that followed therefrom.

This plight of political polarization was also the fate by which the

Hellenic world's successor, Orthodox Christendom, was overtaken in the sequel to its still more amazing victory, in the hour of its own birth, over a Syriac society which had been re-established in the form of the Arab Caliphate. On the morrow of the Arabs' attempt to take Constantinople in A.D. 673–7, Orthodox Christendom came within an ace of committing suicide when an Anatolic and an Armeniac army corps threatened to engage in a fratricidal strife for supremacy. The situation was saved by the genius of the Emperors Leo III and his son Constantine V, who persuaded the rival army corps to liquidate their feud by agreeing to merge themselves in a unitary East Roman Empire that made an irresistible appeal to their loyalty by presenting itself as a Rome risen from the dead. This raising of a ghost, however, is not a means of salvation that can be embraced with impunity; and, in saddling an infant Orthodox Christendom with the incubus of an absolute authoritarian state, Leo Syrus gave an unfortunate, and in the long run fatal, turn to this society's political development.

If we now take examples of the aftermaths of unsuccessful assaults in the history, not of the victorious respondent, but of the foiled assailant, we shall find that the consequent challenges have proved severe *a fortiori*.

The Hittites, for example, were left so desperately weak by over-exertion in their unsuccessful attempt to conquer the Asiatic territories of Egypt in the fourteenth and thirteenth centuries B.C. that they were subsequently submerged by the wave of a post-Minoan Völkerwanderung, and henceforth survived only in a cluster of fossil communities astride the Taurus. The aftermath of the Siceliot Greeks' abortive aggression against their Phoenician and Etruscan competitors took the milder form of a political paralysis which did not cripple their artistic and intellectual activities.

(2) AFTERMATHS OF SUCCESSFUL ASSAULTS

(a) EFFECTS ON THE BODY SOCIAL

We have observed in an earlier part of this Study that, in encounters between contemporaries in which the assailant's impact has resulted in a successful penetration of the assaulted body by the assailant's cultural radiation, the two parties to the encounter usually prove to have been already in process of disintegration; and we have also observed that one of the criteria of disintegration is the schism of the body social into a minority that has become merely dominant instead of creative and a proletariat that has become morally alienated from its former leaders, who have now become merely 'masters'. This social schism is likely to have occurred already in the body social of a society whose cultural radiation is successfully penetrating the body social of one of its neighbours; and the social symptom that is the most signal consequence of this always untoward and often undesired success is an aggravation of the problem which the alienation of an internal proletariat presents in any case.

A proletariat is intrinsically an awkward element in a society, even when it is a purely home-grown product; but the awkwardness is sharply accentuated if its numerical strength is reinforced, and its cultural pattern variegated, by an intake of alien population. History furnishes striking examples of empires which have been unwilling to add to their problems by increasing their alien proletariats. The Roman Emperor Augustus deliberately refused to allow his armies to attempt to extend his frontiers beyond the Euphrates. The Austrian Hapsburg Empire, both during the eighteenth century and afterwards during the period of German victories in the first half of the First World War, similarly displayed a reluctance to extend its frontiers south-eastwards and thereby to increase the Slav elements in its already all too variegated population. The United States of America, after the conclusion of the same war, secured the same end by entirely different means, namely by drastically reducing, through the enactments of A.D. 1921 and 1924, the number of the would-be immigrants whom it would permit to enter its territory from overseas. In the nineteenth century the Government of the United States had proceeded on the optimistic principle to which the Jewish novelist, Israel Zangwill, gave the nickname of 'the melting-pot'. It was assumed, that is to say, that all immigrants, or, at least, all immigrants from Europe, could be rapidly converted into 'dyed-in-the-wool' patriotic Americans, and that therefore, since the vast territories of the Union were industrially under-populated, the Republic would do well to welcome all, on the principle of 'the more the merrier'. After the First World War a more sombre view prevailed. It was felt that 'the melting-pot' was in danger of being overworked. Whether the exclusion of alien proletarian physical bodies would ensure the exclusion of alien proletarian spiritual ideas—'dangerous thought', in the Japanese phrase—was, of course, another question, to which the answer proved to be in the negative.

The social price that a successfully aggressive civilization has to pay is a seepage of its alien victims' exotic culture into the life-stream of the aggressor society's internal proletariat and a proportionate widening of the moral gulf that already yawns between this alienated proletariat and a would-be dominant minority. The Roman satirist Juvenal, writing early in the second century of the

Christian Era, had noted that the Syriac Orontes was flowing into the Tiber. In a Modern Western Society that had radiated its influence over the whole habitable globe, not only the little Orontes but also the great Ganges and great Yangtse had flowed into the Thames and the Hudson, while the Danube had reversed its direction and had deposited a cultural alluvium of Ruman and Serb and Bulgar and Greek proselytes upstream in an over-filled melting-pot at Vienna.

The effects of a successful assault on the body social of the assaulted party are more complex, without being less pernicious. On the one hand we shall find that a culture-element which has been harmless or beneficial in the body social in which it is at home is apt to produce novel and devastating effects in an alien body into which it has intruded—a law which is summarized in the proverb: 'One man's meat is another man's poison.' On the other hand we shall find that, when once an isolated culture element has succeeded in forcing an entry into the life of an assaulted society, it tends to draw after it other elements of the same provenance.

Examples of this devastating play of an expatriated culture-element invading an alien social milieu have already come to our notice. We have noticed, for instance, some of the tragedies that had been inflicted on divers non-Western societies by the impact of the Western world's peculiar political institution. The essential feature of the Western political ideology had been its insistence on taking as its principle of political association the physical accident of geographical propinquity. At the genesis of a Western Christian society, we have seen the emergence of this ideal in Visigothia making life intolerable for a local Jewish diaspora. The havoc thus worked in Visigothia began to afflict the World outside the home-land of Western Christendom when a puissant wave of Modern Western cultural influence carried with it into one quarter of the World after another this peculiar Western political ideology, which was now keyed up to a new intensity by the impact of the new spirit of Democracy upon the old institution of Territorial Sovereignty embodied in parochial states.

We have seen how, in the course of the hundred years ending in A.D. 1918, Linguistic Nationalism disrupted a Danubian Hapsburg Monarchy. This revolutionary revision of the political map also bestowed the doubtful blessing of an ephemeral political liberation on the submerged peoples of a former United Kingdom of Poland–Lithuania, which had been partitioned between the Hapsburg, Hohenzollern, and Romanov empires towards the end of the eighteenth century. After the collapse in A.D. 1918 of the three partitioning empires, a megalomaniac Polish aspiration to re-establish the frontiers of A.D. 1772 as park-walls for a privileged Polish nation's *Lebensraum* provoked a passionate resistance from Lithuanians and Ukrainians who had formerly been the Poles' partners and not the Poles' subjects in the supra-national commonwealth constituted in A.D. 1569. The deadly feuds of these three peoples during the following years, inspired by the evil spirit of Linguistic Nationalism, prepared the way, first for the new Russo-German partition in A.D. 1939 and finally, after appalling agonies, for the Russian Communist tyranny established in A.D. 1945.

The havoc worked by a Modern Western refinement of a traditional Western institution in the East European marches of the Western world was not so tragic as the effect of the same virus of nationalism in the Ottoman body politic, since neither the unpractical anarchy of an eighteenth-century Poland–Lithuania nor the fitfully enlightened monarchy of the Austrian Hapsburgs could compare with the Ottoman millet system in point of value as an alternative solution for the common problem of finding a practicable political constitution for a commonwealth consisting of geographically intermingled communities which bore a greater resemblance to the trades and professions than to the territorially segregated nationalities of Western Europe. The Procrustean methods by which the Ottoman millets were wrenched and hacked into the exotic shape of sovereign independent national states have been noticed on a previous page of this part, and need not be recapitulated here. Here we have only to note that the shocking cruelties that accompanied the partition of the British Indian Empire into the mutually hostile 'national' states of India and Pakistan, and of the British mandated territory of Palestine into the mutually hostile states of Israel and Jordan, were likewise examples of the baneful effects of a Western ideology of nationalism radiated into a social environment in which geographically intermingled communities had previously been enabled to live together in virtue of being organized in millets.

The destructive potentialities that culture-elements are apt to display when they have been torn out of their proper framework and introduced into an alien social milieu are also illustrated by examples on the economic plane. The demoralizing effect of an imported Western Industrialism, for example, was particularly conspicuous in South-East Asia, where an exotic industrial revolution, speeded up by importunate Western economic enterprise, had produced a geographical mixture of socially still unannealed communities in the process of gathering the human fuel for its economic furnace.

'Everywhere in the Modern World economic forces have strained the relations between Capital and Labour, Industry and Agriculture, Town and Country; but in the Modern East the strain is greater because of a corresponding cleavage along racial lines. . . . The foreign Oriental is not merely a buffer between European and native but a barrier between the native and the Modern World. The cult of efficiency merely built up a monumental Western skyscraper on Eastern soil, with the natives in the basement; all inhabited the same country, but the building was of a different world, the Modern World to which the native had no access. In this plural economy, competition is much keener than in the Western World. "There is materialism, rationalism, individualism, and a concentration on economic ends, far more complete and absolute than in homogeneous Western lands; a total absorption in the exchange and market, a capitalist world with the business concern as subject, far more typical of Capitalism than one can imagine in the so-called capitalist countries, which have grown slowly out of the past and are still bound to it by a hundred roots."[1] ... Thus, although these several dependencies have in appearance been remodelled along Western lines, they have in fact been remodelled as economic systems, for production and not for social life. The mediaeval state has, quite suddenly, been converted into a modern factory.'[2]

Our second 'law' of cultural radiation and reception is the tendency of a culture-pattern that has established itself in an emitting body social to re-assert itself in a receiving body social through a reassemblage and reunion there of constituent culture-elements that have become separated in the process of transmission. This tendency has to contend with the opposing tendency of an assaulted society to resist, but such resistance can generally do no more than slow down the process. As we watch this arduous process of infiltration making a headway that carries it to the bitter end of introducing the whole besieging host of Midian inside a beleaguered Israel's defences, the astonishing aspect of this excruciating miracle is not, of course, the needle's obstructiveness but the camel's importunity. The intruding culture-elements are not so separable as they might be supposed to be, and 'one thing leads to another'.

Assaulted societies are not, indeed, always blind to the consequences that are likely to follow from allowing even the most apparently trivial and innocuous exotic culture-element to make an entry. We have already taken note of certain historic encounters in which an assaulted society has succeeded in repelling its assailant's attack, without having given him a chance of making even a tem-

[1] Boeke, Dr. J. H.: 'De Economische Theorie der Dualistische Samenleving', in *De Economist*, 1935, p. 781.
[2] Furnivall, J. S.: *Progress and Welfare in Southeast Asia* (New York 1941, Secretariat, Institute of Pacific Relations), pp. 42-44. The picture drawn in outline in the passage just quoted is amplified ibid., pp. 61-63.

porary lodgement; and an uncompromising policy of self-insula-
tion that has won these rare victories has also been tried in other
cases where it has proved a failure. We have called this policy
Zealotism, from the name of the Jewish party which sought to
reject or expel the Hellenic culture, 'lock, stock, and barrel', from
the 'Holy Land'. The Zealot's characteristic êthos is emotional and
intuitive, but the policy may also be pursued on coolly rational
grounds. A classic case of the latter spirit is presented by the
severance of relations between Japan and the Western world,
which was gradually carried through, after mature reflection, by
Hideyoshi and his Tokugawan successors in the course of fifty-one
years ending in A.D. 1638. It is more surprising to find a similar
awareness of the inherent interdependence of all the divers elements
in an intrusive alien culture-pattern leading, by a similar train of
reasoning, to a similar conclusion in the mind of an old-fashioned
ruler of a secluded and backward Arab country.

The rationalist Zealot's state of mind is piquantly illustrated by
a conversation which took place in the nineteen-twenties between
the Zaydī Imām Yahyā of Sanʿā and a British envoy whose mission
was to persuade the Imām to restore peacefully a portion of the
British Aden Protectorate which he had occupied during the
World War of A.D. 1914–18. In a final interview, after it had become apparent that the mission would not attain its object, the
British envoy, wishing to give the conversation another turn,
complimented the Imām upon the soldierly appearance of his new-
model army. Seeing that the Imām took the compliment in good
part, he went on:

'And I suppose you will be adopting other Western institutions as
well!'

'I think not,' said the Imām with a smile.

'Oh, really? That interests me. And may I venture to ask your
reasons?'

'Well, I don't think I should like other Western institutions,' said the
Imām.

'Indeed? And what institutions, for example?'

'Well, there are parliaments,' said the Imām. 'I like to be the Government myself. I might find a parliament tiresome.'

'Why, as for that,' said the Englishman, 'I can assure you that responsible parliamentary representative government is not an indispensable
part of the apparatus of our Western civilization. Look at Italy. She has
given that up, and she is one of the great Western Powers.'

'Well, then there is alcohol,' said the Imām. 'I don't want to see that
introduced into my country, where at present it is happily almost
unknown.'

'Very natural,' said the Englishman; 'but, if it comes to that, I can assure you that alcohol is not an indispensable adjunct of Western civilization either. Look at America. She has given up that, and she too is one of the great Western Powers.'

'Well, anyhow,' said the Imām, with another smile which seemed to intimate that the conversation was at an end, 'I don't like parliaments and alcohol *and that kind of thing.*'

The moral of the story is that, in manifesting the perspicacity of his insight, the Imām had implicitly indicted the infirmity of his purpose. In adopting for his army the rudiments of Western technique, he had already introduced the thin edge of a wedge; he had started a cultural revolution which would leave the Yaman-ites, in the end, with no alternative but to cover their nakedness with a complete ready-made outfit of Western clothes.

If the Imām had met his Hindu contemporary, the Mahatma Gandhi, that is what he would have been told by the Hindu states-man-saint. In calling upon his fellow Hindus to revert to spinning and weaving their cotton by hand, Gandhi was indeed showing them a way to extricate themselves from the visible meshes of a Western economic spider's web; but this Gandhian policy was based on two assumptions, which must both be justified in the event, if the policy was to achieve its aim. The first assumption was that the Hindus would be prepared to make the economic sacrifices which the policy entailed; and of course they were not. But, even if Gandhi had not been disappointed in his expectations of his countrymen's economic disinterestedness, his policy would have been brought to naught by the falsity of its second implicit assump-tion, which was a misapprehension of the intrusive culture's spiritual quality. Gandhi allowed himself to see nothing more in the Late Modern Western civilization than the secular social structure, in which Technology had been substituted for Religion. It did not apparently occur to him that his masterly use of con-temporary methods of political organization, publicity, and propa-ganda was as 'Western' as the cotton mills against which he was tilting. But one must go farther than that; for Gandhi himself was a product of cultural radiation from the West. The spiritual event that had liberated Gandhi's 'soul force' was an encounter, in the sanctuary of the soul, between the spirit of Hinduism and the spirit of the Christian Gospel embodied in the life of the Society of Friends. The saintly Mahatma and the martial Imām were in one and the same boat.

In general terms of encounters between civilizations, when the assaulted party has failed to prevent even one single pioneer element of the aggressively radioactive culture from making a lodgement in its body social, its only chance of survival lies in making a psychological revolution. It may still be able to save itself by abandoning the Zealot attitude and adopting the 'Herodian's' opposite tactics of learning to fight the assailant with his own weapons. To take an example from the 'Osmanlis' encounter with the Late Modern West, Sultan 'Abd-al-Hamīd II's grudging policy of Westernization at the minimum was a failure, whereas Mustafā Kemāl Atatürk's whole-hearted Westernization to the maximum offered a practical way of salvation. It is futile to suppose that a society can Westernize its army and in other respects carry on as before, and the futility of such a supposition has been illustrated already in the cases of Petrine Russia, nineteenth-century Turkey, and the Egypt of Mehmed 'Alī. It is not merely that a Westernized army needs underpinning by a Westernized science and industry, education and medicine. The army officers themselves acquire Western notions quite irrelevant to their professional skill, especially if they are sent abroad to learn their profession; and the histories of all three countries display the paradoxical feature of groups of army officers heading 'liberal' revolutions. Such a spectacle was provided by the abortive Russian 'Decembrist' revolution of A.D. 1825, by the abortive Egyptian revolution led by 'Arābī Pasha in A.D. 1881, and by the Turkish revolution of the Committee of Union and Progress in A.D. 1908, which was not abortive, but which ran into disaster within ten years of its start.

(b) RESPONSES OF THE SOUL

(i) Dehumanization

In turning our attention from the social to the psychological consequences of encounters between contemporaries, we shall find it convenient, again, to give separate consideration to the respective effects on the parties playing the antithetical roles of 'agent' and 'reagent', assailant and assaulted; and it will be best to examine the effect on the agent first, since it is he who has taken the initiative in the encounter.

The representatives of an aggressively radioactive civilization that has been successful in penetrating an alien body social are prone to succumb to the hybris of the Pharisee who thanks God that he is not as other men are. A dominant minority is apt to look down on the recruits conscripted into its internal proletariat from a subjugated alien body social as infra-human 'under-dogs'. The nemesis attending this particular vein of hybris is peculiarly ironical. In treating as an under-dog the fellow human creature who happens to be momentarily at his mercy, the 'top-dog' is unconsciously reaffirming a truth to which he is intending to give the lie. The truth is that all souls are equal in the sight of their Creator; and the only result achieved by the human being who seeks to rob his fellows of their humanity is to divest himself of his own. All manifestations of inhumanity are not, however, equally heinous.

The least inhuman form of inhumanity is apt to be displayed by representatives of a successfully aggressive civilization in whose culture-pattern religion is the governing and orienting element. In such a society the denial of the underdog's humanity will take the form of an assertion of his religious nullity. A dominant Christendom will stigmatize him as an unbaptized heathen; a dominant Islam, as an uncircumcised unbeliever. At the same time, it will be recognized that the under-dog's inferiority can be cured by religious conversion, and in many cases the top-dogs have exerted themselves to effect this cure, perhaps even against their own interests.

The potential universality of the Church was symbolized, in the visual art of Medieval Christendom, in the convention by which one of the three Magi came to be portrayed as a Negro; and, in the practice of an Early Modern Western Christendom, which had forced its presence upon all other living human societies by the feat of mastering oceanic navigation, the same sense of the Church's universality had shown its sincerity in the readiness of the Spanish and Portuguese *conquistadores* to go to all lengths of social intercourse, including marriage, with converts to a Tridentine Roman Catholic Christianity, irrespective of 'colour'. The Spanish conquerors of Peru and the Philippines were so much more eager to impart their religion than to impart their language that they endowed the native languages of the conquered peoples with the means of resisting Castilian by developing these languages as vehicles for the conveyance of the Catholic liturgy and literature.

In thus demonstrating the sincerity of their religious convictions, the Spanish and Portuguese empire-builders had been anticipated by the Muslims, who, from the outset, had intermarried with their converts without regard to difference of race. But the Muslims had gone farther than this. The Islamic society had inherited, from a precept enshrined in texts of the Qur'ān, a recognition that there were certain non-Islamic religions which, in spite of their inadequacy, were authentic partial revelations of divine truth. This recognition, originally accorded to Jews and Christians, came to be extended to Zoroastrians and Hindus. However, the Muslims signally failed to rise to this relatively enlightened level when confronted with sectarian differences between *Sunnah* and *Shī'ah* within their own religious community. Here they showed themselves in as bad a light as Christians, whether of the 'Early Church' or of the 'Reformation period', in similar circumstances.

The next least noxious form of top-dog's denial of under-dog's humanity is an assertion of under-dog's cultural nullity in a society that has broken out of a traditional religious chrysalis and has translated its values into secular terms. In the history of the cultural aggression of the civilizations of the second generation, this was the connotation of the distinction drawn between Hellenes and 'Barbarians'; and in the Late Modern Western world this cultural dichotomy of Mankind had found exponents in the French in their relations with North American Indians in the eighteenth century, with Maghribīs and Vietnamese in the nineteenth century, and with African Negroes south of the Sahara in the twentieth century of the Christian Era. The same attitude had been adopted by the Dutch in their relations with the Malay peoples of Indonesia; and Cecil Rhodes had sought to kindle the same cultural ideal in the hearts of Dutch-speaking and English-speaking South Africans when he coined his slogan; 'Equal rights for every civilized man south of the Zambesi.'

In South Africa this spark of idealism had been smothered, after the establishment of the Union in A.D. 1910, by the eruption of a narrow and violent Afrikaner Dutch nationalism, bent on asserting its ascendancy over its South African fellow countrymen of Bantu, Indonesian, and Indian origin in the name of a superiority based neither on culture nor on religion but on race. The French, on the other hand, had gone to impressive lengths in giving political effect to their cultural convictions. In Algeria, for example, full French citizenship had, since A.D. 1865, been open to native Algerian subjects of the Islamic faith on condition of their acquiescing in the jurisdiction of the French civil law, including the crucial department of civil law known as personal statute which the status of full French citizenship automatically imposed on its recipients.

The sincerity of the French in acting on their ideal of opening all political and social doors to anyone who had successfully graduated in the French version of a Late Modern Western culture was demonstrated by an incident which, in vindicating the honour of France, had an appreciable effect on the outcome of the Second World War. After the fall of France in June 1940 it was a question of great moment whether the Vichy Government or the Fighting French Movement would succeed in rallying the African territories of the French Empire to its cause. At this juncture the Governor of the Chad Province of French Equatorial Africa was a French citizen of Negro African race; and this Negro Frenchman by cultural adoption duly exercised his official responsibility by opting in favour of the Fighting French Movement, thus giving that Movement, hitherto based entirely on London, its first foothold in the French Empire.

The cultural, like the religious, criterion for drawing the line between top-dog and under-dog is one which, however much open to objection it may be, does not fix an impassible gulf between the two fractions into which it divides the human family. The 'Heathen' can cross the line by conversion; the 'Barbarian' can cross the line by passing an examination. The decisive downward step in top-dog's descent is when he labels under-dog not 'Heathen' or 'Barbarian' but 'Native'. In stigmatizing members of an alien society as 'Natives' in their own homes, top-dog is denying their humanity by asserting their political and economic nullity. By designating them as 'Natives' he is implicitly assimilating them to the non-human fauna and flora of a virgin New World that has been waiting for its human discoverers to enter in and take possession. On these premises the fauna and flora may be treated either as vermin and weeds to be extirpated or as natural resources to be conserved and exploited.

In previous contexts we have found the classical practitioners of this abominable philosophy in those Eurasian Nomad hordes that had succeeded occasionally in establishing their rule over conquered sedentary populations. In their treatment of fellow human beings as if they were either game or livestock, the Ottoman empire-builders were as ruthlessly and as sublimely logical as the French empire-builders were in their treatment of their subjects as Barbarians; and, while it was true that unemancipated French subjects were vastly better off than Ottoman *ra'īyah*, it was also true that a human domestic animal which an 'Osmanli shepherd of men had trained to become a human sheep-dog found open to his talents an even more brilliant career than awaited an African *évolué* when he succeeded in becoming a French official or man of letters.

In the Late Modern Age the English-speaking Protestant West European pioneers of a Western society's overseas expansion had been the worst offenders in committing the Nomad empire-builders' sin of making 'Natives' out of human souls; and in this repetition of an old crime the most sinister feature had been the proneness to go over the edge of a further downward step to which the 'Osmanlis never descended, and to clinch their assertion of the Natives' political and economic nullity by stigmatizing them as the spawn of 'inferior races'.

Of the four stigmata with which under-dog had been branded by top-dog, this stigma of racial inferiority was the most malignant, and that for three reasons. In the first place, it was an assertion of under-dog's nullity as a human being without any qualification, whereas the appellations 'Heathen', 'Barbarian', and 'Native', injurious though they might be, were merely denials of this or that particular human quality and refusals of this or that corresponding particular human right. In the second place, this racial dichotomy of Mankind differed from the religious, cultural, and politico-economic dichotomies in fixing a gulf that was impassable. In the third place, the racial stigma differed from the religious and the cultural (though not in this respect from the politico-economic) in singling out for its criterion the most superficial, trivial, and insignificant aspects of human nature—the colour of the skin or the shape of the nose.

(ii) *Zealotism and Herodianism*

When we turn to examine the response of the assaulted party, we find that he seems to have a choice between the contrasted lines of action for which we have already found, and used in various parts of this Study, names taken from the narratives in the New Testament.

In that age Hellenism was pressing hard upon Jewry on every plane of social activity. No Jew could escape or ignore, turn where he would, the question of becoming or not becoming a Hellene. The Zealot faction was recruited from people whose impulse was to try to fend off the aggressor and to retreat into the spiritual fastness of their own Jewish heritage. The faith which animated them was a conviction that, if they abided by their ancestral tradition, observing the whole of it and nothing else, they would be given, from the jealously guarded source of their spiritual life, a supernatural strength which would enable them to repel the aggressor. The Herodian faction, on the other hand, was recruited from the supporters of an opportunist statesman whose Idumaean origin worked together with his personal genius to enable this son of a recently incorporated Gentile province of the Maccabaean kingdom to take a less prejudiced view of the problem. The policy of Herod the Great was to learn from Hellenism every accomplishment that it might prove necessary for the Jews to acquire for the judicious and practical purpose of equipping themselves to hold their own and to lead a more or less comfortable life in the Hellenizing world that was their inescapable social environment.

There had been Jewish Herodians long before the days of Herod. We can trace the beginnings of a voluntary self-Hellenization of the immigrant Jewish community in Alexandria right back to the infancy of that melting-pot city on the morrow of its founder's death; and, even in the hill-country of Judaea, the High Priest Joshua-Jason, who is the archtype of the Herodian school of statesmanship, was busy before 160 B.C. on his devil's work (as it appeared in Zealot eyes) of seducing his younger colleagues into an indecent exposure of their bodies in an Hellenic palaestra and a vulgar screening of their heads under the broad brim of an Hellenic *petasus*; and this provocation had evoked a contemporary Zealot reaction, as is recorded in the two Books of Maccabees. Nor was Jewish Zealotism crushed out of existence by the catastrophe of the Roman sack of Jerusalem in A.D. 70, nor even by its conclusive repetition in A.D. 135; for the Rabbi Johanan ben Zakkai responded to this challenge by endowing Jewry with an inertly rigid institutional framework and a passively obstinate psychological habitus that enabled it to preserve its distinctive communal life in the frail clay tenement of a politically impotent diaspora.

Jewry, however, was not the only Syriac community, nor the Syriac society the only Oriental civilization, to be divided into an Herodian and a Zealot camp by the challenge of Hellenism. The Zealot-insurrections of Syrian plantation slaves in Sicily in the second century B.C. were balanced at Rome, in the ensuing Imperial Age, by an Herodian inflow of a stream of Syriac freedmen-converts to Hellenism. Conversely, the Herodianism of the more well-to-do and sophisticated stratum of the Syriac society, which an Hellenic dominant minority was prepared to take into social partnership, was balanced by the conscription of other Syriac higher religions besides Judaism for the spiritually irrelevant and desecrating Zealot fatigue duty of serving as instruments for the waging of a secular cultural warfare. Zoroastrianism, Nestorianism, and Monophysitism, and Islam all followed Judaism's lead in making this spiritually disastrous deviation from Religion's true path. Yet the last three of these perverted religious movements eventually made atonement for their Zealot aberration by the Herodian act of translating into their liturgical languages the classical works of Hellenic philosophy and science.

If we pass on now to glance at the psychological reactions manifested in societies that encountered a Medieval Western Christendom, we shall find the most thorough-going practitioners of Herodianism known to history in those former pagan Scandinavian barbarian invaders who, as a result of one of the earliest and most signal Western cultural victories, became the Norman exponents and propagators of the Western Christian way of life. The Normans proceeded to embrace not only the religion but also the language and the poetry of the Romance-speaking native population of the successor-state that they had carved out for themselves in the Gallic heart of the Carolingian Empire. When the French-named Norman minstrel Taillefer lifted up his voice to inspire his fellow knights as they were riding into the battle of Hastings, he did not recite to them the *Völsungasaga* in Norse but the Song of Roland in French; and, before William the Conqueror of England high-handedly promoted the growth of a nascent Western Christian civilization in the backward and isolated province that he had won by the sword, other Norman adventurers had embarked on the enterprise of enlarging the bounds of the Western Christian world in the opposite quarter at the expense of Orthodox Christendom and Dār-al-Islām in Apulia, Calabria, and Sicily. More remarkable still was the Herodian acceptance of a Western Christian culture by the Scandinavians who had remained in their own homelands.

This receptive attitude of the Northmen towards alien cultures was not limited to that of Western Christendom. We find it also in the influence exercised by Byzantine and Islamic art and institutions on the Normans of Sicily; in the tincture of Far Western Christian Celtic culture acquired by the Ostmen in Ireland and by the Norse settlers in the Western Isles; and in the adoption of the Orthodox Christian culture by the Russian Scandinavian conquerors of Slav barbarians in the basins of the Dniepr and the Neva.

In other societies encountered by Medieval Western Christendom we find the Herodian and Zealot impulses much more evenly balanced. For instance, the Zealot reaction of Dār-al-Islām against the Crusades was to some extent set off by the Norman-minded Herodianism of the Cilician Armenian Monophysite converts to a Western Christian way of life.

Our pair of antithetical psychological reactions can also be detected in the histories of an Orthodox Christendom's and a Hindu world's respective encounters with an aggressive Iranic Muslim civilization. In the main body of Orthodox Christendom under the Ottoman Empire, a majority clung to an ancestral religion whose ecclesiastical independence they had chosen to preserve at the price of submitting to an alien political régime. Yet this Zealotism was partially offset, even on the religious plane, by a minority who became Muslim from motives of social or political ambition; and much larger numbers succumbed to Herodianism in the more trivial, yet none the less significant, ways of learning their masters' language and aping their dress. The reactions of the Hindus to the Mughal Rāj took much the same lines; but, in India, conversion to the religion of the conquerors was on a much more extensive scale, particularly among the socially depressed and recently pagan converts to Hinduism in Eastern Bengal, whose descendants in the twentieth century of the Christian Era came to constitute the detached eastern province of Pakistan.

The encounters of contemporaries with the Modern West have already been sketched in an early chapter of the present part of this Study. If we were to re-examine those records from our present psychological standpoint, we should find in all of them alternations of, and conflicts between, the opposing impulses of Zealotism and Herodianism. The case of the Far Eastern society in Japan may be selected as a particularly clear-cut example. After an early experiment in Herodianism the Japanese entered on a rigorously and successfully maintained Zealot phase when the Tokugawa Shogunate severed relations between Japan and the West. A small Herodian minority persisted, however, in those crypto-Christians who remained secretly loyal to their proscribed alien faith for more than two hundred years, until, after the Meiji Revolution of A.D. 1868, it became possible for them at last to come out into the open again. Shortly before that date they had, however, been reinforced by a second, and different, Japanese Herodian movement animating crypto-researchers who, by this time, were secretly studying, through a Dutch medium, the new science of a secularized Late Modern West. After the Meiji Revolution this newfangled Herodianism secured control of Japanese policy, with results which were to startle the World.

But was this latest phase entirely Herodian? Here we are brought up against a certain ambivalence in one, and perhaps in both, of our chosen terms of comparison. For Zealotism the end is clear. It is to reject 'the Greeks' formidable gifts'. But the means are various, ranging, as they do, from the positive method of open war in the style of the Maccabees to the negative method of self-isolation, whether by governmental action through the closing of a frontier, as in Japan, or by the action of individuals who maintain the peculiarity of a peculiar people by private enterprise after the fashion of the Jews of the Dispersion. For Herodianism, on the other hand, the means are clear. They are to accept 'the gifts of the Greeks'—whether these be religions or dynamos—with open arms. But what about the end? For those most thorough-going of all Herodians, the Scandinavians, Northmen, or Normans, the end —pursued, perhaps, unconsciously, but at any rate effectively attained—was a complete fusion with the encountered civilization. It is a commonplace of Medieval Western history that the Normans passed with surprising rapidity through the phases of conversion, leadership, and disappearance. On an earlier page of this Study we quoted a couple of lines from a contemporary observer, William of Apulia:

> Moribus et linguâ, quoscumque venire videbant,
> Informant propriâ, gens efficiatur ut una.

'They convert to their own customs and language those who join their standards, so that the result is a racial merger.'

But is that always the Herodian objective? If we have interpreted correctly the policy of Herod the Great, this eponymous hero of Herodianism believed—wrongly, as we have suggested in examining other cases—that a homoeopathic dose of Hellenism would be the best means of ensuring the survival of Jewry; and the modern Herodianism of Japan was undoubtedly nearer to the policy that we have attributed to Herod than to the practice of the Normans. Modern Japanese statesmen had formed the opinion that nothing short of a technological revolution which would turn Japan into a Great Power in the Western style could enable the Japanese society to preserve its separate identity; and this was a pursuit of the Zealot end by Herodian means. Confirmation of this diagnosis is to be found in the decree of A.D. 1882, by which a technologically Westernizing Japanese Government provided for the official organization of a State Shintō, in which a resuscitated pre-Buddhist paganism was to be utilized as a vehicle for the deification of a living Japanese people, community, and state. This was contrived by re-activating the symbolism of an archaistic cult of an Imperial Dynasty which was reputed to be the divine offspring of the Sun Goddess. This cult offered its hereditary collective divinity for worship here and now in the epiphany of a god perpetually incarnate in the person of the reigning emperor.

The difficulties inherent in the application of our alternative terms, which at first seemed to present so simple a dichotomy, become apparent wherever we turn. How, for example, should we classify the Zionist movement? It had drawn down upon itself the disapproval of the manifestly Zealot puritan devotees of the ritualistic tradition, in whose eyes the Zionists were guilty of impiety in presuming to bring about, on their own initiative and by force, a physical return to the Promised Land which it was God's prerogative to accomplish in His own good time; but it had also drawn down upon itself the disapproval of the no less manifestly Herodian assimilationists, who deplored the irrational belief that the Jews were 'a peculiar people', and who went to various lengths in accepting the Late Modern liberal thesis that the Jewish faith was, like other faiths, a chrysalis that had served its purpose.

Two of the greatest figures of the twentieth century—Lenin and Gandhi—present us with an equally baffling enigma; for both of them seem, like the Roman god Janus, to face both ways at once. A monotonous and interminable anthology of abuse of the West and all its works could be culled from their writings, yet their teaching is saturated with elements of the Western tradition—

Lenin's teaching with the materialist tradition that stems from Marx; Gandhi's teaching with the Christian tradition as transmitted through the followers of George Fox. When Gandhi condemns the Hindu institution of Caste, he is preaching a Western gospel in a not very receptive Hindu mission field.

Regarded as alternative policies open to members of the bodies politic of assaulted societies, Zealotism and Herodianism, except in a few simple—and perhaps over-simplified—examples with which we opened this discussion, seem to fade into a mist of self-contradiction; but we have to remember that it was not as sociopolitical policies that we set out to discuss them, but as responses of individual souls. As such they may be regarded as examples of the alternative reactions which we have called Archaism and Futurism, and which we have examined in an earlier part of this Study when we were considering the 'schism in the human soul' which manifests itself in civilizations that have broken down and gone into disintegration. In that context we defined archaism as an attempt to get back to one of those happier states which, in Times of Troubles, are regretted the more poignantly—and perhaps idealized the more unhistorically—the farther that they are left behind. This definition clearly covers Zealotism. In the same context we characterized Archaism as follows:

'An air of failure or, where there is not positive failure, futility surrounds practically all the examples of Archaism that we have been examining, and the reason is not far to seek. The archaist is condemned, by the very nature of his enterprise, to be for ever trying to reconcile past and present. . . . If he tries to restore the past without taking the present into consideration, then the impetus of life ever moving onward will shatter his brittle construction into fragments. If, on the other hand, he consents to subordinate his whim of resuscitating the past to the task of making the present workable, his Archaism will prove a sham.'[1]

Futurism was defined in that context as an attempt to escape from a distasteful present by taking a leap into an unknown and unknowable future; and this manœuvre, too, courts disaster. As for Herodianism, it is an imitation, at second hand, of another society's institutions and êthos; and at best this will be a parody of a possibly not very admirable original, while, at worst, it will be a discordant combination of incompatible elements.

(iii) *Evangelism*

Was the uniform self-defeat of Zealotism and Herodianism the last word that the oracle of history had to say, when asked for

---

[1] Page 513 of the previous volume of this Abridgement.

light on the spiritual consequences of encounters? If it were indeed the last, then the outlook for Mankind would be forbidding, for then we might be driven to the conclusion that our present enterprise of Civilization was an impracticable attempt to climb an unscalable pitch.

This great enterprise was initiated, as we may recollect, by a new departure in which Human Nature's powers of imagination, intrepidity, and versatility proved a match for the difficulties besetting the change of orientation which Mankind managed to achieve at that momentous stage in human history. A Primitive Man who had long since been brought to a halt by an Epimethean direction of his faculty of mimesis backward, towards his stick-in-the-mud elders and ancestors, now re-liberated his Promethean *élan* by redirecting this same socially indispensable faculty towards creative personalities who offered themselves to him as pathfinding pioneers. How far, a latter-day inquirer was bound to ask himself, was this new move going to carry these primitive culture-heroes' descendants? And, when its momentum had been exhausted, would they be able to draw upon a hidden store of psychic energy by repeating the creative act? If the answer to this last question were to be in the negative, it would be a bad look out for a half-baked Man in Process of Civilization.

The Zealot was a man who looked backward; the Herodian, who thought that he was looking forwards, was actually a man looking sideways and trying to copy his neighbours. Was this the end of the story?

Perhaps the true answer was that this might well be the end if the whole story was comprised in the history of Civilization, but not if Man's attempt at Civilization was only one chapter in the story of a perennial encounter between Man and God. In the myth of the Flood as recounted in the Book of Genesis, the sequel to a cataclysm in which Adam's brood had been all but annihilated by their outraged Maker was the Creator's promise to Noah and his salvaged crew that 'the waters shall no more become a flood to destroy all flesh'; and indeed we have already discovered, in the act of registering the failure of Archaism and Futurism, that there is a third possibility.

When Life is challenged by the emergence of some new dynamic force or creative movement from within, the living individual or society is not thereby condemned to make the futile choice between breaking down by perpetuating what in a previous context we called an enormity, and breaking down by detonating a revolution. There also lies open a middle way of salvation in which a mutual adjustment between the old order and the new departure can arrive at a harmony on a higher level. This is, in fact, the process which we analysed in the part of this Study in which we were discussing the growths of civilizations.

Similarly, when life is challenged by a breakdown which has become an accomplished fact, an individual or a society that is striving to recapture from Fate the initiative in its fight for life is not condemned to make the no less futile choice between an attempt to jump clear of the present into the past or an attempt to jump clear into an unattained future. Here, too, there lies open the middle way of a withdrawal through a movement of Detachment, followed by a return which reveals itself as Transfiguration. Perhaps we may give substance to these abstract terms if we turn once again to the first century of the Christian Era and to the obscure corner of the Roman Empire where the Zealots and the Herodians, to whose party names we have ventured to give a wider connotation, were exploring their respective blind alleys, and if we now focus our attention, not on either of these groups of sectaries, but on one of their contemporaries.

Paul was brought up in a Gentile Tarsus as a Pharisee—a cultural isolationist—and at the same time and place he received a Greek education and found himself a Roman citizen. The Zealot and the Herodian path thus both lay open in front of him, and as a young man he opted for Zealotism. But, when he was plucked out of this perverse initial Zealot course by his vision on the road to Damascus, he did not become an Herodian. There was revealed to him a creative way which transcended both these other two courses. He traversed the Roman Empire preaching neither Judaism versus Hellenism nor Hellenism versus Judaism, but a new way of life, which drew, without prejudice, on the spiritual wealth of both those contending cultures. No cultural frontier could stand in this Gospel's way, for the Christian Church was not just a new society of the same species as the civilizations whose encounters with one another we have been investigating; it was a society of a different species.

NOTE. 'ASIA' AND 'EUROPE': FACTS AND FANTASIES

In the introduction to his history, Herodotus professes to reproduce a Persian exposition of the motive that had impelled the Achaemenidae to take the offensive against the Hellenes. The Persians, according to his account, believed that they had inherited a blood-feud; they regarded themselves as saddled with a duty to exact vengeance from the Hellenes for the siege and sack of Troy. Thus both the great wars, the Trojan and the Persian, were incidents in an historically continuous Feud between 'Europe' and 'Asia'. Needless to say, the Persians were, as a matter of history, entirely unaware of any such obligation; not being students of Homer, they were presumably ignorant of the Trojan War—if this had indeed been an authentic historical event. Needless to say, also, the Herodotean picture is historically fantastic, assuming, as it does, that there was a solidarity of feeling between Trojans and Persians as fellow 'Asians'. We can illustrate the absurdity of this by imagining a strictly similar presentation of an historic feud between Europe and America, and representing that a Darius–Washington felt impelled to avenge on 'Europe' the antecedent aggression of an Agamemnon–Cortés against Mexico.

None the less, the Herodotean myth is of interest and importance in that it put into circulation the concept of 'Europe' and 'Asia' as rival and opposing entities—entities which still survive on our maps with a continental frontier between them, drawn along the long range of somewhat insignificant hills called the Ural Mountains. Herodotus did not invent this concept, for 'Asia' was already a current synonym for the Persian Empire in the *Persae* of Aeschylus, which was produced in 472 B.C.; but 'the Feud between Europe and Asia' is the dominant and unifying theme of Herodotus' work, and the masterliness of his workmanship is largely responsible for the subsequent vogue of this fifth-century Hellenic fantasy.

This fantasy had been begotten when some imaginative Hellenic mind had given a revolutionary change of meaning to the two traditional Hellenic geographical names 'Europe' and 'Asia' by transferring them from the mariner's chart to the publicist's political map and to the sociologist's diagram of the habitats of cultures. This feat of imagination had been unluckily inspired. The mariner's distinction between the opposite coasts of the chain of waterways between the Mediterranean and the Black Sea was natural and useful for its purpose, but this chain of waterways has never coincided with a political frontier from the dawn of human history down to the time of writing the present work except during the two brief periods 547–513 B.C. and 386–334 B.C. As for the identification of the mariner's 'continents' with the domains of diverse cultures, the historian cannot lay his finger on any period at all in which there was any significant cultural diversity between the 'Asiatic' and 'European' occupants of the all but contiguous opposite banks of a Bosphorus and a Hellespont that are no broader than the Hudson and not nearly so broad as the Amazon.

The Hellenic mariner's term 'Asia' to denote the continent which set the eastward limit to his freedom of movement on his own element in the Aegean Sea seems to have been derived from the contemporary local name of a marsh in the valley of the River Caÿster; and recent archaeological discovery has shown that the name was that of a thirteenth-century West Anatolian principality named in the Hittite public records.

'Asia' is possibly not the only Hittite name that found its way into the Greek vocabulary. It has been conjectured that *basileus*, the obviously un-Greek word in Greek for 'king', derives from the name of an actual

Hittite king, Biyassilis, who ruled at Carchemish, on the Euphrates, in the fourteenth century B.C., at about the time when Achaean pirates were making their first contacts with the Pamphylian coast. If this derivation is correct it puts *basileus* on a par with *kral*, the word for 'king' in several Slavonic languages, which is known to derive from the name of Karolus Magnus, *alias* Charlemagne. The origin of the term 'Europe' is more doubtful. It might be a Greek travesty of the Phoenician word *'ereb* (corresponding to the Arabic *gharb*), meaning the dark quarter where the sun sets in the west; or, if it was not a technical term borrowed from Phoenician mariners, but was a native Greek word, it might signify the 'broad faced' *terra firma* in contrast to the islands; or it might be the name of a goddess who was 'broad faced' because she was bovine.

However that may be, the two names established the mariner's distinction between the mainland and the islands. Feeling his way northward along the Asiatic or the European coast of the mainland, he made his passage through three successive straits—the Dardanelles, the Bosphorus, and the Straits of Kerch—but, when he had navigated the last-named, had crossed the Sea of Azov, and had ascended the River Don to the head of fluvial navigation, he had reached a point where the opposing continents lost their separate identities. For the landsmen north of the Black Sea, whether the Nomad of the Eurasian Steppe or the Eurasian peasant of the Black Earth belt which extends from the eastern slopes of the Carpathians to the western slopes of the Altai, the distinction between Europe and Asia could have no intelligible meaning.

The dichotomy of Europe and Asia was one of the least useful of the legacies which the Modern West had accepted from the Hellenic world. The schoolroom distinction between 'Russia-in-Europe' and 'Russia-in-Asia' had always been meaningless but had probably done no one any harm. The parallel distinction between 'Turkey-in-Europe' and 'Turkey-in-Asia' had been the source of a great deal of confused thinking. The real frontiers between the habitats of the civilizations have nothing to do with such antique fictions. There is an unquestionable geographical reality which we call Eurasia. It is so large, and so irregularly shaped, that we may break off from it, for our convenience, a number of sub-continents. Of these the most sharply defined, thanks to its Himalayan land-frontier, is India. Europe is another, no doubt; but Europe's land-frontier, unlike India's, has always been more of a *limen* than a *limes*, and certainly lies a long way west of the Ural Mountains.

X

CONTACTS BETWEEN CIVILIZATIONS IN TIME

XXXIV. A SURVEY OF RENAISSANCES

(1) INTRODUCTION—'THE RENAISSANCE'

A FRENCH writer, E. J. Delécluze (A.D. 1781–1863), seems to have been the first to use the term *la renaissance*[1] (rebirth) to describe the impact made by a dead Hellenic civilization on Western Christendom at a particular time and place, namely Northern and Central Italy in the Late Medieval period. This particular impact of the dead on the living is very far from being the only example of its kind that history affords, and we shall here adopt the term as a general name for such phenomena and proceed to an examination of them. In so doing, we shall have to be careful not to include more than we intend. In so far as this Hellenic culture in the provinces of art and literature—for the term in its conventional use is limited to these—came to Italy through contact with Byzantine scholars, it was not, of course, an encounter in time with a dead civilization but an encounter in space with a living one, and belongs to the subject discussed in the previous Part of this Study. Again, when 'Greece crossed the Alps' and the Italian Renaissance affected the art and literature of France and other Transalpine Western countries, this, in so far as it came through contemporary Italy and not direct from 'ancient' Greece was, again, not strictly a renaissance, but was a transmission of the acquisitions of a pioneer section of a society to other sections of the same society, and, as such, belongs to the subject of 'Growth' and has been discussed, in this context, in the Third Part of this Study. But these logical distinctions may seem somewhat fine drawn, and in practice it may prove both difficult and unnecessary to distinguish between a 'pure' renaissance, in the sense of a direct encounter with a dead society, and a renaissance alloyed in one or other of the manners just indicated.

We must also observe, before plunging into our exploration of renaissances, that these phenomena have to be distinguished from two other types of encounter between the present and the past.

---

[1] The earliest English use of the term cited in *O.E.D.* is dated A.D. 1845. Matthew Arnold started the practice of anglicizing the word and writing 'renascence'.

One is the relationship of Apparentation-and-Affiliation between a dying or dead civilization and its embryo or infant successor. This is a subject about which we have already written at length and it may be regarded as a normal and necessary phenomenon, as is implied in our application to it of the analogy of parenthood and sonship. A renaissance, on the other hand, is an encounter between a grown-up civilization and the 'ghost' of its long-dead parent. Though common enough, it may be described as abnormal, and will be found on examination to be often unwholesome. The other type of encounter between present and past from which renaissances are to be distinguished is the phenomenon which we have called Archaism, using this word to denote attempted reversions to an earlier phase in the development of the society to which the archaizers themselves belong.

One more point of distinction between these three types of encounter between present and past has still to be established. In the relation of Apparentation-and-Affiliation it is obvious that the two societies in contact are at very different, indeed opposite, stages of development. The parent is a disintegrating society in its dotage; the offspring is a new-born 'muling and puking' infant. Again, an archaizing body has obviously fallen in love with a state of affairs very different from its own; otherwise, why archaize? A society entering on a renaissance, on the other hand, is perhaps more likely than not to call up the ghost of its parent as that parent was when he had reached the same stage of development as the offspring has now reached. It is as if Hamlet could choose the kind of paternal ghost that he was to encounter on the battlements: either a father whose beard was 'a sable silvered' or, alternatively, a father who was of his son's own age.

(2) RENAISSANCES OF POLITICAL IDEAS AND INSTITUTIONS

The Late Medieval Italian renaissance of Hellenism exerted a more enduring influence on Western life on the political plane than on either the literary or the artistic. Moreover, these political manifestations not only outlived the aesthetic but also forestalled them. They began when the Lombard cities passed out of the control of their bishops into the hands of communes administered by boards of magistrates responsible to the citizens. This resuscitation of the Hellenic institution of the city state in eleventh-century Italy proceeded, as a result of the radiation of Italian culture into Transalpine provinces of Western Christendom, to make a corresponding impact on the peoples of the Western feudal monarchies. Both in its earlier and narrower and in its later and wider field the influence of this Hellenic *revenant* was the same. The superficial effect was to propagate a cult of constitutional government, which was eventually to confer upon itself the Hellenic title of Democracy, but the difficulties and failures of constitutionalism opened the way for the equally Hellenic figure of the Tyrant, first in the Italian city states and afterwards on a more extended and, consequently, a more disastrous scale.

Another Hellenic ghost presented itself on the medieval stage when Charlemagne was crowned as a Roman Emperor by Pope Leo III in St. Peter's on Christmas Day A.D. 800. That institution, too, had a long history ahead of it. The most devoutly pedantic Hellenizer among these ghost emperors was the Saxon Otto III (reigned A.D. 983–1002), who transferred the seat of his government to Rome—a site which at that date lay in a patch of common ground on which the domains of the two Christendoms overlapped. In installing himself in the former Imperial City, Otto III had hoped to fortify the sickly counterfeit of the Roman Imperial Power that had been palmed off on Western Christendom by reinforcing it with tougher metal from a Byzantine mint. As we have seen in another context, Otto III's experiment, which collapsed after his early death, was repeated more than two centuries later, in much more favourable circumstances, and with much more alarming results, by a man of genius, Frederick II Hohenstaufen.

Many centuries later, Rousseau popularized the Plutarchan version of Hellenism. Consequently the French revolutionists never tired of allusions to Solon and Lycurgus and dressed both their ladies and their Directors in what were supposed to be 'classical' costumes. What could be more natural than that the first Napoleon, when he wanted to raise himself above the rank of 'consul', should style himself 'emperor' and should confer on his son and heir the title 'King of Rome', which had been borne by candidates for the medieval Western office of 'Holy Roman Emperor' until they were crowned at Rome by the Pope (a consecration which many of them failed to achieve)? As for the second (*soi-disant* third) Napoleon, he actually wrote, or caused to be published under his name, a life of Julius Caesar. Finally Hitler paid his tribute to the ghost of a ghost by establishing his country residence on a crag overhanging an enchanted Barbarossa's holy cave at Berchtesgaden and by accepting the regalia of Charlemagne, stolen from a Hapsburg museum.

But another and more benevolent ghost hovers round the institution of Western Christian monarchy. The religious sanction given to the formal revival of the Roman Empire in the West on Christmas Day, A.D. 800, when a Frankish king was created Roman Emperor in virtue of being crowned by the Pope, had no precedent in Hellenic history. The ceremony performed on that day in Rome had, however, a pertinent precedent in a ceremony performed at Soissons in A.D. 751, when the Austrasian major-domo Pepin had been created King of the Franks in virtue of being crowned and anointed by Pope Zacharias's representative, Saint Boniface. This Western rite of ecclesiastical consecration—already customary in Visigothic Spain—was a revival of an Israelite institution recorded in the Books of Samuel and Kings. The consecrations of King David by the prophet Samuel and of King Solomon by Zadok the priest and Nathan the prophet are the precedents for all the coronations of kings and queens in Western Christendom.

(3) RENAISSANCE OF SYSTEMS OF LAW

We have already seen that a Roman Law which, in the course of ten centuries ending with its codification by Justinian, had been slowly and laboriously elaborated to meet the needs, first of the Roman people and afterwards of the whole Hellenic society, had been rapidly left stranded by the collapse of the way of life which it had been designed to regulate—and this not only in the Western but also in the Eastern half of the Hellenic world. Thereafter the symptoms of decay were followed by the symptoms of new life on the legal, as on the political, plane. The impulse to provide a live law for a living society did not find its first vent in any move to reanimate a Roman Law that, in the eighth century of the Christian Era, was perched, high up above contemporary heads, like a Noah's Ark on the roof of the mighty mausoleum of an extinct Hellenic culture. Each of the two new Christian societies, Eastern and Western, demonstrated the sincerity of its belief in a Christian dispensation by attempting, first, to create a Christian law for a would-be Christian people. In both Christendoms, however, this new departure was followed by a renaissance, first of the Mosaic law contained in the Scriptures which Christendom had inherited from Jewry, and secondly of the Roman law as petrified in the Code of Justinian.

In Orthodox Christendom the Christian new departure was announced, in the joint reign of the two Syrian founders of the East Roman Empire, Leo III and his son Constantine V, in the promulgation, in A.D. 740, of 'a Christian law book', which was 'a deliberate attempt to change the legal system of the Empire by the application of Christian principles'.[1] It was, however, almost inevitable that the birth of a new Christian law should be followed by a renaissance of the Jewish law which the Christian Church, perhaps unwisely and certainly not wholly happily, had insisted on including in the Canon of its own Scriptures. Whether Mosaic or Christian, however, the legal system established by the Syrian emperors proved less and less adequate for coping with the growing complexities of Byzantine society, and in the years following A.D. 870 the founder of the Macedonian Dynasty, Basil I, and his sons and successors gave notice that they 'had totally rejected and discarded the imbecilities promulgated by the Isaurians', that is by the foregoing Syrian emperors. With this hearty depreciation of their predecessors the Macedonian emperors nerved themselves to the task of restoring to life the Code of Justinian. In doing so they imagined that they were being truly Roman, much as, in the province of architecture, the Gothic revivalists of the nineteenth century imagined that they were being truly Gothic. But the trouble about all revivals or renaissances is that they are not, and in the nature of things cannot be, 'the genuine article'. They differ from the genuine article very much as the waxworks at Madame Tussaud's differ from the people who pass through the turnstiles to look at them.

The plot of the legal drama in which a Christian new departure was dogged by the successively raised ghosts of Moses and Justinian can be seen likewise working itself out on a Western stage, on which the role of Leo Syrus was played by Charlemagne.

'The Carolingian legislation ... marks the emergence of the new social consciousness of Western Christendom. Hitherto the legislation of the Western kingdoms had been of the nature of a Christian appendix to the old barbarian tribal codes. Now, for the first time, a complete break was made with the Past, and Christendom enacted its own laws, which covered the whole field of social activity in Church and State and referred all things to the single standard of the Christian êthos. This was inspired neither by Germanic nor [by] Roman precedent.'[2]

In Western, as in Orthodox, Christendom, however, the ghost of Moses trod hard on the Apostles' and the Evangelists' heels.

'The Carolingian Emperors gave the law to the whole Christian people in the spirit of the kings and judges of the Old Testament, declaring the Law of God to the people of God. In the letter which Cathaulf addressed to Charles at the beginning of his reign, the writer speaks of the king as the earthly representative of God, and he counsels Charles to use the

[1] Bury, J. B., in his edition of Edward Gibbon, *The History of the Decline and Fall of the Roman Empire*, vol. v (London 1901, Methuen), Appendix II, p. 526.
[2] Dawson, Christopher: *Religion and the Rise of Western Culture* (London 1950, Sheed & Ward), p. 90.

Book of Divine Law as his manual of government, according to the precept of Deuteronomy xvii. 18–20, which commands the King to make a copy of the Law from the books of the priests, to keep it always with him, and to read it constantly, so that he may learn to fear the Lord and keep His laws, lest his heart be lifted up in pride above his brethren and he turn aside to the right hand or to the left.'[1]

Yet, in Western, as in Orthodox, Christendom, a resurgent Moses was overtaken by a resurgent Justinian.

In the course of the eleventh century of the Christian Era the Imperial Law School established by official action at Constantinople in A.D. 1045 found its counterpart in Western Christendom at Bologna in the spontaneous emergence there of an autonomous university dedicated to the study of the *Corpus Iuris* of Justinian; and, though in Western Christendom a resuscitated Roman Law failed eventually to serve the purpose of underpinning a resuscitated Roman Empire, it did potently serve the alternative purpose of fostering the revival, on Western ground, of an earlier Hellenic political institution, the sovereign independent parochial state. The civil lawyers educated by Bologna and her daughter universities became the administrators, not of an abortive Western 'Holy Roman Empire', but of effective Western parochial sovereign states, and the efficiency of their professional services was one of the causes of the progressive victory of this institution over all the alternative forms of political organization that were latent in Western Christendom's original social structure.

While the Bolognese civilians were providing the cities of North and Central Italy with administrators whose competence enabled the communes to overthrow their prince-bishops and to launch out on a career of civic self-government, the canonists were supplementing the Bolognese school of civil law with a sister faculty of ecclesiastical law after the publication of Gratian's encyclopaedic *Decretum* (A.D. 1140–50). The canonists also made their contribution to the development of the parochial secular state, though they were aiming in the opposite direction. Their actual achievement is, indeed, one of the sombre ironies of history.

It might be said that the Holy See employed the canonists as the instruments of their wordy warfare with the Papacy's secular rival, the Holy Roman Empire; but a more accurate picture is presented by the statement that the canonists took possession of the Holy See. All the great Popes from Alexander III (A.D. 1159–81), who held the ecclesiastical fort against Frederick Barbarossa, through Innocent III (A.D. 1198–1216), who gave his world a foretaste of what

[1] Dawson, Christopher: *Religion and the Rise of Western Culture* (London 1950, Sheed & Ward), pp. 90–91.

Papal absolutism in the political sphere might mean, and Innocent IV (A.D. 1243–54), who encountered the great *Stupor Mundi* with a stubborn unscrupulousness quite equal to his own, down to Boniface VIII (A.D. 1294–1303), who collided disastrously with the strong monarchies of France and England—all these, and also most of the lesser Popes who filled the gaps between them, were not theologians (students of God) but canonists (students of Law). The first result was the downfall of the Empire; the second was the ruin of the Papacy, which never thereafter, until galvanized into new life *after* (and not before) the catastrophe of the Protestant secession, recovered from the moral and religious discredit in which its legalism had involved it. The downfall of both Empire and Papacy cleared the way in the West for the advance of the parochial state.

(4) RENAISSANCES OF PHILOSOPHIES

This field presents a pair of nearly contemporary renaissances at opposite ends of the Eurasian continent, namely the revival of the Confucian philosophy of the Sinic world in that East Asian civilization's offspring, the Far Eastern society, and the revival of the Aristotelian philosophy of the Hellenic world in Western Christendom.

Our first example might be ruled out of court on the ground that the Confucian philosophy did not in fact die with the society which had produced it but merely weathered a period of hibernation, and that what has not died is constitutionally disqualified from reappearing as a 'ghost'. We must admit the force of this objection but beg that it may be overlooked; for the re-establishment by the T'ang Emperor, T'ai T'sung, in A.D. 622, of an official examination in the Confucian Classics as a method of selecting recruits for the imperial civil service does present the essential characteristics of a renaissance, and it also marks the fact that, in the political field, the Taoists and Buddhists had let slip an opportunity for supplanting the Confucians which had seemed to be within their grasp during the post-Sinic interregnum, when the prestige of the Confucians had been damaged by the collapse of the universal state with which they had come to be identified.

The contrast between this political failure of the Buddhist Mahāyāna and the success with which the Christian Church seized and harvested its political opportunities in Western Europe brings out the fact that, in comparison with Christianity, the Mahāyāna was a politically incompetent religion. The patronage of the parochial princes of Northern China, which it enjoyed during the best part of three centuries following the collapse of the United Tsin Empire, was of no more avail to the Mahāyāna than the more potent patronage of the Kushan Emperor Kanishka had been at an earlier period. As soon, however, as the encounter on Far Eastern ground between the Mahāyāna and Confucianism was transferred from the political to the spiritual plane, the fortunes of their almost bloodless war were dramatically reversed. A modern Chinese authority on the subject tells us that 'the Neo-Confucianists more consistently adhere to the fundamental ideas of Taoism and Buddhism than do the Taoists and Buddhists themselves'.[1]

When we pass from the renaissance of a Sinic Confucian philosophy in Far Eastern history to the renaissance of an Hellenic Aristotelian philosophy in Western Christian history, we find the plot of the play taking a different turn. Whereas Neo-Confucianism succumbed spiritually to a Mahāyāna, Neo-Aristotelianism imposed itself on the theology of the Christian Church, in whose official view Aristotle could not be other than a heathen. In each case the party in power was worsted by an opponent who had nothing to recommend him but his intrinsic merits. In the Far Eastern case a philosophic civil service succumbs to the spirit of an alien religion; in the Western case an established church succumbs to the spirit of an alien philosophy.

The ghost of Aristotle in Western Christendom displayed the same astonishing intellectual potency as a living Mahāyāna in a Far Eastern world.

'It was not [from the Roman tradition] that [Western] Europe derived the critical intelligence and the restless spirit of scientific inquiry which have made [the] Western Civilisation the heir and successor of the Greeks. It is usual to date the coming of this new element from the [Italian] Renaissance and the revival of Greek studies in the fifteenth century, but the real turning-point must be placed three centuries earlier. . . . Already at Paris in the days of Abelard (*vivebat* A.D. 1079–1142) and John of Salisbury (*vivebat circa* A.D. 1115–1180) the passion for dialectic and the spirit of philosophical speculation had begun to transform the intellectual atmosphere of [Western] Christendom; and from that time forward the higher studies were dominated by the technique of logical discussion—the *quaestio* and the public disputation which so largely determined the *form* of Mediaeval [Western] Philosophy, even in its greatest representatives. "Nothing", says Robert of Sorbonne, "is known perfectly which has not been masticated by the teeth of disputation;" and the tendency to submit every question, from the most obvious to the most abstruse, to this process of mastication not only

[1] Fung Yu-lan: *A Short History of Chinese Philosophy* (New York 1948, Macmillan), p. 318.

encouraged readiness of wit and exactness of thought but, above all, developed that spirit of criticism and methodic doubt to which Western culture and Modern Science have owed so much.'[1]

A ghost of Aristotle that set this abiding impress on the spirit, as well as on the form, of Western thought also produced a passing effect on its substance; and, though the impress here was less durable, it nevertheless went deep enough to require a long and arduous campaign of mental strife as the price of its eventual effacement.

'In [the] whole picture of the Universe [as seen by Medieval Western eyes] there is more of Aristotle than of Christianity. It was the authority of Aristotle and his successors which was responsible even for those features of this teaching which might seem to us to carry something of an ecclesiastical flavour—the hierarchy of heavens, the revolving spheres, the intelligences which moved the planets, the grading of the elements in the order of their nobility, and the view that the celestial bodies were composed of an incorruptible fifth essence. Indeed, we may say [that] it was Aristotle rather than Ptolemy who had to be overthrown in the sixteenth century, and it was Aristotle who provided the great obstruction to the Copernican theory.'[2]

By the seventeenth century of the Christian Era, when the native intellectual genius of the West reasserted itself on 'Baconian' lines by setting out to explore the world of Nature, the theology of the Church had become so entangled in Aristotelianism that Giordano Bruno forfeited his life and Galileo incurred ecclesiastical censure for scientific heresies which had no relation whatever to the Christian religion as it appears in the New Testament.

Before the seventeenth century, Transalpine Western scientists and philosophers had attacked the Schoolmen for their subservience to Aristotle—'their dictator' as Bacon called him—while the fifteenth-century Italian humanists had attacked them for their bad Latin. But Aristotelian theology was proof against the sneers of the connoisseurs of a classical style. It is true that these critics extracted from the name of the eminent Aristotelian scholar Duns Scotus the pejorative word 'dunce', signifying not an ignorant person but a devotee to an obsolete system of learning; but, by the time of writing, the humanists' turn had come. In the twentieth century of the Christian Era, when natural science and technology appeared to be carrying all before them, it might have seemed that the 'dunces' were to be sought in the dwindling remnant of the once preponderant 'Classical Side'.

---

[1] Dawson, Christopher: *Religion and the Rise of Western Culture* (London 1950, Sheed & Ward), pp. 229–30.
[2] Butterfield, H.: *The Origins of Modern Science, 1300–1800* (London 1949, Bell), pp. 21–22.

(5) RENAISSANCES OF LANGUAGES AND
LITERATURES

A living language is primarily a form of speech, as is suggested by the fact that the word itself stems from the Latin word for tongue; its literature is, as it were, its by-product. When, however, the ghosts of a language and literature are raised from the dead, the relation between the two is inverted. The learning of the language is merely a painful prerequisite for reading the literature. When we learn 'vocative, mensa, O table' we are not acquiring a new vocabulary for the expression of our feelings when we stub our toes against a table-leg in the dark, but are taking a first short step towards the distant objective of reading Virgil, Horace, and the rest of the Latin classics. We do not attempt to speak the language, and, when we try to write it, it is only in order that we may the better appreciate the work of the 'ancient' masters.

The first step towards reoccupying a long since derelict literary empire is a work that may require the mobilization of a living political empire's resources. The typical monument of a literary renaissance in its first phase is an anthology, corpus, thesaurus, lexicon, or encyclopaedia compiled by a team of scholars at the instance of a prince; and the princely patron of such works of co-operative scholarship has been, more often than not, the ruler of a resuscitated universal state that has, itself, been the product of a renaissance on the political plane. Of the five outstanding representatives of this type—Asshurbanipal, Constantine Porphyrogenitus, Yung Lo, K'ang Hsi, and Ch'ien Lung—the last four had all been such. In this task of collecting, editing, annotating, and publishing the surviving works of a 'dead' classical literature, the Far Eastern Emperors of a resuscitated Sinic universal state had far outdistanced all their competitors.

It is true that the size of Asshurbanipal's two clay libraries of Sumerian and Akkadian classical literature was an unknown quantity for modern archaeologists who had learnt of the assemblage and dispersal of these two great Assyrian collections by recovering some of the tablets in the course of their excavations on the site of Nineveh; for, within perhaps not more than sixteen years of the royal scholar's death, the contents of both his libraries had been scattered broadcast over the ruins of the hateful city that had been stormed and sacked in 612 B.C. Asshurbanipal's collection may have been larger than the Confucian Canon of the Sinic classics, which was not facilely impressed on soft clay but was laboriously engraved on hard stone, at Si Ngan, the imperial capital of the T'ang Dynasty, between A.D. 836 and 841, and was printed a century later, with a commentary, in an edition running to 130 volumes. Yet we may guess with some confidence that the number of cuneiform characters in Asshurbanipal's collection fell far short of the number of Sinic characters contained in the collection which Yung Lo, the second Emperor of the Ming Dynasty, assembled in A.D. 1403–7, for this ran to no fewer than 22,877 books filling 11,095 volumes, exclusive of the table of contents. Compared with this, the Hellenic collection of the East Roman Emperor Constantine Porphyrogenitus (reigned A.D. 912–59) sinks into insignificance, though even this is staggering to a Western mind.

When we pass from these preliminary tasks to the scholar's conceit of producing imitations of the classical literatures to which he has devoted his labours, we must leave it to statisticians to determine whether the number of essays in the Sinic classical style produced by candidates for the Chinese imperial civil service examinations in the course of the 1,283 years that elapsed between their reinstitution in A.D. 622 and their abolition in A.D. 1905 was greater or less than the number of exercises in the writing of Latin and Greek prose and verse produced by scholars and schoolboys of the Western world between the fifteenth century and the time of writing. But in the use of resuscitated classical languages for serious literary purposes neither the West nor the Far East could stand comparison with the line of Byzantine historians, including such masters of the art as a tenth-century Leo Diaconus and a twelfth-century Anna Comnena, who found their medium of literary expression in a renaissance of the Attic Greek *koinê*.

It will probably have occurred to the reader that our remarks about literary renaissances so far seem to be singularly inapplicable to the literary renaissance—*The* Renaissance, in fact—which occupies the forefront in his own mind. Surely the Italian renaissance of Hellenic literature in the Late Medieval period, though it may have had its patrons among political grandees such as Lorenzo dei Medici, was essentially a spontaneous movement of unorganized scholarship. Perhaps it was—though the patronage of the fifteenth-century Popes, more particularly Pope Nicholas V (A.D. 1447–55), is not to be underrated. This Pope employed hundreds of classical scholars and copyists of ancient manuscripts, gave 10,000 gulden for a translation of Homer into Latin verse, and assembled a library of 9,000 volumes. However, if we allow our minds to travel back over the previous course of Western history, through several centuries running back from the age of 'the Renaissance', we shall find something much more in line with the examples that we have been considering. We shall find Charlemagne, the resuscitator of the universal state of a dead civilization, tentatively aligning himself with Asshurbanipal, Yung Lo, and Constantine Porphyrogenitus.

The abortive first attempt at a literary renaissance of Hellenism in Western Christendom was coeval with the birth of the Western Christian civilization. The English Church had owed its organization at the end of the seventh century to a Greek refugee from an Eastern Orthodox Christian territory conquered by Islam, Archbishop Theodore of Tarsus, and the prophet of the Hellenic renaissance in the West was a Northumbrian, the Venerable Bede (A.D. 673–735). Another Northumbrian, Alcuin of York (A.D. 735–804), carried the seed to the court of Charlemagne, and, before the movement was prematurely extinguished by a blast of barbarism from Scandinavia, its cultivators had not only begun to revive the Hellenic literary culture in its Latin dress but had even acquired a smattering of Greek. Alcuin had dared to dream that, supported by the patronage of Charlemagne, he would be able to conjure up the ghost of Athens on the soil of Frankland. It was a fleeting vision; and, when Western Christendom began to re-emerge from what has been called 'the darkness of the ninth century', the ghost admitted was not that of the Hellenic Classical literature; it was the ghost of 'Aristotil and his philosophie'.[1] The centuries of the Schoolmen had to come and go before the vision of Alcuin was realized.

If we pause at this point to consider why the hopes of Alcuin and his friends were deferred for so many centuries, we discover a difference between the encounters in space, to which the previous part of this Study was devoted, and the encounters in time which we are now considering. An encounter in space is a collision in space, and collisions are usually accidents. Military prowess or new skills in navigating the oceans or the desiccation of the Steppe may be the culturally irrelevant causes which lead to one society's falling upon another, with the cultural consequences that we have described. An encounter in time (a renaissance), on the other hand, is an act of necromancy, the calling up of a ghost; and the necromancer will fail to call up the ghost until he has learnt the tricks of his trade. In other words, a Western Christendom could not entertain an Hellenic ghost, or guest, until its own house was fit to receive the visitor. The Hellenic library was physically present all the time, but it could not be effectively opened until the Westerner was competent to read its contents.

For example, there was never a time, even at the blackest nadir of a Western Dark Age, when the Western Christian society did

---

[1] This is what the 'Clerk of Oxenford', in Chaucer's *Prolog*, had, or wished to have, 'at his beddes head'.

not physically possess the works of Virgil and did not retain sufficient knowledge of Latin to construe his sentences. Yet there were
at least eight centuries, from the seventh to the fourteenth inclusive, during which Virgil's poetry was beyond the comprehension
of the most gifted Western Christian students, if we take as our
standard of understanding an ability to grasp the meaning which
Virgil had intended to convey and which had been duly com-
prehended by his like-minded contemporaries and by posterity
down to, let us say, the generation of Saint Augustine. Even Dante,
on whose spirit the first glimmer of an Italian renaissance of Hellenism was beginning to dawn, saw in Virgil a figure which the
historical Virgil would have taken, not for his own human self, but
for some augustly mythical personage such as Orpheus.

Similarly, there was never a time at which the Western society
did not possess the philosophical works of Aristotle, competently
translated into Latin by the Late Hellenic man of letters, Boëthius
(A.D. 480–524); yet there were six centuries, reckoning from the
date of Boëthius's death, during which his translations were beyond
the comprehension of the most acute Western Christian thinkers.
When, at last, the Western Christians were ready for Aristotle, they
got him, by a roundabout route, through Arabic translations. In
offering to a sixth-century Western Christendom his Latin
translations of Aristotle, Boëthius was like a benevolent but ill-
judging uncle who presents, let us say, the poems of Mr. T. S.
Eliot to his nephew on his thirteenth birthday. The nephew, after
a brief inspection, places the book in the darkest corner of his
small library and, quite sensibly, forgets all about it. Six years
later—the equivalent of centuries on the reduced time-span of an
individual adolescence—the nephew encounters these poems again
as an Oxford undergraduate, falls under their spell, purchases them
from Messrs. B. H. Blackwell, and is unfeignedly surprised to discover, on returning home for the vacation, that the book had been
standing on his shelves all the time.

As it was with Virgil and with Aristotle, so it was also with the
masterpieces of Greek literature, stored in the Byzantine libraries,
which were to be the staple food of the Italian Hellenic renaissance
on its literary side. Western Christendom had been in close contact with the Byzantine world, at least from the eleventh century
onwards. During the first half of the thirteenth century Frankish
conquerors were in actual occupation of Constantinople and Greece.
Culturally nothing came of this at that time; for in the West the
'Classics' were as yet 'caviare to the general'. It might be said, in
explanation, that these contacts were hostile contacts that would
not dispose the Westerner favourably towards a Byzantine library

of Hellenic literature; but to this it must be answered that political and ecclesiastical contacts were no less hostile in the fifteenth century, when 'the Renaissance' was in full bloom. The reason for the difference in the cultural consequences is plain; a renaissance of a dead culture will occur only when an affiliated society has raised itself to the cultural level at which its predecessor was standing at the time when it was accomplishing the achievements that have now become candidates for resuscitation.

When we look into the deaths of the literary renaissances in Western Christendom and China, we find that they held sway unchallenged until overthrown by a masterful alien intruder in the shape of a Modern Western civilization which captivated the soul of Western Christendom in the course of the seventeenth century and the soul of China at the turn of the nineteenth and twentieth centuries of the Christian Era. The Western society had been left to wrestle with its Hellenic ghost without external interference; but the war of pamphlets at the turn of the seventeenth and eighteenth centuries, which Swift called 'The Battle of the Books', and in which the disputants were arguing the question of the relative merits of 'the Ancients' and 'the Moderns', had shown which way the wind was blowing. The question at issue seemed to be whether the Western culture was to remain rooted to the spot, paralysed by a retrospective admiration for, and imitation of, 'the Ancients', or was to go forward into the unknown, leaving 'the Ancients' behind. Thus put, the question could admit of only one sensible answer, but the question itself begged a previous question, and that was whether a retrospective admiration and imitation of 'the Ancients' —what we may call the 'Modern Western classical education' in the widest sense of that term—had in fact cramped 'modern' development.

The answer to this question was manifestly favourable to 'the Ancients', and it was significant that some of the pioneers of Hellenic studies, Petrarch and Boccaccio for example, had also been leading lights in the development of vernacular Italian literature. So far from checking the progress of the vernacular literatures, the renaissance of Hellenic studies had given it fresh impetus. The mastery of Ciceronian Latin achieved by Erasmus had not lured his fellow Westerners into abandoning the literary cultivation of their own mother tongues. It is quite impossible to assess the cultural nexus of cause and effect between, for example, English sixteenth-century Hellenic studies and the outburst of an English poetry of unexampled brilliance at the end of the same century. Did Shakespeare's 'little Latin and less Greek' assist the composition of his plays? Who shall say? It may be thought that Milton had too much Latin and Greek, but, if he had had none of either, we should have had no *Paradise Lost* and no *Samson Agonistes*.

(6) RENAISSANCES OF VISUAL ARTS

The renaissance of one or other of the visual arts of a dead civilization in the history of its successor is a common phenomenon. We may cite as examples the renaissance of 'the old Kingdom's' style of sculpture and painting, after a lapse of two thousand years, in a latter-day Egyptiac world of the Saïte Age in the seventh and sixth centuries B.C.; the renaissance of a Sumeric style of carving in bas-relief in a Babylonic world of the ninth, eighth, and seventh centuries B.C.; and the renaissance, in miniature, of an Hellenic style of carving in bas-relief, of which the finest examples were Attic masterpieces of the fifth and fourth centuries B.C., on the ivory of Byzantine diptychs in the tenth, eleventh, and twelfth centuries of the Christian Era. These three visual renaissances, however, were all left far behind, both in the range of ground covered and in the ruthlessness of the eviction of previous occupants, by the renaissance of Hellenic visual arts in Western Christendom which made its first epiphany in a Late Medieval Italy and spread thence to the rest of the Western world. This evocation of the ghost of Hellenic visual arts was practised in the three fields of architecture, sculpture, and painting, and in each field the *revenant* style made so clean a sweep that, when its force was spent, there ensued a kind of aesthetic vacuum in which Western artists were at a loss to know how to express their long-submerged native genius.

The same strange tale of a house swept and garnished by the drastic hands of ghostly visitants has to be told in telling of each of these three provinces of Western visual art, but the most extraordinary episode of the three was the triumph of an Hellenic *revenant* over the native genius of the West in the province of sculpture in the round; for in this field the thirteenth-century Northern French exponents of an original Western style had produced masterpieces equal in merit with the best work of the Hellenic, Egyptiac, and Mahāyānian Buddhist schools, whereas, in the field of painting, Western artists had not yet shaken off the tutelage of the more precocious art of a sister Orthodox Christian society, and in the field of architecture the Romanesque style—which, as its latter-day label indicates, was a variation on a theme inherited from the latest age of an antecedent Hellenic civilization—had already been overwhelmed by an intrusive 'Gothic' which had originated, as we have already mentioned, in the Syriac world of the 'Abbasid and Andalusian Caliphates.

For a twentieth-century Londoner's enlightenment, the combatants in a mortal struggle between a twice-defeated native Western visual art and its Syriac and Hellenic assailants were still standing, turned to stone, in the architecture and sculpture of the chapel added to Westminster Abbey under the auspices of King Henry VII. The vaulting of the roof is a late triumph of an expiring Gothic style. In the host of erect stone figures *in excelsis* which gaze down at an Italianate Hellenized trinity of recumbent bronze figures on the tombs below, a Transalpine school of native Western Christian sculpture sings a silent swan-song between frozen lips. The centre of the stage is held by the Hellenizing masterpieces of Torrigiani (A.D. 1472–1522), who, contemptuously ignoring the uncouth milieu in which he had deigned to execute his competently polished work, was looking around him complacently, in the confident expectation that these fruits of a Florentine master's exile would be the cynosure of every Transalpine sightseer's eyes. For we learn from Benvenuto Cellini's autobiography that this same Torrigiani was a man of 'most arrogant spirit', and that he was given to boasting of his 'gallant feats among those beasts of Englishmen'.[1]

A 'Gothic' architecture which thus continued to hold its own until the first quarter of the sixteenth century in London—and the first half of the seventeenth century in Oxford—had by then long since been driven off the field in Northern and Central Italy, where it had never succeeded so decisively as in Transalpine Europe in displacing the Romanesque style.

The sterility with which the Western genius had been afflicted by a renaissance of Hellenism in the domain of architecture was proclaimed in its failure to reap any harvest from the birth-pangs of the Industrial Revolution. A mutation of industrial technique that had begotten the iron girder had thrust into the Western architect's hands an incomparably versatile new building material at a time when the Hellenizing architectural tradition was evidenty exhausted. Yet the architects who had been presented by the blacksmith with an iron girder, and by Providence with a clean slate, could think of no better way of filling an opportune vacuum than to cap an Hellenic renaissance with a 'Gothic' revival.

The first Westerner to think of frankly turning the iron girder to account without bashfully drawing a 'Gothic' veil over its

---

[1] Benvenuto Cellini: *Autobiography*, English translation by J. A. Symonds (London 1949, Phaidon Press), Book I, chapter xii, p. 18.

vulgarity was not a professing architect but an imaginative amateur; and, though he was a citizen of the United States, the site on which he erected his historic structure overlooked the shores of the Bosphorus, not the banks of the Hudson. The nucleus of Robert College—Hamlin Hall, dominating Mehmed the Conqueror's Castle of Europe—was built by Cyrus Hamlin in A.D. 1869–71; yet it was not until the following century that the seed sown by Hamlin began to bear fruit in North America and in Western Europe.

The sterilizing of the West's artistic genius was no less conspicuous in the realms of painting and sculpture. Over the span of more than half a millennium running from the generation of Dante's contemporary Giotto (died A.D. 1337), a Modern Western school of painting, which had unquestioningly accepted the naturalistic ideals of Hellenic visual art in its post-archaic phase, had worked out, one after another, diverse methods of conveying the visual impressions made by light and shade, until this long-sustained effort to produce the effects of photography through prodigies of artistic technique had been stultified by the invention of photography itself. After the ground had thus inconsiderately been cut away from under their feet by an operation of Modern Western science, the painters made a 'Pre-Raphaelite Movement' in the direction of their long-since repudiated Byzantine masters, before they thought of exploring a new world of psychology which Science had given them to conquer in compensation for the old world of natural appearance which she had stolen from them and presented to the photographer. So arose an apocalyptic school of Western painters who made a genuinely new departure by frankly using paint to convey spiritual experiences instead of visual impressions; and Western sculptors were, within the limits of their own medium, now setting forth on the same exciting quest.

(7) RENAISSANCES OF RELIGIOUS IDEALS AND INSTITUTIONS

The relation of Christianity to Judaism was as damningly clear to Jewish eyes as it was embarrassingly ambiguous for Christian consciences. In Jewish eyes the Christian Church was a renegade Jewish sect which, on the evidence of its own unauthorized appendix to the Canon of Scripture, had sinned against the teaching of the misguided and unfortunate Galilean Pharisee whose name these traitors to Pharisaism had impudently taken in vain. In Jewish eyes, Christianity's allegedly miraculous captivation of the Hellenic society was by no means 'the Lord's doing'. The posthumous triumph of a Jewish rabbi who had been saluted by his followers, in Gentile style, as the son of a god by a human mother was a pagan exploit of the same order as the earlier triumphs of kindred legendary 'demigods' such as Dionysus and Heracles. Judaism flattered herself that she could have anticipated Christianity's conquests if she had stooped to conquer by descending to Christianity's level. Though Christianity had never repudiated the authority of the Jewish Scriptures—indeed, she had bound them up with her own—she had made her facile conquests by betraying, as Jewish eyes saw it, the two cardinal Judaic principles, the First and Second of the Ten Commandments, Monotheism and Aniconism (no 'images'). So now, in face of a still impenitent Hellenic paganism, plainly visible under a veneer of Christianity, the watchword for Jewry was to persevere in bearing witness to the Lord's everlasting Word.

This 'patient deep disdain' with which a sensationally successful Christianity continued to be regarded by an unimpressed and unshaken Jewry would have been less embarrassing for Christians if Christianity herself had not combined a sincere theoretical loyalty to a Jewish legacy of Monotheism and Aniconism with those practical concessions to the polytheism and idolatry of Hellenic converts for which she was arraigned by her Jewish critics. The Christian Church's reconsecration of the Jewish Scriptures as the Old Testament of the Christian Faith was a weak spot in Christianity's armour through which the shafts of Jewish criticism pierced the Christian conscience. The Old Testament was one of the foundation stones on which the Christian edifice rested; but so, too, was the doctrine of the Trinity, the cult of the Saints, and the representation, not only of the Saints but also of the divine Three Persons, in three-dimensional as well as two-dimensional works of visual art. How could Christian apologists answer the Jewish taunt that the Church's Hellenic practice was irreconcilable with her Judaic theory? Some reply was required which would convince Christian minds that there was no substance in these Jewish arguments, for the tellingness of these arguments lay in the responsive conviction of sin which they evoked in Christian souls.

After the nominal conversion, *en masse*, of an Hellenic Gentile world in the course of the fourth century of the Christian Era, the domestic controversy within the bosom of the Church tended to overshadow the polemics between Christians and Jews; but the theological warfare on this older front seems to have flared up again in the sixth and seventh centuries in consequence of a puritanical house-cleaning in Jewry which, in the Palestinian Jewish community, had been taken in hand towards the close of the fifth century. This domestic campaign, within Jewry, against a Christian-like laxity in the matter of mural decoration of synagogues had its repercussions on the Jewish-Christian battlefront. But, when we turn to the parallel controversy within the Christian Church between iconophiles and iconophobes, we are struck with its persistence and ubiquity. We find this 'irrepressible conflict' bursting out in almost every province of Christendom and in almost every succeeding century of the Christian Era. It is unnecessary here to catalogue a long list of examples beginning with the thirty-sixth canon of the Council of Elvira (*circa* A.D. 300–11), which forbids the exhibition of pictures in churches.

In the seventh century of the Christian Era a new factor was introduced into the argument in the shape of a new actor who made a sensationally brilliant appearance on the historical stage. Yet another religion now sprang, as Christianity had sprung, but this one full-grown, from the loins of Jewry. Islam was as fanatically monotheist and aniconist as any Jew could desire, and the sensational successes of its devotees in the military—and soon also in the missionary—field gave Christendom something new to think about. Much as the military and missionary triumphs of the devotees of Communism had induced in Modern Western souls a heart-searching reappraisal of traditional Western social and economic arrangements, so the triumphs of the Primitive Muslim Arab conquerors supplied fresh fuel for the controversies that had long been smouldering round the problem of Christian 'idolatry'.

In A.D. 726 the ghost of a Judaic iconophobia, long hovering in the wings, was brought into the centre of the stage by the Iconoclastic Decree of the great East Roman Emperor, Leo Syrus. This attempt to impose what amounted to a renaissance in the religious field by means of political authority proved a failure. The Papacy identified itself enthusiastically with the popular 'idolatrous' opposition, and thereby took a long step towards emancipating itself from Byzantine authority. The subsequent, possibly half-hearted, move made in the West by Charlemagne in the direction of the policy of Leo Syrus received a decisive snub from Pope Hadrian I. The West had to wait nearly eight centuries more for its Judaic renaissance; and when this came it was a movement from below upwards; its Leo Syrus was Martin Luther.

In the Protestant Reformation in Western Christendom, Aniconism was not the only Judaic ghost that succeeded in reasserting itself. A Judaic Sabbatarianism simultaneously captivated the secessionists from the Roman Catholic Church; and the renaissance of this other element in Judaism is less easy to explain, because the extreme meticulousness to which a post-exilic Jewry had carried its observance of its Sabbath was a peculiar people's response to a peculiar challenge; it was a part of the Jewish diaspora's technique for preserving its corporate existence. The Protestants' professed objective was a return to the pristine practice of the Primitive Church; yet here we see them obliterating a difference between Primitive Christianity and Judaism on which the Primitive Church had insisted. Could these 'Bible Christians' be unaware of the numerous passages in the Gospels in which Jesus was reported to have defied the Sabbatarian taboo? Could it have escaped their notice that Paul, whom they delighted to honour, had made himself notorious by repudiating the Mosaic Law? The explanation was that these religious enthusiasts, in Germany, England, Scotland, New England, and elsewhere, were in the grip of one of the most potent of renaissances and were bent on turning themselves into imitation-Jews, as enthusiastic Italian artists and scholars had been bent on turning themselves into imitation-Athenians. Their practice of inflicting on their children at baptism some of the most un-Teutonic sounding proper names to be found in the Old Testament was a revealing symptom of this mania for calling a dead world back to life.

We have already introduced, by implication, a third element in the Judaic renaissance of Western Protestantism, namely bibliolatry, the idolization of a sacred text as a substitute for the idolization of sacred images. No doubt, great cultural benefit had accrued, not only to devout Protestants or Puritans, but to Western souls in general, from the translation of the Bible into the vernacular languages and from the constant reading of it by generations of simple people who read very little else. This had immeasurably enriched the vernacular literatures and stimulated popular education. The 'Bible stories', over and above whatever might be their religious value, had become a folklore far surpassing in human interest anything available to Western Man from any native source. For a more sophisticated minority, the critical study of the sacred text had been an apprenticeship in a higher criticism which could be, and duly had been, applied thereafter in all fields of scholarship. At the same time the moral and intellectual nemesis of deifying holy scriptures was a Protestant servitude from which a still priest-ridden Tridentine Catholicism had remained free. The determination to regard as the unerring Word of God an Old Testament which was being more and more plainly shown to be a collection, or rather an amalgamation, of human compositions of varying degrees of religious and historical merit, had set a religious premium on an obstinate stupidity which had led Matthew Arnold to accuse the virtuous middle classes of his own Victorian Age of living in a 'Hebraizing backwater'.

XI
LAW AND FREEDOM IN HISTORY

XXXV. THE PROBLEM

(1) THE MEANING OF 'LAW'

DURING the hundred years which preceded A.D. 1914 Western Man was very little troubled with the problem with which we have now to grapple, because either type of solution seemed as satisfactory as the other. If human destiny were ruled by super-human law, that law was the highly satisfactory Law of Progress. If, on the other hand, there were no such law, it could safely be assumed that the activities of free and intelligent human beings would secure the same result. By the middle of the twentieth century the situation was evidently very different. Civilizations were known to have collapsed in the past, and the pretentious skyscraper erected by Modern Western Man was now seen to be displaying ominous fissures. Was there a Law, such as Oswald Spengler had laid down, in his pontifical work, *The Decline of the West*, published A.D. 1919, that this civilization should go the way of its predecessors, or were we free to retrieve our mistakes and fashion our own destiny?

The first step in our inquiry should be to make up our minds what in this context we mean by 'law'. We obviously do not mean the man-made legislation from which, by a metaphor so familiar that we hardly notice it, the term had been transferred to the context with which we are now concerned. The 'law' with which we are now concerned resembles this familiar man-made institution in being a set of rules governing human affairs, but it differs in that it is not made by Man and cannot be altered by him. We have already noticed in an earlier part of this Study that this idea of law is apt, in the act of being translated to the metaphysical plane, to become polarized into two apparently antithetical concepts. For minds in whose mental vision the personality of the human legislator looms larger than the law which he administers, the metaphysical 'law' governing the Universe is regarded as the 'law' of an omnipotent God. For other minds, in whose vision the person of the legislator or ruler is eclipsed by the notion of the law that he administers, the metaphysical 'law' governing the Universe is conceived of as the impersonal law of a uniform and inexorable Nature.

Each of these concepts presents both consoling and horrifying features. The horrifying feature of 'the laws of Nature' is their inexorability, and yet this carries with it its compensation. Since these laws are inexorable, they are ascertainable by human intelligence. A knowledge of Nature is within Man's mental grasp, and this knowledge is power. Man can learn Nature's laws to harness her for his own purposes. In this undertaking Man had been amazingly successful. He had actually split the atom—and with what results?

A human soul that has been convicted of sin and convinced that it cannot achieve its own reformation without the help of God's grace will opt, like David, to fall into the hand of the Lord. An inexorability in punishing, as well as in exposing, Man's sin, which is the Last Judgement of 'the laws of Nature', can be overcome only by accepting the jurisdiction of the 'Law of God'. The price of this transfer of spiritual allegiance is a forfeiture of that exact and definitive intellectual knowledge which is the material prize and the spiritual burden of human souls that are content to be Nature's masters at the cost of being her slaves. 'It is a fearful thing to fall into the hands of the Living God'; for, if God is a spirit, His dealings with human spirits will be unpredictable and inscrutable. In appealing to the Law of God, a human soul has to abandon certainty in order to embrace hope and fear; for a law that is the expression of a will is animated by a spiritual freedom which is the very antithesis of the uniformity of Nature; and an arbitrary law may be inspired by either love or hate. In casting itself upon the Law of God, a human soul is apt to find what it brings to it. Hence Man's notions of God have ranged from a vision of God the Father to a vision of God the Tyrant; and both visions are consonant with the image of God as a personality in the anthropomorphic guise beyond which the human imagination seems unable to penetrate.

(2) THE ANTINOMIANISM OF MODERN WESTERN HISTORIANS

The idea of a 'Law of God' had been wrought out by the travail of the souls of Israelite and Iranian prophets in response to the challenges of Babylonic and Syriac history, while the classic exposition of the concept of 'laws of Nature' had been fashioned by philosophic observers of the disintegration of the Indic and Hellenic worlds. But the two schools of thought are not logically incompatible with each other, and it is quite conceivable that these two kinds of Law should be in operation side by side. 'The Law of God' reveals a single constant aim pursued by the intelligence and will of a personality. 'Laws of Nature' display the regularity of a recurrent movement, as of a wheel revolving round its axis. If we could imagine a wheel coming into existence without the creative act of a wheelwright, and then revolving for ever without serving any purpose, these repetitions would indeed be vain; and this was the pessimistic conclusion drawn by Indic and Hellenic philosophers, who saw 'the sorrowful wheel of existence' turning for ever *in vacuo*. In real life we find no wheels without wheelwrights, and no wheelwrights without drivers who commission these artificers to build wheels and fit them to carts, in order that the repetitive revolutions of the wheels may convey the carts to the destination intended by the drivers. 'Laws of Nature' make sense when they are pictured as the wheels that God has fitted to His own chariot.

A belief that the whole life of the Universe was governed by the 'Law of God' was an inheritance from Judaism that was shared by the Christian and Muslim societies, and it had been expressed in two strikingly similar but entirely independent works of genius, the *De Civitate Dei* of Saint Augustine and the *Prolegomena* to a *History of the Berbers* by Ibn Khaldūn. The Augustinian version of the Judaic view of history had been taken for granted by Western Christian thinkers for more than a thousand years, and had found its last authoritative expression in Bossuet's *Discours sur l'Histoire Universelle*, published in A.D. 1681.

The Late Modern Western rejection of this theocentric philosophy of history can be both explained and excused; for the picture presented by Bossuet was found, when subjected to analysis, to accord neither with Christianity nor with common sense. Its defects are unsparingly exposed by R. G. Collingwood, a twentieth-century writer who achieved distinction both as an historian and as a philosopher.

'Any history written on Christian principles will be of necessity universal, providential, apocalyptic, and periodized. . . . If challenged to explain how he knew that there was in History any objective plan at all, the mediaeval historian would have replied that he knew it by revelation; it was part of what Christ had revealed to Man concerning God. And this revelation not only gave the key to what God had done in the past; it showed us what God was going to do in the future. The Christian revelation thus gave us a view of the entire history of the World, from its creation in the past to its end in the future, as seen in the timeless and eternal vision of God. Thus mediaeval historiography looked forward to the end of History as something fore-ordained by God and through revelation foreknown to Man. It thus contained in itself an eschatology.

In Mediaeval thought the complete opposition between the objective purpose of God and the subjective purpose of Man, so conceived that God's purpose appears as the imposition of a certain objective plan upon

History quite irrespective of Man's subjective purposes, leads inevitably to the idea that Man's purposes make no difference to the course of History, and that the only force which determines it is the Divine Nature.'[1]

In thus misrepresenting Christian revelation, the medieval-minded Early Modern Western historians were exposing themselves to attack both from Late Modern scientific dogmatism and from Late Modern agnostic scepticism. These historians (to quote Collingwood again) 'fell into the error of thinking they could forecast the future', and, 'in their anxiety to detect the general plan of History, and their belief that this plan was God's and not Man's, they tended to look for the essence of History outside History itself, by looking away from Man's actions in order to detect the plan of God'.

'Consequently the actual detail of human actions became for them relatively unimportant, and they neglected that prime duty of the historian, a willingness to bestow infinite pains on discovering what actually happened. This is why mediaeval historiography is so weak in critical method. That weakness was not an accident. It did not depend on the limitation of the sources and materials at the disposal of scholars. It depended on a limitation, not of what they could do, but of what they wanted to do. They did not want an accurate and scientific study of the actual facts of History; what they wanted was an accurate and scientific study of the divine attributes, a theology . . . which should enable them to determine *a priori* what must have happened and what must be going to happen in the historical process.

'The consequence of this is that, when Mediaeval historiography is looked at from the point of view of a merely scholarly historian, the kind of historian who cares for nothing except accuracy in facts, it seems not only unsatisfactory but deliberately and repulsively wrong-headed; and the nineteenth-century [Western] historians, who did in general take a merely scholarly view of the nature of History, regarded it with extreme lack of sympathy.'[2]

This hostility towards a medieval conception was not peculiar to a generation of latter-day historians whose complacent agnosticism reflected the pleasant tranquillity of their lives. At a higher temperature it also animated their predecessors and their successors. To take the latter first: a twentieth-century generation that was tasting the unpleasant experience of being driven from pillar to post by human dictators, bent on putting their subjects through five-year plans, would have revolted in disgust against the suggestion that a six-thousand-year plan was being imposed on them by

[1] Collingwood, R. G.: *The Idea of History* (Oxford 1946, Clarendon Press), pp. 49, 54, 55.
[2] Ibid., pp. 55, 56.

a dictatorial Deity. As for eighteenth-century Western Man, whose immediate predecessors had paid for their fidelity to medieval concepts by inflicting on themselves the agony of the Wars of Religion, he could not afford to dismiss Bossuet's thesis as a ridiculous and outmoded superstition. For him it was 'the enemy', and *Écrasez l'Infâme* was the watchword of the Age of Voltaire. There was here no essential difference between the Deists, who were prepared to admit the Deity's existence provided that, like a Hanoverian king in Great Britain, he reigned but did not govern, and the atheists who abolished God as a preface to a Declaration of Nature's Independence. Henceforth the laws of nature were free to be entirely inexorable and consequently were in process of becoming completely intelligible. It was the Age of the Newtonian self-adjusting Universe and of Paley's Divine Watchmaker, who had simultaneously wound up his watch and his business.

Thus was the 'Law of God' dismissed as a delusion of the darkness from which Late Modern Western Man was emerging; but, when the Men of Science set themselves to take over this estate from which God had been evicted, they found that there was one province in which their writ, the 'laws of Nature', could not be made to run. Science could explain non-human nature; it could even explain the workings of the human body, which happened to be very like those of the bodies of other mammals; but, when it was a question of the activities of Mankind, not as animals but as human beings in process of civilization, Science recoiled. Here was a chaos unamenable to her laws; a meaningless succession of events that a twentieth-century English novelist who was also poet laureate called Odtaa, standing for 'one damned thing after another'. Science could not make sense of it, so it was left to a less ambitious fraternity, the historians.

The eighteenth-century metaphysical cartographers had partitioned the Universe. On the one side of their dividing line they had found an orderly province of non-human affairs in which the 'laws of Nature' were believed to be in force, and which was therefore held to be progressively accessible to human exploration by cumulative intellectual enterprise; on the other side they had left a chaotic province of human history from which, as they saw it, no more could be extracted than interesting stories which could be recorded with increasing accuracy but which could not 'prove' anything; and this is what someone (alleged to be the American automobile manufacturer Henry Ford) meant when he said that History was 'bunk'. The chief feature of the period that had followed, down to the time of writing, was that Science had set itself to annex, with varying degrees of success, sundry provinces of the domain originally left to the historians—such provinces as, for example, those of anthropology, economics, sociology, and psychology. In the dwindling remainder of their territory, on which an ever-advancing Science had not yet set foot, the historians continued to pursue their 'fact-finding' activities, undisturbed.

But the fundamental faith of Western Man had 'always been a belief that the Universe was subject to Law and was not given over to Chaos; and a deist or atheist Late Modern version of this faith was the belief that the Law of the Universe was a system of 'laws of Nature'. The domain of these laws had, in truth, been continually extended. The great names in the history of Science had been the names of those who had seen through the superficial appearance of Chaos to an underlying Order. The work for which Newton, Darwin, and Einstein, for instance, were famous had been work of this clarifying kind. And who would presume to draw a line beyond which these intellectual *conquistadores* must not extend their operations? A proclamation that one province of the Universe— the metropolitan province occupied by Man in Process of Civilization—had been reserved by some undesignated higher authority as a sanctuary for Chaos might satisfy antinomian historians, but would be regarded as blasphemy by all right-minded devotees of Science.

As a matter of fact, Modern Western historians were apt to be much less antinomian than they supposed, on the admission of a distinguished mid-twentieth-century practitioner of the historian's craft.

'The men of a given generation are generally unaware of the degree to which they envisage their contemporary history within an assumed framework, ranging events into certain shapes or running them into certain moulds which are sometimes adopted almost as in a day-dream. They may be sublimely unconscious of the way their minds are constricted by their routine formulation of the story; and only when the World is different, and there emerges a new generation not locked from birth in the accepted framework, does the narrowness of that framework become apparent to everybody. . . . It is a mistake for writers of history and other teachers to imagine that if they are not Christian they are refraining from committing themselves, or working without any doctrine at all, discussing History without any presuppositions. Amongst historians, as in other fields, the blindest of all the blind are those who are unable to examine their own presuppositions, and blithely imagine therefore that they do not possess any.'[1]

This is the picture of a prisoner unconscious of his chains, and in this context we cannot forbear to quote for a second time a

[1] Butterfield, Herbert: *Christianity and History* (London 1949, Bell), pp. 140 and 146.

passage which, by reason of its urbanity and the brilliance of the book which it prefaced, had become a classic profession of the antinomian unfaith.

'One intellectual excitement has . . . been denied me. Men wiser and more learned than I have discerned in History a plot, a rhythm, a predetermined pattern. These harmonies are concealed from me. I can see only one emergency following upon another as wave follows upon wave; only one great fact with respect to which, since it is unique, there can be no generalisations; only one safe rule for the historian: that he should recognise in the development of human destinies the play of the contingent and the unforeseen.'[1]

And yet an historian who thus publicly declared his allegiance to the dogma that History is just 'one damned thing after another' had, in calling his book *A History of Europe*, committed himself, almost in the same breath, to a predetermined pattern in which the history of one indistinguishable 'continent' was equated with the whole history of Mankind; and he had arrived at this Late Modern Western historical convention by unconsciously subscribing to the articles of a current Western *religio historici*. The unconscious mental operations required for believing in the existence of 'Europe' were so elaborate that the number of tacitly accepted articles must have run to at least thirty-nine.

[1] Fisher, H. A. L.: *A History of Europe* (London 1935, Eyre & Spottiswoode), vol. i, p. vii.

XXXVI. THE AMENABILITY OF HUMAN AFFAIRS TO 'LAWS OF NATURE'

(1) A SURVEY OF THE EVIDENCE

(a) THE PRIVATE AFFAIRS OF INDIVIDUALS

LET us start, for the purpose of our inquiry, by assuming that it is an open question whether 'laws of Nature' have or have not any footing in the history of Man in Process of Civilization. We shall have then to examine various departments of human affairs in order to find out whether the question proves, on closer scrutiny, to be rather less open than we are at present assuming it to be. It might be convenient to take our first soundings among the ordinary affairs of private people, a subject to which modern historians had made magnificent contributions under the heading of Social History. Here the difficulty that confronts us in seeking to find laws governing the histories of civilizations is notably absent. The number of recorded civilizations is inconveniently small for purposes of generalization—less than two dozen; and of some of these our knowledge is very fragmentary. Private individuals, on the other hand, are numbered by the million, and their behaviour, under Modern Western conditions, had been subjected to elaborate statistical analysis, on the basis of which practical men made predictions on which they risked not only their reputations but their money. Those who controlled industry and commerce confidently assumed that such and such a market would absorb such and such a supply of goods. They would sometimes be mistaken, but more often they would not, otherwise they would have had to go out of business.

A business activity which most clearly illustrated the applicability of a law of averages to the affairs of individuals was insurance. We must beware, no doubt, of too hastily enlisting all forms of insurance in support of an argument for the applicability of 'laws of nature' to human affairs in the sense in which we are using the latter term. Life insurance was concerned with the prospects of the human body, and physiology was clearly within the domain of Science. At the same time it would not be denied that the soul had some say in the matter; for physical life might be prolonged by prudence and be shortened by various forms of imprudence, ranging from heroism through folly to bestiality. Marine insurance of ships and their cargoes similarly involved the study of meteorology, which was also a department of Science, though at present a somewhat unruly one. But when we come to insurance against burglary or fire it would appear that the insurance companies were gambling on laws of averages applied to the distinctively human qualities of criminality and carelessness.

(b) THE INDUSTRIAL AFFAIRS OF A MODERN WESTERN SOCIETY

The statistical patterns discernible in the fluctuations of demand and supply in the dealings between caterers and their customers notoriously manifested themselves in a succession of 'booms' and 'slumps'; but the pattern of these business cycles had not yet, at the time of writing, been worked out with sufficient precision to have emboldened the insurance companies to open up a new branch of their business by quoting premiums for insurance against the formidable risks arising from them. Scientific investigators had, however, already learnt a good deal about the subject.

In the intellectual history of an industrial Western society, the phenomenon of trade cycles had been discovered empirically from direct social observation before it was confirmed statistically. The earliest known description of it had been given in A.D. 1837 by a British observer, S. J. Loyd, afterwards Lord Overstone. In a book first published in A.D. 1927 an American student of business cycles, W. C. Mitchell, had declared his belief that 'the characteristics of business cycles may be expected to change as economic organization develops'. On the basis of 'business annals', compiled by another American scholar, W. L. Thorp, from non-statistical evidence, a third American scholar, F. C. Mills, had calculated that the mean wave-length of a 'short' trade cycle was 5·86 years in the early stages of industrialization, 4·09 years in the succeeding age of rapid transition, and 6·39 years in the subsequent age of comparative stability.

Other economists had propounded other cycles, some of which were believed to have much longer wave-lengths. Others had suggested that these 'waves' showed a tendency to subside into a state of equilibrium. There was no general agreement among them about these, and the study was, in fact, in its infancy. We need not pursue it further. The point that we are concerned to make is that, within two hundred years of the outbreak of the Industrial Revolution in Great Britain, the fathers of a Western economic science were engaged in disentangling, from the mass of data presented to them by economic history, a body of laws governing an economic department of human activity in which Man's distinctive qualities came into play.

(c) THE RIVALRIES OF PAROCHIAL STATES:
THE 'BALANCE OF POWER'

After having found the economists using the results of their researches to explore the working of laws applicable to economic history, we naturally turn to the political sphere of activity to see whether anything of the kind may be feasible there also; and, as a field of operations in this political sphere, we will select the rivalries and wars of the parochial states of the Modern Western world. The Modern period of Western history may be taken to have begun towards the end of the fifteenth century with the Italianization of the state system of Transalpine Europe, so that we have something over four centuries at our disposal for the purposes of our present inquiry.

'Every schoolboy knows'—Macaulay's optimistic estimate—that on four occasions, separated from one another by just over one hundred years, the English (or British) people, taking advantage of the comparative immunity afforded by their island fastness, first repelled and then helped to destroy a continental Power which was offering, or threatening, to supply Western Christendom with a universal state, or at any rate was, in traditional language, 'upsetting the balance of power'. On the first occasion the offender was Spain—Spanish Armada, 1588; on the second occasion, the France of Louis XIV—Blenheim, 1704; on the third occasion, the France of the Revolution and Napoleon—Waterloo, 1815; on the fourth occasion the Germany of Wilhelm II—Armistice Day, 1918—subsequently recrudescent under Hitler—Normandy, 1944. Here is an unmistakably cyclical pattern, viewed from an insular angle, a set of four 'great wars', spaced out with curious regularity, each one larger than its predecessor, both in the intensity of its warfare and in what we will call the area of belligerency. The first of the series is an affair of Atlantic states—Spain, France, the Netherlands, England. The second brings in the Central European states, and even Russia if one regards the Russo-Swedish War as a kind of annexe of the 'War of the Spanish Succession'. The third (Napoleonic) bout brings in Russia as a leading belligerent, and may be taken to include the United States of America, if one regards 'the War of 1812' as an annexe of the Napoleonic War. Into the fourth, America enters as a leading belligerent, and the general character of the struggle was indicated by the fact that its successive bouts had been named the First and Second World Wars.

Each of these four wars for the prevention of the establishment of a Modern Western universal state had been separated from its successor and from its predecessor by a time-span of about a century. If we proceed to examine the three inter-war centuries, we find in each case what might be called a midway or supplementary war or group of wars, in each case a struggle for supremacy not in Western Europe as a whole but in its central area, Germany. Since these wars were predominantly Central European, Great Britain did not engage in any of them up to the hilt, while there were some of them in which she did not interfere at all; and consequently they are not so certainly included in what 'every schoolboy (meaning, of course, every British schoolboy) knows'. The first of these intermediate wars was the Thirty Years War (1618–48), the second consisted for the most part of the wars of Frederick 'the Great' of Prussia (1740–63), and the third is associated with Bismarck, though it includes much else, and should be dated 1848–71.

Finally it might be claimed that this drama in four acts had an overture: that it opens not with Philip II of Spain, but with the Hapsburg-Valois 'Italian wars' of two generations earlier. These wars were started by the sensationally futile but ominous invasion of Italy by King Charles VIII of France; and its date, 1494, has often been used by educational authorities as a convenient hard-and-fast line to separate the Late Medieval from the Early Modern period. It is two years later than the Christian conquest of the last remaining Muslim territory in Spain and the first landing of Columbus in the West Indies.

All this can be set out in tabular form; and an examination of the war-and-peace cycles in post-Alexandrine Hellenic history[1] and in post-Confucian Sinic history[1] yielded historical 'patterns' curiously similar in their structure and in their time-spans to those here descried in the course of Modern Western history.

(d) THE DISINTEGRATIONS OF CIVILIZATIONS

If we look back for a moment at our cyclic pattern of the wars of the Modern Western society, we may be struck by the fact that this is not simply a case of a wheel revolving four times *in vacuo* and coming round each time to the position in which it had started. It is also a case of a wheel moving forward along a road in a particularly ominous direction. On the one hand, here are four cases of states banding together to defend themselves against an overmighty and presumptuous neighbour and eventually showing him that his pride has led him to a fall. On the other hand, there is a point which the cyclic pattern does not bring out, but which a

[1] For these the reader must consult *A Study of History* in its unabridged form, vol. ix.

Successive Occurrences of the War-and-Peace Cycle in Modern and post-Modern Western History

Phase	Overture (A.D. 1494–1568)	First Regular Cycle (A.D. 1568–1672)	Second Regular Cycle (A.D. 1672–1792)	Third Regular Cycle (A.D. 1792–1914)	Fourth Cycle (A.D. 1914–)
(i) Premonitory Wars (the Prelude)	. . .	. . .	1667–8[1]	. . .	1911–12[2]
(ii) The General War	1494–1525[3]	1568–1609[4]	1672–1713[5]	1792–1815[6]	1914–45[10]
(iii) The Breathing-space	1525–36	1609–18	1713–33	1815–48	. . .
(iv) Supplementary Wars (the Epilogue)	1536–59[7]	1618–48	1733–63[8]	1848–71[9]	. . .
(v) The General Peace	1559–68	1648–72	1763–92	1871–1914	. . .

[1] Louis XIV's attack on the Spanish Netherlands.

[2] The Turco-Italian War of 1911–12; The Turco-Balkan Wars of 1912–13.

[3] 1494–1503, 1510–16, and 1521–5.

[4] 1568–1609 in the Spanish Hapsburg Monarchy; 1562–98 in France.

[5] 1672–8, 1688–97, and 1702–13.

[6] 1792–1802, 1803–14, and 1815.

[7] 1536–8, 1542–4 [1544–6 and 1549–50, England v. France], [1546–52, Schmalkald League of Protestant Princes in the Holy Roman Empire v. Charles V], 1552–9.

[8] 1733–5, 1740–8, and 1756–63.

[9] 1848–9, 1853–6, 1859 [1861–5, civil war in the United States; 1862–7, French occupation of Mexico], 1864, 1866, and 1870–1.

[10] The recrudescent general war of 1939–45 was heralded by a splutter of premonitory wars: the Japanese attack on China, launched in Manchuria in 1931; the Italo-Abyssinian War of 1935–6; the War of 1936–9 in Spain; and the fateful one-day campaign in the Rhineland on the 7th March, 1936, which was to pay for its bloodlessness at compound interest in the holocausts of the years 1939–45.

very elementary knowledge of history does reveal: each of these four bouts of warfare was more extensive, more violent, more destructive, materially and morally, than its predecessor. In the histories of other societies, such as the Hellenic and the Sinic, such bouts of warfare have ended in all the contending pieces being swept off the board except one, which then establishes a universal state.

This self-amortization of a cyclic rhythm, which proves to be the dominant tendency in struggles for existence between parochial states, has previously come to our notice in our study of the disintegrations of civilizations; and it is not surprising that there should be this affinity between the rhythms of two processes that are manifestly bound up with each other. Our study of the breakdowns in which the disintegrations originate has shown us that a frequent occasion, symptom, or even cause of breakdown has been the outbreak of an exceptionally violent war between the parochial states of which the society has been composed. The replacement of the contending states by an œcumenical empire is apt to be followed, not by the entire cessation of outbreaks of violence, but their reappearance in new forms, as civil wars or social upheavals; and so the process of disintegration, though temporarily arrested, continues.

We have observed also that disintegrations, like the wars of parochial states, have run their course in a series of rhythmic fluctuations, and we have ascertained, from the examination of a number of examples, that the cyclic rhythm of Rout-and-Rally, in which the dominant tendency towards disintegration has fought out its long battle with a resistance movement, has been apt to take a run of three and a half beats—rout, rally, relapse, rally, relapse, rally, relapse—in accomplishing the historical journey from the breakdown of a civilization to its final dissolution. The first rout throws the broken-down society into a Time of Troubles, which is relieved by the first rally, only to be followed by a second and more violent paroxysm. This relapse is followed by a more durable second rally, manifesting itself in the establishment of a universal state. This, in its turn, experiences a relapse and a recovery, and this last recovery is followed by the final dissolution.

It will be seen that the drama of Social Disintegration has—to judge from performances up to date—a more precise and regular plot than the drama of the Balance of Power, and if we study our table of universal states we shall find that—in cases in which the course of events is not disturbed by the impact of alien bodies social—a span of some four hundred years is apt to be occupied by the movement of rout, rally, relapse, and more effective rally, running from the initial breakdown to the establishment of the universal state; and a further period of about the same length by the ensuing movement of recurrent relapse, last rally and final relapse, running from the establishment of the universal state to its dissolution. But a universal state is apt to die hard, and a Roman Empire which went to pieces in the socially backward western provinces on the morrow of the catastrophe at Adrianople in A.D. 378 (just on four hundred years after its establishment by Augustus) did not go the same way in the central and eastern provinces till after the death of Justinian in A.D. 565. Similarly a Han Empire, which met with its second stroke in A.D. 184 and which broke up thereafter into the Three Kingdoms, managed to reconstitute itself for a moment in the Empire of the United Ts'in (A.D. 280–317) before going into its final dissolution.

(e) THE GROWTHS OF CIVILIZATIONS

When we turn our attention from Social Disintegration to Social Growth, we shall recollect our finding, in a previous stage of this Study, that Growth, like Disintegration, exhibits a cyclically rhythmic movement. Growth takes place whenever a challenge evokes a successful response that, in turn, evokes a further and different challenge. We have not found any intrinsic reason why this process should not repeat itself indefinitely, even though a majority of the civilizations that had come to birth down to the time of writing might have failed, as a matter of historical fact, to maintain their growth by failing to make, for more than a small number of times in succession, a response that had been both an effective answer to the challenge that had called it forth and at the same time a fruitful mother of a new challenge requiring a different response.

We have seen, for example, that, in the history of the Hellenic civilization, the initial challenge of anarchic barbarism evoked an effective response in the shape of a new political institution, the city-state; and we have noticed that the success of this response evoked a new challenge, this time on the economic plane, in the shape of a rising pressure of population. This second challenge evoked a number of alternative responses of unequal efficacy. There was the disastrous Spartan response of annexing by force the food-bearing lands of Sparta's Hellenic neighbours; there was the temporarily effective Corinthian and Chalcidian response of colonization, the winning for Hellenes of new fields to plough overseas in lands wrested from the more backward peoples of the western basin of the Mediterranean; and there was the permanently effective Athenian response of increasing the aggregate productivity of this enlarged Hellenic world, after its geographical expansion had been brought to a halt by the resistance of Phoenician and Tyrrhenian competitors, through an economic revolution in which subsistence farming was replaced by cash-crop farming and by industrial production for export in exchange for imports of staple foods and raw materials.

This successful response to an economic challenge evoked, as we have seen, a further challenge on the political plane; for the now economically interdependent Hellenic world required a political régime of law and order on an œcumenical scale. The existing régime of parochial city-state dispensations, which had fostered the rise of an autarkic agricultural economy in each isolated patch of plain, no longer provided an adequate political structure for an Hellenic society whose economic structure had now come to be unitary. This third challenge was not met in time to save the growth of the Hellenic civilization from being cut short by a breakdown.

In the growth of the Western civilization we can also descry a series of successive challenges evoking successful responses, and this series is longer than the Hellenic in that the third challenge met with a successful response as well as the first and the second. The initial challenge was the same anarchic barbarism of an interregnum that had confronted the Hellenes, but the response was a different one, namely the creation of an œcumenical ecclesiastical institution in the shape of the Hildebrandine Papacy; and this provoked a second challenge; for a growing Western Christendom which had achieved ecclesiastical unity then found itself in need of a politically and economically efficient parochial state system. The challenge was met by a resuscitation of the Hellenic institution of the city-state in Italy and Flanders. This solution, however, which served well enough in certain areas, failed to meet the requirements of the territorially extensive feudal monarchies. Could the solution of the problem of creating efficient parochial organs of Western political and economic life, which had been attained in Italy and Flanders through the city-state system, be made available for the rest of the Western world by translating this Italian and Flemish efficiency into nation-wide terms?

This problem, as we have seen, was solved in England, first on the political plane by injecting efficiency into the medieval Transalpine institution of Parliament, and afterwards on the economic plane through the Industrial Revolution. This Western Industrial Revolution, however, like the Athenian economic revolution in Hellenic history, had the effect of replacing a parochial economic autarky by an œcumenical economic interdependence. Thus the

Western civilization found itself confronted, as a result of its successful response to a third challenge, with the same new challenge that had faced the Hellenic civilization after its successful response to its second challenge. At the time of writing, midway through the twentieth century, this political challenge had not yet been successfully met by Western Man, but he had come to be acutely conscious of its menace.

These brief glances at the growths of two civilizations suffice to show that there is no uniformity between their histories in respect of the number of the links in the concatenation of interlocking rounds of challenge-and-response through which social growth had been achieved; and an examination of the histories of all other sufficiently well-documented civilizations would confirm that conclusion. The upshot of our present inquiry therefore seems to be that the operation of 'laws of Nature' is as inconspicuous in the histories of the growths of civilizations as it is conspicuous in the histories of their disintegrations. In a later chapter we shall find that this is no accident, but is inherent in an intrinsic difference between the growth-process and the disintegration-process.

(f) 'THERE IS NO ARMOUR AGAINST FATE'

In studying the operation of 'laws of Nature' in the histories of civilizations, we have found that the rhythm in which these laws reveal themselves is apt to be generated by a struggle between two tendencies of unequal strength. There is a dominant tendency which prevails, in the long run, against repeated counteracting moves in which the recalcitrant opposing tendency asserts itself. The struggle sets the pattern. The persistence of the weaker tendency in refusing to resign itself to defeat accounts for the repetitions of the encounter in a series of successive cycles; the dominance of the stronger tendency makes itself felt by bringing the series to a close sooner or later.

On these lines we have watched struggles for existence between parochial states following—through three or four cycles of wars fought on one side for the overthrow, and on the other side for the maintenance, of a balance of power—a course that in each case ends in the overthrow of the balance. We have likewise watched the struggle between a broken-down society's tendency to disintegrate and a counter effort to restore it to a lost state of health— a course that, in each case, ends in dissolution. In studying the operation of 'laws of Nature' in the economic affairs of an industrial Western society, we have found expert investigators of trade cycles surmising that these repetitive movements might prove to be waves rippling on the surface of waters that were, all the time, flowing in a current whose headway would eventually bring these rhythmic fluctuations to an end. In the same connexion we may remind ourselves of our finding that, when and where a conflict between a disintegrating civilization and bands of recalcitrant barbarians beyond its pale had passed over from the war of movement into a stationary warfare along the *limes* of a universal state, the passage of time had usually militated against the defenders of the *limes* and to the advantage of its barbarian assailants, until in the end the dam had burst and the flood of barbarism had swept the pre-existing social structure off the map.

These are all illustrations of our more general finding that cyclical movements in human history, like the physical revolutions of a cartwheel, have a way of forwarding, through their own monotonously repetitive circular motion, another movement with a longer rhythm which, by contrast, can be seen to be a cumulative progress in one direction, which ultimately reaches its goal and, in reaching it, brings the series to an end. There is, however, no warrant for interpreting these victories of one tendency over another as illustrations of 'laws of Nature'. Empirically observed matters of fact are not necessarily the outcomes of inexorable fate. The burden of proof here lies with the determinist, not with the agnostic—a consideration that Spengler, with his dogmatic and undocumented determinism, failed to take into account.

However, without prejudice to the still open issue between Law and Freedom in History, we propose, before attempting to carry our argument farther, to take note of several other episodes in which some tendency has reasserted itself against successive rebellions against it. In such resolutions of conflicting forces Spengler would see the hand of 'Fate', but, whether his dogma of inevitability was right or wrong, he hardly attempts to prove it. We will begin with the situation created by the establishment, through military prowess, of an Hellenic ascendancy in South-West Asia.

Though this Hellenic ascendancy was little less than a thousand years old when, in the seventh century of the Christian Era, it was overthrown by the Arab Muslim war-bands, Hellenism had never succeeded, south of the Taurus, in becoming anything more than an exotic alien culture, feebly radiating its influence into an incorrigibly Syriac or Egyptiac country-side from its outposts in a few Hellenic or Hellenized cities. Hellenism's capacity to achieve mass-conversions had been put to the test by the Seleucid Hellenizer Antiochus Epiphanes (reigned 175–163 B.C.) when he set out to make Jerusalem as Hellenic as Antioch; and the resounding defeat of this cultural military enterprise had portended the ultimate total disappearance of the intrusive culture. Its always sickly existence was prolonged for centuries by reason of the fact that the Romans took over control from the weakening Seleucidae and Ptolemies. The Hellenic ascendancy over the Syriac and Egyptiac societies had been imposed and maintained by force of arms; and, so long as the subjugated societies had reacted by replying in kind, they had been courting defeat. In the next chapter of the story, the mass-conversion of the population of the Oriental provinces to Christianity, in the third century of the Christian Era, might have seemed to have done for Hellenism incidentally what Antiochus had tried to do and failed; for in these provinces the Catholic Christian Church had captivated a subject native peasantry and an urban Hellenic 'ascendancy' alike; and, since Christianity had been making its triumphal progress in an Hellenic dress, it looked as if the Orientals had now at last inadvertently received, in association with Christianity, a culture which they had rejected so vehemently when it had been offered to them unadulterated and undisguised. But that would have been a mistaken estimate. Having accepted a Hellenized Christianity, the Orientals set themselves to de-Hellenize their religion by adopting successive heresies, of which Nestorianism was the first. In thus resuming the Oriental resistance movement against Hellenism in the non-military form of theological controversy, the Orientals had hit upon a new technique of cultural warfare in which they eventually prevailed.

This anti-Hellenic cultural offensive presented itself over several centuries in the cyclic pattern with which we are already familiar. The Nestorian wave rose and fell, to be followed by the Monophysite wave, and this in turn by the Muslim wave, which carried all before it. It might be said that the Muslim victory was a reversion to the crude method of military conquest. It is true, no doubt, that the Muslim Arab war-bands can hardly be regarded as anticipators of the non-violent non-resistance doctrines of Tolstoy and Gandhi. They 'conquered' Syria, Palestine, and Egypt during the years A.D. 637–40, but it was a conquest of much the same order as that achieved by Garibaldi in A.D. 1860, when he 'conquered' Sicily and Naples with a force of 1,000 volunteers in red shirts, supported by two little guns which were taken round for show, without being provided with any ammunition. The Kingdom of the Two Sicilies was conquered by the martial missionary of *Italia Una* because it wanted to be conquered, and the feelings of the populations of the Oriental provinces of the Roman Empire towards the Arab war-bands were not altogether unlike those of the Sicilians toward Garibaldi.

In the example just given we see a succession of heretical protests against an undesired uniformity, of which the third succeeded.

The history of France since the twelfth century of the Christian Era presents the same pattern in a different context. Since that century the Roman Catholic Church in France had been engaged in a never more than temporarily successful struggle to establish the ecclesiastical unity of France as a Catholic country against an impulse towards secession which had kept on reasserting itself in some new form after each previous manifestation had been suppressed. A revolt against Catholic Christianity which had taken the form of Catharism at its first outbreak in Southern France in the twelfth century was stamped out there in the thirteenth century, only to re-emerge in the same region in the sixteenth century as Calvinism. Proscribed as Calvinism, it promptly reappeared as Jansenism, which was the nearest approach to Calvinism possible within the Catholic fold. Proscribed as Jansenism, it reappeared as Deism, Rationalism, Agnosticism, and Atheism.

In other contexts we have noted the fate of a Judaic monotheism to be perpetually beset by a repeatedly resurgent polytheism, and also the fate of the kindred Judaic conception of the One True God's transcendence to be no less repeatedly beset by yearnings for a God Incarnate. Monotheism put down the worship of Baal and Ashtoreth, only to find a jealous Yahweh's proscribed rivals slily creeping back into the fold of Jewish orthodoxy in the guise of personifications of the Lord's 'Word', 'Wisdom', and 'Angel', and afterwards establishing themselves within the fold of Christian orthodoxy in the doctrine of the Holy Trinity and in the cults of God's Body and Blood, God's Mother, and the Saints. These re-encroachments of polytheism evoked a whole-hearted reassertion of monotheism in Islam, and a less thoroughgoing reassertion of it in Protestantism, and these two puritan movements, in their turn, had been plagued by the soul's irrepressible appetite for a plurality of gods, to reflect the apparent plurality of natural forces in the Universe.

(2) POSSIBLE EXPLANATIONS OF THE CURRENCY OF 'LAWS OF NATURE' IN HISTORY

If the repetitions and uniformities which we have discerned in the course of this Study are accepted as real, there would seem to be two possible explanations of them. The laws governing them may be either laws current in Man's non-human environment imposing themselves on the course of History from the outside, or they may be laws inherent in the psychic structure and working of Human Nature itself. We will begin by looking into the former hypothesis.

The day-and-night cycle, for example, manifestly affects the everyday life of ordinary people, but we can dismiss it from our consideration in the present context. The farther that Man advances from the primitive state, the more capable he becomes of 'turning night into day' as and when he requires. Another astronomical cycle to which Man had once been a slave was the annual cycle of the seasons. Lent became a season of Christian abstinence because, countless ages before Christianity dawned on the World, the tail-end of winter was regularly a season when Man had to go short, whether this might be spiritually good for him or not. But, here again, Western and Westernizing Man had emancipated himself from Nature's law. By means of cold storage and of rapid transport over the technologically unified surface of the planet, any meat, vegetable, fruit, or flower could now be purchased at any season of the year in any part of the World, by anyone who had the money to pay for it.

The familiar annual round was possibly not the only astronomical cycle to which the Earth's flora was subject and to which Man was therefore indirectly enslaved in so far as he was dependent on agriculture for subsistence. Modern meteorologists had brought to light indications of weather cycles with a much longer timespan. In an investigation of the irruptions of the Nomads out of 'the Desert' into 'the Sown' we found some indirect evidence of a weather cycle with a time-span of six hundred years, each of these cycles consisting of alternating bouts of aridity and humidity. This hypothetical cycle seemed, at the time of writing, to be less well-established than certain other cycles of the same class, with wave-lengths running only into double or perhaps single figures, which appeared to govern fluctuations in the yield of crops artificially sown and harvested under modern conditions. It had been suggested that there was a correspondence between these weather-and-harvest cycles and the economic industrial cycles plotted by certain economists. But the preponderance of recent expert opinion was against this view. The brilliant suggestion of Stanley Jevons, a Victorian pioneer in this field of inquiry, that trade cycles might be the effects of fluctuations in the radioactivity of the Sun, as advertised by the appearance and disappearance of sun-spots, had quite gone out of favour. Jevons himself, in later years, agreed that 'periodic collapses [of trade] are really mental in their nature, depending on variations of despondency, hopefulness, excitement, disappointment, and panic'.[1]

A. C. Pigou, a Cambridge economist, had expressed, in A.D.

---

[1] Jevons, W. Stanley: *Investigations in Currency and Finance*, 2nd ed. (London, 1909, Macmillan), p. 184.

1929, the view that the importance, whatever this might be, of harvest variations as a factor determining fluctuations in industrial activity, was substantially less at the time when he was writing than it had been fifty or a hundred years earlier. G. Haberler, writing twelve years later than Pigou, had taken the same view, and is quoted here as a sample of orthodox economic opinion at the time of writing.

'The waning, like the waxing, of prosperity . . . must be due, not to the influence of "disturbing causes" from outside, but to processes that run regularly within the world of business itself.

'The mysterious thing about [these fluctuations] is that they cannot be accounted for by such "external" causes as bad harvests due to weather conditions, diseases, general strikes, lock-outs, earthquakes, the sudden obstruction of international trade channels, and the like. Severe decreases in the volume of production, real income, or level of employment as a result of crop failures, wars, earthquakes, and similar physical disturbances of the productive processes rarely affect the economic system as a whole, and certainly do not constitute depressions in the technical sense of business-cycle theory. By depressions in the technical sense we mean those long and conspicuous falls in the volume of production, real income, and employment which can only be explained by the operation of factors originating within the economic system itself, and in the first instance by an insufficiency of monetary demand and the absence of a sufficient margin between price and cost.

'For various reasons it seems desirable, in the explanation of the business cycle, to attach as little importance as possible to the influence of external disturbances. . . . The responses of the business system seem *prima facie* more important in shaping the business cycle than external shocks. Secondly, historical experience seems to demonstrate that the cyclical movement has a strong tendency to persist, even where there are no outstanding extraneous influences at work which can plausibly be held responsible. This suggests that there is an inherent instability in our economic system, a tendency to move in one direction or the other.'[1]

There is another and very different natural cycle which cannot be overlooked, namely the human generation cycle of birth, growth, procreation, senescence, and death. Its significance in a particular field of history was vividly illustrated for the writer of this Study by a conversation which came his way in A.D. 1932 at a public luncheon in the city of Troy, New York State. Finding himself seated next to the local Director of Public Education, he asked him what, among his manifold professional duties, was the job that he was finding most interesting. 'Organizing English lessons for

[1] Haberler, G.: *Prosperity and Depression* (Geneva 1941, League of Nations), p. 10.

grandparents' was his prompt reply. 'And how, in an English-speaking country, does anyone manage to arrive at being a grand-parent without having mastered English?', the British visitor thoughtlessly went on to ask. 'Well, you see,' said the Director, 'Troy is the principal centre of the linen collar manufacturing industry in the United States, and, before the Immigration Restriction Acts of 1921 and 1924, most of the labour-force here was recruited from foreign immigrants and their families. Now the immigrants who came from each of the principal emigrant-exporting countries had a way of cleaving as close as they could to their own familiar past by continuing to consort with other birds of the same feather. Immigrants of the same national origin were not only apt to work side by side in the same factories; they were apt to live next door to one another in the same blocks of tenements; and so, when the time came for them to retire, most of them knew little more English than they had known when they had first landed on American shores. They did not have to know any more up to this point in the American chapter of their life, because they commanded the services of home-bred interpreters. Their children had arrived in America young enough to go to the public school before entering the factory in their turn, and the combination of an American education with, let us say, an Italian infancy had made them thoroughly bilingual; they talked English in the factory, street, and store, and Italian in their parents' homes, almost without noticing that they were constantly switching back and forth from one language to the other; and their effortless and ungrudging bilingualism was highly convenient for their old parents. Indeed, it abetted their parents' inclination, after their retirement, to forget even the smattering of English that they had once picked up during their working life in the factory. However, this is not the end of the story; for in due course the retired immigrants' children married and had children of their own; and, for these representatives of a third generation, English was the language of the home as well as the school. Since their own parents had married after having been educated in the United States, one of them would be of non-Italian origin as often as not, and then English would be the *lingua franca* in which the father and mother would communicate with one another. So the American-born children of bilingual parents would not know their grandparents' Italian mother tongue, and, moreover, would have no use for it. Why should they put themselves out in order to learn a foreign lingo that would convict them of an un-American origin which they were eager to slough off and consign to oblivion? So the grandparents found that their grandchildren could not be induced to communicate with them in the only language in which the grandparents were able to talk with any ease; and they were thus confronted suddenly, in their old age, with the appalling prospect of being unable to establish any human contact with their own living descendants. For Italians and other non-English-speaking Continental Europeans with a strong sense of family solidarity, this prospect was intolerable. For the first time in their lives, they now had an incentive for mastering the hitherto unattractive language of their adopted country, and last year they thought of applying to me for help. Of course I was eager to arrange special classes for them; and, though it is notorious that the enterprise of learning a foreign language becomes more difficult progressively as one grows older, I can assure you that these English lessons for grandparents have been one of the most successful and rewarding pieces of work that we have ever taken in hand in our department.'

This tale of Troy shows how a series of three generations can achieve, through the cumulative effect of two successive caesuras, a social metamorphosis which could never have been achieved by representatives of a single generation within the span of a single lifetime. The process by which an Italian family transformed itself into an American family could not be analysed or described intelligibly in terms of a single life. An interaction between three generations was required to bring it about. And, when we turn from changes of nationality to consider changes of religion and of class, we find that here, too, the family, and not the individual, is the intelligible unit.

In a class-conscious Modern England which in A.D. 1952 was fast dissolving under the writer's eyes, it had usually taken three generations to make 'gentlefolk' out of a family of working-class or lower-middle-class antecedents; and in the field of religion the standard wave-length seems to have been the same. In the history of the eradication of paganism in the Roman world, the intolerantly devout Christian-born Emperor Theodosius I followed the ex-pagan convert Constantine I, not in the next generation, but in the next but one; and, in the history of the eradication of Protestantism in seventeenth-century France, there was the same interval between the intolerantly devout Catholic-born Louis XIV and his ex-Calvinist grandfather Henry IV. In France at the turn of the nineteenth and twentieth centuries it took the same number of generations to breed genuinely devout Catholics among the grandchildren of officially converted bourgeois agnostics or atheists who had re-embraced Catholicism because the Church had acquired a new value for them as a traditional institution which might serve as a barrier against a rising tide of socialism and other ideologies which threatened to abolish the economic inequality between the *bourgeoisie* and the working class. In the Syriac world, again, under the Umayyad Caliphate, it took three generations to breed genuinely devout Muslims among the descendants of ex-Christian or ex-Zoroastrian grandparents who had embraced Islam in order to make themselves acceptable to the Primitive Muslim Arab ruling class. The duration of the Umayyad régime, which stood for the conqueror's ascendancy, was determined by the three-generation period that had to elapse in order to bring the original converts' Muslim-born grandchildren on to the stage of History. The Umayyad agents of an Arab ascendancy were supplanted by the 'Abbasid exponents of the equality of all Muslims when, in the name of Islamic religious principles, the genuinely devout Muslim grandchildren of cynical converts tried conclusions with the Laodicean Muslim grandchildren of Laodicean Muslim Arab conquerors.

If a concatenation of three generations thus proves to be the regular psychic vehicle of social change in the three fields of religion, class, and nationality, it would not be surprising to find a concatenation of four generations playing a similar part in the field of international politics. We have already found that, in the field of encounters between civilizations, the time-interval between the creation of an intelligentsia and its revolt against its makers has had an average length of about 137 years in a set of three or four examples; and it is not difficult to see how a concatenation of four generations might also determine the wave-length of a war-and-peace cycle, if we may assume that the agony of a general war makes a deeper impression on the Psyche than is made on it by a comparatively mild round of supplementary wars. If, however, we apply this consideration to the war-and-peace cycles in Modern Western Europe, we shall run up against a stumbling-block in finding that one of the 'supplementary' wars, i.e. the Thirty Years War, though confined in its geographical incidence to Central Europe, was probably more, and not less, devastating, within its narrower geographical range, than the 'general wars' which preceded and followed it.

This war-and-peace cycle is neither the last nor the longest of the apparently genuine, though not exact, regularities and recurrences for which we have to seek an explanation. Each of these cycles of a hundred years or so is only a term in a series which as a whole constitutes what we have called a Time of Troubles following the breakdown of a civilization; and this in its turn runs on, in Hellenic and in Sinic history, for example, into a universal state, which also exhibits the rhythms that we have already noticed.

The whole process, from start to finish, occupies, in general terms, something between eight hundred and a thousand years. Will a psychological explanation of regularities in human affairs, which has served us well enough so far, avail us here? Our answer would have been bound to be in the negative if, in our eyes, the intellectual and volitional surface of the Psyche had been the whole of the Psyche.

In the Western world in the writer's generation a Western science of Psychology was still in its infancy; yet the pioneers had already carried their reconnaissances far enough to enable C. G. Jung to report that the subconscious abyss on whose surface each individual human personality's conscious intellect and will were afloat was not an undifferentiated chaos but was an articulated universe in which one layer of psychic activity could be discerned below another. The nearest layer to the surface appeared to be a Personal Subconscious deposited by a personality's individual experiences in the course of his or her own life up to date; the deepest layer to which the explorers had so far penetrated appeared to be a Racial Subconscious that was not peculiar to any individual but was common to all human beings, inasmuch as the Primordial Images latent there reflected the common experiences of Mankind, deposited during the infancy of the Human Race, if not at a stage before Man had yet become completely human. On this showing, it was perhaps not unreasonable to surmise that, in between the uppermost and the lowermost of the layers of the Subconscious that Western scientists had so far succeeded in bringing within their ken, there might be intermediate layers deposited neither by racial experience nor by personal experience, but by corporate experience of a supra-personal but infra-racial range. There might be layers of experience common to a family, common to a community, or common to a society; and, if, at the next level above the Primordial Images common to the whole Human Race, there should indeed prove to be images expressing the peculiar êthos of a particular society, the impress of these on the Psyche might account for the length of the periods which certain social processes seemed to require in order to work themselves out.

For example, one such social image that was manifestly apt to imprint itself deeply on the subconscious psychic life of the children of a civilization in process of growth was the idol of the parochial sovereign state; and it can readily be imagined that, even after this idol had begun to exact from its devotees human sacrifices as grim as any that the Carthaginians ever paid to Baal Hammon or the Bengalis to Juggernaut, the victims of a demon which these victims themselves had conjured up might well need the poignant experience, not just of a single life-time and not just of one concatenation of three-generation cycles, but of a span of not less than four hundred years, in order to bring themselves to the point of plucking this baneful idolatry out of their hearts and casting it from them. It can also readily be imagined that they might need, not just four hundred years, but eight hundred years or a thousand, to dissociate themselves from the whole apparatus of the civilization whose breakdown and disintegration a Time of Troubles had made manifest, and to open their hearts to receive the impress of some other society of the same species or of the different species represented by the higher religions. For the image of a civilization presumably makes a still more potent appeal to the Subconscious Psyche than the image of any of the parochial states into which civilizations are apt to be articulated on the political plane unless and until they eventually enter into a universal state. From the same angle of mental vision we can likewise understand how a universal state, once established, should sometimes succeed, in its turn, in retaining its hold over its ex-subjects', or even over its actual destroyers', hearts for generations, or perhaps even for centuries, after it has lost its usefulness as well as its power and has become almost as grievously heavy an incubus as the antecedent parochial states that it had been created to liquidate.

'The relation between the external anxieties felt by the representatives of an adult generation—anxieties that are directly conditioned by the social position of the people who feel them—and the inward, automatically operating, anxieties of these people's children in the rising generation is unquestionably a phenomenon of importance over a wide field. . . . The stamp that is set by the procession of successive generations on both the psychic development of the individual and the course of historical change is something that we shall only begin to understand more adequately than we do at present when we have become more capable than we are to-day of taking our observations, and doing our historical thinking, in terms of long chains of generations.'[1]

If the social laws current in the histories of civilizations are indeed reflections of psychological laws governing some infra-personal layer of the Subconscious Psyche, this would also explain why these social laws should be, as we have found them to be, so much more clearly pronounced and more exactly regular in the disintegration-phase of a broken-down civilization's history than in its foregoing growth-phase.

Though the growth-phase, as well as the disintegration-phase, can be analysed into a series of bouts of Challenge-and-Response,

---

[1] Elias, N.: *Über den Prozess der Zivilisation*, vol. ii: *Wandlungen der Gesellschaft: Entwurf zu einer Theorie der Zivilisation* (Basel 1939, Haus zum Falken), p. 451.

we have found it impossible to discern any standard wave-length common to the successive bouts through which social growth takes place, whether we measure the intervals between successive presentations of challenges or the intervals between successive deliveries of effective responses; and we have also seen that, in the growth-phase, these successive challenges and successive responses are infinitely various. By contrast, we have found that the successive stages of the disintegration-phase are marked by repeated presentations of an identical challenge which continues to recur because the disintegrating society continues to fail to meet it; and we have also found that, in all past cases of social disintegration that we have mustered, the same successive stages invariably occur in the same order, each stage taking approximately the same period of time, so that the disintegration-phase, as a whole, presents the picture of a uniform process with a uniform duration in each case. Indeed, as soon as a social breakdown has occurred, the tendency towards variety and differentiation that is characteristic of the growth-phase is replaced by a tendency towards uniformity that shows its power by triumphing sooner or later over interference from outside as well as over recalcitrance from within.

We have observed, for example, how, when first a Syriac and then an Indic universal state was cut short by an intrusive Hellenic civilization prematurely, before it had completed a universal state's standard life-span, the smitten and submerged society could not or would not pass away until, in spite of the disturbing influence of an alien body social, it had duly completed the regular course of a broken-down society's disintegration by eventually re-entering into the interrupted phase and abiding in a re-integrated universal state until the tale of its normal duration was completed.

This striking contrast between the regularity and uniformity of the phenomena of social disintegration and the irregularity and diversity of the phenomena of social growth has been frequently noted in this Study as a matter of historical fact, without any attempt, so far, to account for it. In the present part, which is concerned with the relation between Law and Freedom in human affairs, it is incumbent on us to grapple with this problem; and a key to its solution may be found in the difference between the respective natures of the conscious personality on the surface of the Psyche and the subconscious levels of psychic life underlying it.

The distinctive power conferred in the gift of consciousness is a freedom to make choices; and, considering that a relative freedom is one of the characteristics of the growth-phase, it is only to be expected that, in so far as human beings are free in these circumstances to determine their own future, the course which they follow should be in truth, as it appears to be, a wayward one in the sense of being recalcitrant to the rule of 'laws of Nature'. The reign of Freedom, which thus keeps 'laws of Nature' at bay, is, however, precarious inasmuch as it depends on the fulfilment of two exacting conditions. The first condition is that the conscious personality must keep the subconscious underworld of the Psyche under the will's and reason's control. The second condition is that it must also contrive to 'dwell together in unity' with the other conscious personalities with which it has to dwell together on some terms or other in the mortal life of a *Homo Sapiens* who was a social animal before he was a human being, and a sexual organism before he was a social animal. These two necessary conditions for the exercise of Freedom are actually inseparable from one another; for, if it is true that 'when knaves fall out honest men come by their own', it is no less true that, when persons fall out, the Subconscious Psyche escapes from the control of each and all of them.

Thus the gift of consciousness, whose mission is to liberate the human spirit from the 'laws of Nature' ruling over the subconscious abyss of the Psyche, is apt to defeat itself by misusing, as a weapon of fratricidal conflict between one personality and another, the freedom that is its *raison d'être*; and the structure and working of the Human Psyche account for this tragic aberration without any need for recourse to Bossuet's impious hypothesis of special interventions on the part of an omnipotent but jealous God to make sure that human wills shall reduce each other to impotence by cancelling each other out.

(3) ARE LAWS OF NATURE CURRENT IN HISTORY INEXORABLE OR CONTROLLABLE?

If our foregoing survey has convinced us that human affairs are amenable to laws of Nature, and that the currency of these laws in this realm is also explicable, at least to some extent, we may now go on to inquire whether laws of Nature current in human history are inexorable or controllable. If we here abide by our previous procedure of considering laws of non-Human Nature first before we bring laws of Human Nature into the picture, we shall find that, as far as laws of non-Human Nature are concerned, we have virtually answered the question in the previous chapter.

The short answer is that, though Man is powerless to modify the terms of any law of non-Human Nature or to suspend its operation, he can affect the incidence of these laws by steering his course on lines on which these laws will minister to his own purposes. That is what the 'poet', already quoted, meant when he wrote

> When Men of Science find out something more,
> We shall be happier than we were before.

Western Man's success in modifying the incidence of laws of non-Human Nature on his affairs had been registered in reductions in the rates of insurance premiums. Improvements in charts, followed by the installation of wireless and radar on ships, had diminished the risk of shipwreck; the smudge-pots of Southern California and the gauze-screens of the Connecticut Valley had diminished the risk of frost damage to crops; the devices of inoculation, spraying, and baptism in pest-killing liquids had diminished the danger of pest damage to crops, trees, and flocks; and, for human beings too, by various methods, the incidence of disease had been diminished and the expectation of life lengthened.

When we pass to the realm of laws of Human Nature, we find the same tale being told in rather more faltering accents. The risk of accidents of various kinds had been reduced by improvements in education and discipline. The risk of burglaries had been found to vary inversely with the conditions of the social milieu in which burglars were bred and therefore to be amenable to measures of social betterment.

When we come to consider those alternating flows and ebbs of Western economic activity that had come to be called trade cycles, we find the professional students of them drawing a distinction between controllable and uncontrollable factors, one school going so far as to maintain that these cycles were due to the deliberate action of bankers. The majority, however, held that the rational action of the bankers counted for less than the uncontrolled play of imagination and feeling welling up from the subconscious lower levels of the Psyche. Not *cherchez la banque* but the more familiar *cherchez la femme* would seem to indicate the direction in which the minds of some of the highest authorities in this field were turning:

'One reason why spending money is a backward art in comparison with making money [is that] the family continues to be the dominant unit of organization for spending money, whereas, for making money, the family has been largely superseded by a more highly organised unit. The Housewife, who does a large fraction of the World's shopping, is not selected for her efficiency as a manager, is not dismissed for her inefficiency, and has small chance of extending her sway over other households if she prove capable. . . . It is not surprising that what the World has learned in the art of consumption has been due less to the initiative of consumers than to the initiative of producers striving to win a market for their wares.'[1]

These considerations suggested that the fluctuations in the volume of business activity might continue to escape control so long as the units of consumption continued to be households and the units of production freely competing individuals, firms, or states whose conflicting wills left the economic arena open for the play of subconscious psychic forces. At the same time there seemed no reason why the Hebrew Patriarch Joseph's legendary success, as economic intendant of an Egyptiac world during the last days of the Hyksos régime, in making provision during years of abundance against coming years of scarcity should not be emulated on a global scale in a latter-day economically Westernized world that had become co-extensive with the whole surface of the planet. There seemed no reason why some historic American or Russian Joseph should not one day bring the sum total of Man's economic life under a central control which, whether benevolent or malevolent, would assuredly outrange in its effectiveness the wildest flights of either Mosaic or Marxian fancy.

When we pass from business cycles of a few years' duration to the generation cycle with a wave-length of something between a quarter and a third of a century, we can see that the wastage, to which any cultural heritage was prone, was being reduced on the physical plane by printing, photostating, and other techniques, and on the spiritual plane by the spread of education.

So far, the results of our present inquiry seem to be encouraging; but, when we pass on to social processes of a vastly longer wavelength, such as 'the sorrowful wheel' revolving through eight or ten centuries of breakdown and disintegration, we encounter a question that had been insistently presenting itself to an increasing number of minds in the Western world on the morrow of what had been the second World War within a single generation. When a civilization had broken down, was it doomed already to follow the wrong turning to the bitter end? Or could it retrace its steps? Perhaps the strongest practical motive for the interest that was undoubtedly being taken by the writer's Western contemporaries in a synoptic study of the history of Man in Process of Civilization was an eagerness to take their historical bearings at a moment in the history of their own civilization which they felt to be a turning-point. In this crisis the Western peoples, and the American people perhaps above all, were conscious of a load of responsibility; and,

[1] Mitchell, W. C.: *Business Cycles: the Problem and its Setting* (New York 1927, National Bureau of Economic Research, Inc.), pp. 165-6.

in looking to past experience for light to guide them, they were turning to the only human source of wisdom that had ever been at the disposal of Mankind. But they could not turn to History for light on how they ought to act without first putting the preliminary question: Did History give them any assurance that they were really free agents? The lesson of History, after all, might turn out to be, not that one choice would be better than another, but that their sense of being free to choose was an illusion; that the time, if there had ever been such a time, when choices would have proved effective was now over; and that their generation had passed out of an H. A. L. Fisher phase in which anything might be followed by anything into an Omar Khayyám phase where

> The Moving Finger writes; and, having writ,
> Moves on; nor all thy Piety nor Wit
>   Shall lure it back to cancel half a Line,
> Nor all thy Tears wash out a Word of it.

If we try to answer the question in the light of the evidence presented by the histories of civilizations up to date, we shall have to report that, out of fourteen clear cases of breakdown, we cannot point to one in which the malady of fratricidal warfare had been got rid of by any means less drastic than the elimination of all but one of the war-making states themselves. But in accepting this formidable finding we must not allow ourselves to be discouraged by it; for the inductive method of reasoning is notoriously an imperfect instrument for proving a negative proposition; and, the smaller the number of instances under review, the weaker it is. The experience of some fourteen civilizations over a period of a mere 6,000 years had established no very strong presumption against the possibility that, in response to the challenge by which these pioneering civilizations had been worsted, some other representative of this relatively novel form of society might succeed some day in opening up some hitherto unknown avenue for an unprecedented spiritual advance, by finding some less prohibitively costly device than the forcible imposition of a universal state for curing the social disease of fratricidal war.

If, with this possibility in mind, we now glance back, once again, at the histories of those civilizations which had trodden the whole length of the *via dolorosa* from breakdown to final dissolution, we shall observe that at least some of them had caught sight of a saving alternative solution, even though none of them had succeeded in achieving it.

In the Hellenic world, for example, the vision of a Homonoia or Concord that might do what force could never do had unquestionably been caught by certain rare Hellenic souls under the spiritual stress of a Time of Troubles that had set in with the outbreak of the Atheno-Peloponnesian War of 431–404 B.C. In a post-Modern Western world the same ideal had been embodied in the League of Nations after the War of A.D. 1914–18 and in the United Nations Organization after the War of A.D. 1939–45. In Sinic history during the Sinic society's first rally after its breakdown, Confucius's pious zeal for the revival of the traditional code of conduct and ritual, and Lao-Tse's quietist belief in leaving a free field for the spontaneous operation of the subconscious forces of Wu Wei, had both been inspired by a yearning to touch springs of feeling that might release a saving power of spiritual harmony, and more than one attempt had been made to embody these ideals in working institutions.

The objective on the political plane was to find a middle way between two deadly extremes: the desolating strife of parochial states and the desolating peace imposed through the delivery of the knock-out blow. The reward of success in running the gauntlet of these adamantine Symplegades, whose clashing jaws had crushed every vessel that had attempted to navigate them up to date, might be the Argonauts' legendary experience of bursting out into an open sea hitherto unnavigated by Mankind. It was obvious, however, that this issue could not be ensured by any talismanic blueprint of a federal constitution. The most adroit political engineering applied to the structure of the body social would never serve as a substitute for the spiritual redemption of souls. The proximate causes of breakdown in the warfare of states or in the strife between classes were no more than symptoms of spiritual disease. A wealth of experience had long since demonstrated that institutions were of no avail to save froward souls from bringing themselves and each other to grief. If the prospects of Man in Process of Civilization, on his arduous climb up a precipitous cliff-face towards an unattained and invisible ledge above, evidently depended on his ability to recover a lost control of this pitch, it was no less evident that this issue was going to be decided by the course of Man's relations, not just with his fellow men and with himself, but above all with God his Saviour.

XXXVII. THE RECALCITRANCE OF HUMAN NATURE TO LAWS OF NATURE

SUCH evidences as we have collected of Man's ability to control his own affairs, either by circumventing laws of Nature or by harnessing them to his service, raises the question whether there may not be some circumstances in which human affairs are not amenable to laws of Nature at all. We may begin our exploration of this possibility by inquiring into the rate of social change. If the tempo proves to be variable, this will be evidence, as far as it goes, that human affairs are recalcitrant to laws of Nature in the time-dimension at least.

If the tempo of History should indeed prove to be constant in all circumstances, in the sense that the passage of each decade or century could be shown to generate a definite and uniform quantum of psychological and social change, it would follow that, if we knew the value of either the quantum in the psycho-social series or the time-span in the time series, we should be able to calculate the magnitude of the corresponding unknown quantity in the other series. This assumption had been made by at least one distinguished student of Egyptiac history who had rejected a chronological date presented by astronomy on the ground that to accept it would mean accepting the, to him, inadmissible proposition that the tempo of social change in the Egyptiac world must have been notably quicker during one period of two hundred years' length than it had been during an immediately preceding period of the same length. Yet a host of familiar examples could be cited to show that the proposition at which this eminent Egyptologist shied is in fact an historical truism.

For example: We know that the Parthenon at Athens was built in the fifth century B.C., Hadrian's Olympieum in the second century A.D., and the Church of Saint Sophia at Constantinople in the sixth century A.D. On the principle on which our Egyptologist took his stand, there should be a much shorter interval between the first and the second of these buildings, which are in approximately the same style, than between the second and the third, which are in totally different styles; but here the incontestably certain dates show that, in this case, the shorter of the two intervals was that between the two buildings whose styles were dissimilar.

We should be similarly misled if we were to put our trust in the same *a priori* principle in trying to estimate the relative time-intervals between the equipment of a Roman soldier in the last days of the Empire in the West, of a Saxon soldier of the Holy Roman Emperor Otto I, and of a Norman knight depicted on the Bayeux tapestry. Considering that the round shields and the gladiator's square-rimmed crested helmets with which Otto's soldiers are equipped are mere variants on the equipment of the late Roman Emperor Majorian's soldiers, whereas William the Conqueror's soldiers are equipped with Sarmatian conical helmets and coats of scale armour, with kite-shaped shields, the hypothesis of invariability in the tempo of change would lead us, here also, to fly in the face of the facts by guessing that the interval between Otto I (reigned A.D. 936–73) and William the Conqueror (ruled in Normandy A.D. 1035–87) must have been much longer than the interval between Majorian (reigned A.D. 457–61) and Otto.

Again, anyone who takes a synoptic view of the standard civilian Western male dress as worn in A.D. 1700 and A.D. 1950 will see at a glance that the coat, waistcoat, trousers, and umbrella of A.D. 1950 are merely variations on the coat, waistcoat, breeches, and sword of A.D. 1700, and that both are utterly different from the doublet and trunk-hose of A.D. 1600. In this case, which is the converse of the two preceding, an earlier and shorter period shows far more change than a later and longer one. These cautionary tales are a warning against the danger of confiding in an hypothesis of in-variability in the tempo of change as a basis for trying to estimate the lapse of time that it must have taken for successive strata of the debris of human occupation to accumulate on some site whose history has to be reconstructed solely from the material evidence disinterred by the archaeologist's spade, in default of chronological data furnished by written records.

We may perhaps follow up our opening attack on this hypothesis that the rate of cultural change is invariable by citing a few examples, first of acceleration, then of retardation, and, finally, of an alternating rate.

A familiar example of acceleration is the phenomenon of revolution; for this, as we found in a previous context in this Study, is a social movement generated by an encounter between two communities, one of which happens to have got ahead of the other in one or other of the different fields of human activity. The French Revolution of A.D. 1789, for example, was, in its first phase, a spasmodic effort to catch up with a constitutional progress which a neighbouring Britain had been slowly achieving during the two preceding centuries. Indeed, the Continental Western 'Liberalism' which inspired so many, mostly abortive, revolutions in the nineteenth century had been given the name of Anglomania by some Continental historians.

A common type of acceleration is to be found in the behaviour of marchmen just within the fringe of a civilization, or of barbarians just beyond its pale, who are suddenly inspired to catch up with their more advanced neighbours. The writer of this Study vividly remembers the impression made on him by a visit to the Nordiska Museet at Stockholm in 1910. After passing through a series of rooms displaying samples of Scandinavian palaeolithic, neolithic, bronze-age, and pre-Christian iron-age cultures, he was startled to find himself in a room displaying Scandinavian artifacts in the style of the Italian Renaissance. Wondering how he could have failed to notice the products of the Medieval period, he retraced his steps; and there, sure enough, was a Medieval room; but its contents were insignificant. He then began to realize that Scandinavia had passed in a flash out of a Late Iron Age, in which she had been beginning to create a distinctive civilization of her own, into an Early Modern Age in which she had become an undistinguished participant in a standardized Italianate Western Christian culture. Part of the price of this feat of acceleration had been the cultural impoverishment to which the Nordiska Museet bore witness.

As with Scandinavia in the fifteenth century of the Christian Era, so with the whole of the non-Western but precipitately Westernizing world of the writer's own day. It is a commonplace to remark that the African peoples, for example, were trying to achieve in a generation or two a political, social, and cultural progress that had occupied the West European peoples, whom the Africans were simultaneously imitating and resisting, for a thousand years or more. These peoples tended to exaggerate—and the Western onlooker, perhaps, to underrate—the amount of real acceleration that Africa had achieved.

If revolutions are a dramatic manifestation of acceleration, the phenomenon of retardation is to be seen in a straggler's refusal to keep pace with the movement of the main body. An example may be found in the obstinate retention of the institution of slavery by the Southern States of the North American Union a whole generation after it had been abolished in the neighbouring West Indian islands of the British Empire. Other examples were furnished by groups of colonists who had migrated to 'new' countries and had maintained there the standards prevalent in their homelands at the time when they had left home, long after their cousins in the 'old' country had abandoned those standards and had moved forward. The case was a familiar one, and it was sufficient to mention Quebec, the Appalachian highlands, and the Transvaal in the twentieth century of the Christian Era as compared with France,

Ulster, and the Netherlands at the same date. The previous pages of this Study present many examples of both acceleration and retardation which the reader can recall for himself. It is obvious, for example, that what we have called Herodianism is akin to acceleration and that what we have called Zealotism is akin to retardation. It is also obvious that, since change can be for the worse as well as for the better, acceleration is not necessarily good nor retardation necessarily bad.

A concatenation of alternating changes of speed which runs, not to two, but certainly to three, and possibly to four, terms is to be found in the Modern Western history of the arts of shipbuilding and navigation. The story begins with a sudden acceleration which revolutionized both these arts during the fifty years A.D. 1440–90. This spurt was followed by a retardation which persisted through the sixteenth, seventeenth, and eighteenth centuries, but which was followed in its turn, after that long pause, by another sudden acceleration during the fifty years A.D. 1840–90. In A.D. 1952 the next phase was enigmatical because it was still in progress, but to a layman's eye it looked as if the further technological advances then in progress, notable though these were, might nevertheless prove to fall short of the revolutionary achievements of the Victorian half-century.

'In the fifteenth century . . . there was a swift and momentous change in the building of ships. . . . In the space of fifty years the sea-going sailing-ship developed from a single-master into a three-master carrying five or six sails.'[1]

And this technological revolution not only gave its authors access to all quarters of the Globe; it also gave them an ascendancy over all non-Western mariners whom they might encounter. The new ship's distinctive virtue, in which it surpassed its successors as conspicuously as its predecessors, was its power to keep the sea for an almost unlimited length of time on end without having to call at a port. 'The ship', as it came, during its *floruit*, to be called *par excellence*, was the offspring of a happy marriage between diverse traditional builds and rigs, each of which had peculiar excellences but also consequent limitations. The Western ship that was brought to birth between A.D. 1440 and A.D. 1490 harmonized the strong points of an age-old Mediterranean oar-propelled 'long ship', *alias* galley, with those of no less than three distinct types of sailing-ship: a coeval square-rigged Mediterranean 'round ship', *alias* carrack; a lateen-rigged Indian-Ocean 'caravel' whose fore-runner

---

[1] Bassett-Lowke, J. W., and Holland, G.: *Ships and Men* (London 1946, Harrap), p. 46.

is depicted in the visual records of an Egyptian maritime expedition to the East African land of Punt in the reign of the Empress Hatshepsut (1486–68 B.C.); and a massively built Atlantic-faring sailing-ship which caught Caesar's eye in 56 B.C. when he occupied the peninsula afterwards called Brittany. The new design, which combined the best points of these four types, was complete by the end of the fifteenth century, and the best ships then afloat did not differ in essentials from those of Nelson's day.

Then, after three and a half centuries of retardation, the Western art of shipbuilding found itself on the eve of another outburst of acceleration; and, this time, the work of creation at high speed was to go forward on two parallel lines. On the one hand the steam-engine was to be substituted for sail; and contemporaneously the art of building sailing-ships was to awake from its long sleep and carry the old type forward to a new and hitherto-undreamed-of perfection at which, for some purposes, the sailing-ship was to hold its own in competition with the steamship throughout the creative half-century A.D. 1840–90.

If we now look for an explanation of these accelerations and retardations, which are such striking departures from the uniformity of movement that we should expect in societies wholly subject to the laws of Nature, we shall find our explanation in the formula of Challenge and Response, which we examined and illustrated at length in an earlier part of this Study. Let us take the last case cited, namely the two great accelerations, with a long period of retardation between them, in the history of Western shipbuilding and navigation.

The challenge that evoked the creation of the Modern Western ship within the half-century A.D. 1440–90 was a political one. Towards the close of the Middle Ages, Western Christendom found itself not only foiled in its attempt to break out southeastwards into Dār-al-Islām (i.e. in 'The Crusades'), but seriously threatened by the counter-attack of the Turks up the Danube and along the Mediterranean. The danger of the West's position at this date was accentuated by the fact that the Western Christian society happened to occupy the tip of one of the peninsulas of the Eurasian continent; and a society so precariously situated must sooner or later be pushed into the sea by the pressure of mightier forces thrusting outwards from the heart of the Old World if this besieged society did not forestall disaster by breaking out of its cul-de-sac into wider lands elsewhere. Otherwise it might expect to suffer at the hands of Islam a fate which it had already itself inflicted, many centuries before, on the abortive Far Western Christendom of 'the Celtic Fringe'. In the Crusades the Latin

Christians, choosing the Mediterranean as their war-path and traversing it in vessels of the traditional Mediterranean builds, had been moved by a longing to possess the cradle of their Christian faith. They had failed; and the menacing subsequent advance of Islam had put Islam's foiled Western antagonists between the Devil and the Deep Sea. They chose the Deép Sea and devised the new ship—with consequences surpassing the wildest dreams of the most optimistic of the disciples of the Portuguese Prince Henry the Navigator.

The overwhelming success of the fifteenth-century Western shipwrights' response to the challenge of Islam accounts for the long spell of retardation which followed in the Western shipwright's trade. The second spell of acceleration in this field was due to a very different cause, namely the new economic revolution which began to affect parts of Western Europe towards the end of the eighteenth century. The two outstanding features of this revolution were a sudden increase of population at an accelerating rate and a rise of commerce and manufacturing industry to a preponderance over agriculture. We need not enter here upon the complicated but familiar story of nineteenth-century Western industrial expansion and of the contemporary growth of population, which not only multiplied, to various degrees, the number of inhabitants of the sundry motherlands in the West's West European 'Old World', but also rapidly began to fill the great open spaces in new lands acquired by Western pioneers overseas. It is obvious that oceanic transport would have proved a positively throttling 'bottle-neck' obstructing these developments if the shipbuilders had not responded to the challenge as heartily and as effectively as they had responded four hundred years before.

We have chosen our illustration from the material field of human affairs: a couple of successive technological responses in a particular craft to a couple of challenges, the first political and military, the second economic and social. But the principle of Challenge and Response is the same all the way up and down the scale, whether it be the challenge of empty bellies craving for bread or the challenge of hungry souls craving for God. Whatever it be, the Challenge is always God's offer of Freedom of choice to human souls.

XXXVIII. THE LAW OF GOD

IN the present Part of this Study we are trying to gain some insight into the relation between Law and Freedom in History; and, if we now return to our question, we shall find that we have already reached an answer. How is Freedom related to Law? Our evidence declares that Man does not live under one law only; he lives under two laws, and one of these two is a Law of God which is Freedom itself under another and more illuminating name.

The 'perfect law of liberty', as Saint James calls it in his Epistle, is also a law of Love; for Man's freedom could only have been given to Man by a God who is Love in person, and this divine gift can be used by Man for freely choosing Life and Good, instead of Death and Evil, only if Man, on his side, loves God well enough to be moved by this responsive love of his to commit himself to God by making God's will his own.

> Our wills are ours, we know not how;
> Our wills are ours, to make them thine.[1]

'History is, . . . above everything else, a call, a vocation, a dispensation to be heard and responded to by free human beings—in short, the interaction of God and Man.'[2] Law and Freedom in History prove to be identical, in the sense that Man's freedom proves to be the Law of a God who is identical with Love. But this finding does not dispose of our problem; for, in answering our original question, we have raised a new one. In finding that Freedom is identical with one of two codes of Law we have raised the question of the relation in which these two codes stand to each other. At first sight the answer would seem to be that the Law of Love and the Law of Subconscious Human Nature, which both manifestly have jurisdiction over human affairs, are not only different but are contradictory and even incompatible; for the law of the Subconscious Psyche holds in bondage souls whom God has called to work with Him in freedom. The more searchingly we compare these two 'laws', the wider the moral gulf between them seems to be. If we appraise the Law of Nature by the standard of the Law of Love and see through Love's eyes all that Nature has made, behold, it is very bad.

> Ay, look: high Heaven and Earth ail from the prime foundation:
> All thoughts to rive the heart are here, and all are vain.[3]

[1] Tennyson: *In Memoriam*, in the Invocation.
[2] Lampert, E.: *The Apocalypse of History* (London 1948, Faber), p. 45.
[3] Housman, A. E.: *A Shropshire Lad*, xlviii.

One of the conclusions that have been drawn by human spectators of the moral evil of the Universe is that this chamber of horrors cannot be any God's handiwork. The Epicureans held that it was the undesigned outcome of the fortuitous concourse of indestructible atoms. The Christian, on the other hand, finds himself compelled to choose between two other alternatives, both of which are grievously disconcerting: Either the God who is Love must be the creator of a manifestly ailing Universe, or the Universe must have been created by another God who is not the God of Love.

The heretic Marcion at the beginning of the second century and the poet Blake at the beginning of the nineteenth century of the Christian Era both adopted the latter of these alternatives. Their solution for this moral enigma was to attribute the Creation to a god who was neither loving nor lovable. While the Saviour God won souls by love, the Creator God could only impose a law and exact savage penalties for formal breaches of it. This melancholy task-master god, whom Marcion identified with the Mosaic Jehovah and whom Blake names Urizen and nicknames Nobodaddy, would be bad enough if he performed his duties competently according to his own limited lights; but notoriously he fails to do so, and his failure must be due either to incompetence or to malevolence. Obviously there is no intelligible relation whatever between the World's sins and the World's sufferings.

While Marcion is on strong ground in affirming that Creation is bound up with evil, he is on weak ground in denying that it has anything to do with goodness and love; for the truth is that God's love is the source of Man's freedom, and that a freedom which gives vent for Creation thereby opens the door to sin. Every challenge can be regarded equally as a call from God or as a temptation by the Devil. Marcion's vindication of God's love at the cost of denying His unity is wider of the mark than Irenaeus' vindication of the identity of the Creator and the Redeemer at the cost of identifying with one another two epiphanies of the Godhead which are morally irreconcilable from a human standpoint. Moreover, the testimony of Christian experience to the truth of a logical and moral paradox has been strikingly vindicated by Modern Western science. The travail of striving to reconcile two irreconcilable epiphanies of God, which had tormented the minds of saints and scholars, was declared by at least one school of latter-day Western psychologists to have already tormented a Subconscious Psyche in an antecedent struggle through which the future saint and scholar's moral personality had been originally acquired at a stage of early infancy in which God's future place in the Soul's universe had been occupied by the infant child's Mother.

'As the baby begins ... early in the ... second year of post-natal life
... to draw a distinction between itself and outer reality, it is the Mother
who comes to represent the external world and to mediate its impacts
on the child. But she dawns upon its growing consciousness under two
opposite aspects. She is the child's chief object of love, and its fountain-
head of satisfaction, security, and peace. But she is also Authority, the
chief source of power mysteriously set over the child and arbitrarily
thwarting some of the impulses along whose paths its new life quests
outwards. The frustration of infantile impulse generates anger, hate, and
destructive wishes—what the psychologists generally style aggression—
directed against the thwarting authority. But this hated Authority is also
the loved Mother. The infant is thus faced with the primal conflict. Two
irreconcilable sets of impulses are directed towards the same object, and
that object is the centre of its surrounding universe.'[1]

Thus, according to one psychological theory, the conscious moral
conflict of maturity is subconsciously anticipated in early infancy;
and in the infantile, as in the adult, struggle a spiritual victory
exacts its spiritual price. 'Primitive Love conquers Primitive Hate
by saddling it with the burden of primal guilt';[2] and psychology
thus endorses the Irenaean anti-Marcionite Christian finding that
Love and Hate, Righteousness and Sinfulness, are indissolubly
linked with one another through the chain of Creation:

'Without a mother, no strong love focused on a personal object;
without such love, no conflict of irreconcilable influences, no guilt; and,
without such guilt, no effective moral sense.'[3]

[1] Huxley, J.: *Evolutionary Ethics*, the Romanes Lecture, 1943, reprinted in
Huxley, T. H. and J.: *Evolution and Ethics, 1893–1943* (London 1947, Pilot
Press), p. 107.
[2] Ibid., p. 110.
[3] Ibid.

XII
THE PROSPECTS OF THE WESTERN CIVILIZATION

XXXIX. THE NEED FOR THIS INQUIRY

As he took up his pen to write the present Part of this Study, the writer was conscious of a distaste for his self-imposed task which was something more than a natural shrinking from the hazards of a speculative subject. It was, of course, clear that forecasts made in 1950 might be belied by events long before the manuscript could be printed and published. Yet, if the risk of making himself ridiculous had been a governing consideration in the writer's mind, this would have deterred him from ever embarking on any part of this Study; and, in committing himself to Part Twelve of the work after having already given eleven hostages to fortune, he could take heart from the reflection that at this date the prospects of the Western civilization were at any rate very much less obscure than they had been when, in the early months of the year 1929, he had been drafting the original notes for this Part that were now lying at his elbow. The Great Depression, which was then just about to set in, with all its consequences, which included the Second World War, had, long before 1950, completely swept away the illusion, prevalent in 1929, that things in general were, after all, not so very different from what they had been before 1914.

The writer's distaste for his present subject ought therefore to have been appreciably diminished by the intervening passage of two enlightening decades of history if it had been merely a recoil from the hazards of forecast. His disinclination had, however, little or nothing to do with the difficulty of estimating the Western civilization's prospects, but was rooted in a reluctance to throw overboard one of the cardinal principles governing his approach to his Study. He was distressed by a fear that he might be abandoning a standpoint from which alone it was, in his belief, possible to see in true perspective the whole history of a species of Society of which the Western civilization was but one representative; and his belief in the rightness of this non-Western standpoint had been confirmed, in his judgement, by the results of two decades spent in trying to read the map of history from a non-Western angle of vision.

One of the stimuli that had spurred the writer to embark on the present Study was a revolt against a current Late Modern Western convention of identifying the Western society's history with 'History', writ large. This convention seemed to him the offspring of a distorting egocentric illusion, to which the children of a Western civilization had succumbed like the children of all other known civilizations and primitive societies.[1] The best point of departure from this egocentric assumption seemed to be to adopt the contrary assumption that all the representatives of any species of society are philosophically on a par with one another. The writer had adopted this counter-assumption, and it had seemed to him to justify his faith in it through the first six Parts of the present Study. In his Seventh Part he had found the value of the civilizations to be unequal on the evidence of an assay in which the touchstone had been the part played by their breakdowns and disintegrations in the history of Religion; but the result of this test had not been to re-exalt the Western civilization. On the contrary, the finding had been that the civilizations of the greatest mark and moment had been the civilizations of the second generation—the Syriac, the Indic, the Hellenic, and the Sinic—from the standpoint of an observer who saw the guide-line of History in a progressive increase in the provision of spiritual opportunities for human souls in transit through This World.

The writer's own adoption of this standpoint had reinforced his original reluctance to single out the Western civilization for special treatment. However, in deciding to abide in A.D. 1950 by a plan originally drawn up in A.D. 1927–9, he was bowing to the logic of three facts which had lost none of their cogency during the intervening years.

The first of these facts was that, in the second quarter of the

---

[1] When the Editor of the Abridgement was staying on the slope of Mount Kilimanjaro in A.D. 1935, he was told the Cause of the First World War as understood by the Chagga tribe, who live on the southern side of that mountain. Mount Kilimanjaro was first ascended by a German, Dr. Hans Meyer, in A.D. 1889. When he reached the top, he found there the god of the mountain, who, gratified by an attention that he had never before received, made over to the worthy German mountaineer and his fellow countrymen all the Chagga country, but on one condition, namely that one of the climber's fellow countrymen should ascend the mountain every year (or was it once every five years?) to do homage to him. All went well. The Germans occupied German East Africa, and an industrious party of German mountaineers ascended the mountain at the proper intervals, until, in A.D. 1914, there was a most unfortunate omission of this duty. Justly incensed, the god of the mountain revoked his gift and made the country over to the enemies of the Germans, who declared war upon them and drove them out. This Anglo-German war in the East African heart of the World brought with it incidentally, as is the way with wars, some 'side-show' bouts of fighting in relatively unimportant outlying areas.

The Chagga account of the First World War seems to be as good as many other accounts of it, and indeed better than some, in that it recognizes the importance of the part played by religion in history.

twentieth century of the Christian Era, the Western civilization was the only extant representative of its species that did not show indisputable signs of being in disintegration. Of the seven others, five—namely the main body of Orthodox Christendom and its Russian offshoot, the main body of the Far Eastern civilization and its Korean and Japanese offshoot, and the Hindu civilization —had not only entered into but had passed through their universal state phase; and a scrutiny of the histories of the Iranic and Arabic Muslim civilizations revealed strong evidence that these two societies had also broken down. The Western society alone was possibly still in its growth phase.

The second fact was that the expansion of the Western society and the radiation of the Western culture had brought all other extant civilizations and all extant primitive societies within a world-encompassing Westernizing ambit.

The third fact that seemed to make this inquiry imperative was the alarming fact that, for the first time in the history of the Human Race, all Mankind's eggs had been gathered into one precious and precarious basket.

> Gone are the days when madness was confined
> By seas or hills from spreading through Mankind:
> When, though a Nero fooled upon a string,
> Wisdom still reigned unruffled in Peking;
> And God in welcome smiled from Buddha's face,
> Though Calvin in Geneva preached of grace.
> For now our linked-up globe has shrunk so small,
> One Hitler in it means mad days for all.
> Through the whole World each wave of worry spreads,
> And Ipoh dreads the war that Ipsden dreads.[1]

In a Third World War fought with atomic or bacteriological weapons it seemed improbable that the Angel of Death would overlook even those nooks and corners of Man's terrestrial habitat which, till recently, had been either so uninviting or so inaccessible, or both, as to give their poor, weak, backward inhabitants a virtual immunity against the unwelcome attentions of 'civilized' militarists. In a talk given at Princeton just three weeks before the enunciation of the Truman Doctrine of American support for Greece and Turkey against Russian pressure (12 March, 1947), the writer had given play to the fancy that, if a Westernizing world were to allow itself to fall into a Third World War, the sequel might be a rendering, in real life, of one of Plato's myths, in which the Athenian philosopher imagines the mountain shepherds periodically issuing

[1] Skinner, Martyn: *Letters to Malaya*, I and II (London 1941, Putnam), pp. 34–35.

from their fastnesses in order to build up a new civilization on the vacated site of an old one that has perished in the latest of a number of periodic cataclysms. In the imagery of a collective Subconscious Psyche, shepherds had come to symbolize the unspent and unspoiled primitive human potentialities for creation that God had still held in reserve after He had led a sophisticated majority of Mankind into the temptations that had worsted Cain the husbandman, his son Enoch the city-builder, and their heir Tubal-Cain the smith. Whenever Man in Process of Civilization had come to grief in essaying this most recent, and perhaps most hazardous, of human enterprises up to date, he had always, so far, counted on being able to draw upon the reserve power latent in still primitive brethren of his whom he had driven out of those choicer portions of the Earth that he had appropriated as his own domain, 'to wander about in sheepskins and goatskins in deserts and in mountains'; and, in the past, these comparatively innocent survivors of the children of Abel had heaped coals of fire on the heads of the children of Cain by coming to their murderers' rescue when the Cainites' sins had found them out. A shepherd from Ascra, on the foothills of Mount Helicon, had spoken the prologue to the tragedy of Hellenic history, and shepherds from the Negeb, on the fringes of the Arabian Desert, had stood by the cradle of Christianity in Bethlehem. In his Platonizing *jeu d'esprit* the present writer had suggested in A.D. 1947 that, if the Western civilization in which he and his audience were implicated were to inflict some major catastrophe on the *Oikoumenê*, the task of launching, all over again, a cultural enterprise that had been on foot for the last five or six thousand years might perhaps fall to Tibetans hitherto safely ensconced behind the ramparts of their plateau or to Esquimaux hitherto snugly nestling against an innocently inclement ice-cap that was a less vicious neighbour than any *homo homini lupus*. Within the three and a half years that had elapsed between the delivery of that address and the writing of the present lines in the still peaceful precincts of the same university town, these tentative fancies had been overtaken and ridden down by the march of historical events. At the moment of writing in December 1950, an invading Chinese Communist expeditionary force was reported to be *en route* for Lhasa, while Esquimaux who had formerly been happy in having no foe or friend except Physical Nature found themselves in the fairway of a transpolar bombing-route between the basins of the Volga and the Mississippi, and of a *ventre-à-terre* invasion-route, across the ice-floes of the Behring Straits, from the once sequestered habitat of the primitive denizens of the north-eastern tip of Russia-in-Asia into an Alaska that was divided from the main body of the Continental United States by nothing but a Canadian 'Polish Corridor'.

Thus a now ubiquitous Western society held the fate of all Mankind in its hands at a moment when the West's own fate lay on the finger-tip of one man in Moscow and one man in Washington who, by pressing a button, could detonate an atom-bomb.

These were the facts that led the present writer reluctantly to endorse in A.D. 1950 the conclusion, reluctantly reached in A.D. 1929, that an inquiry into the prospects of the Western civilization was a necessary part of a twentieth-century study of History.

XL. THE INCONCLUSIVENESS OF
A PRIORI ANSWERS

WHAT was the Western civilization's expectation of life in
A.D. 1955? On·first thoughts a student of History might be
inclined to rate the West's current expectations low, considering
the well-known prodigality of Nature. The Western civilization
was, after all, one out of no more than twenty-one representatives
of its species. Was it rational to expect to see the twenty-first
civilization on trial succeed in avoiding the failure that had been
the lot of all the others? Considering the number of failures that
had been the price of each dearly bought success in the past history
of the evolution of Life on Earth, it might appear improbable that,
in the history of a species still so young as the civilizations were,
any representative of the third generation would be cast for the
part of finding some hitherto untravelled way of going on living
and growing indefinitely, or else of creating a mutation that would
generate a new species of Society.

Yet such an inference would have been drawn from the experience of Life, not at the human, but at a pre-human level. It might
be true that, when Nature had been engaged on the evolution of
rudimentary organisms, she had been apt to coin millions of
specimens in order to give herself the off-chance of making a lucky
hit that would produce a novel and superior design. In the evolution
of plants, insects, fishes, and the like, twenty specimens would, no
doubt, have been a ridiculously small number for Nature to work
on; but it would surely be an unwarrantable assumption to suppose that rules of evolution that might be inevitable for animal
or vegetable organisms were also necessarily applicable to such
entirely different 'specimens' as human societies in process of
civilization. In fact, the argument from the prodigality of Nature
is, in the present context, no argument at all. We have raised it
only to dismiss it.

There remain a pair of emotional *a priori* answers to our question which must be considered before we proceed to examine the
testimony of the civilizations themselves. The two emotional
answers were mutually contradictory, and the writer of this Study,
who had been born in A.D. 1889, had lived to see the West begin
to revert from one of these two feelings to the other.

The outlook prevalent among people of the middle class in
Great Britain at the end of the nineteenth century can best be
conveyed by a quotation from a parody, written by two school-

masters, of a schoolboy's notions of history as presented in his examination scripts, and entitled *1066 and All That*.

'History is now at an end; this history is therefore final.'

This *fin-de-siècle* English middle-class outlook was shared by the contemporary children of the German and Northern American victors of the latest bout of Modern Western wars. The beneficiaries from this aftermath of the General War of A.D. 1792–1815 had not, by then, begun to suspect, any more than their English 'opposite numbers', that the Modern Age of Western History had been wound up only to inaugurate a Post-Modern Age pregnant with tragic experiences. They were imagining that, for their benefit, a sane, safe, satisfactory Modern Life had miraculously come to stay in a suddenly inaugurated timeless present. A sense of timelessness seemed to brood, for example, over a sixty-years-long Victorian Age, though, indeed, a casual examination of the pictures in the popular Diamond Jubilee production, *Sixty Years a Queen*, suggested a fast-moving pageant of change in every department of life, ranging from technology to dress.

At that date, English middle-class Conservatives, for whom the millennium had already arrived, and English middle-class Liberals, for whom it lay only just round the corner, were, of course, aware that the English working class's share in the middle class's prosperity was shockingly small, and that British subjects in most of the colonies and dependencies of the United Kingdom were not enjoying a self-government that was the privilege of their fellow subjects in the United Kingdom and in a few other dominions of the British Crown; but these inequalities were discounted by the Liberals as remediable and by the Conservatives as inevitable. Contemporary citizens of the United States at the North were similarly aware that their economic prosperity was not shared by their fellow citizens at the South. Contemporary subjects of the German Reich were aware that the inhabitants of a 'Reichsland' annexed from France were still French at heart and that the rest of the French nation was still unreconciled to the amputation of the ceded departments. The French were still entertaining thoughts of a *revanche*, and the subject population in Alsace-Lorraine were still dreaming the same dream of an eventual liberation as other subject populations in Slesvik, Poland, Macedonia, and Ireland. Such peoples did not acquiesce in the comfortable belief that 'History' was 'at an end'. Yet their unwavering confidence that a, to them, intolerable established system must be borne away, sooner or later, by Time's 'ever-rolling stream' made little impression, at the time, on the torpid imaginations of representatives of the

Powers then in the ascendant. It may be safely said that there was, in A.D. 1897, no living man or woman, even among the most sanguine prophets of nationalist or socialist revolution, who dreamed that a demand for national self-determination was going to break up the Hapsburg, Hohenzollern, and Romanov empires and the United Kingdom of Great Britain and Ireland within the next twenty-five years; or that a demand for social democracy was going to spread from the urban working class of a few precociously industrialized provinces of the Western world to the peasantry of Mexico and China. Gandhi (born A.D. 1869) and Lenin (born A.D. 1870) were then still unknown names. The word 'Communism' stood for a lurid but brief and apparently irrelevant past episode which had come to be regarded as the last eruption of 'History's' now extinct volcano. This ominous outbreak of savagery in the Parisian underworld in A.D. 1871 was written off as an atavistic reaction to the shock of a startling military disaster, and there was no discernible fear of the recrudescence of a conflagration that had been smothered for a quarter of a century under the wet blanket of a bourgeois Third Republic.

This complacent middle-class optimism was no new thing at the time of Queen Victoria's Jubilee. We find it a hundred years earlier in the stately periods of Gibbon and in Turgot's *Second Discourse*, delivered at the Sorbonne in A.D. 1750, *On the Advantages which the Establishment of Christianity has procured for the Human Race*. A hundred years farther back again we can detect it in the casual observations of Pepys. The shrewd diarist detected a rise in the political and economic barometer; '1649 and all that', which included the Massacre of St. Bartholomew and the Spanish Inquisition, were things of the past. Indeed, the generation of Pepys was that in which we have already placed the beginning of the Late Modern Age (A.D. 1675–1875), and this Late Modern Age is one of the great Ages of Faith—Faith in Progress and in Human Perfectibility. Two generations earlier than Pepys we find a more sonorous prophet of this Faith in Francis Bacon.

A Faith that has lived three hundred years dies hard, and we can detect its expression, ten years after it had received its apparent knock-out blow in A.D. 1914, in an address delivered by a distinguished historian and public servant of the prediluvian generation, Sir James Headlam-Morley (A.D. 1863–1929).

'In our analysis of this [Western] culture the first great fact that we will notice is that, though undoubtedly there is a common history and common civilisation for all Western Europe, the people were not joined in any formal political union, nor has the country ever been subjected to one common government. For a moment, indeed, it looked as though

Charlemagne would establish his authority over the whole area; that hope, as we know, was to be disappointed; his attempt to create a new empire failed, as all subsequent attempts have failed. Again and again attempts were made by the later Empire, by the rulers of Spain and France, to unite the whole of Western Europe in one great state or empire. Always we find the same thing: the appeal to local patriotism and personal liberty inspires a resistance which breaks down the efforts of every conqueror. And so there has been as a permanent characteristic of Europe that which critics call anarchy; for the absence of a common rule means struggle, fighting, and war, a ceaseless confusion between rival units of government [contending with one another] for territory and predominance.

'This is a condition which to many is very shocking. Undoubtedly it implies a great expenditure of energy, a great destruction of wealth, at times a great loss of life. There are many, in consequence, who would have preferred to see the gradual establishment of some common government and who, to its disadvantage, contrast the history of Europe with that of Imperial Rome, or—at the present day—of the United States of America. There are many, from the days of Dante onwards, who have longed for that ordered government which might appear to be the true reflex and instrument of Divine Providence. How often do we hear it said that if, on the soil of America, English and Italians and Poles and Ruthenians and Germans and Scandinavians can all live side by side in peace and contentment, why should they not do so in their original homes?

'I have not to-day to discuss ideals of the future; we are concerned with the past, and all that we have to do is to note the fact that this anarchy, this warfare, this rivalry, existed just at the time when the energies of the Continent were at their highest. Let us note also that the energies of the Mediterranean World—the vital force, artistic spirit, intellectual ingenuity—seem gradually but steadily to have decayed, and that the beginning of the decay coincided with the establishment of a common government. May it not be that the friction and disorder was not in reality merely destruction of energy, but the cause by which the energy was produced?'[1]

It is strange to hear Gibbon's reassuring voice still echoing in an England that was now ringing with the dread sound of an apocalyptic trump. By A.D. 1924, however, the antithetical feeling, expressed in a different reading of the significance of an antecedent Hellenic civilization's decline and fall, was already in the ascendant in a stricken Western world.

Five years before Headlam-Morley delivered his address, Paul Valéry had eloquently proclaimed that all civilizations were mortal. Spengler was saying the same thing at the same time. We can now

[1] J. W. Headlam-Morley: 'The Cultural Unity of Western Europe', in *The New Past and other Essays on the Development of Civilization*, edited by E. H. Carter (Oxford 1925, Blackwell), pp. 88–89.

see that the Doctrine of Progress was based on a number of false premisses. But does that admission compel us to accept the Doctrine of Doom? Such would be very simple reasoning. One might as well argue that because Johnny Head-in-Air had fallen into the Slough of Despond, there could therefore be no way across it. Valéry's pessimism and Gibbon's optimism are, both alike, rationalizations of emotions which happened to be superficially appropriate to the brief spans of their respective lives.

XLI. THE TESTIMONY OF THE HISTORIES OF THE CIVILIZATIONS

(1) WESTERN EXPERIENCES WITH NON-WESTERN PRECEDENTS

IN earlier parts of this Study we have tried to gain some insight into the causes of the breakdowns of civilizations and into the process of their disintegrations by surveys of the relevant historical facts; and in studying the breakdowns we found that the cause was, in every case, some failure of self-determination. A broken-down society would prove to have forfeited a salutary freedom of choice through having fallen under the bondage of some idol of its own making. Midway through the twentieth century of the Christian Era the Western society was manifestly given over to the worship of a number of idols; but, among these, one stood out above the rest, namely the worship of the parochial state. This feature of Post-Modern Western life was a terrifying portent on two accounts: first, because this idolization was the true, though unavowed, religion of the great majority of the inhabitants of the Westernizing world, and secondly, because this false religion had been the death of no less than fourteen, and perhaps of sixteen, of the twenty-one civilizations on record.

Fratricidal warfare of ever-increasing violence had been by far the commonest cause of mortality among civilizations of all three generations. In the first generation it had certainly been the destruction of the Sumeric and the Andean, and probably of the Minoan as well. In the second generation it had destroyed the Babylonic, the Indic, the Syriac, the Hellenic, the Sinic, the Mexic, and the Yucatec. In the third generation it had destroyed the Orthodox Christian, both in its main body and in its Russian offshoot, the Far Eastern in its Japanese offshoot, the Hindu, and the Iranic. Of the five remaining civilizations, other than the Western, we may suspect that the Hittite had likewise brought itself to ruin by fratricidal warfare at home before it had run full tilt against a petrified Egyptiac world, and had subsequently succumbed to a barbarian Völkerwanderung. The Mayan civilization had, so far, yielded no evidence of fratricidal warfare. The Egyptiac and the Far Eastern civilization in China seem to have sacrificed their lives to a different idol, namely an œcumenical polity with an increasingly parasitic bureaucracy. The only remaining specimen is the Arabic society, which may have been destroyed by the incubus of a parasitic Nomad institution in a non-Nomad world—the slave-ascendancy of the Egyptian Mamlūks—unless this society affords a solitary case of destruction by an alien assailant.

Moreover, in the Post-Modern chapter of Western history, the devastating effects of the idolization of parochial sovereign states had been enhanced by a demonic drive. The restraining influence of a universal church had been removed. The impact of democracy in the form of nationalism, coupled in many cases with some new-fangled ideology, had made the warfare more bitter, and the impetus given by industrialism and technology had provided the combatants with increasingly destructive weapons.

The Industrial Revolution that had begun to affect the Western world in the eighteenth century of the Christian Era was an unmistakable counterpart of the economic revolution that had overtaken the Hellenic world in the sixth century B.C. In both cases, communities that had previously made their living more or less in isolation, by subsistence farming, had now gone into economic partnership with each other to increase their output and their income by learning to produce and exchange specialized commodities. In so doing they had ceased to be autarkic, and they could no longer resume their autarky even if they had so wished. The effect in both cases had been to give the society a new structure on the economic plane that was incongruous with its structure on the political plane; and the fatal result of this 'faulting' in the social fabric of the Hellenic society has already come to our notice more than once.

One discouraging symptom in Modern Western history had been the emergence, first in Prussia and then in Germany at large, of a militarism that had been deadly in the histories of other civilizations. This militarism had first made its appearance in the reigns of the Prussian kings Frederick William I and Frederick the Great (A.D. 1713–86), at a time when, of all ages of latter-day Western history, the conduct of war had been most formal and its destructiveness at a minimum. In its final phase, up to the time of writing, the mad-dog militarism of a National Socialist Germany could be compared only with the *furor Assyriacus* after its temperature had been raised to the third degree by Tiglath-Pileser III (reigned 746–727 B.C.). Whether the unprecedentedly drastic destruction of the National Socialist war machine had destroyed the will to militarism in all parts of a Westernizing world seemed, at the time of writing, much more doubtful.

To set against these bad omens there were also some more favourable symptoms. There was one ancient institution, no less evil than war, which the Western civilization had got rid of. A society which had succeeded in abolishing slavery might surely take heart from this unprecedented victory of a Christian ideal as it addressed itself to the task of abolishing the coeval institution of war. War and slavery had been twin cancers of civilization ever since this species of society had first emerged. The conquest of one of them was a good omen for the prospects of the campaign against the other.

Moreover, a Western society that was still being worsted by war could take heart from its record on other spiritual battlefields. In its response to the challenge presented by the impact of industrialism on the institution of private property, the Western society had already in many countries made some headway in forcing a passage between the Scylla of unrestricted economic individualism and the Charybdis of totalitarian control of economic activities by the state. There had also been some measure of success in coping with the impact of democracy on education. In throwing open to all an intellectual treasure-house which had been a small minority's jealously guarded and oppressively exploited preserve since the dawn of civilization, the Modern Western spirit of democracy had given mankind a new hope at the cost of exposing it to a new danger. The danger lay in the opening which a rudimentary universal education gave for propaganda, and in the skill and unscrupulousness with which this opportunity had been seized by advertising salesmen, news agencies, pressure groups, political parties, and totalitarian governments. The hope lay in the possibility that these exploiters of a semi-educated public would prove unable to 'condition' their victims so thoroughly as to prevent them from continuing their education to a point at which they would become immune against such exploitation.

But the plane on which the decisive spiritual battle was likely to be fought was neither the military nor the social nor the economic nor the intellectual; for in A.D. 1955 the crucial questions confronting Western Man were all religious.

Had the fanatically positive Judaic religions been discredited beyond repair by the incriminating record of intolerance that had given the lie to their professions? Was there any virtue in the religious toleration into which a disillusioned Western world had subsided toward the close of the seventeenth century of the Christian Era? How long would Western souls find it bearable to go on living without religion? And, now that the discomfort of a spiritual vacuum had tempted them to open the door to such devils as nationalism and fascism and communism, how long was their latter-day belief in toleration likely to stand the test? Toleration had been easy in a lukewarm age in which the varieties of Western Christianity had lost their hold on Western hearts and minds, while these had not yet found alternative objects for their frustrated devotion. Now that they had gone a whoring after other gods, would an eighteenth-century toleration hold its own against a twentieth-century fanaticism?

Wanderers in a Western wilderness, astray from the One True God of their forefathers, who had been taught by a disillusioning experience that parochial states, like sectarian churches, were idols whose worship brought not peace but a sword, might be tempted to seize upon a Collective Humanity as an alternative object of idolization. A 'religion of Humanity' that had missed fire in the frigid mould of a Comtian Positivism had set the World ablaze when it had been fired from the cannon's mouth of Marxian Communism. Would a life-and-death struggle for the salvation of souls, which Christianity had waged and won in its youth against an Hellenic worship of a Collective Humanity embodied in the cults of Dea Roma and Divus Caesar, have to be fought out again, two thousand years later, against some latter-day embodiment of the worship of the same Leviathan? The Hellenic precedent raised the question without revealing the answer.

If we now pass on from the symptoms of breakdown in the Western world to the symptoms of disintegration, we shall recall that, in our analysis of 'Schism in the Body Social', we found unmistakable traces, in a latter-day Western world, of the appearance of the characteristic threefold division into a dominant minority, an internal proletariat, and an external proletariat.

The Western world's external proletariat need hardly detain us, for the former barbarians were being eliminated, not by extermination, but by being transferred to the ranks of a Western internal proletariat which had come to embrace a great majority of the living generation of Mankind. The thus forcibly domesticated barbarians were actually one of the smallest contingents of which this vast twentieth-century internal proletariat of the Western society was composed. A far larger quota had been contributed by children of non-Western civilizations who had been caught in a World-encompassing Western net. A third contingent, the most unhappy and therefore the most actively dissident of the three, consisted of *déracinés* of diverse origins, Western as well as non-Western, who had suffered divers degrees of coercion. There were the descendants of African negro slaves who had been forcibly transplanted across the Atlantic; there were the descendants of Indian and Chinese indentured labourers whose emigration overseas had often in effect been just as involuntary as that of African slaves. Then there were others who had been uprooted without crossing any seas. The most flagrant examples of proletarianization were the 'Poor Whites' in the 'Old South' of the United States and in the Union of South Africa, who had sunk to the social level of their more successful fellow colonists' imported or indigenous African helots. But, over and above all these outstanding unfortunate groups, it could be said that, wherever there were masses of people, rural or urban, who felt that the Western social system was not giving them what they were entitled to have, there was an internal proletariat; for our definition of 'proletariat' has, throughout this Study, been psychological, and we have consistently used it to denote those who felt that they no longer 'belonged' spiritually to the society within which they found themselves included physically.

The proletarian reaction against a dominant minority had found violent expression at various times and in various places, from medieval Peasant Wars to the Jacobinism of the French Revolution. In the middle of the twentieth century of the Christian Era it was expressing itself more powerfully than ever before, and this along two channels. Where the grievances were mainly economic, the channel was Communism; where they were political or racial, the channel was a nationalistic revolt against Colonialism.

In A.D. 1955 the threat to Western civilization from the Russo-Chinese Communist bloc was obvious and menacing. At the same time there were a number of less sensational, but not necessarily less substantial, entries on the other side of the account.

The first point that might come to tell in a menaced Western civilization's favour was the alloy of Russian nationalism in an œcumenical Communism that professed, with a show of Pauline fervour, to have risen superior to all invidious distinctions between Jew and Greek. This vein of insincerity was a flaw in Communism's moral armour. At a moment when, in Eastern Asia, the Western cause was suffering grievous adversity, a Western telepathist who could have looked into the hearts of the close-lipped statesmen in the Kremlin might have learnt that they were watching the spectacular successes of their Chinese allies with mixed feelings. The future of Manchuria, Mongolia, and Sinkiang was, after all, of vastly greater importance for China and for Russia alike than the future of Indo-China, Hong-Kong, and Formosa. It was conceivable that Malenkov or his successor Khrushchev or Khrushchev's possible successor, at present still below the horizon, might become another Tito, and that, after Germany and Japan had been rearmed by the West, and China by the Soviet Union, a frightened West might hail a frightened Russia as 'the White Man's Hope'. The long-since-discredited Kaiser Wilhelm II had called attention to the Yellow Peril and had been thought a fool for his pains; yet some writers still persisted in holding the view that he was not only a well-meaning but also a very clever man; and, significantly, even Hitler had commended the Kaiser's judgement on this one point.

This at first sight unconvincing prognostication had a solid basis in two indisputable facts. Russia was the only major province of the patrimony of the White Race in which the population was increasing in the twentieth century at the rate at which it had increased in the nineteenth century in Western Europe and North America; and Russia was also the province of the White Race's patrimony which marched with the Continental frontiers of China and India. If either or both of these sub-continents, each of which housed nearly a quarter of the human race, were to succeed in carrying the process of Westernization on the technological and organizational planes to a point at which Chinese or Indian man-power would begin to count in the World's military and political balance-sheet in proportion to its mere numbers, it was to be expected that such an invigorated Samson would insist on a drastic revision of the World's hitherto grossly inequitable distribution of territory and natural resources. In such an event, Russia, struggling to preserve her own existence, might find herself involuntarily performing, for a Western world snugly sheltering under her lee, the unrewarding service of acting as a buffer that the main body of Orthodox Christendom had once performed for the same Western world when the explosive quarter had been, not India or China, but a South-West Asia united under a dynamic Primitive Muslim Arab leadership.

These were highly speculative forecasts relating to a future not yet in sight. There was perhaps more solid ground for encourage-ment in the fact that a Western community which had come into headlong collision with the Chinese in Korea and had been des-perately embroiled in Indo-China had managed to come to terms with the Indonesians on the morrow of their liberation from the Japanese, and had voluntarily abdicated its dominion over the Filipinos, Ceylonese, Burmans, Indians, and Pakistanis. The reconciliation between an Asia represented by various communi-ties formerly subject to the British Rāj and a Western society represented by British protagonists in the drama of Late Modern Western Imperialism opened up a prospect that some part, at least, of the vast Asian contingent in a world-wide Western internal proletariat, which had been heading towards secession from a Western dominant minority, might change its course and make for the alternative goal of partnership on terms of equality with its former Western masters.

A similar issue might be hoped for in the Asian and North African provinces of the Islamic world, and also in most of Africa south of the Sahara. A more intractable problem was presented by those areas in which climatic conditions had tempted the Western European not only to establish his rule but also to make his home; and the same problem arose in a less menacing form in regions where non-White populations had been imported to do the more disagreeable and elementary chores of the White Man's work for him. The difference in the degree of menace, as seen from the White standpoint, expressed itself in the statistics of the racial composition of the local population. Where the non-White was indigenous, as for example in South Africa, he usually far outnumbered the dominant White race. Where he had been forcibly imported, as in the United States, the proportions were in the reverse.

In the United States, at the time of writing, the tendency of a 'colour-bar' to harden into a caste distinction on Indian lines was being resisted by the counter-operation of the spirit of Christianity; and, though it was impossible to tell as yet whether this Christian counter-attack was a forlorn hope or 'the wave of the Future', it was a good omen that, in the United States as in India, the redeeming spirit had been at work on both sides. In the hearts of the dominant White majority a Christian conscience that had insisted on abolishing Negro slavery had come to realize that a merely juridical emancipation was not enough, and on the other side a Coloured proletarian minority had shown signs of responding in the same spirit.

The alienation of the internal proletariat is, as we found in an earlier part of this Study, the most conspicuous symptom of the disintegration of a civilization; and, with that in mind, we have been considering what evidence there might be, both of alienation and of reconciliation, within the Western society as it stood in the middle of the twentieth century of the Christian Era. So far, we have been considering those elements of the proletariat which were themselves non-Western in origin but which had been brought within the frontiers of the Western society by the West's world-wide expansion. There remained, needless to say, all that part of the proletariat which was racially indistinguishable from its dominant minority; that vast majority of Western men and women whom 'superior persons' born into a nineteenth-century Western privileged minority referred to under such various names as 'the working classes', 'the lower classes', 'the populace', 'the masses', and even (in a contemptuously quizzical vein) 'the great unwashed'. Here the immensity of the theme is daunting. It must suffice to say that in practically all Western countries, and more particularly in the most highly industrialized and most thoroughly modernized Western countries, there had been, in the past half-century, an immense practical advance towards social justice in every department of life. The political revolution through which India had obtained her emancipation from the British Rāj had not been more remarkable than the social revolution in Great Britain through which a Western country in which power, wealth, and opportunity had been still, within living memory, the close preserve of an odiously small and scandalously over-privileged minority, had transformed itself, with remarkably little ill-feeling on either side, into a community in which a large measure of social justice had been secured at the cost of a minimal sacrifice of individual liberty.

The foregoing survey of facts telling against, as well as facts telling in favour of, the likelihood of the Western civilization's coming to grief through a secession of an internal proletariat suggests two tentative conclusions. In the first place, the forces of reconciliation appeared to be stronger than any corresponding forces at work in the Hellenic society at a corresponding stage in its history. Secondly, this difference in the Western world's favour appeared to be mainly due to the continuing operation of a spirit of Christianity that had not lost its hold over the hearts of Western men and women, even though their minds might have rejected the creed in which the abiding truths of Christianity had been translated into the ephemeral language of a pagan Hellenic philosophy.

This persistent vitality of a higher religion which had once provided a larval Western society with its chrysalis was an element that had been conspicuously lacking in an otherwise comparable Hellenic situation; and it might be conjectured that there was some relation between this apparent invincibility of Christianity's spiritual essence and the paucity and jejunity of the new crop of religions that could be descried raising their heads here and there in a Westernizing world at this time.

We may therefore conclude that the evidence from non-Western precedents bearing on the future of the Western civilization was not decisive.

(2) UNPRECEDENTED WESTERN EXPERIENCES

So far we have been examining elements in the post-Modern Western situation which are comparable with elements in the histories of the other civilizations, but there are also elements in it to which the histories of the other civilizations present no parallels. Two of these unparalleled features leap to the eye. The first is the extent of the mastery that Western Man had acquired over non-human Nature; the second is the accelerating rapidity of the social change that this mastery was bringing about.

Ever since Man's passage from the Lower to the Upper Palaeolithic stage of technological progress, the Human Race had been Lords of Creation on Earth in the sense that, from that time onwards, it had no longer been possible either for inanimate Nature or for any other non-human creature either to exterminate Mankind or even to interrupt human progress. Thenceforth, nothing on Earth, with one exception, could stand in Man's way or bring Man to ruin; but that exception was a formidable one —namely, Man himself. As we have seen, Man had already brought himself to grief in the misconduct of some fourteen or fifteen civilizations. Eventually, in A.D. 1945, the detonation of the atomic bomb had made it clear that Man had now acquired a degree of control over non-human Nature which made it impossible for him to avoid any longer the challenge of the two evils which he had brought on the World in the very act of providing himself with a new species of Society in the shape of societies in process of civilization. These twin evils were two different manifestations of the single evil of war, though it might be convenient to distinguish them by giving them different names—war as ordinarily understood, and class-war: horizontal war and vertical war, in other words.

This was a situation with which the Human Race was very ill-prepared to cope. In considering its prospects, we may manage to simplify our task by giving separate consideration, first to Technology, War, and Government, and then to Technology, Class-conflict, and Employment.

XLII. TECHNOLOGY, WAR, AND GOVERNMENT

(1) PROSPECTS OF A THIRD WORLD WAR

As a result of two world wars, the number of the Great Powers had been reduced from a fluctuating plurality, in which some states, such as Italy, had borne the title by courtesy, though everyone knew that they could not sustain it, to two only—The United States and the Soviet Union. The Soviet Union had established its domination over Eastern Germany as well as over most of the successor-states of the former Hapsburg and Ottoman empires which had been overrun, during the Second World War, by the ephemeral National Socialist German Third Reich. The only reason why Western Germany and the inter-war Austrian Republic had not followed their neighbours into Russia's maw by A.D. 1956 was that they had come, meanwhile, under the protection of the United States and her West European allies. By this date it had become apparent that the substitution of a United States protectorate for an untenable independence was the only insurance against Russian (or Chinese) domination that promised to be effective in the long run for any state anywhere in the World.

This role, which was a new role for the United States in the Old World, had long been familiar to her in the New World. From the days of the Holy Alliance to the days of the Third Reich the Monroe Doctrine had saved the successor-states of the Spanish and Portuguese empires in the Americas from falling under the domination of some European Power at the price of replacing a Spanish or Portuguese colonial administration by a United States hegemony. Benefactors are seldom popular, and unless their benefactions are completely disinterested they may not altogether deserve to be. The feelings of, say, the French towards the United States since A.D. 1945 were not very different from those of, say, the Brazilians at any time within the past hundred years.

However that might be, the Soviet Union and the United States found themselves, in A.D. 1956, confronting one another as the only two Great Powers still surviving on the face of the planet; and in any international balance of power two was bound, at the best, to be an awkward number. It was true that, in contrast with Germany and Japan twenty years earlier, both were economically 'sated' countries, which could find peaceful employment for the whole of their manpower, for many decades to come, in cultivating their own estates. But past history had shown that mutual fear was as potent a source of warlike aggression as economic want. The Russian and American peoples were ill equipped for understanding each other. The Russian people's habitual temper was one of docile resignation, the American's one of obstreperous impatience; and this difference of temper was reflected in a difference of attitude towards arbitrary government. The Russians acquiesced in this as inevitable, whereas the Americans had learnt from their own history to think of it as an evil institution which any people could overthrow at will. The Americans saw their *summum bonum* in a personal liberty which they rather oddly identified with equality, whereas the Russian Communist dominant minority saw their *summum bonum* in theoretical equality which they still more oddly identified with liberty.

These temperamental and doctrinal differences made it difficult for the two peoples to understand and trust each other; and this mutual distrust bred fear, now that the arena in which they menaced one another had been transformed out of all recognition by the unprecedentedly rapid progress of technology, which had made a once wide world shrivel to dimensions so diminutive as to make it henceforth impossible for the rivals to take their stand in this arena without finding themselves within point-blank range of each other.

In a world thus technologically unified, it looked as if a competition for World power between the Soviet Union and the United States might be decided in the long run by the suffrages of those three-quarters of the living generation of Mankind who, five or six thousand years after the dawn of civilization, were still living in the Neolithic Age on the material plane of life, but who had begun to become aware that a higher standard was possible. In exercising a choice, now open to it, between an American and a Russian way of life, this hitherto submerged majority might be expected to choose whichever way of the two seemed to them the more likely to satisfy this awakening majority's revolutionary aspirations. Yet, although the last word might lie with a hitherto submerged non-Western majority of Mankind, it nevertheless seemed probable that, in the short run, the decisive weight in the scales of a Russo-American balance would prove to be, not those three-quarters of the World's population, but that one-quarter of the World's present industrial war-potential that was still located in Western Europe. In global terms it might be said that there was now one sole continent, Eurafrasia, skirted by two large offshore islands, North and South America. On this global view, Russia appeared as the continental, and the United States as the insular Power—much as, in the 'European' inter-parochial wars of the 'Modern' period of Western history, Britain had played the part of the insular Power, and Spain, France, and Germany the part of serving as Britain's successive continental enemies. In the Post-Modern global arena the West European sector was still crucial, because it was the insular Power's Continental bridgehead. In times past, Flanders had been the 'cockpit' of Western Europe, in which its incorrigibly belligerent parochial states had fought their battles. Now the whole of Western Europe appeared to be marked out for serving, in the event of another general war, as the 'cockpit' of a Westernizing world. There was, perhaps, a poetic justice in this transformation of the strategic map; but this did not make the plight of inhabiting a 'cockpit' less unwelcome to West Europeans in general since A.D. 1946 than it had been to Flemings since before the close of the fifteenth century.

The progess of technology has no power to diminish the sway of human feelings over the course of human affairs. Militarism is a matter not of technology but of psychology—the will to fight. Wars are exhilarating when fought elsewhere and by other people. Perhaps they are most exhilarating of all when over and done with; and historians of all civilizations had traditionally regarded them as the most interesting topic in their field. Most armies in the past had been relatively small, and had largely consisted of people who preferred fighting to other occupations. But, since the *levée en masse* in a revolutionary France in A.D. 1792, Modern Western warfare had become a far more serious matter; and the warfare of the future threatened to become more serious still. War was now tending to kill the militarism of peoples who experienced it, and the will of the people is a force to which even an autocratic government has ultimately to yield. Among the countries that had suffered the most severely in the First World War, France had virtually refused to endure the second. Hitler had succeeded in galvanizing the Germans into a further bout of militarism; but in A.D. 1956 it seemed doubtful whether another Hitler—if another were ever to arise—could perform the same *tour de force* again. It was significant that the favourite conventional epithet of the Communist dictators was 'peace-loving'. Napoleon in St. Helena had still described war as a *belle occupation*; but it may be doubted whether he would have applied the phrase to atomic warfare if he could have lived to see its advent.

These reflections were primarily applicable to peoples of advanced civilization who had had first-hand experience of twentieth-century warfare. The traditional submissiveness of the peoples of Asia, on the other hand, had, since time immemorial, taken the political form of passive obedience to arbitrary governments; and the cultural process of Westernization would have to go far beyond the rudimentary accomplishment of acquiring a Western military technique before the Asian peasant-soldier would begin to think of questioning, or defying, orders to sacrifice his life, even in an aggressive war which meant nothing to him personally. How far could mid-twentieth-century Asian governments go in exploiting their subjects' ingrained submissiveness for military purposes? In Western eyes it might look as if the Chinese and Russian peasant-soldier had given his government a blank cheque drawn on his life; yet History had demonstrated that there was a limit beyond which neither a Chinese nor a Russian government could venture with impunity. Chinese régimes, from the Ts'in to the Kuomintang, that had had the temerity to give the screw just one turn too many had repeatedly paid for this slight excess by the forfeiture of their mandate to rule; and in Russian history it had been the same story.

A Czardom that had had the wisdom to take the sting out of the Russian people's sufferings in the Crimean War by conceding the reforms of the eighteen-sixties had paid with its life for its obstinacy in refusing to forestall trouble once again by paying a corresponding ransom for subsequent military reverses, first in the Japanese war of A.D. 1904–5, which had provoked the abortive Russian revolution of the latter year, and afterwards in the First World War, which had provoked the double revolution of A.D. 1917. It seemed, then, that there were limits at which the *moral* of Russia or any other peasant country would collapse. Nevertheless, it seemed likely that the Government of the Soviet Union would face the terrors of a war with the United States rather than make any political concession to the United States that, in Russian eyes, would be tantamount to submission to an American ascendancy.

If it was thus likely that there were circumstances in which the Soviet Union could and would go to war with a Power of its own calibre, was this also to be predicted of the United States? In A.D. 1956 the answer appeared to be in the affirmative. Ever since the first settlement of the oldest of the Thirteen Colonies, the American people had been one of the most unmilitary, yet at the same time one of the most martial, of the nations of the Western world. They had been unmilitary in the sense that they had disliked submitting themselves to military discipline and had had no Gallic ambition to see their country win military glory for its own sake. They had been martial in the sense that, till the date of the closing of the frontier *circa* A.D. 1890, they had always numbered among them a contingent of frontiersmen who were accustomed, not only to bearing arms, but to using them at their own discretion in pursuit of their own private enterprises—a state of affairs that, by then, had long since been obsolete in the greater part of Western Europe. The martial spirit of ten generations of American frontiersmen would have been acknowledged by the North American Indians at any time since the first landing of White men from the British Isles on American coasts; by the English colonists' French rivals in the eighteenth century; and by their Mexican victims in the nineteenth century; and these encounters between the Anglo-American frontiersmen and their competitors for the possession of North America were also evidence that not only the frontiersmen, but the American people as a whole, were prepared, exceptionally and temporarily, to submit themselves to a military discipline without which the frontiersmen's personal spirit and prowess would have been unable to prevail against antagonists of their own cultural level.

The soldierly qualities latent in the American people as a whole had been revealed to their German adversaries in the German-American wars of 1917–18 and 1941–5; but the most impressive demonstration of American valour, discipline, generalship, and endurance had been given in a war in which Americans had been arrayed against Americans. The War of A.D. 1861–5 between the Union and the Confederacy had been the longest, the most stubborn, the costliest in casualties, and the most fertile in technological innovations of all wars waged in the Western world between the fall of Napoleon and the outbreak of the First World War. Moreover the two world wars that, within living memory, had harrowed Germany and Germany's Russian and West European victims as severely as the American Civil War had harrowed the South, had left the United States virtually unscathed. The psychological effects that two world wars in one lifetime had produced on the *moral* of West Europeans had hardly made themselves felt on the American side of the Atlantic; and in A.D. 1956 it could not be doubted that the American people would indeed be prepared to face the terrors of a war with the Soviet Union rather than make any concession to the Soviet Union that, in American eyes, would be tantamount to submission to a Russian ascendancy.

But the foregoing historical evidence, suggesting the likelihood of a will to war in certain circumstances on the part of the American and the Russian people, has to be estimated in the light of the developments of atomic warfare and of the psychological effect of these developments—an effect which, under mid-twentieth-century conditions, would not lag very far behind the technological developments themselves. To die for a country or a cause becomes a gratuitous and meaningless act of heroism if it has become demonstrably certain that the country will perish together with the patriot, and the cause together with the devotee, in one all-comprehending catastrophe.

(2) TOWARDS A FUTURE WORLD ORDER

By A.D. 1955 the abolition of War had, in fact, become imperative; but it could not be abolished unless the control of atomic energy could be concentrated in the hands of some single political authority. This monopoly of the command of the master weapon of the age would enable, and indeed compel, the authority to assume the role of a World Government. The effective seat of this Government, in the conditions of A.D. 1955, must be either Washington or Moscow; but neither the United States nor the Soviet Union was prepared to place itself at the mercy of the other.

In this awkward pass the traditional line of least psychological resistance would, no doubt, have been to resort to the old-fashioned expedient of ordeal by battle. A 'knock-out blow' had, as we have already seen, been the brutal means by which one broken-down civilization after another had passed out of its Time of Troubles into its universal state. But on this occasion the knock-out blow might knock out not only the antagonist but also the victor, the referee, the boxing-ring, and all the spectators.

In these circumstances the best hope for the future of Mankind lay in the possibility that the governments and peoples of the United States and the Soviet Union might have the patience to pursue a policy which had come to be called 'peaceful co-existence'. The greatest menace to the welfare and, indeed, to the continued existence of the Human Race was not the invention of atomic weapons but the rise in living human souls of a temper such as had once prevailed in an Early Modern Western world for about a hundred years beginning with the outbreak of the Western Wars of Religion *circa* A.D. 1560. At the opening of the second half of the twentieth century there were Capitalists and Communists who, like their Catholic and Protestant forerunners, felt it to be impracticable as well as intolerable to acquiesce in leaving the allegiance of Society divided for an indefinite time to come between the true faith (their own) and a damnable heresy (their adversary's). But the history of the Western Wars of Religion bore witness that spiritual issues could not be settled by force of arms; and Mankind's acquisition of atomic weapons gave warning that it would not be open to Capitalists and Communists to learn the futility of religious warfare by the empirical method of prolonged trial that had been practicable for Catholics and Protestants in an age in which Man's worst weapons had been swords, pikes, and muzzle-loading guns.

In circumstances so precarious and obscure, a dogmatic optimism was as unwarrantable as a dogmatic pessimism; and the living generation of Mankind had no choice but to reconcile itself, as best it could, to the knowledge that it was facing issues in which its very existence might be at stake, and that it was impossible to guess what the outcome was going to be. In A.D. 1955 these perennial waifs on board Noah's Ark were in the situation in which Thor Heyerdahl and his five fellow vikings on board a balsa-log raft had found themselves on the morning of the 7th August, 1947. On that fateful morning the westward-flowing current that had borne the raft *Kon-Tiki* 4,300 miles across the Pacific Ocean was now carrying her towards the Raroia Reef. Beyond the line of surf breaking over this barrier the approaching seafarers could descry the feathery tops of palm-trees, and they knew that these palms bedecked idyllic isles set in a still lagoon; but between them and this haven ran the foaming and thundering reef 'in one line from horizon to horizon',[1] and the set of the current and the wind gave the voyagers no chance of circumnavigation. They were heading perforce towards an inevitable ordeal; and, though they might know what were the alternatives awaiting any voyagers in this plight, they could not guess which of these alternatives was to be the ending of their own saga.

If the raft were to disintegrate among the breakers, the crew would be torn in pieces by the knife-edged coral, unless they were saved by speedy drowning from that more painful death. If the raft were to hold together, and if its crew were to succeed in holding on to it until the breakers had defeated their own malice by washing the raft on to the reef high and dry, a shipwrecked crew might swim across the still lagoon beyond and reach one of the palm-crowned islands alive. If the moment of the raft's arrival at the reef should happen to coincide with the flood of one of those high tides that periodically submerged the reef to a depth that compelled the breakers to subside, the *Kon-Tiki* might, after all, clear the death-line in calm water, and so come through unscathed. In the event, a high tide did flow in to lift her battered frame off the reef into the lagoon some days after the surf had cast her up on to a bare coral scree; but on the morning of the 7th August, 1947, no man on board the *Kon-Tiki* could tell which of these alternative destinies was going to be his.

The experience of these six young Scandinavian seafarers on that day was an apt allegory of an ordeal that still lay ahead of

[1] Heyerdahl, Thor: *Kon-Tiki* (Chicago 1950, Rand McNally), p. 242.

Mankind at the opening of the second half of the twentieth century of the Christian Era. An Ark of Civilization that had travelled a time-distance of some five or six thousand years across the ocean of History was making for a reef which its crew would not be able to circumnavigate. This unavoidable danger ahead was the perilous transition between a World partitioned into an American and a Russian sphere and a World united under the control of a single political authority which, in an age of atomic weapons, must supersede the present division of authority sooner or later in one way or another. Was the transition to be pacific or catastrophic, and, if catastrophic, was the catastrophe to be complete and irremediable, or would it be partial and leave behind it elements out of which a slow and painful recovery might ultimately be achieved? At the time when these words were being written no one could foreknow the outcome of the ordeal towards which the World was manifestly moving.

Without waiting, however, for a facile wisdom after the event, an observer might perhaps usefully speculate on the shape of things to come, so long as he confined his consideration of a future world order to elements which an œcumenical dispensation seemed likely to have in common with each of the two demi-mundane dispensations that had been crystallizing respectively round the United States and round the Soviet Union.

In so far as technology could, and did, supply facilities for transport, World Government was already a quite practicable proposition. As soon, however, as we ascend—or descend—from the plane of technology to the plane of human nature, we find the earthly paradise skilfully assembled by the ingenuity of *Homo Faber* being reduced to a fool's paradise by the perversity of *Homo Politicus*. The 'Parliament of Man', whose inauguration the prophet Tennyson seemed to have synchronized approximately with the invention of the aeroplane, was now in being under the more prosaic name of the United Nations Organization; and U.N.O. had not proved as ineffective as its critics sometimes asserted. On the other hand, U.N.O. was evidently incapable of becoming the embryo of a world government. The realities of the distribution of power were not reflected in the clumsiness of a constitution that had embodied the unrealistic principle of 'one state, one vote', and had then found no better means of bringing a fictitious equality of states into line with a harsh reality than the concession to five Powers, one of whom had since been reduced from China to Formosa, of a veto that was denied to their nominal peers. The best prospect in sight for the U.N.O. was that it might evolve from being a forum into becoming a confederacy; but there is a great gulf between any confederacy of independent states and any confederation of peoples with a central government claiming and receiving the direct personal allegiance of every individual citizen of the union; and it was notorious that the history of political institutions knew of no case in which that gulf had been crossed by any other process than a revolutionary leap.

On this showing, U.N.O. seemed unlikely to be the institutional nucleus out of which an eventually inevitable world government would grow. The probability seemed to be that this would take shape through the development, not of U.N.O., but of one or other of two older and tougher political 'going concerns', the Government of the United States or the Government of the Soviet Union.

If the living generation of Mankind had been free to choose between them, there could be little doubt in any Western observer's mind that a decisive majority of all living men and women that were competent to form any judgement on this issue would have opted for becoming subjects of the United States rather than of the Soviet Union. The virtues that made the United States incomparably preferable stood out conspicuously against a Communist Russian foil.

America's cardinal virtue in the eyes of her present and prospective subjects was her transparently sincere reluctance to be drawn into playing this role at all. An appreciable portion of the living generation of American citizens, as well as the ancestors of all American citizens who were not themselves immigrants, had been moved to pluck up their roots in the Old World and to start life again in the New World by a yearning to extricate themselves from the affairs of a continent whose dust they had demonstratively shaken from off their feet; and the buoyancy of the hope with which they had made their withdrawal was matched by the poignancy of the regret with which the living generation of Americans was making its compulsory return. The compulsion was, as we have seen, an aspect of that 'annihilation of distance' which was making the Old and the New World one and indivisible. But the ever-increasing clearness with which this compulsion was being recognized was not diminishing the reluctance with which it was being accepted.

The Americans' second outstanding virtue was their generosity. Both the United States and the Soviet Union were 'sated' Powers, but their economic and social situations were identical only in the general sense that Russia, like America, commanded vast undeveloped resources. In contrast to America, Russia had hardly begun to exploit her potentialities, and the development that she had carried out, at such a cost in human effort and suffering, during the twelve years immediately preceding the German assault upon her in A.D. 1941, had been largely ruined by the invasion. Thereafter the Russians had taken an unjust advantage of finding themselves on the winning side by recouping themselves for a German destruction of Russian industrial plant by seizing and removing plant, not only from a guilty Germany, but also from East and Central European countries that the Russians professed to be liberating from the Nazis, and from Chinese provinces in Manchuria that they professed to be liberating from the Japanese. This was a contrast indeed to the American post-war reconstruction policy, implemented in the Marshall Plan and other measures, in which a number of countries, whose life had been disorganized by the war, were set on their feet again with the help of money voted by the Congress at Washington with the goodwill of the American taxpayer, out of whose pockets all this money had to come. In the past it had been customary for victorious Powers, not to give, but to take, and there had been no departure from this evil custom in the policy of the Soviet Union. The Marshall Plan set a new standard for which there was no comparable historical precedent. It might be said that this generous policy was in America's own interests, on a long and enlightened view; but good deeds are not the less good for being, at the same time, wise.

Citizens of West European countries were, however, now haunted by fears that some American decision, in which the West European peoples might have had no say, might bring Russian atomic weapons down upon their heads as unintended by-products of some impulsive American retort to Russian provocation. Though the satellite states of the American Union enjoyed, in most respects, an enviable freedom of action that was entirely denied to the satellites of the Soviet Union, they did find themselves in much the same helpless plight in these matters of life and death.

In A.D. 1895, in connexion with an Anglo-American dispute about the location of the frontier between British Guiana and Venezuela, an American Secretary of State, Richard Olney, had issued a resonant dispatch which had secured for his name such immortality as it still enjoyed.

'To-day the United States is practically sovereign on this continent, and its fiat is law upon the subjects to which it confines its interposition. Why? It is not because of the pure friendship or good will felt for it. It is not simply by reason of its high character as a civilized state, nor because wisdom and justice and equity are the invariable characteristics of the dealings of the United States. It is because, in addition to all other grounds, its infinite resources, combined with its isolated position, render it master of the situation and practically invulnerable as against any or all other Powers.'

This dictum had not lost any of its cogency in coming to be applicable to a far wider sphere of hegemony than Latin America alone, and, though a non-American might resign himself to the fact that American whips were preferable to Russian scorpions, a 'philosopher' might (in Gibbonian parlance) 'be permitted to enlarge his views' by observing that the virtual monopoly, by a paramount Power, of the determination and execution of policies in which the lives and fortunes of satellite peoples were at stake, was pregnant with a constitutional problem which could be solved only by some form of federal union. The constitutional issues raised by the advent of a supernational order were not likely to be settled easily or rapidly, but at least it was a good omen that the United States was already committed by its own history to an approval of the federal principle.

XLIII. TECHNOLOGY, CLASS-CONFLICT, AND EMPLOYMENT

(1) THE NATURE OF THE PROBLEM

IF the meaning of the word employment may be stretched to cover not only the amount and distribution of work and leisure but also the spirit in which the work is done and the use to which the leisure is put, it would be true to say that the impact of an unprecedentedly potent Western technique on a world-wide Westernizing society that was still articulated into a number of separate classes with widely different standards of living had confronted the heirs of the Western civilization with a problem of employment comparable to the problem of government discussed in the preceding chapter.

Like the problem of government, the problem of employment was nothing new in itself; for, if the primary cause of the break-downs and disintegrations of other civilizations had been a failure to get rid of war by a voluntary and timely expansion of the scope of government from a parochial to an œcumenical range, a secondary cause had been a failure to get rid of class-conflict by voluntary and timely changes in the pressure and product of work and in the enjoyment and use of leisure. In this field, however, as in that, the difference in degree between a latter-day Western and any previous human mastery over non-human Nature was tantamount to a difference in kind. By putting an unprecedentedly powerful new drive into economic production, modern technology had made a customary social injustice seem remediable and therefore feel intolerable. When the newfangled cornucopia of mechanized industry had churned out fabulous wealth for those Western *entrepreneurs* who had sown the seed and reaped the harvest of the Industrial Revolution, why should wealth and leisure still be monopolized by a privileged minority? Why should not this new-found abundance be shared between the Western capitalists and the Western industrial workers, and between the Western industrial workers and an Asian, African, and Indian-American peasantry that had been herded *en masse* into a world-embracing Western society's internal proletariat?

This new dream of the possibility of abundance for all Mankind had generated unprecedentedly insistent and impatient demands for 'freedom from want'; the ubiquity of these demands raised the question whether the productivity of the cornucopia was really as inexhaustible as it was assumed to be; and this question could only be answered by solving an equation in which there were at least three unknown quantities.

The first of these unknown quantities was the extent of technology's potential capacity to satisfy the rising demands of a Human Race which was continuing to multiply and beginning to demand leisure. What were the planet's reserves of irreplaceable material resources in the shape of minerals, and of replaceable material resources in the shape of water-power and crops and livestock and manpower and human skill? How far could the resources so far tapped be made to increase their yield, and how far could Mankind's wasting assets be offset by the tapping of alternative resources hitherto unexploited?

The current findings of Western science seemed to suggest that the capacity of technology was enormous; but at the same time the contemporary reactions of human nature made it evident that there might prove to be practical limitations, on the human plane, to a productivity which might be virtually infinite in abstract terms of technological potentiality. A production that might be technically possible could not be translated into reality unless and until human hands could be found to pull the levers; but the price of this immense potential enhancement of the power over non-human Nature was a proportionate number of turns of the screw in the regimentation of the workers; and their inevitable resistance to such encroachments on their personal freedom was bound to militate against the realization of what was technologically feasible.

What was the extent of the sacrifices of personal freedom that the workers would be prepared to make for the sake of increasing the size of the cake of which they were each demanding a larger slice? How far would the urban industrial workers go in submitting to 'scientific management'? And how far would the primitive peasant majority of Mankind go in adopting Western scientific methods of agriculture and in accepting limitations on a traditionally sacrosanct right and duty of procreation? At this stage the most that could be said was that the potential capacity of technology to increase production was running a race with the natural human refractoriness of the industrial workers and of the peasants. The World's teeming peasantry was threatening to cancel the benefits of technological progress by continuing to raise the numbers of the World's population *pari passu* with each successive increase in the means of subsistence. At the same time the industrial workers were threatening to cancel the benefits of technological progress by limiting production through trades-union restrictive practices *pari passu* with each successive increase in the potentialities of productivity.

(2) MECHANIZATION AND PRIVATE
ENTERPRISE

The outstanding feature on the economic-social plane was the tug-of-war between a regimentation imposed by mechanized industry and an obstinate human reluctance to be regimented. The crux of the situation was the fact that mechanization and police were unfortunately inseparable. An observer might find his impressions affected by the light in which he happened to view the scene. From a technician's angle of vision the recalcitrant industrial workers' attitude might appear childishly unreasonable. Were these people really unaware that every desirable object had its price? Did they think that they could have 'freedom from want' without submitting to the conditions which must be fulfilled before their wants could be satisfied? But an historian might see the spectacle with different eyes. He would recall that the Industrial Revolution had started in an eighteenth-century Britain, at a time and in a place where an exceptionally high degree of freedom from regimentation had been enjoyed by a minority, and that members of this minority had been the creators of the system of mechanized production. The pre-industrial freedom of enterprise which these pioneers of industrialism had inherited from a previous social dispensation had been the inspiration and life-blood of the new dispensation that their initiative had conjured into existence.

Moreover, the industrial *entrepreneur's* pre-industrial spirit of freedom, which had been the mainspring of the Industrial Revolution, had continued to be its driving-force in the next chapter of the story. While, however, the captains of industry had thus continued, for a season, to elude the fate of being crushed by a steamroller of their own manufacture, this fate was the birthmark of the new urban industrial working class, who had felt from the outset the crushing effects upon human life of a triumphal technology's success in mastering non-human Nature. In a previous context we have watched technology liberating Man from the tyrannies of the day-and-night cycle and the cycle of the seasons; but, in the act of setting him free from these ancient servitudes, it had enslaved him to a new one.

The trades-union organizations that were the new industrial working class's characteristic contributions to the new structure of Society were, indeed, legacies from the same pre-industrial paradise of private enterprise that had bred the captains of industry. Looked at as instruments for enabling the workers to hold their own in their struggle with their employers, they were, in fact, creatures of the self-same social dispensation as their capitalist antagonists. Evidence of this community of êthos may be found in the fact that in a Communist Russia the liquidation of the private employers had been followed by the regimentation of the trades-unions, while in National-Socialist Germany the liquidation of the trades-unions had been followed by the regimentation of the private employers. In Great Britain, on the other hand, after the general election of A.D. 1945, under a Labour Government whose programme was to take the ownership of industrial enterprises out of private hands without interfering with personal freedom, the workers in the nationalized industries had never thought of dissolving their trades-unions or of renouncing their right to promote their members' interests by means of all the devices which they had employed against the dispossessed private 'profiteers'; and this course of action could not be disposed of by being declared illogical; for the purpose of trades-unions was to resist regimentation, whether imposed by a private capitalist or by a National Board.

Unfortunately the workers' resistance to regimentation at the hands of an employer had driven them into regimenting themselves. In fighting against the fate of being turned into robots in the factory they had imposed upon themselves the fate of serving as robots in the trades-union, and from this fate there seemed to be no escape. Nor was there any consolation in the fact that their old-time and familiar enemy, the private *entrepreneur*, was himself now being regimented and robotized out of existence. The adversary was no longer a comprehensible human tyrant whose eyes could be damned and whose windows could be broken when tempers were roused. The workers' ultimate adversary was an impersonal collective power that was both more potent and more elusive than any execrable and consequently identifiable human being.

If this abiding self-regimentation of the industrial workers was a gloomy portent, it was also an awe-inspiring spectacle to see the Western middle class beginning to take the road which the Western industrial working class had long been following. The century ending in A.D. 1914 had been the Western middle class's golden age; but the new era had seen this class fall, in their turn, into the adversity to which the Industrial Revolution had condemned the industrial workers. The liquidation of the *bourgeoisie* in Soviet Russia had been a sensational portent; but a more accurate index of what was coming was to be found in the contemporary social histories of Great Britain and other English-speaking countries which had suffered no political revolutions.

During the period between the Industrial Revolution and the outbreak of the First World War the distinguishing psychological characteristic of the Western middle class, in contrast with the 'working' class, both manual and clerical, had been its appetite for work. In the citadel of Capitalism on Manhattan Island there had been a trivial yet significant illustration of this difference of attitude as recently as A.D. 1949. In that year the financial houses on Wall Street were trying, without success, to induce their shorthand-typists, by offers of special remuneration at high overtime rates, to reconsider a collective decision to refuse henceforth to attend at their offices on Saturday mornings. The shorthand-typists' employers were eager to devote their own Saturday mornings to work for the sake of retaining the profits that they would forfeit if they were to submit to this shortening of their own working week; but they had ceased to be able to do their own work without having shorthand-typists in attendance to assist them, and they found themselves unable to persuade these indispensable collaborators in their business of money-making that the game of working on Saturdays was worth the candle. The shorthand-typists took the stand that one day's, or even one half-day's, additional leisure was worth more to them than any monetary inducement for withdrawing their demand for this amenity. Additional money in their pockets was of no use to them if they had to earn it at the price of foregoing the additional leisure without which they would have no time for spending it. In this choice between money and life, they opted for life at the cost of letting the money go, and their employers did not succeed in persuading them to change their minds. By A.D. 1956 it had begun to look as if, so far from the Wall Street shorthand-typists ever being brought round by a monetary inducement to the Wall Street financiers' point of view, the financiers might eventually be converted by economic adversity to the standpoint of the typists; for by this date even Wall Street was beginning to feel a breeze that had already chilled once-sanguine hearts in Lombard Street.

In the twentieth century of the Christian Era the Western middle class's opportunities for doing profitable business were being progressively reduced in one Western centre of capitalist activity after another; and these economic reverses were having depressing effects on the middle-class êthos. This class's traditional zest for work was being sapped by a progressive restriction of the field for private enterprise. Inflation and taxation were making nonsense of its traditional virtues of strenuous earning and thrifty saving. The rising cost of living was conspiring with a simultaneously rising standard of living to reduce the size of its families. The loss of personal domestic service was threatening to undermine its professional efficiency. The loss of leisure was threatening to undermine its culture. Moreover, the middle-class woman—the mother on whom, as scores of biographies showed, the maintenance of high middle-class standards chiefly depended—was being harder hit than the middle-class man.

The progressive exodus of the middle class out of private enterprise into public service or into its psychological equivalent in the service of great non-governmental corporations had been bringing with it gains as well as losses for the Western society. The principal gain was the subordination of the egoistic profit-motive to the altruistic motive of public service, and the social value of this change could be measured by the effects of corresponding changes in the histories of other civilizations. In the histories of the Hellenic, Sinic, and Hindu civilizations, for example, the social rallies inaugurated by the establishment of universal states had been signalized and achieved in large part by the redirection of a hitherto predatory class's abilities to public service. Augustus and his successors had made good civil servants out of predatory Roman business men; Han Liu Pang and his successors had made them out of predatory feudal gentry; Cornwallis and his successors had made them out of predatory commercial agents of the British East India Company. Yet, in each case, though in different ways, the results had revealed characteristic weaknesses, and the ultimate failure was to be explained by the ambivalence of a civil-service êthos, in which the sovereign virtue of integrity was counterbalanced by a lack of zest and by a disinclination to take the initiative or to incur risks. These characteristics were now being displayed by the general run of twentieth-century Western middleclass civil servants, and this did not augur well for their prospects in grappling successfully with the enormous task that would sooner or later confront them, the task of organizing and maintaining a world government.

When we look into the causes of this civil-service êthos, we find that it was the response to the challenge of pressure exerted by a machine which bore no less hardly upon human souls for being constructed out of psychic instead of metallic materials. To tend the machinery of a highly organized state, administering many millions of subjects, was as soul-destroying a task as the performance of any typical set of scientifically managed physical movements in a factory. Red tape, in fact, could prove more constrictive than iron; and red tape had now entered into the civil servant's soul, while the part played by formalities and routine in an overworked civil service was being played by an increasingly rigid and disciplinary party-system in overworked elected legislatures.

The significance of all these tendencies for the prospects of the current 'capitalist' system was not difficult to gauge. The Western middle class's fund of pre-industrial psychic energy had been Capitalism's driving-force. If this energy was now being depotentiated, and was at the same time being diverted from private enterprise into public service, this process spelled Capitalism's doom.

'Capitalism is essentially a process of economic change. . . . Without innovations, no entrepreneurs; without entrepreneurial achievement, no capitalist returns and no capitalist propulsion. The atmosphere of industrial revolutions—of "progress"—is the only one in which Capitalism can survive. . . . Stabilised Capitalism is a contradiction in terms.'[1]

It looked as if the regimentation imposed by industrial technology might be taking the life out of the pre-industrial spirit of private enterprise; and this prospect opened up a further question. Would the technical system of mechanized industry be able to survive the social system of private enterprise? And, if not, would the Western civilization itself be able to survive the death of a mechanized industry, to which it had given hostages by allowing its population to increase in the Machine Age far beyond the numbers that any non-industrial economy could support?

It was indisputable that the industrial system could only work so long as there was some fund of creative psychic energy to drive it, and that hitherto this driving-power had been supplied by the middle class. The ultimate question therefore seemed to be whether there was some alternative source of psychic energy, employable for the same economic purposes, on which a Westernizing world could draw, if the middle-class's energy were to be depotentiated or diverted. If a practical alternative was within reach, the World could afford to look forward with equanimity to the demise of the capitalist system. But, if there was no such alternative, then the outlook was disconcerting. If mechanization spelled regimentation, and if this regimentation had taken the spirit out of an industrial working class and out of a middle class in succession, was it possible for any human hands to handle the almighty machine with impunity?

(3) ALTERNATIVE APPROACHES TO SOCIAL HARMONY

The social problem confronting Mankind was being approached from different angles in different countries. One approach was

[1] Schumpeter, J. A.: *Business Cycles* (New York 1939, McGraw-Hill, 2 vols.), vol. ii, p. 1033.

being made in North America, another in the Soviet Union, and a third in Western Europe.

The North American approach was inspired by the ideal of creating an Earthly Paradise in a New World, and this Earthly Paradise was to be based on a system of private enterprise which the North Americans (including within this term the English-speaking Canadians. as well as the people of the United States) believed that they could maintain in perfect health, whatever its fate elsewhere, by raising the economic and social standards of the wage-earning classes to a middle-class level, and thus counteracting what we have described in the previous section as the natural psychological effects of industrial mechanization. It was an inspiring but perhaps a too simple faith, based, as it was, on a number of illusions, all of which could be reduced to the fundamental illusion of isolationism. The New World was not as 'New' as its admirers could have wished. Human nature, which included Original Sin, had crossed the Atlantic with the first immigrants and with all their successors. Even in the nineteenth century, when isolationism seemed feasible on the political plane, this Earthly Paradise contained an abundance of snakes, and, as the twentieth century advanced and darkened, it became more and more apparent that the duality of worlds, New and Old, was a theory which did not fit the facts. The Human Race was now 'all in the same boat'; and a philosophy of life which was not applicable to the whole of it might not be applicable to any part of it in the long run.

The Russian approach to the problem of class-conflict was inspired, like the American, by the ideal of creating an Earthly Paradise, and had taken shape, like the American, in a policy of getting rid of class-conflict by eliminating class divisions; but here the likeness ended. While the Americans were trying to assimilate the industrial working class to the middle class, the Russians had liquidated the middle class and had banned all freedom of private enterprise, not only for capitalists but also for trades-unions.

In the Communist Russian policy there were strong points which the Soviet Union's Western rivals could not afford to underrate; and the first and greatest of these assets was the êthos of Communism itself. In the long run this ideology might prove an unsatisfying substitute for Religion, but in the short run it offered to any soul whose house was empty, swept, and garnished an immediate satisfaction for one of the deepest of Man's religious needs, by offering him a purpose transcending his petty personal aims. The mission of converting the World to Communism was more exhilarating than the mission of keeping the World safe for the right to take profits or for the right to strike. 'Holy Russia' was a more rousing war-cry than 'Happy America'.

Another strong point in the Russian approach was that Russia's geographical position made it impossible for Russians to entertain the delusion of isolationism. Russia had no 'natural frontiers'. Moreover Marxism, as preached from the Kremlin, made a potent appeal to the World's peasantry from China to Peru, and from Mexico to Tropical Africa. In her social and economic situation, Russia had a much closer affinity than had the United States with the depressed three-quarters of the Human Race for whose allegiance the two Powers were competing. Russia could claim, with a specious appearance of veracity, that she had saved herself by her exertions and would save the rest of the world-proletariat by her example. A part of this proletariat was resident within the United States itself; and the anxiety of certain sections of anti-Communist Americans about the potency of this Marxian appeal was unconcealed and, in some of its manifestations, hysterical.

The West European approach towards the solution of the problem of class conflict—an approach which was most in evidence in Great Britain and in the Scandinavian countries—differed from the American and the Russian in being less doctrinaire than either of them. In countries that were in process of losing power and wealth to the rising giants on the fringes of the Western world at the very time when their local industrial workers were demanding a 'new deal', it was manifestly impracticable for the West European middle class to follow the North American middle class in offering to the working class, with both hands, the two amenities of a middle-class standard of living and an abundance of opportunities for the gratification of personal ambitions. It would have been still more impracticable to offer to the West European working class the strait-waistcoat of a totalitarian régime. Accordingly, the current Anglo-Scandinavian approach was an attempt to find a middle way by experimenting in a combination of private enterprise with governmental regimentation in the interests of social justice. It was a policy that was often identified with 'socialism', a term which was laudatory in the mouths of its British admirers, whereas it was depreciatory in the mouths of its American critics. So far as the British 'welfare state' system was concerned, it had been built up piecemeal and undogmatically by legislative contributions from all political parties.

(4) POSSIBLE COSTS OF SOCIAL JUSTICE

Social life is impossible for Man without some measure of both personal liberty and social justice. Personal liberty is an indispensable condition for any human achievement, good or evil, while social justice is the sovereign rule of the game of human intercourse. An uncurbed personal liberty drives the weakest to the wall, and social justice cannot be enforced up to the hilt without the suppression of the liberty without which human nature cannot be creative. All known social constitutions had been pitched somewhere between these two theoretical extremes. In the working constitutions of both the Soviet Union and the United States, for example, elements of personal liberty and of social justice were combined in diverse ratios; and in the mid-twentieth-century Westernizing world the mixture, whatever it might be, was invariably labelled 'Democracy', because this term, disinterred from the Hellenic political vocabulary—where it had often been used in a pejorative sense—had now come to be an obligatory shibboleth for every self-respecting political alchemist.

Thus used, the term 'Democracy' was simply a smoke-screen to conceal the real conflict between the ideals of Liberty and Equality. The only genuine reconciliation between these conflicting ideals was to be found in the mediating ideal of Fraternity; and, if Man's social salvation depended on his prospects of translating this higher ideal into reality, he would find that the politicians' ingenuity did not carry him far, since the achievement of Fraternity was beyond the reach of human beings so long as they trusted exclusively to their own powers. The Brotherhood of Man stemmed from the Fatherhood of God.

In the trembling balance in which personal liberty and social justice were being weighed against one another, the spanner of technology had been thrown into the anti-libertarian scale. This finding could be illustrated and supported by taking an observation of a coming state of society which was already within sight, though it might not yet be within reach. Let it be assumed, for the sake of the argument, that an almighty technology has already accomplished the next major tasks on its agenda. By thrusting an atomic bomb into Man's hands it will have forced him to abolish war, and at the same time it will have enabled him to reduce the death-rate to an unprecedentedly low minimum by bestowing impartially on all classes and on all races the benefits of preventive medicine. Let it also be assumed—as was, indeed, probable—that these prodigious improvements in the material conditions of life have been carried out at a speed with which cultural changes have failed to keep pace. These assumptions require us to imagine that the peasant three-quarters of Mankind will not yet have lost their habit of reproducing their kind up to the limits of their means of subsistence; and this assumption in turn requires us to imagine them still to be expending on increases in their head of population all the additional means of subsistence that will have been placed in their hands by the establishment of a World Order that will have brought in its train the benefits of peace, police, hygiene, and the application of science to the production of food.

Such prognostications would not be fantastic; they would merely be projections, into the future, of tendencies long current. In China, for example, increases in population had swallowed up increases in the means of subsistence which had been bestowed by the introduction of previously unknown food crops from the Americas in the sixteenth century and by the establishment, in the seventeenth century, of the *Pax Manchuana*. Thanks to the naturalization of maize in China *circa* A.D. 1550, of sweet potatoes *circa* A.D. 1590, and of pea-nuts a few years later, the population had risen from 63,599,541 indicated by the census returns of A.D. 1578 to an estimated figure of 108,300,000 in A.D. 1661. Thereafter it had risen further, to 143,411,559 in A.D. 1741, to a figure of the order of 300,000,000 in the middle of the nineteenth century, and to one of the order of 600,000,000 in the middle of the twentieth century. These figures show not only an increase but an increase in an accelerating geometrical progression—and this in spite of recurrent bouts of plague, pestilence, and famine, battle, murder, and sudden death. The figures of the contemporary movement of population in India, Indonesia, and elsewhere told the same tale.

If such things had been happening yesterday, what was to be expected tomorrow? Though the cornucopia of science had produced an abundance that had falsified Malthusian pessimism up to date, the insuperable finiteness of the area of the Earth's surface must set a ceiling to the progressive increase of Mankind's food-supply; and it seemed as likely as not that this ceiling would be reached some time before the peasantry's habit of breeding up to the limit would have been overcome.

In thus forecasting a posthumous fulfilment of Malthus's expectations, we should also have to forecast that, by the time of 'the great famine', some œcumenical authority would have made itself responsible for looking after the elementary material needs of the whole population of the planet. In such a state of affairs the begetting of children would have ceased to be the private affair of wives and husbands and have become the public concern of a ubiquitous impersonal disciplinary power. The nearest that governments had come hitherto towards intruding on this inner sanctum of private life had been to institute negative or positive rewards for the parents of unusually large families if the authorities were anxious to obtain an increase of manpower for 'labour' or for 'cannon-fodder'; but they had no more dreamed of forbidding their subjects to restrict the size of their families than they had dreamed of compelling them to multiply. Indeed, the freedom to beget or not to beget had been so heedlessly taken for granted that, even as late as A.D. 1941, it had not occurred to President Roosevelt to raise the number of axiomatic human freedoms consecrated in his Atlantic Charter from four to five by explicitly putting on record the sacred right of parents to determine the size of their own families. It now looked as if the future might show that there had been an unintentional logic in Roosevelt's artless silence on this point, since it appeared that, in the last resort, a novel 'freedom from want' could not be guaranteed to Mankind unless a familiar 'freedom to beget' were taken away from them. The problem of how this was to be done raised some very delicate questions.

If the time were indeed to come when the begetting of children would have to be regulated by an external authority, how was this curtailment of personal liberty likely to be received, on the one hand by the peasant majority of Mankind, and on the other hand by a minority whom an industrial technology had already emancipated from the peasant's bondage to an unquestioned custom? The controversy between these two sections of the Human Race was likely to be bitter, since each would have a grievance against the other. The industrial workers would resent the assumption that it was morally incumbent on them to provide sustenance for an unrestricted increase in the number of peasant mouths. The peasantry, on their side, would feel aggrieved at being threatened with the loss of their traditional freedom to reproduce their kind on the plea that this was the only alternative to starvation; for this sacrifice would be demanded of them at a time when the gulf between their own pauper standard of living and that of the industrial workers in Western or Westernized countries would probably have become greater than it had ever been before.

A progressive widening of this gulf was, in truth, one of the consequences that must be expected, if we are right in forecasting that, at the time when global food production would be reaching its ceiling, the peasantry would still be expending most of its additional supply of commodities on increasing its numbers, and the industrialized workers expending most of theirs on raising their standard of living. In this situation the peasantry would not see why, before they were called upon to renounce the most sacred of human rights, the affluent minority should not be called upon to part with a larger quota of their provocative superfluities. Such a demand would strike a sophisticated Western élite as preposterously unreasonable. Why should a Western or Westernized élite, which owed its prosperity to its intelligence and foresight, be penalized to pay for the peasantry's improvident incontinence? This demand would seem the more unreasonable, considering that a sacrifice of Western standards would not exorcize the spectre of world-wide famine but would merely keep it at bay for an inconsiderable period, during which the sacrifice would be reducing the most advanced peoples to the level of the laggards.

So harsh a reaction as this would be of no help towards solving the problem; and, indeed, it could be foreseen that, if such a food crisis as we have forecast were eventually to occur, the predominant reaction of Western Man would not be along these unsympathetic lines. Cool calculations of enlightened self-interest, a humane desire to alleviate suffering, and a sense of moral obligation that would be the surviving spiritual legacy of a dogmatically discarded Christianity—a combination of motives that was already inspiring a number of international efforts to raise standards of living in Asian and African countries—would impel Western Man to play the part of the Good Samaritan rather than that of the Priest or the Levite.

If and when this controversy broke out, it seemed likely to be carried from the plane of economics and politics on to the plane of religion, and this on several accounts. In the first place, the peasantry's persistence in breeding up to the limits of its food supply was the social effect of a religious cause which could not be modified without a change in the peasantry's religious attitude and outlook. The religious outlook which made the peasantry's breeding habits so resistant to argument might not have been irrational in origin, for it was a survival from a primitive state of society in which the household had been the optimum social and economic unit of agricultural production. A mechanized technology had now done away with the social and economic environment in which the worship of family fecundity had made economic and social sense; but the persistence of the cult when there was no longer any sense left in it was a consequence of the relative slowness of the Psyche's pace on the subconscious level in comparison with the pace of the intellect and the will.

Without a religious revolution in the souls of the peasantry, it was hard to see how the World's Malthusian problem was to be solved; but the peasantry was not the only party to the situation that would have to achieve a change of heart if Mankind was to find a happy issue out of an impending catastrophe. For, if it was true that 'Man doth not live by bread alone', then a complacently prosperous Western minority had something to learn from an unworldly vein in the êthos of the peasantry.

Western Man had brought himself into danger of losing his soul through his concentration on a sensationally successful endeavour to increase his material well-being. If he was to find salvation, he would find it only in sharing the results of his material achievement with the less materially successful majority of the Human Race. The birth-controlling agnostic engineer had as much to learn from the incontinent and superstitious peasant as the peasant from the engineer. What part the World's historic higher religions might be destined to play in enlightening both parties and bringing them to a mutual understanding was a question that could not be answered yet.

(5) LIVING HAPPY EVER AFTER?

If we could imagine a World Society in which Mankind had first rid itself of war and class-conflict and had gone on to solve the population problem, we might surmise that Mankind's next problem would be the role of leisure in the life of a mechanized society.

Leisure had already played a part of capital importance in history; for, if necessity had been the mother of Civilization, leisure had been its nurse. One of the distinctive features of Civilization had been the pace at which this new way of life had developed its potentialities; and this impetus had been imparted to the civilizations by a minority of a minority—by the purposeful few among a privileged class, whose privilege had been the enjoyment of leisure. All the great achievements of Man in the arts and sciences had been the fruits of the profitably employed leisure of this creative minority. But the Industrial Revolution had upset—and this in several different ways—the previous relation between leisure and life.

The most momentous of these changes had been psychological. Mechanization had set up in the industrial worker's mind a tension between his feelings towards his work and his feelings towards his leisure to which neither the peasant majority nor the privileged minority had been subject in a pre-industrial age. In an agrarian society a cycle of the seasons that had been the husbandman's calendar had also settled for a leisured minority the allocation of their time between holding court and going to war or between sitting in parliament and going hunting, shooting, and fishing. The peasantry and their rulers alike had taken both work and leisure for granted as alternating phases in a Yin-and-Yang rhythm beaten out by the perpetually recurring cycles of day and night and summer and winter. Each phase was a relief from the other. But this pre-industrial interdependence and parity of work and leisure had been deranged when the worker had been transformed into a tender of machines which could go on working, day and night, all the year round. The chronic industrial warfare which the worker now found himself impelled to wage in order to prevent the machines and their masters from working him to death had impregnated his mind with a hostility to the life of toil that his peasant forebears had taken as a matter of course; and this new attitude towards work had brought with it a new attitude towards leisure; for, if work was intrinsically evil, then leisure must have an absolute value in itself.

Human nature's reaction against the routine of the factory and the office had, by the middle of the twentieth century, already gone so far as to make the value of freedom from an excessive pressure of work count for more than the value of the remuneration that the worker could secure by working at full stretch. But at the same time the so far unchecked advance of technology was playing a sardonic practical joke on its human victims. When it was not threatening to work them to death, it was threatening to reduce them to 'unemployment'. So trades-union restrictive practices which had been devised as a form of organized inefficiency for putting a brake on the killing drive of the machine had come to serve the workers' further purpose of spinning out the residue of an employment that was apparently being snatched out of human hands altogether.[1] It was possible to foresee an *Earthly Paradise Regained* in which a régime of 'full employment' would also be one in which the ration of work that could be doled out to each individual would occupy so small a fraction of his day that he would have almost as much leisure as the long-extinct 'idle rich' privileged class of which his ancestors had been taught to disapprove. In such circumstances the use made of leisure would evidently become more important than it had ever been before.

How would Mankind use this prospective universal leisure? The question, which was a disturbing one, had been raised by Sir Alfred Ewing in a presidential address to the British Association on the 31st August, 1932.

'Some may envisage a distant Utopia in which there will be perfect adjustment of labour and the fruits of labour, a fair spreading of employment and of wages and of all the commodities that machines produce. Even so, the question will remain: How is Man to spend the leisure he has won by handing over nearly all his burden to a tireless mechanical

---

[1] The idea that, one day, the machines would 'grow up' and dispense with their human assistants had been elaborated in Samuel Butler's *Erewhon*, published A.D. 1870.

slave? Dare he hope for such spiritual betterment as would qualify him to use it well? God grant that he may strive for that and attain it. It is only by seeking [that] he will find. I cannot think that Mankind is destined to atrophy and cease through cultivating what, after all, is one of his most God-given faculties—the creative ingenuity of the engineer.'

The *Pax Romana* fell a very long way short of the future that we are now envisaging in respect of the ease that it provided for human existence; yet, even so, the author of a treatise on *Sublimity in Style*, writing at an undetermined date during the Roman Empire's heyday, felt that the relaxation of tension due to the establishment of the Hellenic universal state had led to a deterioration of human quality.

'One of the cancers of the spiritual life in souls born into the present generation is the low spiritual tension in which all but a few chosen spirits among us pass their days. In our work and in our recreation alike, our only objective is popularity and enjoyment. We feel no concern to win the true spiritual treasure that is to be found in putting one's heart into what one is doing and in winning a recognition that is truly worth having.'

These findings of an Hellenic critic were endorsed, at the beginning of the Modern Age of Western history, by one of the pioneers of the modern scientific spirit. The following passage is to be found in *The Advancement of Learning*, which was published by Francis Bacon in A.D. 1605.

'For as it has been well observed, that the arts which flourish in times while virtue is in growth, are military; and while virtue is in state, are liberal; and, while virtue is in declination, are voluptuary: so I doubt that this age of the World is somewhat upon the descent of the wheel. With arts voluptuary I couple practices joculary; for the deceiving of the senses is one of the pleasures of the senses.'

'Practices joculary' would cover a good deal of the use of leisure in the wireless and television age. The raising of the working class to the material standards of the middle class was apparently being accompanied by a proletarianization of the life of a large portion of the middle class on the spiritual plane.

The guests at Circe's banquet had soon found themselves penned in Circe's sty; the open question had been whether they were going to remain there indefinitely. Was this a fate to which the Human Race was likely to resign itself? Would the Human Race really be content to 'live happy ever after' in a Brave New World in which the only change from a monotony of insipid leisure would be a monotony of mechanical work? Such a forecast surely failed to take account of a creative minority that had been the salt of the Earth in all ages of history. The gloomy diagnosis of the author of the Late Hellenic treatise on *Sublimity in Style* had over-looked an all-important element in the situation under his eyes; he appears to have been unaware of the Christian martyrs.

It may seem—and indeed it is—a far cry from a prospect of technological unemployment to an expectation of another Day of Pentecost; and the reader may incline to ask the sceptic's question: 'How may these things be?' Midway through the twentieth century of the Christian Era it was not possible to tell how they might be; yet something might already be said to suggest that such a hope was not merely 'wishful thinking'.

One of the devices by which Life achieves the *tour de force* of keeping itself alive is by compensating for a deficit or surplus in one department by accumulating a surplus or incurring a deficit in another. We might therefore expect that, in a social milieu in which there is a deficit of freedom and a surplus of regimentation in the economic and political spheres, the effect of such a law of Nature would be to stimulate freedom and to relax the tyranny of regimentation in the sphere of Religion. Such, undeniably, had been the course of events in the days of the Roman Empire.

One lesson of this Hellenic episode was that in Life there is always an irreducible minimum of psychic energy that will insist on discharging itself through one channel or another; but it is equally true that there is also a maximum limit to the quantity of psychic energy which Life has at its disposal. From this it follows that, if a reinforcement of energy is required for putting a greater drive into one activity, the requisite additional supply will have to be obtained by making economies of energy in other quarters. Life's device for economizing energy is mechanization. For example, by making the beating of the heart and the alternating inflation and deflation of the lungs automatic, Life had released human thought and will for other uses than the continuous maintenance of physical vitality from moment to moment. If a conscious act of thought and act of will had never ceased to be required for the initiation of each successive breath and each successive heart-beat, no human being would ever have had any margin of intellectual or volitional energy to spare for doing anything else but just keeping alive; or, to make the same point more accurately, no sub-human being would ever have succeeded in becoming human. On the analogy of this creative effect of the economy of energy in the life of Man's body physical, we might surmise that, in the life of his body social, Religion would be likely to be starved so long as thought and will were preoccupied with economics (as they had been in the West since the outbreak of the Industrial Revolution) and with politics (as they had been in the West since the Western renaissance of a deified Hellenic state). Conversely, we might infer that the regimentation that was now being imposed on the Western society's economic and political life would be likely to liberate Western souls for fulfilling the true end of Man by glorifying God and enjoying Him once again.

This happier spiritual prospect was at least a possibility in which a dispirited generation of Western men and women might catch a beckoning gleam of kindly light.

XIII
CONCLUSION

XLIV. HOW THIS BOOK CAME TO BE WRITTEN

WHY do people study History? The present writer's personal answer would be that an historian, like anyone else who has had the happiness of having an aim in life, has found his vocation in a call from God to 'feel after Him and find Him'. Among innumerable angles of vision the historian's is only one. Its distinctive contribution is to give us a vision of God's creative activity on the move in a frame which, in our human experience of it, displays six dimensions. The historical angle of vision shows us the physical cosmos moving centrifugally in a four-dimensional frame of Space–Time; it shows us Life on our planet moving evolutionarily in a five-dimensional frame of Life–Time-Space; and it shows us human souls, raised to a sixth dimension by a gift of the Spirit, moving, through a fateful exercise of their spiritual freedom, either towards their Creator or away from Him.

If we are right in seeing in History a vision of God's creation on the move, we shall not be surprised to find that, in human minds whose innate receptivity to the impress of History is presumably always much the same on the average, the actual strength of the impression varies in accordance with the recipient's historical circumstances. Mere receptivity has to be reinforced by curiosity, and curiosity will be stimulated only when the process of social change is vividly and violently apparent. A primitive peasantry had never been historical-minded, because their social milieu had always spoken to them, not of History, but of Nature. Their festivals had not been a Fourth of July, a Guy Fawkes' Day, or an Armistice Day, but the unhistorical red- and black-letter days of the annually recurrent agricultural year.

Even, however, for the minority whose social milieu spoke to them of History, this exposure to the radiation of an historical social environment was not in itself enough to inspire an historian. Without a creative stirring of curiosity, the most familiar and impressive monuments of History will perform their eloquent dumbshow to no effect, because the eyes to which they will be addressing themselves will be eyes that see not. This truth that a creative spark cannot be struck without a response as well as a challenge was borne in upon the Modern Western philosopher-pilgrim Volney when he visited the Islamic world in A.D. 1783–5. Volney came from a country which had been drawn into the current of the histories of civilizations as recently as the time of the Hannibalic War, whereas the region that he was visiting had been a theatre of History for some three or four thousand years longer than Gaul and was proportionately well stocked with visible relics of the past. Yet, in the last quarter of the eighteenth century of the Christian Era, the living generation in the Middle East were squatting among the amazing ruins of extinct civilizations without being moved to inquire what these monuments were, whereas this same question drew Volney from his native France to Egypt, and, in his wake, the goodly company of French *savants* who seized the opportunity offered to them by Bonaparte's military expedition fifteen years later. Napoleon knew that he was striking a note to which even the uneducated rank and file of his army would respond when he reminded them, before going into action on the decisive battlefield of Imbābah, that forty centuries of History were looking down on them from the Pyramids. We may be sure that Murād Bey, the commander of the opposing Mamlūk force, never thought of wasting his breath by addressing any similar exhortation to his own incurious comrades.

The French *savants* who visited Egypt in Napoleon's train distinguished themselves by finding a new dimension of History for a Modern Western society's insatiable curiosity to conquer; and, since that date, no fewer than eleven lost and forgotten civilizations —the Egyptiac, the Babylonic, the Sumeric, the Minoan, and the Hittite, together with the Indus culture and the Shang culture, in the Old World, and the Mayan, Yucatec, Mexic, and Andean civilizations in the New World—had been brought to life again.

Without the inspiration of curiosity no one can be an historian; but this is not enough by itself; for, if it is undirected, it can issue only in the pursuit of an aimless omniscience. The curiosity of each of the great historians had always been canalized into the task of answering some question of practical significance to his generation which could be formulated, in general terms, as 'How has this come out of that?' If we survey the intellectual histories of the great historians, we find that in the majority of cases some momentous, and usually also shocking, public event had been the challenge that had inspired a response in the form of an historical diagnosis. This event might be one that they themselves had witnessed, or in which they had even played an active part, as Thucydides had in the Great Atheno-Peloponnesian War and Clarendon in the Great Rebellion; or it might be an event long past, the repercussions of which could still arouse a response in a sensitively historical mind, as the intellectual and emotional challenge of the decline and fall of the Roman Empire stimulated Gibbon when he was musing among the ruins of the Capitol centuries later. The creative stimulus might be a momentous event which seemed to provide cause for satisfaction, such, for example, as the mental challenge which Herodotus received from the Persian War. But, for the most part, it is the great catastrophes of history which, in challenging Man's natural optimism, call out the historian's finest efforts.

An historian born, as was the present writer, in A.D. 1889, who was still alive in A.D. 1955, had indeed already heard a long peal of changes rung on the historian's elemental question: 'How has this come out of that?' How, first and foremost, had it happened that he had lived to see the immediately preceding generation's apparently reasonable expectations so rudely disappointed? In liberal-minded middle-class circles in democratic Western countries in a generation born round about A.D. 1860, it had seemed evident, by the close of the nineteenth century, that a triumphantly advancing Western civilization had now carried human progress to a point at which it could count on finding the Earthly Paradise just round the next corner. How was it that this generation had been so grievously disappointed? What, exactly, had gone wrong? How, through the welter of war and wickedness which the new century had brought in its train, had the political map come to be changed out of all recognition, and a goodly fellowship of eight Great Powers come to be reduced to two, both of them located outside Western Europe?

The list of such questions might be indefinitely elaborated, and they furnished themes for an equally large number of historical inquiries. Thanks to his professional good fortune in being born into a Time of Troubles that was, by definition, an historian's paradise, the present writer was, in fact, moved to interest himself in each of the historical conundrums flung at him by current events. But his professional good fortune did not end here. He had been born just in time to receive a still undiluted Early Modern Western 'Renaissance' education in Hellenism. By the summer of A.D. 1911 he had been studying Latin for fifteen years and Greek for twelve; and this traditional education had the wholesome effect of rendering its recipients immune against the malady of cultural chauvinism. An Hellenically educated Westerner could not easily fall into the error of seeing in Western Christendom the best of all possible worlds, nor could he consider the historical questions that his own contemporary Western social milieu was putting to him without referring them to the oracles of a Hellas in which he had found his spiritual home.

He was, for example, unable to observe the disappointment of his liberal-minded elders' expectations without being reminded of Plato's disillusionment with a Periclean Attic democracy. He could not live through the experience of the outbreak of war in A.D. 1914 without realizing that the outbreak of war in 431 B.C. had brought the same experience to Thucydides. As he found his own experience revealing to him, for the first time, the inwardness of Thucydidean words and phrases that had meant little or nothing to him before, he realized that a book written in another world more than 2,300 years ago might be the depository of experiences which, in the reader's world, were only just beginning to overtake the reader's own generation. There was a sense in which the two dates A.D. 1914 and 431 B.C. were philosophically contemporaneous.

It will be seen that in the present writer's social milieu there were two factors, neither of them personal to himself, which had a decisive influence on his approach to a study of History. The first was the current history of his own Western world and the second was his Hellenic education. By perpetually interacting with one another, they made the writer's view of History binocular. When the historian's elemental question 'How has this come out of that?' was put to the writer by some current catastrophic event, the form that the question was apt to assume in his mind was: 'How has this come out of that in Western as well as in Hellenic history?' He thus came to look upon History as a comparison in two terms.

This binocular view of History might have been appreciated and approved by Far Eastern contemporaries in whose then likewise still traditional education the classical language and literature of an antecedent civilization had played a no less predominant part. A Confucian literatus would, like the present writer, have found himself unable to encounter any passing event without being reminded by it of some classical parallel that would have, for him, a greater value, and even perhaps a more vivid reality, than the post-classical occurrence that had set his mind working on its congenial task of chewing the cud of a familiar classical Sinic lore. The principal difference in mental outlook between this Late Ch'ing Confucian-minded Chinese scholar and his Late Victorian Hellenic-minded English contemporary might prove to be that the Chinese student of human affairs could still remain content to make his historical comparisons in two terms only, whereas the Late Victorian Englishman, when once he had begun to think historically in two terms, could no longer rest till he had extended his cultural gamut to a wider range.

For a Chinese student receiving his traditional classical education towards the end of the nineteenth century of the Christian Era, it would still be a novel idea that any civilization other than the Sinic and its Far Eastern successor could be deserving of any serious consideration; but a similarly blinkered vision was impossible for any Westerner of the same generation.

It was impossible because, within the preceding four hundred years, the Western society to which he belonged had thrust itself into contact with no less than eight other representatives of its own species in the Old World and the New; and it had since become doubly impossible for Western minds to ignore the existence, or to deny the significance, of other civilizations besides its own and the Hellenic, because, within the last century, these insatiably questing Westerners, who had already conquered a previously virgin Ocean in the wake of Columbus and da Gama, had gone on to unearth a previously buried past. In a generation which had acquired this wide historical horizon, a Western historian who had been led by his Hellenic education to make historical comparisons in two terms, could not be content until he had collected, for comparative study, as many specimens as he could find of the species of Society of which the Hellenic and the Western were merely two representatives.

When he had succeeded in multiplying his terms of comparison more than tenfold, he could no longer ignore the supreme question which his original comparison in two terms had already threatened to raise. The most portentous single fact in the Hellenic civilization's history was the eventual dissolution of a society whose breakdown had been registered in 431 B.C. by the outbreak of the Great Atheno-Peloponnesian War. If there was any validity in the writer's procedure of drawing comparisons between Hellenic history and Western, it would seem to follow that the Western society must, at any rate, be not immune from the possibility of a similar fate; and, when the writer, on passing to his wider studies, found that a clear majority of his assemblage of civilizations were already dead, he was bound to infer that death was indeed a possibility confronting every civilization, including his own.

What was this 'Door of Death' through which so many once flourishing civilizations had already disappeared? This question led the writer into a study of the breakdowns and disintegrations of civilizations; and thence he was led on into a complementary study of their geneses and growths. And so this Study of History came to be written.

ARGUMENT

I. INTRODUCTION

I. THE UNIT OF HISTORICAL STUDY

THE intelligible units of historical study are not nations or periods but 'societies'. An examination of English history, chapter by chapter, shows that it is not intelligible as a thing-in-itself but only as a part of a larger whole. This whole contains parts (e.g. England, France, the Netherlands) that are subject to identical stimuli or challenges but react to them in different ways. An example from Hellenic history is introduced to illustrate this. The 'whole', or 'society', to which England belongs is identified as Western Christendom; its extension in space at different dates is measured, and its origins in time. It is found to be older, but only slightly older, than the articulation of its parts. Exploration of its beginnings reveals the existence of another society which is now dead, namely the Graeco-Roman or Hellenic society, to which ours is 'affiliated'. It is also obvious that there are a number of other living societies—the Orthodox Christian, the Islamic, the Hindu and the Far Eastern societies—and also certain 'fossilized' relics of, at this stage, unidentified societies such as the Jews and the Parsees.

II. THE COMPARATIVE STUDY OF CIVILIZATIONS

The purpose of this chapter is to identify, define, and name all the societies—or, rather, civilizations, for there are also primitive or non-'civilized' societies—which have come into existence so far. The first method of search to employ is to take the existing civilizations already identified, examine their origins, and see if we can find civilizations now extinct to which these are affiliated as Western Christendom has been found to be affiliated to the Hellenic civilization. The marks of this relationship are (*a*) a universal state (e.g. the Roman Empire), itself the outcome of a time of troubles, followed by (*b*) an interregnum, in which appear (*c*) a Church and (*d*) a Völkerwanderung of barbarians in an heroic age. The Church and the Völkerwanderung are the products, respectively, of the internal and external 'proletariats' of a dying civilization. Employing these clues we find that:

The Orthodox Christian society is, like our own Western society, affiliated to the Hellenic society.

Tracing the Islamic society back to its origins we find that it is itself a fusion of two originally distinct societies, the Iranic and the

Arabic. Tracing these back to their origin we find, behind a thousand years of 'Hellenic intrusion', an extinct society, to be called the Syriac society.

Behind the Hindu society we find an Indic society.

Behind the Far Eastern society we find a Sinic society.

The 'fossils' are found to be survivals from one or other of the extinct societies already identified.

Behind the Hellenic society we find the Minoan society, but we observe that the Hellenic society, unlike the other affiliated societies so far identified, did not take over a religion discovered by the internal proletariat of its predecessor. It might therefore be regarded as being not strictly affiliated to it.

Behind the Sinic society we find a Shang culture.

Behind the Indic society we find an Indus culture that stands in some relation to a contemporary Sumeric society.

As offspring of the Sumeric society we find two more societies, a Hittite and a Babylonic.

The Egyptiac society had no predecessor and no successor.

In the New World we can identify four societies: the Andean, the Yucatec, the Mexic, and the Mayan.

Thus we have, in all, twenty-one specimens of 'civilizations'; and, if we divide the Orthodox Christian society into Orthodox-Byzantine (in Anatolia and the Balkans) and Orthodox-Russian, and the Far Eastern into Chinese and Japanese-Korean, we have twenty-three.

III. THE COMPARABILITY OF SOCIETIES

(1) *Civilizations and Primitive Societies*

Civilizations have at any rate one point in common, that they are a separate class from primitive societies. These latter are very much more numerous but also very much smaller individually.

(2) *The Misconception of 'the Unity of Civilization'*

The erroneous idea that there is only one civilization, namely our own, is examined and dismissed; also the 'Diffusionist' theory that all civilization had its origin in Egypt.

(3) *The Case for the Comparability of Civilizations*

Civilizations are, relatively speaking, a very recent phenomenon in human history, the earliest of them having originated no more than six thousand years ago. It is proposed to treat them as 'philosophically contemporaneous' members of a single 'species'. The half-truth 'History does not repeat itself' is exposed as constituting no valid objection to the procedure proposed.

(4) *History, Science, and Fiction*

These are 'three different methods of viewing and presenting the objects of our thought and, among them, the phenomena of human life'. The differences between these three techniques are examined and the uses of Science and Fiction in the presentation of the theme of History are discussed.

II. THE GENESES OF CIVILIZATIONS

IV. THE PROBLEM AND HOW NOT TO SOLVE IT

(1) *The Problem Stated*

Of our twenty-three 'civilized' societies sixteen are affiliated to previous civilizations but six have emerged direct from primitive life. Primitive societies existing to-day are static, but it is clear that they must originally have been dynamically progressive. Social life is older than the human race itself; it is found among insects and animals, and it must have been under the aegis of primitive societies that sub-man rose to the level of man—a greater advance than any civilization has as yet achieved. However, primitive societies, as we know them, are static. The problem is: why and how was this primitive 'cake of custom' broken?

(2) *Race*

The factor that we are looking for must be some special quality in the human beings who started civilizations or some special features of their environment at the time or some interaction between the two. The first of these views, namely, that there is some innately superior race, e.g. the Nordic Race, in the world, which is responsible for the creation of civilizations, is examined and rejected.

(3) *Environment*

The view that certain environments, presenting easy and comfortable conditions of life, provide the key to an explanation of the origin of civilizations is examined and rejected.

V. CHALLENGE AND RESPONSE

(1) *The Mythological Clue*

The fallacy in the two views already examined and rejected is that they apply the procedure of sciences which deal with material things to a problem that is really spiritual. A survey of the great myths in which the wisdom of the human race is enshrined suggests the possibility that man achieves civilization, not as a result of superior biological endowment or geographical environment, but as a response to a challenge in a situation of special difficulty which rouses him to make a hitherto unprecedented effort.

(2) *The Myth applied to the Problem*

Before the dawn of civilization the Afrasian Steppe (the Sahara and the Arabian Desert) was a well-watered grassland. The prolonged and progressive desiccation of this grassland presented its habinitants with a challenge to which they responded in various ways. Some stood their ground and changed their habits, thus evolving the Nomadic manner of life. Others shifted their ground southwards, following the retreating grassland to the tropics, and thus preserved their primitive way of life—which they are still living today. Others entered the marshes and jungles of the Nile Valley and—faced with the challenge that it presented—set to work to drain it, and these evolved the Egyptiac civilization.

The Sumeric civilization originated in the same way and from the same causes in the Tigris–Euphrates Valley, and the Indus culture in the Indus Valley.

The Shang culture originated in the Yellow River Valley. The nature of the challenge which started it is unknown, but it is clear that the conditions were severe rather than easy.

The Mayan civilization arose in answer to the challenge of a tropical forest; the Andean in answer to that of a bleak plateau.

The Minoan civilization arose in answer to the challenge of the sea. Its founders were refugees from the desiccating coasts of Africa who took to the water and settled in Crete and other Aegean islands. They did not, in the first instance, come from the nearer mainlands of Asia or Europe.

In the cases of the affiliated civilizations the challenge that brought them into existence must have come primarily not from geographical factors but from their human environment, i.e. from the 'dominant minorities' of the societies to which they are affiliated. A dominant minority is, by definition, a ruling class that has ceased to lead and has become oppressive. To this challenge the internal and external proletariats of the failing civilization respond by seceding from it and thereby laying the foundations of a new civilization.

VI. THE VIRTUES OF ADVERSITY

The explanation of the geneses of civilizations given in the last chapter rests on the hypothesis that it is difficult rather than easy conditions that produce these achievements. This hypothesis is now brought nearer to proof by illustrations taken from localities where civilization once flourished but subsequently failed and where the land has reverted to its original condition.

What was once the scene of the Mayan civilization is now again tropical forest.

The Indic civilization in Ceylon flourished in the rainless half of the island. This is now entirely barren, though the ruins of the Indic irrigation system remain as evidence of the civilization that once flourished here.

The ruins of Petra and Palmyra stand on small oases in the Arabian Desert.

Easter Island, one of the remotest spots in the Pacific, is proved by its statues to have been once a centre of the Polynesian civilization.

New England, whose European colonists have played a predominant part in the history of North America, is one of the bleakest and most barren parts of that continent.

The Latin townships of the Roman Campagna, till recently a malarial wilderness, made a great contribution to the rise of the Roman Power. Contrast the favourable situation and poor performance of Capua. Illustrations are also drawn from Herodotus, the Odyssey, and the Book of Exodus.

The natives of Nyasaland, where life is easy, remained primitive savages down to the advent of invaders from a distant and inclement Europe.

VII. THE CHALLENGE OF THE ENVIRONMENT

(1) *The Stimulus of Hard Countries*

A series of pairs of contiguous environments is adduced. In each case the former is the 'harder' country and has also had the more brilliant record as an originator of one form or other of civilization: the Yellow River Valley and the Yangtse Valley; Attica and Boeotia; Byzantium and Calchedon; Israel, Phoenicia, Philistia; Brandenburg and the Rhineland; Scotland and England; the various groups of European colonists in North America.

(2) *The Stimulus of New Ground*

We find that 'virgin soil' produces more vigorous responses than land which has already been broken in and thus rendered 'easier' by previous 'civilized' occupants. Thus, if we take each of the affiliated civilizations, we find that it has produced its most striking early manifestations in places outside the area occupied by the 'parent' civilization. The superiority of the response evoked by new ground is most strikingly illustrated when the new ground has to be reached by a sea-passage. Reasons for this fact are given, and also for the phenomenon that the drama develops in homelands and epic in overseas settlements.

(3) The Stimulus of Blows

Various examples from Hellenic and Western history are given to illustrate the point that a sudden crushing defeat is apt to stimulate the defeated party to set its house in order and prepare to make a victorious response.

(4) The Stimulus of Pressures

Various examples show that peoples occupying frontier positions, exposed to constant attack, achieve a more brilliant development than their neighbours in more sheltered positions. Thus the 'Osmanlis, thrust up against the frontier of the East Roman Empire, fared better than the Qaramanlis to the east of them; Austria had a more brilliant career than Bavaria thanks to being exposed to the prolonged assault of the Ottoman Turks. The situation and fortunes of the various communities in Britain between the fall of Rome and the Norman Conquest are examined from this point of view.

(5) The Stimulus of Penalizations

Certain classes and races have suffered for centuries from various forms of penalization imposed upon them by other classes or races who have had the mastery over them. Penalized classes or races generally respond to this challenge of being excluded from certain opportunities and privileges by putting forth exceptional energy and showing exceptional capacity in such directions as are left open to them—much as the blind develop exceptional sensitiveness of hearing. Slavery is perhaps the heaviest of penalizations, but out of the hordes of slaves imported into Italy from the Eastern Mediterranean during the last two centuries B.C. there arose a 'freedmen' class which proved alarmingly powerful. From this slave world, too, came the new religions of the internal proletariat, among them Christianity.

The fortunes of various groups of conquered Christian peoples under 'Osmanli rule are examined from the same standpoint—particularly the case of the Phanariot Greeks. This example and that of the Jews are used to prove that so-called racial characteristics are not really racial at all but are due to the historical experiences of the communities in question.

VIII. THE GOLDEN MEAN

(1) Enough and Too Much

Can we say simply: the sterner the challenge the finer the

response? Or is there such a thing as a challenge too severe to evoke a response? Certainly some challenges which have defeated one or more parties that have encountered them have ultimately provoked a victorious response. For example, the challenge of expanding Hellenism proved too much for the Celts but was victoriously answered by their successors the Teutons. The 'Hellenic intrusion' into the Syriac world evoked a series of unsuccessful Syriac responses—the Zoroastrian, the Jewish (Maccabaean), the Nestorian, and the Monophysite—but the fifth response, that of Islam, was successful.

(2) *Comparisons in Three Terms*

None the less, it can be proved that challenges can be too severe: i.e. the *maximum* challenge will not always produce the *optimum* response. The Viking emigrants from Norway responded splendidly to the severe challenge of Iceland but collapsed before the severer challenge of Greenland. Massachusetts presented European colonists with a severer challenge than 'Dixie' and evoked a better response, but Labrador, presenting a severer challenge still, proved too much for them. Other examples follow: e.g. the stimulus of blows can be too severe, especially if prolonged, as in the effect of the Hannibalic War on Italy. The Chinese are stimulated by the social challenge involved in emigrating to Malaya but are defeated by the severer social challenge of a white man's country, e.g. California. Finally, varying degrees of challenge presented by civilizations to neighbouring barbarians are reviewed.

(3) *Two Abortive Civilizations*

This section is a continuation of the argument of the last example in the preceding section. Two groups of barbarians on the frontiers of Western Christendom in the first chapter of its history were so stimulated that they began to evolve rival civilizations of their own which were, however, nipped in the bud, namely the Far Western Celtic Christians (in Ireland and Iona) and the Scandinavian Vikings. These two cases are considered and the consequences that might have ensued if these rivals had not been swallowed and absorbed by the Christian civilization radiating from Rome and the Rhineland.

(4) *The Impact of Islam on the Christendoms*

On Western Christendom the effect of this impact was wholly good, and Western culture in the Middle Ages owed much to Muslim Iberia. On Byzantine Christendom the impact was excessive and evoked a crushing re-erection of the Roman Empire under Leo the Syrian. The case of Abyssinia, a Christian 'fossil' in a fastness encircled by the Muslim World, is also noticed.

III. THE GROWTHS OF CIVILIZATIONS

IX. THE ARRESTED CIVILIZATIONS

(1) *Polynesians, Eskimos, and Nomads*

It might seem that, once a civilization had been brought into existence, its growth would be a matter of course; but this is not so, as is proved by the record of certain civilizations which have achieved existence but then failed to grow. The fate of these arrested civilizations has been to encounter a challenge on the border-line between the degree of severity which evokes a successful response and the greater degree which entails defeat. Three cases present themselves in which a challenge of this kind has come from the physical environment. The result in each case has been a *tour de force* on the part of the respondents which has so engrossed the whole of their energies that they have had none left over for further development.

The Polynesians achieved the *tour de force* of inter-insular voyaging between Pacific islands. It eventually defeated them and they relapsed into primitive life on their several now isolated islands.

The Eskimos achieved an extraordinarily skilled and specialized annual cycle adapted to life on the shores of the Arctic.

The Nomads achieved a similar annual cycle as herdsmen on the semi-desert Steppe. The ocean with its islands and the desert with its oases have many points in common. The evolution of Nomadism during periods of desiccation is analysed. It is noted that hunters become agriculturists before taking the further step of becoming Nomads. Cain and Abel are types of the agriculturist and the Nomad. Nomad incursions into the domains of civilizations are always due either to increased desiccation 'pushing' the Nomad off the Steppe or to the breakdown of a civilization creating a vacuum which 'pulls' the Nomad in as a participant in a Völkerwanderung.

(2) *The 'Osmanlis*

The challenge to which the Ottoman system was a response was the transference of a Nomad community to an environment in which they had to rule sedentary communities. They solved their problem by treating their new subjects as human flocks and herds, evolving human equivalents of the sheep-dogs of the Nomad in the form of a slave 'household' of administrators and soldiers. Other examples of similar Nomad empires are mentioned, the Mamlūks for instance; but the 'Osmanli system surpassed all others in efficiency and duration. It suffered, however, like Nomadism itself, from a fatal rigidity.

(3) *The Spartans*

The Spartan response to the challenge of over-population in the Hellenic World was to evolve a *tour de force* which in many respects resembles that of the 'Osmanlis, with the difference that in the Spartan case the military caste was the Spartan aristocracy itself; but they too were 'slaves', enslaved to the self-imposed duty of holding down permanently a population of fellow-Greeks.

(4) *General Characteristics*

Eskimos and Nomads, 'Osmanlis and Spartans have two features in common: specialization and caste. (In the former pair, dogs, reindeer, horses, and cattle supply the place of the human slave castes of the 'Osmanlis.) In all these societies the human beings are degraded by specialization as boat-men, horse-men or warrior-men to a subhuman level in comparison with the all-round men, the ideal of Pericles' funeral speech, who alone are capable of achieving growth in civilization. These arrested societies resemble the societies of bees and ants, which have been stationary since before the dawn of human life on Earth. They also resemble the societies portrayed in 'Utopias'. A discussion of 'Utopias' follows, in which it is shown that 'Utopias' are generally the products of civilizations in decline and are attempts, in so far as they have a practical programme, to arrest the decline by pegging the society at its actual level at the moment.

X. THE NATURE OF THE GROWTHS OF CIVILIZATIONS

(1) *Two False Trails*

Growth occurs when the response to a particular challenge is not only successful in itself but provokes a further challenge which again meets with a successful response. How are we to measure such growth? Is it to be measured by an increasing control over the society's external environment? Such an increasing control can be of two kinds: increasing control over the human environment, which normally takes the form of conquest of neighbouring peoples, and increasing control over the physical environment, which is expressed in improvements in material technique. Examples are then adduced to show that neither of these phenomena—neither political and military expansion nor improvement in technique—is a satisfactory criterion of real growth. Military expansion is normally a result of militarism, which is itself a symptom of decline. Improvements in technique, agricultural or industrial, show little or no correlation with real growth. In fact, technique may well be improving at a time when real civilization is declining, and vice versa.

(2) *Progress towards Self-determination*

Real progress is found to consist in a process defined as 'etherialization', an overcoming of material obstacles which releases the energies of the society to make responses to challenges which henceforth are internal rather than external, spiritual rather than material. The nature of this etherialization is illustrated by examples from Hellenic and modern Western history.

XI. AN ANALYSIS OF GROWTH

(1) *Society and the Individual*

Two traditional views are current as to the relation of society to the individual: one represents a society as simply an aggregate of 'atomic' individuals, and the other regards the society as an organism and the individuals as parts of it, inconceivable except as members or 'cells' of the society to which they belong. Both these views are shown to be unsatisfactory, and the true view is that a society is a system of relations between individuals. Human beings cannot be themselves without interacting with their fellows, and a society is a field of action common to a number of human beings. But the 'source of action' is in the individuals. All growth originates with creative individuals or small minorities of individuals, and their task is twofold: first the achievement of their inspiration or discovery, whatever it may be, and secondly the conversion of the society to which they belong to this new way of life. This conversion could, theoretically, come about in one or other of two ways: either by the mass undergoing the actual experience which has transformed the creative individuals, or by their imitation of its externals—in other words, by *mimesis*. In practice the latter is the only alternative open in the case of all but a small minority of mankind. Mimesis is 'a short cut', but it is a route by which the rank and file, *en masse*, can follow the leaders.

(2) *Withdrawal and Return: Individuals*

The action of the creative individual may be described as a twofold motion of withdrawal-and-return: withdrawal for the purpose of his personal enlightenment, return for the task of enlightening his fellow men. This is illustrated from Plato's parable of the Cave, from Saint Paul's analogy of the seed, from the Gospel story and from elsewhere. It is then shown in practical action in the lives of great pioneers: Saint Paul, Saint Benedict, Saint Gregory the Great, the Buddha, Muhammad, Machiavelli, Dante.

(3) *Withdrawal and Return: Creative Minorities*

Withdrawal followed by Return is also characteristic of the sub-societies which form the constituent parts of 'societies' in the proper sense. The period in which such sub-societies make their contributions to the growth of the societies to which they belong is preceded by a period in which they are markedly withdrawn from the general life of their society: for example, Athens in the second chapter of the growth of the Hellenic Society; Italy in the second chapter of the growth of the Western Society; and England in its third chapter. The possibility that Russia may be going to play a similar role in the fourth chapter is considered.

XII. DIFFERENTIATION THROUGH GROWTH

Growth as described in the foregoing chapter clearly involves differentiation between the parts of a growing society. At each stage some parts will make an original and successful response; some will succeed in following their lead by mimesis; some will fail to achieve either originality or mimesis, and succumb. There will also be increasing differentiation between the histories of different societies, and it is obvious that different societies have different predominating characteristics, some excelling in art, some in religion, others in industrial inventiveness. But the fundamental similarity in the purposes of all civilizations is not to be forgotten. Each seed has its own destiny, but the seeds are all of one kind, sown by the same Sower, in the hope of the same harvest.

IV. THE BREAKDOWNS OF CIVILIZATIONS

XIII. THE NATURE OF THE PROBLEM

Of twenty-eight civilizations that we have identified (including the arrested civilizations in the list) eighteen are dead and nine of the remaining ten—all, in fact, except our own—are shown to have already broken down. The nature of a breakdown can be summed up in three points: a failure of creative power in the creative minority, which henceforth becomes a merely 'dominant' minority; an answering withdrawal of allegiance and mimesis on the part of the majority; a consequent loss of social unity in the society as a whole. Our next task is to discover the causes of such breakdowns.

XIV. DETERMINISTIC SOLUTIONS

Some schools of thought have maintained that the breakdowns of civilizations are due to factors outside human control.

(i) During the decline of the Hellenic Civilization writers, both pagan and Christian, held that the decay of their society was due to 'cosmic senescence'; but modern physicists have relegated cosmic senescence to an unbelievably distant future, which means that it can have had no effect on any past or present civilizations.

(ii) Spengler and others have maintained that societies are organisms, with natural transitions from youth and maturity to decay, like living creatures; but a society is not an organism.

(iii) Others have held that there is something inevitably dysgenic in the influence of civilization on human nature, and that after a period of civilization the race can only be restored by an infusion of barbaric 'new blood'. This view is examined and dismissed.

(iv) There remains the cyclic theory of history, as found in Plato's *Timaeus*, Virgil's Fourth Eclogue, and elsewhere. This probably originated in Chaldaean discoveries concerning our own solar system, and the vastly wider vision of modern astronomy has deprived the theory of its astronomical basis. There is no evidence in favour of the theory and much against it.

XV. LOSS OF COMMAND OVER THE ENVIRONMENT

The argument of this chapter is the converse of that in chapter X (1), where it was shown that an increase in control over the physical environment, as measured by improvement in technique, and an increase in control over the human environment, as measured by geographical expansion or military conquest, are not the criteria or causes of growth. Here it is shown that the decline of technique and the geographical contraction caused by military aggression from outside are not the criteria or causes of breakdowns.

(1) *The Physical Environment*

Several examples are adduced to show that the decay of technical achievement has been a result, not a cause, of breakdown. The abandonment of the Roman roads and of the Mesopotamian irrigation system was a result, not a cause, of the breakdowns of the civilizations that had formerly maintained them. The oncoming of malaria which is said to have caused breakdowns of civilizations is shown to have been a result of the breakdowns.

(2) *The Human Environment*

Gibbon's thesis that 'the Decline and Fall of the Roman Empire' was due to 'Barbarism and Religion' (i.e. Christianity) is examined and rejected. These manifestations of the external and internal proletariats of the Hellenic society were consequences of a breakdown of the Hellenic society that had already taken place. Gibbon does not begin his story far enough back; he mistakes the Antonine period for a 'golden age' when it was really an 'Indian summer'. Various examples of successful aggression against civilizations are passed in review, and it is shown that in every case the successful aggression occurred *after* the breakdown.

(3) *A Negative Verdict*

Aggression against a society still in process of growth normally stimulates it to greater effort. Even when a society is already in decline, aggression against it may galvanize it into activity and give it a further lease of life. (The editor adds a note on the meaning of 'breakdown' as a technical term used in this Study.)

XVI. FAILURE OF SELF-DETERMINATION

(1) *The Mechanicalness of Mimesis*

The only way in which the uncreative majority can follow the leadership of the creative leaders is by mimesis, which is a species of 'drill', a mechanical and superficial imitation of the great and inspired originals. This unavoidable 'short cut' to progress entails obvious dangers. The leaders may become infected with the mechanicalness of their followers, and the result will be an arrested civilization; or they may impatiently exchange the Pied Piper's pipe of persuasion for the whip of compulsion. In that case the creative minority will become a 'dominant' minority and the 'disciples' will become a reluctant and alienated 'proletariat'. When this happens the society enters on the road to disintegration. The society loses capacity for self-determination. The following sections illustrate ways in which this comes about.

(2) *New Wine in Old Bottles*

Ideally each new social force released by creative minorities should beget new institutions through which it can work. Actually it works more often than not through old institutions designed for other purposes. But the old institutions often prove unsuitable and intractable. One of two results may follow: either the break-up of the institutions (a revolution) or their survival and the consequent perversion of the new forces working through them (an 'enormity'). A revolution may be defined as a delayed and consequently explosive act of mimesis; an enormity as a frustration of mimesis. If the adjustment of institutions to forces is harmonious, growth will continue; if it results in a revolution, growth becomes hazardous; if it results in an enormity, breakdown may be diagnosed. Then follow a series of examples of the impact of new forces upon old institutions, the first group being impacts of the two great new forces at work in the modern Western Society:

the impact of Industrialism on slavery, e.g. in the Southern States of the U.S.A.;

the impact of Democracy and Industrialism on war, as seen in the intensification of warfare since the French Revolution;

the impact of Democracy and Industrialism on the parochial state, as shown in the hypertrophy of nationalism and the failure of the free trade movement in the Modern Western World;

the impact of Industrialism on private property, as illustrated by the rise of Capitalism and Communism;

the impact of Democracy on education, as illustrated by the rise of the Yellow Press and of Fascist dictatorships;

the impact of Italian efficiency on Transalpine governments, as illustrated (except in England) by the emergence of despotic monarchies;

the impact of the Solonian revolution on the Hellenic city-states, as illustrated by the phenomena of *tyrannis*, *stasis*, and *hegemony*;

the impact of Parochialism on the Western Christian Church, as illustrated by the Protestant Revolution, the 'Divine Right of Kings', and the eclipse of Christianity by patriotism;

the impact of the Sense of Unity on Religion, as illustrated by the rise of bigotry and persecution;

the impact of Religion on Caste, as shown in the Hindu Civilization;

the impact of Civilization on the Division of Labour, showing itself as esotericism in the leaders (who become ἰδιῶται) and lop-sidedness in the followers (who become βάναυσοι). The latter defect is illustrated from cases of penalized minorities, e.g. the Jews, and from aberrations of modern athleticism;

the impact of Civilization on Mimesis, which is directed no

longer, as in primitive societies, towards the traditions of the tribe, but towards pioneers. Too often the pioneers selected for imitation are not creative leaders but commercial exploiters or political demagogues.

(3) *The Nemesis of Creativity: Idolization of an Ephemeral Self*

History shows that the group which successfully responds to one challenge is rarely the successful respondent to the next. Various examples are given, and it is shown that this phenomenon corresponds with certain fundamental postulates of both Greek and Hebrew thought. Those who have succeeded once are apt, on the next occasion, to be found 'resting on their oars'. The Jews, having responded to the challenges of the Old Testament, are worsted by the challenge of the New. The Athens of Pericles dwindles into the Athens of Saint Paul. In the Italian *Risorgimento* the centres which have responded in the Renaissance prove ineffective, and the lead is taken by Piedmont, which has had no part in previous Italian glories. South Carolina and Virginia, leading states of the U.S.A. in the first and second quarters of the nineteenth century, have failed to make a recovery from the Civil War comparable with that of the previously undistinguished North Carolina.

(4) *The Nemesis of Creativity: Idolization of an Ephemeral Institution*

Idolization of the city-state proved, in the later stages of Hellenic history, a snare into which the Greeks fell but not the Romans. A 'ghost' of the Roman Empire caused the breakdown of the Orthodox Christian society. Illustrations are also given of the hampering effects of the idolization of kings, parliaments, and ruling castes, whether bureaucracies or priesthoods.

(5) *The Nemesis of Creativity: Idolization of an Ephemeral Technique*

Illustrations from biological evolution show that perfect 'technique' or perfect adaptation to an environment often proves an evolutionary 'cul de sac', and that the less specialized and more 'tentative' organisms show greater survival power. The amphibians are contrasted favourably with the fishes, and the rat-like ancestors of man with their contemporaries, the giant reptiles. In the industrial sphere the success of a particular community in the first stages of a new technique, e.g. in the invention of the paddlesteamer, makes that community slower than others to adopt the more efficient screw-propeller. A brief review of the history of the art of war from David and Goliath to the present day shows that, at each stage, the inventors and beneficiaries of one innovation proceed to rest on their oars and allow the next innovation to be made by their enemies.

(6) *The Suicidalness of Militarism*

The three previous sections have presented illustrations of 'resting on one's oars', which is the passive way of succumbing to the nemesis of creativity. We now pass on to the active form of aberration, summarized in the Greek formula κόρος, ὕβρις, ἄτη (surfeit, outrageous behaviour, and destruction). Militarism is an obvious example. The reason why the Assyrians brought ruin on themselves was not because, like the victors reviewed at the end of the previous chapter, they allowed their armour to 'rust'. From a military standpoint they were continuously and progressively efficient. Their ruin came because their aggressiveness exhausted them—besides rendering them intolerable to their neighbours. The Assyrians are an example of a military frontier province turning its arms against the interior provinces of its society. The similar cases of the Austrasian Franks and Timur Lenk are also examined, and other examples are cited.

(7) *The Intoxication of Victory*

A theme similar to that of the preceding paragraph is illustrated from a non-military sphere by the example of the Hildebrandine Papacy, an institution which failed after raising itself and Christendom from the depths to the heights. It failed because, intoxicated by its own success, it was tempted to make illegitimate use of political weapons in pursuit of inordinate aims. The controversy over Investiture is examined from this standpoint.

V. THE DISINTEGRATIONS OF CIVILIZATIONS

XVII. THE NATURE OF DISINTEGRATION

(1) *A General Survey*

Is disintegration a necessary and invariable consequence of breakdown? Egyptiac and Far Eastern history show that there is an alternative, namely petrifaction, which was also nearly the fate of the Hellenic civilization and may be the fate of our own. The outstanding criterion of disintegration is the schism of the body social into three fractions: dominant minority, internal proletariat, and external proletariat. What has already been said about these fractions is recapitulated, and the plan of the following chapters is indicated.

(2) *Schism and Palingenesia*

The apocalyptic philosophy of Karl Marx proclaims that the class war will be followed, after the Dictatorship of the Proletariat, by a new order of society. Apart from Marx's particular application of the idea, this is what actually happens when a society falls into the tripartite schism already noticed. Each of the fractions achieves a characteristic work of creation: the dominant minority a universal state, the internal proletariat a universal church, and the external proletariat barbarian war-bands.

XVIII. SCHISM IN THE BODY SOCIAL

(1) *Dominant Minorities*

Though militarists and exploiters are conspicuous among the characteristic types in dominant minorities, there are also nobler types: the legists and administrators who maintain the universal states, and the philosophic inquirers who endow societies in decline with their characteristic philosophies, e.g. the long chain of Hellenic philosophers from Socrates to Plotinus. Examples are cited from various other civilizations.

(2) *Internal Proletariats*

The history of the Hellenic society shows an internal proletariat recruited from three sources: citizens of the Hellenic states disinherited and ruined by political or economic upheavals; conquered peoples; victims of the slave-trade. All alike are proletarians in feeling themselves 'in' but not 'of' the society. Their first reactions are violent, but these are followed by 'gentle' reactions culminating in the discovery of 'higher religions' such as Christianity. This religion, like Mithraism and its other rivals in the Hellenic world, originated in one of the other 'civilized' societies conquered by Hellenic arms. The internal proletariats of other societies are examined and similar phenomena observed: e.g. the origins of Judaism and Zoroastrianism in the internal proletariat of the Babylonic society were similar to those of Christianity and Mithraism in the Hellenic society, though, for reasons given, their later development was different. The transformation of the primitive Buddhist philosophy into the Mahāyāna provided a 'higher religion' for the Sinic internal proletariat.

(3) *The Internal Proletariat of the Western World*

Abundant evidence can be adduced of the existence of an internal proletariat here—among other things, the existence of an 'intelligentsia' recruited from the proletariat as an agent of the dominant minority. The characteristics of an intelligentsia are discussed. The internal proletariat of the modern Western society has, however, shown itself markedly unfertile in the production of new 'higher religions', and it is suggested that this is due to the continued vitality of the Christian Church from which Western Christendom was born.

(4) External Proletariats

So long as a civilization is growing, its cultural influence radiates into and permeates its primitive neighbours to an indefinite distance. They become a part of the 'uncreative majority' which follows the creative minority's lead. But when a civilization has broken down the charm ceases to act, the barbarians become hostile, and a military frontier establishes itself which may be pushed far afield but ultimately becomes stationary. When this stage has been reached, time works on the side of the barbarians. These facts are illustrated from Hellenic history. Violent and gentle responses by the external proletariat are pointed out. The pressure of a hostile civilization transforms primitive fertility religions of the external proletariat into religions of the Olympian 'divine war-band' type. The characteristic product of triumphant external proletariats is epic poetry.

(5) External Proletariats of the Western World

Their history is reviewed and violent and gentle responses of the external proletariats are illustrated. Owing to the overwhelming material efficiency of the modern Western society, barbarism of the historic type has almost disappeared. In two of its remaining strongholds, Afghanistan and Sa'udi Arabia, native rulers are protecting themselves by adopting imitations of Western culture. However, a new and more atrocious barbarism has become rampant in the ancient centres of Western Christendom itself.

(6) Alien and Indigenous Inspirations

Dominant minorities and external proletariats are handicapped if they have an alien inspiration. For example, universal states founded by alien dominant minorities (such as British India) are less successful in making themselves acceptable than indigenous universal states like the Roman Empire. Barbarian war-bands provoke much more stubborn and passionate opposition if, like the Hyksos in Egypt and the Mongols in China, their barbarism is tinged with the influence of an alien civilization. On the other hand the 'higher religions' produced by internal proletariats generally owe their attractiveness to an alien inspiration. Nearly all the 'higher religions' illustrate this fact.

The fact that the history of a 'higher religion' cannot be understood unless two civilizations are taken into account—the civilization from which it has derived its inspiration and the civilization in which it has taken root—shows that the assumption on which this Study has hitherto been based—the assumption that civilizations, taken in isolation, are 'intelligible fields of study'—begins at this point to break down.

XIX. SCHISM IN THE SOUL

(1) *Alternative Ways of Behaviour, Feeling, and Life*

When a society begins to disintegrate, the various ways of behaviour, feeling, and life characteristic of individuals during the growth stage are replaced by alternative substitutes, one (the former in each pair) passive, the other (the latter) active.

Abandon and self-control are alternative substitutes for creativity; truancy and martyrdom for the discipleship of mimesis.

The sense of drift and the sense of sin are alternative substitutes for the *élan* which accompanies growth; the sense of promiscuity and the sense of unity for the 'sense of style' which is the subjective counterpart of the objective process of differentiation which accompanies growth.

On the plane of life there are two pairs of alternative variations upon the movement towards a transfer of the field of action from the macrocosm to the microcosm which underlies the process previously described as etherialization. The first pair of alternatives—archaism and futurism—fail to achieve this transfer and breed violence. The second pair—detachment and transfiguration—succeed in making the transfer and are characterized by gentleness. Archaism is an attempt to 'put back the clock', futurism an attempt at a short cut to an impossible millennium on Earth. Detachment, which is a spiritualization of archaism, is a withdrawal into the fortress of the soul, an abandonment of 'the world'. Transfiguration, which is a spiritualization of futurism, is the action of the soul which produces the 'higher religions'. Examples of all four ways of life and of their relations to each other are given. Finally, it is shown that some of these ways of feeling and life are primarily characteristic of souls in dominant minorities, others of souls in proletariats.

(2) '*Abandon*' *and Self-control* are defined, with examples.

(3) *Truancy and Martyrdom* are defined, with examples.

(4) *The Sense of Drift and the Sense of Sin*

The sense of drift is due to a feeling that the whole World is ruled by Chance—or Necessity, which is shown to be the same thing. The wide range of the belief is illustrated. Certain predestinarian religions, e.g. Calvinism, are productive of remarkable energy and confidence, and the cause of this, at first sight, curious fact is considered.

Whereas the Sense of Drift normally acts as an opiate, the Sense of Sin should be a stimulus. The doctrines of *Karma* and 'Original Sin' (which combine the ideas of sin and determinism) are discussed. The Hebrew Prophets furnish the classic case of the recognition of sin as being the true, though not the obvious, cause of national misfortunes. The teaching of the Prophets was taken over by the Christian Church and was thus introduced to a Hellenic world which for many centuries had been unconsciously preparing itself to receive it. The Western society, though inheriting the Christian tradition, seems to have discarded the sense of sin, which is an essential part of that tradition.

(5) *The Sense of Promiscuity*

This is a passive substitute for the sense of style characteristic of civilizations in course of growth. It manifests itself in various ways. (*a*) *Vulgarity and Barbarism in Manners.* The dominant minority shows itself prone to 'proletarianization', adopting the vulgarities of the internal and the barbarisms of the external proletariat, until, in the final stage of dissolution, its way of life has become indistinguishable from theirs. (*b*) *Vulgarity and Barbarism in Art* is the price commonly paid for the abnormally wide diffusion of the art of a disintegrating civilization. (*c*) *Lingue Franche.* The intermingling of peoples leads to confusion and mutual competition of languages; some of them spread as 'lingue franche', and in every case their expansion entails a corresponding debasement. Many examples are examined as illustrations. (*d*) *Syncretism in Religion.* Three movements are to be distinguished: the amalgamations of separate schools of philosophy; the amalgamations of separate religions, e.g. the dilution of the religion of Israel by combination with the neighbouring cults, which was opposed with ultimate success by the Hebrew Prophets; and the amalgamation or syncretism of philosophies and religions with one another. Since philosophies are a product of dominant minorities and 'higher religions' a product of internal proletariats, the interaction here is comparable with that illustrated in (*a*) above. Here, as there, the proletarians move some way towards the position of the dominant minority, but the dominant minority moves a

far greater distance towards the position of the internal proletariat. For example, the Christian religion employs for its theological exegesis the apparatus of Hellenic philosophy, but this is
a small concession compared with the transformation undergone
by Greek philosophy between the ages of Plato and of Julian.
(e) *Cuius regio eius religio?* This section is a digression arising out
of the case of the philosopher-emperor Julian considered at the
end of the previous section. Can dominant minorities make up
for their spiritual weakness by using political force to impose the
religion or philosophy of their choice? The answer is that, subject
to certain exceptions, they will fail, and the religion which seeks
the support of force will grievously injure itself thereby. The one
apparently striking exception is the case of the spread of Islam,
and this is examined and shown to be not really as much of an
exception as it at first appears to be. An opposite formula, *religio
regionis religio regis*, is nearer the truth: a ruler who, from cynicism
or conviction, adopts the religion of his subjects prospers thereby.

(6) *The Sense of Unity*

This is the 'active' antithesis of the passive feeling of promiscuity. It expresses itself materially in the creation of universal
states, and the same spirit inspires the concepts of an omnipotent
law or an omnipresent godhead pervading and ruling the Universe.
These two concepts are examined and illustrated. In the latter
connexion the career of Yahweh, the 'jealous god' of the Hebrews,
is traced from his beginnings as the 'jinn' of a Sinaitic volcano
to his eventual sublimation as the historic vehicle for a purified
and exalted conception of the One True God who is worshipped
by the Christian Church, and an explanation is offered of his
triumph over all his rivals.

(7) *Archaism*

This is an attempt to escape from an intolerable present by
reconstructing an earlier phase in the life of a disintegrating society.
Ancient and modern examples are given, the modern including
the Gothic Revival and the artificial revival, for nationalistic
reasons, of a variety of more or less extinct languages. Archaizing
movements generally either prove sterile or transform themselves
into their opposite, namely:

(8) *Futurism*

This is an attempt to escape the present by a leap into the darkness of an unknown future. It involves a scrapping of the traditional

links with the past, and is in fact revolutionism. In art it expresses itself as iconoclasm.

(9) *The Self-transcendence of Futurism*

As archaism may fall into the gulf of futurism, so futurism may rise to the heights of transfiguration. In other words, it may abandon the forlorn attempt to find its Utopia on the terrestrial plane and may seek it in the life of the soul, untrammelled by time and space. In this connexion the history of the post-Captivity Jews is examined. Futurism expressed itself in a series of suicidal attempts to create a Jewish Empire on Earth, from Zerubbabel to Bar Kōkabā; transfiguration, in the establishment of the Christian religion.

(10) *Detachment and Transfiguration*

Detachment is an attitude which finds its most uncompromising and exalted expression in a philosophy professing to represent the teaching of the Buddha. Its logical conclusion is suicide, for real detachment is possible only for a god. The Christian religion, on the other hand, proclaims a God who has voluntarily abandoned a detachment which it was clearly within His power to enjoy. 'God so loved the World. . . .'

(11) *Palingenesia*

Of the four ways of life here examined, transfiguration is the only one which presents a thoroughfare, and it does so by a transference of the field of action from the macrocosm to the microcosm. This is true also of detachment, but, whereas detachment is only a withdrawal, transfiguration is a withdrawal and return: a palingenesia, not in the sense of a rebirth of another example of an old species but in the sense of a birth of a new species of society.

XX. THE RELATION BETWEEN DISINTEGRATING SOCIETIES AND INDIVIDUALS

(1) *The Creative Genius as a Saviour*

In the growth stage creative individuals lead successful responses to successive challenges. In the disintegration stage they appear as saviours *of* or *from* the disintegrating society.

(2) *The Saviour with the Sword*

These are the founders and maintainers of universal states, but all the works of the sword prove ephemeral.

(3) *The Saviour with the Time Machine*

These are the archaists and futurists. These, too, take to the sword and suffer the swordsman's fate.

(4) *The Philosopher masked by a King*

This is Plato's famous remedy. It fails on account of the incompatibility between the detachment of a philosopher and the coercive methods characteristic of political potentates.

(5) *The God incarnate in a Man*

Various imperfect approximations fall by the way and Jesus of Nazareth alone conquers death.

XXI. THE RHYTHM OF DISINTEGRATION

Disintegration proceeds not uniformly but by an alternation of routs and rallies. For example, the establishment of a universal state is a rally after the rout of a time of troubles, and the dissolution of a universal state is the final rout. As there is found to be usually one rally followed by a rout in the course of a time of troubles and one rout followed by a rally in the course of a universal state, the normal rhythm seems to be rout–rally–rout–rally–rout–rally–rout: three-and-a-half beats. This pattern is exemplified in the histories of several extinct societies, and then applied to the history of our own Western Christendom with a view to ascertaining what stage in its development our society has reached.

XXII. STANDARDIZATION THROUGH DISINTEGRATION

As differentiation is the mark of growth, so standardization i- the mark of disintegration. The chapter concludes with an indicas tion of the problems standing over for examination in the forthcoming volumes.

VI. UNIVERSAL STATES

XXIII. ENDS OR MEANS?

The course of the work down to the present point is summarized, and reasons are given for proceeding to a further examination, in successive Parts, of universal states, universal churches, and barbarian war-bands. Are universal states to be regarded simply as the final phases of civilizations or as prologues to further developments?

XXIV. THE MIRAGE OF IMMORTALITY

The citizens of universal states not only, in most cases, welcome their establishment but believe them to be immortal, and continue in this belief, not only when the universal state is obviously on the verge of dissolution but after it has disappeared, with the result that the institution reappears as a 'ghost' of its former self, e.g. the Roman Empire of the Graeco-Roman world as the Holy Roman Empire in the affiliated society of Western Christendom. An explanation may be found in the fact that a universal state marks a rally after a time of troubles.

XXV. *SIC VOS NON VOBIS*

The institutions of a universal state fail in the long run to preserve its existence, but at the same time serve the purposes of other institutions, more particularly, the purposes of the higher religions of the internal proletariats.

(1) *The Conductivity of Universal States*

The universal state, by imposing order and uniformity, provides a medium of high conductivity, not only geographically between what had previously been separate parochial states, but also socially between the different classes of society.

(2) *The Psychology of Peace*

The tolerance which the rulers of universal states find necessary for their own maintenance favours the spread of higher religions, as is illustrated by the common idea (expressed, for example, in Milton's Nativity Ode) that the Roman Empire was providentially ordained for the benefit of the Christian Church. Such toleration is not, however, universal or absolute. At the same time this tolerance, in the form of anti-militarism, will prove advantageous to aggressive outsiders—barbarians or neighbouring civilizations.

(3) *The Serviceability of Imperial Institutions*

Communications. Roads, sea routes, and their orderly maintenance serve others beside the Government, e.g. Saint Paul's use of Roman roads. Will the higher religions of the present day make similar use of the world-wide system of communications provided by modern technology? If so, they will encounter problems which can be illustrated by the histories of Christian missions in non-Christian worlds at earlier dates.

Garrisons and Colonies serve purposes of civilization as well as of government, but also contribute to the pammixia and proletarianization which mark disintegrating societies. The most obvious beneficiaries are the barbarian war-bands, but the higher religions profit also. Illustration from the development of Islam. Mithraism spread from garrison to garrison along the frontier of the Roman Empire and Christianity from colony to colony, e.g. the significance of Corinth and Lyons, both of them colonies founded by the Roman Government, in the early history of the Christian Church.

Provinces. Contrasted policies illustrated from the history of the Sinic universal state, and the use of provincial organization by a higher religion illustrated from the development of the Christian Church.

Capital Cities. Various factors influence their location. The original capital of the conquerors who found the universal state may not prove permanently suitable. A survey of capitals and their migrations follows. Some capitals which have lost their political significance remain memorable as headquarters of religions.

Official Languages and Scripts. The problems confronting the rulers of universal states in the choice of official languages and their various solutions. The currency of some languages, e.g. Aramaic and Latin, has extended, in time and space, far beyond the empires in which they originally prevailed.

Law. Here again the rulers of universal states have differed greatly from one another in the extent to which they have imposed their own systems on their subjects. The legal systems of universal states have been utilized by communities for which they were not designed, e.g. the use of Roman Law by the Muslims and by the Christian Church, and the use of the Code of Hammurabi by the authors of the Mosaic Law.

Calendars; Weights and Measures; Money. The problems of calendar-making and the close association of calendars with religion. Our methods of measuring time are still part Roman, part Sumerian, and the French Revolution failed to revolutionize them. Weights and measures: the battle of the decimal and duodecimal systems. Money: its significance, and origin in Greek cities; its subsequent spread through the absorption of these cities into the Lydian and Achaemenian empires. Paper money in the Sinic world.

Standing Armies. The Roman Army a source of inspiration to the Christian Church.

Civil Services. Civil service problems illustrated by a comparison of the policies of Augustus, Peter the Great, and the British Rāj in India. Civil service *éthos* in the Sinic and British Indian services.

The Roman Civil Service training of three great churchmen founders of Western Christendom.

Citizenship. Extension of citizenship a privilege conferred by the rulers of universal states; it helps to produce the egalitarian conditions in which the higher religions flourish.

VII. UNIVERSAL CHURCHES

XXVI. ALTERNATIVE CONCEPTIONS OF THE RELATIONS BETWEEN UNIVERSAL CHURCHES AND CIVILIZATIONS

(1) *Churches as Cancers*

Since churches grow in the decaying bodies social of universal states, they are naturally regarded as cancers, both by their contemporary opponents and by a school of modern historians. Reasons are given for regarding this view as mistaken; religions tend to quicken rather than destroy the sense of social obligation in their votaries.

(2) *Churches as Chrysalises*

Each of the civilizations of the third generation alive today has as its background a church, through which it is affiliated to a civilization of the second generation. The indebtedness of the Modern Western civilization to the Christian Church is analysed. By contrast, the civilizations of the second generation were affiliated to their predecessors by other links, and this fact suggests a revision of our hitherto accepted plan of the course of history.

(3) *Churches as a Higher Species of Society*

(a) *A New Classification*

The rises and falls of civilizations compared with the revolutions of a wheel whose purpose is to carry forward the chariot of Religion. The steps in religious progress represented by the names of Abraham, Moses, the Hebrew Prophets, and Christ are to be seen as products, respectively, of the disintegrations of the Sumeric, Egyptiac, Babylonic, and Hellenic societies. Does the forthcoming unification of the World today offer a prospect of a further advance? If so, the higher religions now existing have difficult lessons to learn.

(b) *The Significance of the Churches' Past*

An admission that the record of the Churches hitherto seems to disqualify them for the role here assigned to them.

(c) The Conflict between Heart and Head

The impact of Modern Science on Religion was not the first conflict of its kind. The conflict between the early Christian Church and Hellenic philosophy had ended in a compromise, in which the philosophers accepted the 'Truth' of Christian Revelation provided that that Revelation clothed itself in the language of the philosophers. These outworn Hellenic garments have long since become a source of embarrassment, enlisting the Christian Church in a number of non-religious lost causes with which Christianity had no concern. Religion must surrender to Science every province of intellectual knowledge to which Science can establish a title. Religion and Science are concerned with different kinds of truth, and the modern psychology of the Subconscious Psyche throws a profound light on the nature of the difference.

(d) The Promise of the Churches' Future

The distinguishing mark of the Churches is that they all have as a member the One True God. This differentiates them from all other types of societies, and the consequences of this difference are elucidated.

XXVII. THE ROLE OF CIVILIZATIONS IN THE LIVES OF CHURCHES

(1) Civilizations as Overtures

An examination of the vocabulary of technical terms which the Christian Church took over from the Hellenic civilization and transformed to new uses is an example of 'etherialization' and suggests that the Hellenic civilization served as an overture to Christianity.

(2) Civilizations as Regressions

The subsequent degradation of these same technical terms when taken over for secular use by the Western society which has emerged from, and emancipated itself from, the Christian Church.

XXVIII. THE CHALLENGE OF MILITANCY ON EARTH

The break-away of the affiliated civilization from the Church is due to false steps on the part of the Church, and these are an inevitable consequence of the embodiment of the spirit of Religion in an ecclesiastical institution for the purpose of 'militancy on Earth'. Three types of false step are noted: (i) a political imperialism gives reasonable cause for offence to secular authorities as an interference with the proper discharge of their own duties; (ii) the economic success which inevitably attends the discharge of economic duties 'heartily, as to the Lord and not unto men'; (iii) the idolization by a Church of its corporate self.

Can Religion promise no Golden Age ahead at the end of the journey? In an Other World perhaps, but not in this one. Original Sin presents an unsurmountable obstacle. This World is a province of the Kingdom of God, but it is a rebellious province, and, in the nature of things, it will always remain so.

VIII. HEROIC AGES

XXIX. THE COURSE OF THE TRAGEDY

(1) *A Social Barrage*

An heroic age is the social and psychological consequence of the crystallization of a *limes*, or military frontier, between the universal state of a disintegrating civilization and the trans-frontier barbarians. It may be likened to a barrage or dam across a valley, creating a reservoir above it, and the implications of this simile are elaborated in this and the following sections of the chapter.

(2) *The Accumulation of Pressure*

The pressure on the *limes*, or barrage, increases as the trans-frontier barbarians learn the military techniques of the civilization that they are 'up against'. The guardians of the civilization find themselves reduced to employing barbarians themselves, and these mercenaries turn against their employers and strike at the heart of the empire.

(3) *The Cataclysm and its Consequences*

The triumphant barbarians are inevitably ruined by their own success, being totally unfitted to cope with the crisis that they have created. None the less, in their agony, they give birth to heroic legends, and ideals of conduct such as are expressed in the Homeric *Aidôs* and *Nemesis* and the Umayyad *Hilm*. The heroic age of disorder ends with surprising suddenness, and is followed by a 'dark age' in which the forces of law and order gradually reassert themselves. The 'interregnum' ends, and a new civilization begins.

(4) *Fancy and Fact*

Hesiod's curious scheme of 'Ages'—Gold, Silver, Bronze, and Iron, in which an 'Age of Heroes' is inserted between the Bronze and the Iron Ages. The 'Age of Heroes' is, in fact, the Age of

Bronze described over again, in terms not of historic fact but of Homeric fancy. The glamour of the epic poetry produced by triumphant barbarism deceived Hesiod, the poet of the 'dark age' following. It also deceived, for example, the forerunners of the Third Reich who glorified the 'blond beasts' of 'Nordic' barbarism. Yet the barbarians served as a link through which those civilizations of the second generation that produced higher religions were affiliated to civilizations of the first generation.

NOTE: *'The Monstrous Regiment of Women'*

An explanation of how demonic women came to play so conspicuous a part in the tragedies of heroic ages, not only in legend but also in fact.

IX. CONTACTS BETWEEN CIVILIZATIONS IN SPACE

XXX. AN EXPANSION OF THE FIELD OF STUDY

Civilizations, which can be studied adequately in separation from each other in their phases of genesis, growth, and breakdown, cease to be intelligible fields of study in their final phase of disintegration. Their contacts in this phase have now to be studied. Certain geographical areas—Syria and the Oxus-Jaxartes Basin—have been conspicuous in the histories of these contacts, and it is no accident that these same areas and their immediate surroundings also contain the birthplaces of the higher religions.

XXXI. A SURVEY OF ENCOUNTERS BETWEEN CONTEMPORARY CIVILIZATIONS

(1) *A Plan of Operations*

We propose to begin by examining the encounters between the Modern West and all the other contemporary civilizations. The modern period of the history of the Western society can be dated from two events, one just before the close of the fifteenth century of our era, and the other just after the beginning of the sixteenth. The first was the mastering of the technique of oceanic navigation; the second was the break-up of the 'medieval' Western Christian Commonwealth which had been put together and held together by the Papacy. 'The Reformation' was, of course, a stage in a long process of evolution which had begun in the thirteenth century and was not completed till the seventeenth. But 'the Reformation' itself overtook the same generation as had witnessed the voyages of Columbus and da Gama. We shall next step backward in time and examine the contacts of the West in its 'medieval' phase with the two rival societies which it encountered; and then the contacts of the Hellenic society, concluding with a glance at some earlier contacts of the same order.

In dealing with the contacts of the Modern West, we shall find that these chapters of history, though known to us in detail up to date, are most of them—perhaps all of them—unfinished, and leave off on a note of interrogation.

(2) Operations according to Plan

(a) Encounters with the Modern Western Civilization

(i) *The Modern West and Russia.* The original patrimony of Russian Orthodox Christendom had suffered from invasions and conquests at the hands of the Western parochial state of Poland–Lithuania from the fourteenth century onwards—losses not fully retrieved until A.D. 1945. The radiation of the Western culture received a welcoming ('Herodian') response from Peter the Great, but, after two centuries of Westernization on lines approved in the West itself, the Petrine régime was tried and found wanting in the ordeal of the First World War, and was supplanted by an heretical Westernizing régime: Communism.

(ii) *The Modern West and the Main Body of Orthodox Christendom.* In this society, which had been politically clamped together under the rule of an alien universal state, the Ottoman Empire, modern Western culture penetrated, not from above downwards, as in Russia, but from below upwards, from the seventeenth century onwards. This might have led to the Westernizing of the Pādishāh's empire under Phanariot Greek influence. Unfortunately nationalist movements prevailed and led to the break-up of the empire into parochial states. Russia failed to secure the leadership of these peoples, either on Pan-Orthodox or on Pan-Slav lines, though a Russian Pan-Communist régime has now been imposed upon some of them.

(iii) *The Modern West and the Hindu World.* Here the West imposed itself in the form of an alien universal state, replacing another alien universal state, the Muslim Mughal Rāj, which had already gone into liquidation. The British Rāj employed an Indian élite, much as the Ottoman Pādishāh had employed an Eastern Orthodox Christian élite. This Indian élite eventually succeeded (where the Phanariots had failed) in Indianizing the Rāj while preserving it intact, with the large exception of the secession of Pakistan. The strong and weak points of the British Indian Civil Service are discussed, and the population problem indicated as the cloud on the horizon of India's future.

(iv) *The Modern West and the Islamic World.* At the opening of the Modern Western period the two sister Islamic societies, Arabic and Iranic, blocked all the overland lines of access to other parts of the World from the domains of the Western and Russian societies, but a sensational reversal of fortune to Islam's disadvantage was about to follow. Since this change in the balance of power the rulers of a number of Muslim states have been pursuing policies of Petrine 'Herodianism' with varying degrees of success. The Islamic world embraces the homelands of three out of the four primary civilizations of the Old World, and the natural agricultural wealth of these areas has now been reinforced by the discovery that they are rich in oil. In consequence they have become the 'Naboth's Vineyard' of a twentieth-century World in which the West and Russia are in conflict.

(v) *The Modern West and the Jews.* The Jewish Diaspora did not fit into the Western system of homogeneous territorial states. In an historical survey starting, not from the opening of the Modern Age of Western history, but from the beginnings of the Western Christian society itself, three phases may be noted. In the first phase (*e.g.* in the history of Visigothia) the Jews, though unpopular and ill-treated, were found useful, since, in that age, the Western Christians were (as Cecil Rhodes said of the Oxford dons) 'children in finance'. In the next phase, the Western Christians had learnt to 'be their own Jews', and the Jews were expelled (e.g. from England in A.D. 1291). In the third phase, the Western society was financially competent enough to allow the Jews back again (e.g. to England in A.D. 1655) and to welcome their *expertise* in business. The Liberal age which then ensued unhappily did not prove to be the end of the story. The section concludes with examinations of Anti-Semitism and of Zionism.

(vi) *The Modern West and the Far Eastern and Indigenous American Civilizations.* These civilizations had had no previous contact with the West before it presented itself in its Modern phase. To all appearance (though this may be deceptive) the American civilizations were completely obliterated. The stories of the impact of the Modern West on China and on Japan run curiously parallel. In both cases there is a reception of Western culture in its Early Modern religious form, followed by rejection; and, at a later date, an impact of Late Modern Western technology. The differences between the two histories are largely accounted for by the fact that China is a vast and sprawling empire and Japan a close-knit insular community. Both societies were, at the time of writing, in eclipse: China under Communism and Japan under American control. Both, like India, were facing a population problem.

(vii) *Characteristics of the Encounters between the Modern West and its Contemporaries.* 'Modern Western' civilization is 'middle-class' civilization. Those non-Western societies which had developed a middle class welcomed the Modern Western êthos. If a ruler of a non-Western civilization that had no indigenous middle class wished to 'Westernize', he had to create an artificial middle class for his purpose in the form of an intelligentsia. These intelligentsias ultimately turn against their masters.

(b) Encounters with Medieval Western Christendom

(i) *The Flow and Ebb of the Crusades.* Medieval Western Christendom entered on a period of expansion in the eleventh century, followed by a period of collapse and withdrawal on some frontiers, though not on others, two centuries later. The causes of this expansion and subsequent retreat are analysed.

(ii) *The Medieval West and the Syriac World.* The Crusaders and their Muslim adversaries had much in common. Norman 'Franks' and Saljūq Turks were, both alike, ex-barbarians recently converted to the higher religion of the society which they had entered and, in many respects, dominated. The cultural radiation of the Syriac civilization into the less advanced Western Christian society affected poetry, architecture, philosophy, and science.

(iii) *The Medieval West and Greek Orthodox Christendom.* There was a greater antipathy between these two Christian Societies than between either of them and its Muslim neighbours. This mutual antipathy is illustrated by citations, on the one side, from the Lombard Bishop Liutprand's account of his mission to Constantinople and, on the other side, from the picture of the Crusaders in Anna Comnena's *History*.

(c) Encounters between Civilizations of the first two Generations

(i) *Encounters with the post-Alexandrine Hellenic Civilization.* The Hellenic civilization in this phase had encounters with every contemporary civilization in the Old World, and the results of the consequent Hellenic radiation were not worked out and completed until several centuries after the Hellenic society itself had gone into dissolution. The Hellenic culture spread far beyond the conquests of Hellenic armies, e.g. into the Sinic world.

The career of Alexander marks an expansion in Hellenic history comparable with the conquest of the Ocean in the history of Western Christendom; but, whereas the West, in its Modern phase, was emancipating itself from its chrysalis religion, Christianity, the

Hellenic civilization, having had no such religious chrysalis, was becoming increasingly hungry for religion.

(ii) *Encounters with the pre-Alexandrine Hellenic Civilization.* A conflict between three antagonists for mastery of the Mediterranean Basin, the rivals of the pre-Alexandrine Hellenic society being the Syriac society and a fossilized remnant of the Hittite society, namely, the Etruscans. The Syriac society manifested itself both in the Phoenician sea-power and, in the later stages of the story, in the Achaemenian Empire. The most important cultural conquest of the Greeks in this period turned out to be the Hellenization of Rome, which was achieved indirectly through a previous Hellenization of the Etruscans.

(iii) *Tares and Wheat.* The only fruitful results of encounters between civilizations are the works of peace. A glance at contacts between civilizations of the first generation, Indic and Sinic, Egyptiac and Sumeric, follows.

XXXII. THE DRAMA OF ENCOUNTERS BETWEEN CONTEMPORARIES

(1) *A Concatenation of Encounters*

On the military level, a challenge from one side leads to a challenge from the other, and this, after redressing the balance, passes over into a counter-aggression and provokes a retort in turn. A chain of such encounters between 'East' and 'West' is traced from the Achaemenian Empire's assault on Greece down to the twentieth-century reactions of non-Western peoples against Western imperialism.

(2) *Diversities of Responses*

A military response is not the only one possible. Communist Russia reinforces armaments with ideological warfare. Where a military response has been impossible, or has been tried and failed, some conquered peoples have reacted by maintaining their identity as communities by an intensive cultivation of their religion. A classic case of this response is that of the Jews since their dispersion. The supreme response is the creation of a higher religion which in due course takes the conquerors captive.

XXXIII. THE CONSEQUENCES OF ENCOUNTERS BETWEEN CONTEMPORARIES

(1) *Aftermaths of Unsuccessful Assaults*

The result of the successful repulse of an assault may be the militarization of the victor, with ultimately disastrous results.

Thus a victory over the Achaemenian invader led, within fifty years, to the breakdown of the Hellenic civilization.

(2) *Aftermaths of Successful Assaults*

(a) *Effects on the Body Social.* The social price that a successfully aggressive civilization has to pay is a seepage of its alien victims' culture into its own life-stream. The effect on the victims of assault is of the same order, but more complex. The introduction of Western ideals and institutions into non-Western societies often produces disconcerting results, for 'one man's meat is another man's poison'. The attempt to introduce one element of an alien culture, while excluding the rest, is doomed to failure.

(b) *Responses of the Soul*

(i) *Dehumanization.* The successful assailant succumbs to *hubris* and regards the conquered as 'under-dogs'. Thus the brotherhood of Man is denied. When 'under-dog' is regarded as a 'heathen' he may recover human status by conversion; when regarded as a 'barbarian' he may recover human status by passing an examination; but when he is regarded as a 'native' he has no hope, short of the overthrow or the conversion of his master.

(ii) *Zealotism and Herodianism.* The terms imply a clear-cut distinction between rejection and acceptance of the conqueror's êthos, but a closer examination suggests that the distinction is not as clearcut as it looks at first. The point is illustrated by a consideration of modern Japan, and of the careers of Gandhi and Lenin.

(iii) *Evangelism.* The self-defeat of the original Zealots and Herodians is set against the achievement of St. Paul.

NOTE. *'Asia' and 'Europe': Facts and Fantasies*

'Asia' and 'Europe' originated as names of the opposite mainland coasts confronting Hellenic mariners on a voyage from the Aegean to the Black Sea. The attribution of political and cultural significance to the terms has led to nothing but confusion. 'Europe' is a sub-continent, with an ill-defined frontier, of the continent of 'Eurasia'.

X. CONTACTS BETWEEN CIVILIZATIONS IN TIME

XXXIV. A SURVEY OF RENAISSANCES

(1) *Introduction—'the Renaissance'*

The origin of the term 'renaissance' is stated, and the meaning given to it in this *Study* explained.

(2) *Renaissances of Political Ideas and Institutions*

The late Medieval Italian renaissance began earlier, and exercised a more enduring influence on the political plane than on the literary or the artistic. City states; secular monarchies; the Holy Roman Empire. Ecclesiastical coronation a renaissance of an Old Testament rite.

(3) *Renaissances of Systems of Law.*

The revivals of Roman Law in Eastern Orthodox Christendom and in Western Christendom, and their consequences for Church and State.

(4) *Renaissances of Philosophies*

The revivals of the Sinic Confucian philosophy in the Far Eastern society in China and of the Hellenic Aristotelian philosophy in Medieval Western Christendom were parallel events in several respects. The former survived until worsted by an intruding Modern Western êthos at the beginning of the twentieth century. The latter was shaken by the Hellenic literary renaissance of the fifteenth century and was finally worsted by the 'Baconian' scientific movement of the seventeenth century.

(5) *Renaissances of Languages and Literatures*

A conspicuous part was played by dynastic rulers in launching renaissances in this department, e.g. the prodigious libraries assembled by certain Chinese emperors. The Italian renaissance of Hellenic languages and literatures had an abortive forerunner in the 'Carolingian renaissance', which, in turn, had its roots in a renaissance in Northumbria. Renaissances cannot succeed until the society seeking to call up the 'ghost' of a dead civilization has itself reached the appropriate stage of development for performing the act of necromancy.

(6) *Renaissances of the Visual Arts*

A number of examples are cited, besides the Western instance popularly known as 'the Renaissance'. The course of this last is traced in architecture, sculpture, and painting. In all three departments the ultimate result was to sterilize originality.

(7) *Renaissances of Religious Ideals and Institutions*

The contemptuous attitude of Judaism to its successful Christian offspring, and the uneasy and ambiguous attitude of the Christian Church towards the Jewish ideals of monotheism and aniconism, are discussed. The Sabbatarianism and bibliolatry of

the Protestant movement from the sixteenth century onwards
furnish a clear example of a powerful and popular renaissance of
Judaism within the Western Christian fold.

XI. LAW AND FREEDOM IN HISTORY
XXXV. THE PROBLEM

(1) *The Meaning of Law*

The 'Law of Nature' distinguished from the 'Law of God'.

(2) *The Antinomianism of Modern Western Historians*

The notion that History reveals the workings of a Divine
Providence, as maintained down to the time of Bossuet, has since
been discredited. But the men of science, whose Law of Nature
has replaced the Law of God in most departments of inquiry, have
felt constrained to leave History in a state of lawlessness where
anything may be expected to follow from anything else, as in the
view of H. A. L. Fisher.

XXXVI. THE AMENABILITY OF HUMAN
AFFAIRS TO 'LAWS OF NATURE'

(1) *A Survey of the Evidence*

(*a*) *The Private Affairs of Individuals.* Insurance companies rely
on a calculable regularity in human affairs.

(*b*) *The Industrial Affairs of a Modern Western Society.* Economists find themselves able to calculate wave-lengths of trade
cycles.

(*c*) *Rivalries of Parochial States: the Balance of Power.* The
fairly regular recurrences of war and peace cycles in the histories
of several civilizations.

(*d*) *The Disintegrations of Civilizations.* Regularities in the rout-
and-rally alternations, with suggested explanations.

(*e*) *The Growths of Civilizations.* The regularity traceable in
breakdown and disintegration phases is here absent.

(*f*) *'There is no armour against Fate.'* Further illustrations are
given of the persistence with which a tendency, thwarted first at
one point and then at another, sometimes ultimately wins through.

(2) *Possible explanations of the currency of Laws of Nature in
History*

The uniformities that we have discerned may be due to the
working either of laws current in Man's non-human environment
or of laws inherent in the psychic structure of Man himself. These
alternatives are examined, and it is found that Man's dependence

on the laws of non-human Nature diminishes with Man's progress in technology. The succession of human generations is found to have great significance, three generations being the time-span of several kinds of changes in mental habit. The laws of the Subconscious Psyche, which psychologists were only just beginning to discover at the time of writing, are next considered as an influence on the course of history.

(3) *Are Laws of Nature current in History inexorable or controllable?*

As regards the laws of non-human Nature, Man cannot alter them, but he can harness them to his own purposes. As regards the laws affecting human nature itself, a more cautious answer seems to be called for. The result will depend on Man's relations, not just with his fellow men and himself, but above all with God his Saviour.

XXXVII. THE RECALCITRANCE OF HUMAN NATURE TO 'LAWS OF NATURE'

This recalcitrance is illustrated by a number of examples of 'challenge and response'. Faced with a challenge, Man is free, within limits, to alter the pace of change.

XXXVIII. THE LAW OF GOD

Man does not live under the Law of Nature only, but also under the Law of God, which is Perfect Freedom. Contrasted views of the nature of God and His Law are examined.

XII. THE PROSPECTS OF THE WESTERN CIVILIZATION

XXXIX. THE NEED FOR THIS INQUIRY

The ensuing inquiry marked a departure from the standpoint, adopted and hitherto maintained throughout this *Study*, of treating all the civilizations known to history synoptically. The departure is justified by the facts that the Western society is the only one surviving that is not manifestly in disintegration, that in many respects it had become world-wide, and that its prospects were, in fact, the prospects of a 'Westernizing world'.

XL. THE INCONCLUSIVENESS OF *A PRIORI* ANSWERS

There was no reason for supposing, on pseudo-scientific grounds, that, because all other civilizations had perished or were perishing, the West was bound to go the same way. Emotional reactions, such as 'Victorian' optimism and 'Spenglerian' pessimism, were equally void of cogency as evidence.

XLI. THE TESTIMONY OF THE HISTORIES OF THE CIVILIZATIONS

(1) *Western Experiences with Non-Western Precedents*

What light do our previous studies of breakdowns and disintegrations throw on our present problem? We have noted war and militarism as being the most potent cause of the breakdown of a society. The West has so far wrestled unsuccessfully with this disease. On the other hand it has achieved unprecedented successes in other directions: e.g. the abolition of slavery; the growth of democracy and education. The West also now displays the ominous division into dominant minority and internal and external proletariats. On the other hand, some remarkable successes have been achieved in coping with the problems of a diversity of internal proletariats within the Westernizing world.

(2) *Unprecedented Western Experiences*

The mastery of Man over non-human nature and the accelerating rapidity of social change are both without parallel in the histories of earlier civilizations. The plan of the following chapters is indicated.

XLII. TECHNOLOGY, WAR, GOVERNMENT

(1) *Prospects of a Third World War*

Characteristics of the United States of America and of the Soviet Union, and of the attitude of the rest of the human race towards each of them.

(2) *Towards a Future World Order*

The prospects of the human race compared with Heyerdahl's raft, *Kon-tiki*, on approaching the reef. A future World Order would inevitably be something very different from the present United Nations Organization. The qualifications of the American nation for leadership are discussed.

XLIII. TECHNOLOGY, CLASS-CONFLICT, AND EMPLOYMENT

(1) *The Nature of the Problem*

The triumphs of modern technology had led to an unprecedented demand for 'freedom from want'; but would Mankind be prepared to pay the price required for the satisfaction of this demand?

(2) *Mechanization and Private Enterprise*

Modern technology had entailed a mechanization, or regimentation, not only of the manual workers, but also of their employers (nationalization, &c.), of the civil service ('red tape'), and of the politicians (party discipline). The working-class organs of resistance (trade unions) had required further regimentation. The authors of the Industrial Revolution, on the other hand, had come out of a non-regimented society.

(3) *Alternative Approaches to Social Harmony*

The American, the Russian, and the West European, especially the British, approaches analysed and compared.

(4) *Possible Costs of Social Justice*

Social life impossible without some measure both of personal liberty and of social justice. Technology tilts the balance in favour of the latter. What, in an age when the death-rate was being lowered by preventive medicine, were going to be the consequences of an uncontrolled 'personal liberty' to propagate the human species? The prospects of a Great Famine ahead are discussed, and the conflicts that it seemed likely to engender.

(5) *Living happy ever after?*

Suppose that the World Society found a successful solution of all these problems, would the human race thenceforth 'live happy ever after'? No, because 'original sin' is born again in every child that comes into the World.

XIII. CONCLUSION

XLIV. HOW THIS BOOK CAME TO BE WRITTEN

The writer, born into the age of the Late Victorian optimism, and encountering the First World War in early manhood, was struck by the parallels between the experience of his own society in his own lifetime and those of the Hellenic society, a study of which had provided the staple of his education. This raised in his mind the questions: Why do civilizations die? Is the Hellenic civilization's fate in store for the Modern West? Subsequently his inquiries were extended to include the breakdowns and disintegrations of the other known civilizations, as further evidence for throwing light on his questions. Finally, he proceeded to investigate the geneses and growths of civilizations, and so this *Study of History* came to be written.

INDEX

Indus culture, extinction of, 9; Sumeric Civilization, 140, 147.
Industrial revolutions, 256, 275, 313.
Industrialism: 'drive' imparted by, 215–16; impact of, on non-Western World, 223–4; increased power, 320–38, 348.
Innocent III, Pope, 246.
Innocent IV, Pope, 247.
Institutions: as carriers, 54; churches as, 116; nature of, 119; see also POLITICAL INSTITUTIONS.
Insurance, 268–9, 289.
Intelligentsias: alien cultures in, 218; genesis of, 185–6; revolt of, against dominant minority, 185–8; spiritual malaise of, 163.
Io, Hellenic goddess, 212.
Iranic Muslim Civilization: breakdown of, 304, 312; geographical range of, 167–8; Orthodox Christian Civilization, contact with, 233; Orthodox Christian Civilization (Russian branch), contact with, 168; position of, at end of 15th century, 167; Syriac Civilization, affiliation to, 82; Time of Trouble, 173.
'Irāq, irrigation system in, 171.
Irenaeus, Saint, 23, 33, 300–1.
Ishtar, worship of, 26, 88, 211.
Isis, worship of, 16, 26, 88, 90, 210, 218.
Islam: aniconism of, 259; as barbarians' heresy, 144; as chrysalis, 82; Christianity, relation to, 189; conversions to: — Greek, 156; — Hindus, 163, 233; — mass, 51, 191–2; Monophysite and Nestorian Christians, 191; disintegration in a Syriac world, 84; die-hard spirit of, 98; exclusiveness of, 228; fetish worship, 90; genesis of, 142, 203; Greek philosophy, presentation in terms of, 95; liturgical language of, 49; Monotheism of, 89, 259, 279; myths of, 84; political purposes, diversion to, 232; polytheistic tendencies, 279; propaganda of, 18, 25; race-feeling, absence of, 228, 230–1; religious appeal of, 57; Sharī'ah, the, 54; spiritual merits of, 30–31; spiritual message of, 89; Sunnah and Shī'ah, feud between, 228; tolerant spirit of, 192, 228.
Islamic Civilization: competition in 20th century, 170–1; intelligentsia in, 185; position of in 20th century, 171; Western Civilization, contact with, 167 seqq., 214.
Israel: kingdom of, 88, 172; estab-

lishment of, 223; Jewish diaspora, 178; Jewish title to, 235; prospects of, 179; war with Arab States (1948–9), 177.
Israelites, 28.
Italy: as education of Western Europe, 150, 200, 241–2; autocracy in, 112; balance of power of, 200; Crusades, participation in, 190; Fascism: — as substitute for Christianity, 148; — Communist influence on, 188; — establishment of régime, 98; — foundation of Rome, 56; Florence, 154; Jews, treatment of, 175; law, systems of, 52; Lombards, conquest of, 52; political ability, lack of, 188; neo-paganism in, 79; Iuppiter Dolichênus, worship of, 31.
Ivan IV, 'the Terrible', Tsar of Muscovy, 168.

Japan: aggression by, 184; capital cities of, 42–43; Christianity, attitude towards, 18, 181, 234; colonization policy, 184; defeat of in 1945, 182, 184; Dutch relations with, 234; Imperial House, the, 235; intelligentsia, 185–6; Meiji Revolution, 234; militarism of, 182; population, pressure of, 183; Portuguese, relation to, 181–2, 217; position of, after Second World War, 183–4; rearmament of, 316; Shintoism in, 417; United States, relations with, 182; Western World, relations with, 168, 179–84, 217, 225, 234–5; Westernization in 19th century, 20; Xenophobia in, 181; Zealotism and Herodianism in, 234–6; see under TOKUGAWA SHOGUNATE.
Japanese language, 45.
Jerome, Saint, 4.
Jerusalem: as temple-state, 44, 206; Crusaders' Kingdom of, 190; Hellenization of, attempted, 277; siege of, 206.
Jesuits: in China, 44; in India, 24 n., 25, 26, 44; in Russian Orthodox Christendom, 151.
Jevons, W. Stanley, 280.
Jewishness, nature of, 178–9.
Jews: the, as a peculiar people, 235, 259–60; as God's chosen people, 258; as fossil of Syriac Society, 82, 171–2; assimilation of, to Gentiles, 176–8; Babylonian captivity, 28, 33, 43, 206, 216–17; causes of ill-treatment of, in Western World, 174–5; diaspora, 172 seqq., 178, 186, 217,